PITTSBURGH ORIGINAL TEXTS

Dikran Y. Hadidian
General Editor

2

Samaritan Documents
Relating to Their History, Religion and Life

SAMARITAN DOCUMENTS
RELATING TO THEIR HISTORY, RELIGION AND LIFE

TRANSLATED AND EDITED
BY
JOHN BOWMAN

PICKWICK *Publications* · Eugene, Oregon

Pickwick Publications
An imprint of Wipf and Stock Publishers
199 W 8th Ave, Suite 3
Eugene, OR 97401

Samaritan Documents
Relating to their History, Religion, and Life
By Bowman, John

ISBN 13: 978-0-915138-27-2
Publication date 01/26/2009
Previously published by Pickwick, 1977

ACKNOWLEDGEMENTS

The author desires to express his grateful thanks to all who in various ways and at different times and places, either in person or by letter or in their writings, gave him of their knowledge and skill. He would like in particular to mention the names of the late Professor Paul Kahle, the late Professor Edward Robertson, the late Moses Gaster and Professor Leon Nemoy, Dikran Y. Hadidian, the editor of the series, Mrs. Patricia Johnson who typed the work and the Faculty of Arts of Melbourne University who provided the funds for the typing.

In this year of Grace, 1976

Prof. John Bowman
Department of Middle Eastern Studies
University of Melbourne,
Australia

SAMARITAN DOCUMENTS RELATING TO THEIR HISTORY, RELIGION AND LIFE

CONTENTS

INTRODUCTION

The present volume of documents relating to Samaritan History, Religion and Life is basically intended as a companion to The Samaritan Problem, Pittsburgh Theological Monograph Series Number 4, as giving translations of texts by Samaritan authors mentioned therein. But this is not the only aim of this work. It attempts to make accessible in English examples from a variety of Samaritan documents which provide us with a first hand picture of Samaritan views about their history, their religion and hopes for the future.

Samaritan literature is religious literature; it is not merely religion centered, but its very bounds are set by religion, for religion and life are synonymous for the Samaritan. It is not a very extensive literature: though there is quite a mass of material, it falls into a limited number of categories. The Samaritan Torah or Pentateuch, their entire Bible is basic. In their Divine Service it is read either in Ḳataf i.e. digest form or *in extenso*. The Samaritans like the Jews are totally devoted to the Torah, but that which should unite Samaritans and Jews separates them. The Samaritan Torah, basically the same as the Jewish Torah, has small but significant differences which serve as the ground for the existence of the Samaritans as a separate sect. The Samaritan Tenth Commandment is one such difference.

The second section of the present book gives a selection from Samaritan Chronicles, the earliest of which is the Tolidah in Hebrew. The Tolidah seeks to establish the claim of the Samaritans to have the only valid succession of Priests back not only to Aaron but to Adam! In the same work the claim has been introduced that they actually possess the very copy of the

Torah written by Aaron's great grandson; this latter is an attempt by them to justify the authenticity of their peculiar text of the Torah and the claims they make based on statements therein that differ from the Jewish Hebrew text of the Torah.

Also included in this section is a translation of a short selection from the Samaritan Book of Joshua in Arabic. While Hebrew versions of the Samaritan Joshua do exist, it is unlikely that they are anything other than Hebrew translations of the Arabic. Part of the Samaritan Book of Joshua is clearly dependent on the Biblical Book of Joshua, which like the rest of the Jewish Hebrew Bible (apart from the Pentateuch) is not recognised by the Samaritans as Divine Revelation. True the Samaritan Book of Joshua too is not part of their Canon of Scripture, but they at least since the later Middle Ages have all set considerable store by it; before that it seems to have been recognised only by sectarians within the Samaritan fold.

The third example of Samaritan historiography is from the Chronicle Adler, which is in Hebrew and is a nineteenth century production. Like the Samaritan Book of Joshua it blames Eli not only for the schism between Samaritans (who see themselves as the true Israel) and the Jews, but also for bringing the period of Divine Grace and Favor to an end and causing Divine Disfavor which has existed till today. It is interesting to see how a Jewish sect which hived off from Judaism in the first half of the fourth century B.C. seeks to rewrite Biblical history from its own viewpoint. The Samaritan Chronicles are naturally coy about the exile of the Israelites towards the last quarter of the eighth century B.C. With them much prominence is given to the Babylonian Exile of the Jews.

The fourth Samaritan Chronicle is that by Abu'l Fatḥ. It is in Arabic and belongs to the fourteenth century. Of Samaritan Chronicles it has the most claim to being regarded as a historical work. Even so, polemic and apologetic are not wanting from its pages. The three sections chosen for translation and inclusion in our pages dealing with Abu'l Fatḥ's remarks on Samaritan sects are important; so too are his allegations about the Septuagint translation, though this latter tells us more about Abu'l Fatḥ's methods of apologetics and polemics than gives us any new information about the Septuagint.

The third section of the book gives examples of Samaritan Bible commentaries in Arabic. The first two are from an 18th century commentator Ibrahim ibn Ya'ḳub on Ex. 21 and Lev. 23. The second two are from the Kitab al Tabbaḥ of Abu'l Hasan al-Surī of the 11th century A.D.: on Deut. 6:4-9 i.e. Shema: on Deut. 34:1-4 i.e. on Moses going up to the top of Mt. Pisgah and the LORD showing him the whole land that Israel was to inherit: on Deut. 34:5-9 i.e. on the death of Moses: on Deut. 34:10-12 with special reference to v.10 'And there has not arisen a prophet since in Israel like Moses' a verse which is very important for Samaritans for whom Moses is what Muhammad is for Muslims.

Ibrahim ibn Ya'kub's style of commenting is conditioned by the legal material he is commenting on e.g. Ex. 21 slaves and slavery: and Lev. 23 the appointed feasts of the LORD. Abu'l Hasan al-Surī when commenting in the major part of his book on halakic (i.e. legal) matters in the Torah e.g. on uncleanness and laws relating to that state, can be as terse. The sections we give however from Abu'l Hasan al-Surī here are haggadic (i.e. homiletic). While there is more freedom in handling the latter type of commenting on the Bible text, even it, compared with a Jewish haggadic Midrash, sticks closely to the very words of Scripture. Basically there is a real difference between Samaritan and Jew in the importance given to the words of haggadah. With the Samaritans it must be accepted, with the Jews acceptance is kept for halakot which must be followed.

The fourth section deals with haggadic Midrash. Our first example is Abu'l Hasan al-Suri on Angels, from his Kitab al-Tabbaḥ. Whether the Samaritan priests had at one stage frowned on belief in the existence of angels, by the 11th century, as witness Abu'l Hasan, a priest could write a brief treatise attesting their existence. However in the Samaritan Targum which is presumably not later than the 4th century A.D. as Marḳah's discourses are in part based on it, there are mentions of angels. In the Samaritan Targum (Gen. 5:24) the disappearance of Enoch was not because God took him, but because it was the Angels who did. Further in Gen. 9:6 the Hebrew Bible statement 'for God made man in His own image' becomes 'for in the image of the angels made He man'. It will be observed however that Abu'l Hasan al-Suri does not individualize angels or give them personal names. In Marḳah individualization of the angels seems to be indicated; but with Marḳah there was acceptance of ideas which the strict priestly party was not willing to accept until the fourteenth century and later when we hear that the babe Moses in the basket of bulrushes was guarded by four angels, Kebala', Penuel, Anusa and Zilpah,[1] whose names apparently were derived by extraordinary exegesis of the Hebrew text of Gen. 32:31; Ex. 14:25; Num. 4:20; and Ex. 17:15 respectively.

The second example of haggadic midrash is from the Memar Marḳah and in this case is on the Day of Vengeance (Deut. 32:33 Sam. reading of the Jewish Hebrew text "Vengeance is Mine"). The post-talmudic tractate on the Kuthim i.e. the Samaritans, makes it clear that at the time of its composition Jews held that Samaritans did not believe in the resurrection of the dead. As the reader will see Marḳah in discoursing on the Day of

Vengeance and Recompense, did teach belief in the resurrection of the dead. If tractate Kuthim is right, it may be speaking of different Samaritans from those that Markah sought to reach. Markah lived in the time of Baba Raba who tried to reunite Samaritans of the old orthodox priestly party and break away laicising Dositheans. After Baba's death there was a reaction; the reunion failed and the priests held to their own old ways and beliefs until one thousand years later in the 14th century when there was a second ecumenical movement which succeeded. This time the priests were left with their old powers, but were prepared to accept Dosithean teachings into their liturgy. The third example of haggadic Midrash in Phinehas on the Taheb. This is in Hebrew and is a very late composition but is worth including since its views on the Taheb i.e. the Samaritan Saviour, is not a returning or a second Moses, but is modelled on Noah. The fourth and last example is a selection from the *Molad Mošeh* a haggadic Midrash on the Birth of Moses. This is now accepted by all Samaritans, priests included; but it is unlikely this was the case before the 14th century that the old orthodox priestly party would have accepted it. If one compares Abu'l Hasan al-Suri's version of the death of Moses with that given by the Memar Markah one is left with the impression that while the *Molad Mošeh* and the Memar Markah share in their attitude to Moses, it is quite foreign to Abu'l Hasan al-Suri, a priest of the 11th century who kept to the old ways. The views of Moses represented in the *Molad Mošeh* are the sort of views however that became orthodox from the 14th century on.

In the sixth section of our work we give an example of Samaritan halakah. Just as the Karaites, though they pushed aside the Talmud with its post-Biblical developments of the laws of the Torah and claimed they would live by the Law alone as set out in the Bible, could not manage without usages of of their own, so too the Samaritans. In the Samaritan Hilluk we have such an attempt to fill in the gaps in the Torah according to Samaritan usage. They would not admit there were gaps, nor any problem existed. Certainly they do not put such compendia as the Hilluk or even the two much earlier works, Abu'l Hasan al-Suri's Kitab al-Tabbaḥ and Yusuf b. Salama's al-Kafi on even a level with the Torah. While the Samaritans did not attempt like the Rabbanite Jews to make the Torah cover all aspects of life, there were matters like marriage which were clearly within the orbit of the Law but about which the Torah was not explicit. In the present section a translation is given of the section on Marriage in the Samaritan compendium the Hilluk. Thereafter translations are given of the texts of two Samaritan Marriage Documents, which have both differences from, and similarities with Jewish Ketubot i.e. marriage documents. With the provisions set out in Hebrew marriage documents we have evidence from the [2]Aramaic Papyri from Egypt of the Fifth Century B.C. which predate the Samaritan secession from the Jewish Community. The Samaritan Marriage Document in its provisions however does not seem aware of later Jewish modifications not earlier than the 1st century B.C. It is perhaps fitting to close this section with a translation of a Samaritan Bill of Divorce. The Bible does mention a Bill of Divorce but does not give its text. Here again the Samaritan priests supplied the deficiency.

Of all Samaritan literature the one area which is the most prolific is the liturgy. It had been my intention to devote a major section to translations from the liturgy, but I decided against this as the Samaritan Liturgy deserved a whole book to itself if one is to present it in all its ramifications. One hesitates to say diversity, for there is a sameness about much of it. However as an Epilogue to this selection of Documents illustrating Samaritan History, Religion and Life we include a few of the shorter pieces which are still used today by the Samaritans in Israel.

FOOTNOTES

1. See M. Heidenheim, *Bibliotheca Samaritana* ii 29, v.6; Peniel and Kebula' only, *ibid.* p.205, v.18 reprint Philo Press, Amsterdam 1971.

2. See A. E. Cowley, *Aramaic Papyri of the Fifth Century B.C.* Clarendon Press, Oxford, 1923, p.54ff., 131f., 153.

CHAPTER 1

<u>THE SAMARITAN TEN WORDS OF CREATION</u>, the English of which is given below, came from the old area of Nablus where the old Samaritan quarter used to be. It was found in the nineteenth century in the ruins near the Ḥiṣn Ya'ḳūb mosque, on the minaret of which, built in upside down, is the Nablus Samaritan Decalogue inscription. Both inscriptions may well have originally come from the same building; both end with 'Arise LORD, return LORD!'. Rosen, the first to publish the Samaritan Ten Words of Creation,[1] has already given an English translation of this inscription, but in view of its importance and almost perfect condition it is included here; Montgomery gives also a facsimile of it.[2] Undoubtedly something similar to the theological conception of the creation of the world by the Divine Memra or Logos underlies the selection of the nine passages in the first chapter of Genesis, where 'And God said' occurs; but the fact that for the tenth Word of God we have Exod. 3:6, God's word to Moses from the burning bush, surely is significant. Whereas the Rabbis (M. A<u>b</u>o<u>t</u> 5:1) knew that the world was created by Ten Words, it is usually understood that they found the first Word implied in Gen. 1:1. Doubtless for both Jew and Samaritan, the choice of the number ten for the Words of creation was influenced by God's Ten Words or Ten Commandments given at Sinai; the Samaritan Ten Words of Creation underline this connection by giving as their tenth Word of Creation God's revelation of Himself to Moses. The fact that God's personal revelation to Moses is chosen as the tenth Word is significant not only as pointing towards the great theophany at Sinai, the new Creation by God's Ten Words, but also as highlighting Moses emphasizing

his significance for the Samaritans.

It is unfortunate that we do not have a similar Jewish inscription with its own version of the Ten Words of Creation. Even if we had it, it is not likely that the Biblical verses would have been as truncated as they are in the Samaritan inscription, although in modern times we do indeed find abbreviated inscriptions of the Ten Commandments in synagogues. The Samaritans were charged by the Jews with having their Law in Notarikon,[3] which cannot in this connection mean shorthand, but must refer to the Samaritan practice of 'plucking' (*ḳaṭaf*) the Law, i.e. taking a few words out of a verse or passage and making them represent the whole verse. Actually the reason for this (see below) was not in any way, sinister, but merely represented an attempt to retain the primacy of the reading of the Law as part of divine worship. However, the Samaritans during worship do not in fact ḳaṭaf, or read mere snippets of, each parašiyyah of the first chapter of Genesis. On the contrary, all of it is read. Now this inscription is in the nature of a ḳaṭaf of Genesis ch.1; but whereas *ḳeṭafim* exist in liturgical Mss. for the rest of the Torah, including even the Ten Commandments, the ḳeṭaf of the first chapter of the Bible occurs only here and in the Malef.[4] As we will see,[5] this chapter was and is repeated by the Samaritans in full and without abbreviation more frequently than any other chapter of the Bible. It could, of course, be argued that the intractability of stone and the lack of available space have led to the abbreviating in this inscription. While that is a feasible argument, it does not explain why the engraver was not content to regard Gen. 1:1 as the first Word, which would have enabled him to stop with Gen. 1:31 in line 11 of the inscription, and thus save himself at least the two lines taken by Exod. 3:6.

(Gen. 1:1) In the beginning God created.
(Gen. 1:3) And God said, Let there be light.

(Gen. 1:6)	And God said, Let there be a firmament.
(Gen. 1:9)	And God said, Let the waters be gathered together.
(Gen. 1:11)	And God said, Let the earth put forth vegetation.
(Gen. 1:14)	And God said, Let there be lights.
(Gen. 1:20)	And God said, Let the waters bring forth swarms.
(Gen. 1:24)	And God said, Let the earth bring forth.
(Gen. 1:26)	And God said, Let us make man.
(Gen. 1:29)	And God said, Behold, I have given you.
(Gen. 1:31)	And God saw every thing that he had made, and behold, it was very good.
(Exod.3:6)	And he said, I am the God of thy father, the God of Abraham, The God of Isaac, and the God of Jacob.
(Exod.36:6)	The LORD, the LORD, merciful and gracious.
(Num.10:35)	Arise, O LORD.

THE ḲIṢE HA-BERI'AH

The sections of Creation are chanted at the beginning of every Samaritan service. They comprise the *ḳaṣim* of Gen. 1:1 - 2:3, *ḳaṣim* being the small parašiyyot into which the text of the Samaritan Torah is divided; they correspond to the ṣĕtumot and pĕtuḥot of the Masoretic Bible, and in fact in some cases they agree with them. Here, in Gen. 1:1 - 2:7, the ḳaṣim and the pĕtuḥot are in complete agreement. At the end of each book of the Samaritan Pentateuch the number of ḳaṣim contained therein is given, just as in the Hebrew Bible the number of pĕtuḥot and sĕtumot in each book of the Law is likewise given. The division of the text of the Jewish Pentateuch into pĕtuḥot and sĕtumot is very old.[6] The Samaritan system of sectionalization does not have the dual system of pĕtuḥot and sĕtumot; sometimes the Samaritan ḳaṣim agree with either a pĕtuhah or a sĕtumah, or begin with one and end with the other. While in some cases there is no agreement at all, it is significant that agreement does occur especially in connection with those parts of the Law which are read in both communities on festivals. Both Jew and

Samaritan had to face the fact that with the weekly reading of a large parašah in the triennial or annual cycle, there was no certainty that the passage appropriate to a particular feast-day would occur exactly when required; that is why in the synagogue to this day additional lessons are read on festivals from a second scroll. One could regard such readings as supplementary, but however unlikely it may seem, these readings from a second scroll on a festival may be a survival of a time when the liturgy was restricted to the reading of the Law and there were no *piyyuṭim*. That this latter view merits serious consideration may be seen from the fact that in M. Meg. 5:3 the portions fixed to be read on festivals agree strikingly with the corresponding Samaritan sections. We know also that in the Temple[7] the first chapter of Genesis was used liturgically section by section. There, however, the verses were not recited all at once, but each day of the week had its appropriate verses telling of the acts of creation on that day. The Karaites have continued this liturgical usage of the first chapter of Genesis, reading on any one day only the section dealing with the creation brought about on that day.

Perhaps we may therefore say that the sectionalization of the Law into ḳaṣim by the Samaritans, and into pĕṯuḇoṯ and sĕṯumoṯ by the Jews, was originally prompted by liturgical requirements. The process may have begun prior to the Samaritan-Jewish schism. Certainly such sectionalization is part of the earliest Masorah. It is interesting to see how the Samaritan *ḳiṣe ha-beri'ah* ('sections of Creation') are separated from each other by brief exclamations of praise. The Samaritan liturgy probably consisted once of nothing more than the reading of the Law, with such brief exclamations of praise interjected here and there; from these spontaneous exclamations there were eventually evolved the set hymns and prayers of the developed liturgy. As the hymns grew and took up more space and time in the service, the place of the readings from the Law was correspondingly diminished. The weekly reading of a parašah in the annual cycle remained. The Samaritans have always been conservative; what is now retained as the preparatory service for the eve of Sabbath is probably the old Sabbath morning service or a part thereof: it consists of readings of small parašiyyot. In the present Sabbath morning service the whole Law is read - but in the form of a digest, or ḳaṭaf.[8] This ḳaṭaf is basic for all services, but on festivals parašiyyot relating to the particular occasion are inserted and read in full. Presumably, each of the parašiyyot from which the individual phrases of the ḳaṭaf are taken, were once read in full; but in order to make place for the addition of the hymns, which since the fourth century assume such a large place in the liturgy, the readings in the Law were subsequently condensed. They were not entirely dispensed with, however. It would be tempting to think that the festival readings of the Law from the second scroll in the Jewish synagogue likewise mark the last survival of a service once based entirely, or at least in very large measure, on readings in the Law.[9] The Jewish synagogue did not adopt the ḳaṭaf form, but instead dropped the readings from the Law, except for the weekly reading of the large parašah in the triennial or annual cycle, and the reading from the second scroll on festivals.

THE SECTIONS OF THE CREATION

(Gen. 1:1) In the beginning God created the heavens and the earth. (1:2) Now the earth was without form and void, and darkness was upon the face of the deep; and the spirit of God was moving over the face of the waters. (1:3) And God said, 'Let there be light'; and there was light. (1:4) And God saw that the light was good; and God separated the light from the darkness. (1:5) And God called the light Day, and the darkness he called Night. And there was evening and there was morning, one day,

> Blessed be our God! Praised be our God!
> Exalted is our God! Holy is our God.

He who is God in heaven and on earth, let Him be blessed. There is no might which endures save His might; nor is there any who can perform the like of His works. Blessed be He who is to be blessed. Blessed be our God for ever, and blessed be His name for ever. There is none like God, O Jeshurun! God is to be praised. There is no God but one. The LORD our God is one LORD. (1:6) And God said, "Let there be a firmament in the midst of the waters, and let it separate the waters from the waters". (1:7) And God made the firmament and separated the waters which were under the firmament from the waters which were above the firmament. And it was so. (1:8) And God called the firmament Heaven. And there was evening and there was morning, a second day.

> Our God is to be praised. There is no God but one.
> The LORD our God is the one LORD.

(1:9) And God said, "Let the waters under the heavens be gathered together into one place, and let the dry land appear". And it was so. (1:10) And God called the dry land Earth, and the waters that were gathered together He called Seas. And God saw that it was good. (1:11) And God said, "Let the earth put vegetation, plants yielding seed, and fruit trees bearing fruit in which is their seed, each according to its kind, upon the earth". And it was so. (1:12) And the earth brought forth vegetation, plants yielding seed according to their own kinds, and trees bearing fruit in which is their seed, each according to its kind. (1:13) And there was evening and there was morning a third day.

Our God is to be praised: there is no God but one.
The LORD our God is the one LORD.

(1:14) And God said, "Let there be lights in the firmament of the heavens to separate the day from the night; and let them be for signs and for seasons and for days and years, (1:15) and let them be lights in the firmament of the heavens to give light upon the earth." And it was so. (1:16) and God made the two great lights, the greater light to rule the day, and the lesser light to rule the night; and He made the stars also. (1:17) And God set them in the firmament of the heavens to give light upon the earth, (1:18) to rule over the day and over the night, and to separate the light from the darkness. And God saw that it was good. (1:19) And there was evening, and there was morning, a fourth day.

Our God is to be praised. There is no God but one,
The LORD our God is the one LORD.

(1:20) And God said, "Let the waters bring forth swarms of living creatures, and let birds fly above the earth across the firmament of the heavens". (1:21) And God created the great sea monsters and every living creature that moves, with which the waters swarm, according to their kinds, and every winged bird according to its kind. And God saw that it was good. (1:22) And God blessed them, saying, "Be fruitful, and multiply, and fill the waters in the seas, and let birds multiply on the earth." (1:23) And there was evening and there was morning, a fifth day.

And God is to be praised. There is no God but one.
The LORD our God is the one LORD.

(1:24) And God said, "Let the earth bring forth living creatures according to their kinds: cattle, and creeping things, and beasts of the earth, according to their kinds." And it was so. (1:25) And God made the beasts of the earth according to their kinds, and the cattle according to their kinds, and everything that creeps upon the ground according to its kind. And God saw that it was good. (1:26) And God said, "Let us make man in Our image, after Our likeness; and let them have dominion over the fish of the sea, and over the birds of the air, and over the cattle, and over all the earth, and over every creeping thing that creeps upon the earth." (1:27) And God created man in His own image, in the image of God He created him; male and female He created them. (1:28) And God blessed them, and God said to them, "Be fruitful, and multiply, and fill the earth and subdue it; and have dominion over the fish of the sea, and over the birds of the air, and over every living thing that moves upon the earth." (1:29) And God said, "Behold, I have given you every plant yielding seed which is upon the face of all the earth, and every tree with seed in its fruit; you shall have them for food. (1:30) And to every beast of the earth, and to every bird of the air, and to everything that creeps on the earth, to everything that has the breath of life, I have given every green plant for food." And it was so. (1:31) And God saw every thing that He had made, and behold, it was very good. And there was evening and there was morning, a sixth day. (2:1) Thus the heavens and the earth were finished, and all the host of them. (2:2) And on the sixth day God finished His work which He had done, and He rested on the seventh day from all His work which He had done. (2:3) And God blessed the seventh day and hallowed it, because on it God rested from all His work which He had done in creation.

(2:4) These are the generations of the heavens and of the earth when they were created. In the day that the LORD God made the earth and the heavens, (2:5) when no plant of the field was yet in the earth, and no herb of the field had yet sprung up, for the LORD God had not caused it to rain upon the earth, and there was no man to till the ground; (2:6) but a mist went up from the earth and watered the whole face of the ground. (2:7) Then the LORD God formed man of dust from the ground, and breathed into his nostrils the breath of life; and man became a living being.

> Blessed be our God. Praised be our God.
> Exalted is our God. Holy is our God.
> He who is God in heaven and on earth, let Him be blessed. There is no might which endures save His might; nor is there any who can perform the like of His works. Blessed be He who is to be blessed. Blessed be our God for ever, and blessed be His name for ever. There is none like God, O Jeshurun! God is to be praised. There is no God but one. The LORD our God is the one LORD.

SAMARITAN DECALOGUE INSCRIPTIONS

In the translation which follows, the form of the Samaritan Decalogue is given as it is found in four ancient inscriptions.[10] These are not the only existing Samaritan Decalogue inscriptions; another is in the house of Mr. Kaplan, city archaeologist for Tel Aviv, but it is certainly much later than these four, being from the ninth century A.D., as is still another Samaritan Decalogue inscription found near Yabneh. My own impression of these four inscriptions is that they are of the third or fourth century A.D.

The Leeds Samaritan Decalogue inscription, now in the Department of Semitic Languages and Literatures, University of Leeds, on indefinite loan from the Leeds City Museum, came to Leeds about 1863, from Nablus. The next inscription is that built into the wall of the minaret of the Ḥiṣn Ya'ḳub mosque at Nablus, and probably came from a former Samaritan synagogue. The third inscription is at Bīr Ya'ḳūb near Sychar. This is the smallest of the four and the roughest in finish. The Leeds and Nablus inscriptions were carefully lined before the letters were engraved, just as a scroll is lined before being written on. What is even more noteworthy is that the letters hang from the lines, as do those of the Habakkuk Scroll from the Dead Sea. The fourth inscription is the one in the Palestine Museum, which was discovered in 1935 near Nablus. This stone, now broken into two pieces, was a comparatively long slab which presumably served as a lintel of some large building. It is a well executed piece of work, lovingly finished with a decorative leaf border.

The Leeds and the Nablus inscriptions stand close together as to their epigraphy. The Palestine Museum inscription and the Sychar stone, although unlike in shape and finish, also resemble one another epigraphically. Wright regarded the Leeds stone as at least three or four hundred years old, but perhaps much older. Montgomery[11] would date the Leeds inscription and the Nablus Decalogue as "anterior to the disruption of the Samaritan community by Justinian", thus following Rosen. Blau, on the other hand, thought that they came from the first Samaritan Temple on Mount Gerizim, destroyed by John Hyrcanus, which is extremely unlikely; it is more likely that they came from the second Samaritan Temple built after Bar Kokhba's revolt in the thirties of the second century A.D., if indeed they came from the Temple and not from a synagogue. Be that as it may, the second Samaritan Temple was destroyed finally in the time of the Emperor Zeno (A.D. 474-491), and Samaritan synagogues as well suffered much at this same time. There is no need to argue that we must go on further, to Justinian's time, for the reduction of the Samaritan community which resulted from his edict of 529, "De Haereticis et Manichaeis et Samaritis". To be sure, at that time steps were taken to destroy Samaritan synagogues, and the rebuilding of them was forbidden. But while the Samaritans were still able to cause trouble in 529, they were already at a low ebb after 486. The Palestine Museum inscription is listed by the Museum as of the third or fourth century A.D., and the Sychar inscription stands well together with it not only in epigraphy but also in certain textual features as well. If therefore the Museum's dating of its inscription is right, I should provisionally suggest a somewhat similar date for the Sychar inscription.

In the translation of these four inscriptions I have superimposed them one upon the other, indicating as far as possible what is actually represented in each. Owing to the fragmentary condition of the Leeds inscription and that from Sychar, one cannot say with certainty what had been the form of the first and second commandments in the Leeds Decalogue, or of the first, second and third commandments in the Bīr Ya'ḳūb Decalogue at Sychar. Certainly the Nablus inscription did not have Exod. 20:2, 'I am the LORD your God' as a preamble before the first commandment, ibid., 20:3, 'You shall have no other gods before Me', since the Samaritan Pentateuch Exod. 20:2 is not regarded as part of the first commandment, but rather as a preamble. In the Palestine Inscription Exod. 20:2 appears not as a preamble, but as the first commandment, and Exod. 20:7, 'You shall not take the name of the LORD your God in vain', is omitted. Since in this inscription we have both the beginning and the end of the Ten Commandments, and since there are no major lacunae due to the defacement of the writing, it must be assumed that Exod. 20:2 is deliberately regarded as the first commandment, in order to make up the total of ten after the normal Samaritan second commandment, Exod. 20:7, has been omitted.

The Samaritan Pentateuch divides the Ten Commandments in the same way as do the Roman Catholic and Lutheran Churches,[12] with the exception of the ninth commandment. The coveting of the neighbor's house and the coveting of his wife are not two separate prohibitions, forming the ninth and tenth commandments, but rather one prohibition, making the ninth commandment. In this way space is left by the Samaritans for their own tenth commandment. Just as the inscriptions reduce the previous nine commandments (ten to all but the Samaritans), by stripping them of midrashic additions, to something like their basic form, so do they deal also with their own rather lengthy tenth commandment. It would be rash to assume that the Samaritans had a tradition which defined the basic forms of the Ten Words; and even if they had one, it could not have been consistent, since in these four inscriptions, for example, we have three different abbreviated forms of their ninth commandment, Bīr Ya'ḳūb-Sychar inscription going farthest in reducing it to 'you shall not covet', while the Palestine Museum inscription makes 'You shall not covet your neighbor's house' cover also the prohibition of coveting his wife.

The basic element in the Samaritan tenth commandment is the place where God may be worshipped - sacrificially. The inscriptions of Bīr Ya'ḳūb-Sychar, Leeds, and Nablus agree in giving as their tenth commandment Deut. 27:5a; but Leeds adds Deut. 27:8, which is not included in the selection of verses from Deut. 27 which forms, *inter alia*, the tenth commandment in the Samaritan Pentateuch. The Palestine Museum inscription cites as its tenth commandment Deut. 27:4b which, while indeed a part of a verse incorporated in the tenth commandment of the Samaritan Pentateuch, has no reference to the setting up of an altar at the place of worship; however, this inscription explicitly mentions Mount Gerizim. The Nablus inscription ends with citations of snippets from Num. 10:35-36, which verses are not represented in the Samaritan Pentateuch text of the tenth commandment; but it must be noted that these concluding words, here within the frame, are in the Samaritan inscription of the Ten Words of Creation appended outside the frame. The Leeds inscription in its margin cites Deut. 33:4, which is not a part of the tenth commandment, but is a frequent liturgical refrain with the Samaritans.

The Ten Commandments are read in full in the Samaritan Morning Service at the synagogue on the second and last Sabbaths of the month. On the second Sabbath it is the Exodus text which is recited, on the last Sabbath the Deuteronomic. The reading of the Ten Commandments in full comes within the recitation of either the Exodus or the Deuteronomic ḳaṭaf. On the other Sabbaths a Decalogue ḳaṭaf, exactly the same for inclusion in either the Exodus ḳaṭaf or the Deuteronomy ḳaṭaf, is recited. The interesting thing is that even the extra Samaritan tenth commandment is abbreviated. Only two commandments other than the tenth are represented here, their second and third, i.e. the prohibition of taking the LORD'S name in vain and the commandment to keep the Sabbath. To be sure, Exod. 20:6 which is part of the Midrash on the first commandment (in the Samaritan enumeration) is also quoted at the beginning of the ḳaṭaf.

The Samaritan Decalogue inscriptions are virtually ḳeṭafim; but there are no similar complete ḳeṭafim of the Ten Commandments in the liturgy with which they might be compared. It is possible that the Samaritan Decalogue inscriptions discussed above are older than the fourth century A.D., and while there is a close relationship between the Nablus and the Leeds inscriptions, the latter quotes as part of its tenth commandment a verse in Deut. 27 which does not form part of the official Samaritan text of this commandment. However, the Samaritan tenth commandment known to Origen[13] is exactly the same as that of the Samaritan Pentateuch, which indicates perhaps that the Leeds inscription antedates the final fixing of the Samaritan text of the tenth commandment, whenever that may have taken place, but certainly before Origen's time.

(PM)	(1)	I am the LORD your God (Exod. 20:2).
(PM)	(2)	You shall have no other gods before Me (Exod. 20:3).
(N)	(1)	
(N)	(2)	You shall not take the name of the LORD your God in vain (Exod. 20:7).

(L., PM)	(3)	Observe the Sabbath day, to keep it holy (Exod. 20:8).	
(L., BY) (PM, N)	(4)	Honor your father and your mother (Exod. 20:12).	
(L., BY) (PM, N)	(5)	You shall not kill (Exod. 20:13).	
(L., BY) (PM, N)	(6)	You shall not commit adultery (Exod. 20;14).	
(L., BY) (PM, N)	(7)	You shall not steal (Exod. 20:15).	
(L., BY) (PM, N)	(8)	You shall not bear false witness against your neighbor (Exod. 20:16).	
(BY)	(9)	You shall not covet (L., PM, N.) your neighbor's house (Exod. 20:17).	
(L., N.)		You shall not covet your neighbor's wife	
(BY, L., N)	(10)	And there you shall build an altar to the Lord your God (Deut. 27:5).	[PM: This which I command you this day, on Mount Gerizim (Deut. 27:3-4]
(L.)		And you shall write upon the stones all the words of this law very plainly (Deut. 27:8).	
(N.)		Arise, O LORD! Return, O LORD! (Num. 10:35-36).	
(L.)		Moses commanded us a law, as a possession for the assemply of Jacob (Deut. 33:4).	

A different example of Samaritan Decalogue inscriptions is the Kefar Bilo inscription published by the second President of Israel, the late Mr. Ben-Zebi.[14] The inscription consists of ten lines, and is apparently complete; what makes it all the more remarkable is that it not only has no Samaritan tenth commandment, but also omits the third Commandment, 'Observe the Sabbath day, to keep it holy' and the fourth Commandment, 'Honor your father and your mother'. Furthermore, it abbreviates the eighth Commandment to 'You shall not bear ' ('false witness' being omitted). The Samaritan ninth Commandment appears in the same brief form as in the Bīr Ya'ḳūb - Sychar inscription: 'You shall not covet'. Like the Palestine Museum inscription, the Kefar Bilo stone takes 'I am the LORD your God' (Exod.20:2) as its first Commandment, and Exod. 20:3 as its second Commandment, but reduces the latter to 'You shall have no other gods'. Its principal difference from other Samaritan inscriptions is that it takes Exod. 20:4 as its third Commandment. 'You shall not make for yourself'. However, this verse is not regarded by the Samaritan Pentateuch as a separate commandment, but with Exod. 20:3 forms part of the Samaritan first Commandment. The Palestine Museum Inscription, in taking Exod. 20:2 as its first Commandment, breaks with the usual Samaritan tradition; in this the Kefar Bilo stone is similar to the Palestine Museum stone, but it goes even further in making Exod. 20:4 a separate commandment, as does the official Jewish enumeration of the Ten Commandments, followed by the Protestants. Even so, the Kefar Bilo stone has only nine Commandments, unless Gen. 1:1, 'In the beginning God created', is to be regarded as its first Commandment. It would perhaps be better at this point to cease using the word Commandment and adopt instead the term 'Ten Words'. There are Ten Words of Creation, as we have seen above, the Nablus Ten Words of Creation add Exod. 3:6 after the enumeration of the Words from the first chapter of Genesis. This was done perhaps in order to link up the Divine Words of Creation with the Divine Words of Revelation of the Moral Law at Sinai. The Kefar Bilo inscription, on the other hand, links up the Words delivered at Sinai with God's work of Creation. It is God the Creator who is also God the Lawgiver.

(Gen. 1:1)	In the beginning God created.	
(Exod. 20:2)	I am the Lord your God.	(1 PM)
(Exod. 20:3)	You shall have no other gods.	(1 N)
(Exod. 20:4)	You shall not make for yourselves.	
(Exod. 20:7)	You shall not take	(2 N)
(Exod. 20:13)	You shall not kill	(5L, BY, PM, N)
(Exod. 20:14)	You shall not commit adultery.	(6L, BY, PM, N)
(Exod. 20:15)	You shall not steal.	(7L, BY, PM, N)
(Exod. 20:16)	You shall not bear (false witness)	(8L, BY, PM, N)

(Exod. 20:17) You shall not covet. (9 BY)

THE SAMARITAN BIBLE AND THE TEN COMMANDMENTS

The treatment of the Ten Commandments in the Samaritan Pentateuch is no more than the result of the application of a general principle which affects the whole Samaritan Pentateuch, although in the case of the Ten Commandments it has been carried out at once both rigorously and mildly. This principle is harmonization. The Samaritans claim to believe literally that nothing can or must be taken away from the Law or be added to it (cf. Deut. 4:2). They claim that their text of the Law is perfect, while that of the Jews is defective. In a sense, if one were to compare the Jewish and Samaritan recensions as they are now, there might at first glance appear to be verisimilitude in this view. We must remember that basically the Jewish and Samaritan Pentateuchs are one and the same. True, there are different readings here and there. These fall into three distinct categories. The first category are such as might have arisen owing to the variations which result from even the most careful scribal transmission, and not always did the Samaritan text preserve the inferior reading. The second category are dogmatic alterations, e.g., the reading 'Gerizim' in the Samaritan text for 'Ebal' in the Masoretic (Deut. 27:4), and the substitution of 'the place which God has chosen' in the Samaritan for 'the place which God shall choose' in the Masoretic. The third category - and it is with this last that we are most concerned - are the cases within the same books of the Pentateuch, or within different books, where whole passages are inserted in the Samaritan text, which were taken from some other part dealing with the same event or with something that was regarded as relevant.

Presumably, when the Samaritan Jewish schism took place, the Samaritans took over the same Torah as the one which was in the hands of the post-exilic Jewish community. It may have been Manasseh, the grandson of Eliashib, who took this text of the Law to Shechem after his expulsion from the ranks of the priesthood at Jerusalem as a result of his marrying Sanballat's daughter. Obviously, the Samaritan priests had to answer some awkward questions when Mount Gerizim was made the site of the sanctuary instead of Zion. The name of Gerizim had to be intruded into the Law. We know that the descendants of those who were left after the fall of the Northern Kingdom came to Jerusalem at least from time to time to keep the festivals, etc. This had to be stopped - a task that was perhaps made somewhat easier by the intransigence of Ezra and Nehemiah. Moreover, it is always the tendency with reformers or dissenters to claim that they have discovered the original truth in its pure state. So also with the Samaritans who argued that since the Law was perfect, God must have told the people of Israel where they were to bring their offerings in the time between the entry into Canaan and the capture of Jerusalem. Also, since the Law was Mosaic, this information as to the site of the sanctuary must have been given to Moses.

Furthermore, Jacob is reported to have told his wives in justification of his handling of the breeding arrangements of Laban's flock that the idea had been suggested to him by the angel of God in a dream, Gen. 31:11-13, although in the preceding chapter it is not stated that Jacob's conduct in this matter had been divinely inspired; hence something must be wrong with the recension the Samaritans had received from the Jews. For if the Law is perfect - as it undoubtedly is - surely an account should have been given previously of this angelic message; and since no such account is found in the Jewish recension, it was added after Gen. 30:35 from Gen. 31:11-13. Similarly, in Exodus there are quite a number of occasions where God gives an order to Moses to be transmitted by him and Aaron to Pharaoh. In the Jewish recension it is then stated that Moses and Aaron spoke to Pharaoh, and we are led to assume that they delivered the message, although the order itself is not repeated. The Samaritan version makes good this lack - if such it be thought to be - by repeating the message verbatim, although changing, where necessary, the first or second person to third, in order to make it quite clear that the order was carried out *au pied de la lettre*. Examples of this procedure are Samaritan. The following references are according to the chapter and verse division of the Hebrew Bible. The extra verses appearing in the Samaritan Bible are here marked with the accompanying "b", following Von Gall's numeration. Exod. 7:18b = 7:15 beg. 16, 17; 7:29b = 7:26 end, 27, 28; 8:1b = 8:1a; 8:19b = 8:16, 17, 18; 9:5b = 9:1b-5; 9:19b = 9:13-19. The Samaritan priests could no doubt argue that the Jewish recension of the Law was defective in such cases. To the modern scholar the Samaritan recension is clearly stamped as secondary by the filling of these so-called gaps. But it put into the hands of the Samaritan priests a useful tool for 'restoring' texts and passages to uphold their claim that they represented 'true' Israel, and by applying this method liberally they diverted attention from the particular 'restorations' which were made for dogmatic reasons. The interesting thing is that such alterations and harmonizations affect in the main, apart from the tenth Commandment, history and not Law. A fruitful field for harmonization and restoration was provided by those passages in the Book of Numbers which deal with events recapitulated in the early chapters of Deuteronomy. Actually the Masoretic text in Num. 21:33f. provides a precedent for this harmonizing and restorative procedure, for Num. 21:33f. is verbally identical with Deut. 3:1f., except for the change of the person from first to third, while Num. 21:35 is an abbreviation of Deut. 3:3, and, as Gray[15] remarks, "In view of these facts there can be little doubt that the story of Og has been incorporated in Numbers from Deuteronomy". The Samaritans proceeded to insert Deut. 1:6-8 after Num. 10:10; Deut. 1:20-23a after Num. 12:16; Deut. 1:27-33 after Num. 13:33; Deut. 1:42 after Num. 14:40; Deut. 3:24-25, 26b-28; Deut. 2:2-6 after Num. 20:13; Deut. 2:9 after Num. 21:11; Deut. 2:17-19 after Num. 21:12; Deut. 2:24-25 after Num. 21:20; Deut. 2:28-29 beg. after Num. 21:22; Deut. 2:31 after Num. 21:23a; Deut. 3:21f after Num. 27:23. The same thing was probably carried on in Hebrew texts within the Jewish community, as is shown by the witness of the Septuagint to the Hebrew text underlying it in Num. 27:18, which had been influenced by Deuteronomy, whereas the Samaritan and the Masoretic Hebrew had not. Nevertheless, this cross-fertilization of those parts of the Pentateuch which have been recapitulated in Deuteronomy was carried on to the account of the theophany at Sinai and the revelation delivered there. For the Samaritan it was only logical to proceed to apply the same method to the Exodus narrative here.

Yet in the case of the Ten Commandments the Samaritan Pentateuch has to a large extent retained the differences which are found in the Masoretic text between the forms of the Ten Commandments in Exodus and Deuteronomy; compare e.g., Samaritan Exod. 20:10-11 and Deut. 5:14-15, although Exod. 20:8 has 'observe the Sabbath day' as in Deut. 5:12, instead of 'remember', as in the Masoretic Exod. 20:8.

Another example of harmonization is that Samaritan Exod. 20:17 and Deut. 5:21 (18) insert in the list of things not to be coveted 'his field' which is found only in the Masoretic Deut. 5:21 (18). Furthermore, the additional Samaritan tenth Commandment is alike in Exodus and Deuteronomy. It is drawn from the first half of Deut. 11:29, followed by Deut. 27:2, plus the first part of Deut. 27:3 and Deut. 27:4, down to Gerizim (so read, instead of Ebal); then Deut. 27:5-7. The commandment ends with

Deut. 11:30. We note first that harmonization has taken place between two passages in Deuteronomy, with the difference that the passages drawn upon were left as they were where they were, but the product of harmonization was inserted where there was reference to neither passage. What has happened is that the commandment to set up on Mount Ebal (or Gerizim) the stones inscribed with the words of the Law and an altar for the sacrifices required by the Law was inserted between Deut. 11:29 and Deut. 11:30; the second part of Deut. 11:29, which commands the setting of the blessing upon Mount Gerizim and of the curse upon Mount Ebal, remains in the text of Deut. 11:29 as it stands in that chapter of Deuteronomy; yet when Deut. 11:29 is drawn upon to make with Deut. 27:2-7 the Samaritan tenth Commandment, the verses from Deut. 27 replace the second part of Deut. 11:29. This tenth Commandment, developed in Deuteronomy from Deuteronomic verses for the Deuteronomic Decalogue, is affixed also to the Exodus Decalogue.

But the influence of Deuteronomy on the Exodus account of the theophany did not stop with the addition of an extra tenth Commandment. The Exodus description of the people's reaction to the theophany is filled out by skillful interweaving of the parallel account in Deuteronomy: e.g., after Exod. 20:19 (beg.) 'and said to Moses', Deut. 5:24-27 is inserted and substituted for the middle part of Ex. 20:19. Thereafter follows Exod. 20:19 (end) - 22 (beg.). Exod. 20:22 (beg.) reads, 'And the LORD said to Moses' followed by direct speech, and Deut. 5:25-27 also uses direct speech for God's words to Moses, but what was said by God according to Exodus and Deuteronomy is not the same. Yet all the Law was God-given; there could not be two accounts of what God had said at Sinai. Therefore the Samaritan inserts the words of God found in Deut. 5:28-29 into the Exodus narrative here. However, what God has said according to Exodus 20:19 is not excluded, but is deferred until the reader has noted first what God had said according to the Deuteronomy account. Even more interesting is the fact that we have here a case of double intrusion. The section from Deut. 5:28-30 which has also been inserted into the Exodus account here, has itself been conflated with Deut. 18:18-22; i.e. after Deut. 5:29 as it stands in the Samaritan conflated Exodus text we find Deut. 18:18-22, and then revert to Deut. 5:30-31 before returning to Exod. 20:22. Yet Deut. 5:28-30 as it stands in its proper context in Deuteronomy has not been conflated with Deut. 18:18-22. The next change is in Exod. 20:24, where instead of 'in every place where I cause My name to be remembered' the Samaritan reads 'in the place where I have caused My name to be remembered'.

When we review the alterations and additions to the text in these closing verses of Exod. 20 we find that through the intrusion of Deut. 18:18ff. the Samaritan doctrine of the Taheb or Messiah, based on Deut. 18:18, is brought into close connection with the Ten Commandments. It was on Mount Gerizim that the Taheb was to rediscover the hidden Tabernacle vessels, and after the altar of incense was set up again, the high priest of the Samaritans was to make atonement for Israel, and the new age was to commence. The collocation of these verses from Deut. 18 with the Samaritan tenth Commandment was probably already fixed in the Samaritan text of Exodus by the first century A.D. In the Fourth Gospel the Samaritan woman at Jacob's well in Sychar stresses that 'our fathers worshipped on that mountain', (John 4:20), and when Jesus declares that the day is coming when both Mount Zion and Mount Gerizim will no longer be places of paramount importance for the worship of God, who could be worshipped anyway only in spirit and in truth, the woman asks Him if He is the Messiah 'who will tell us all things' (John 4:25). Jesus replies that He is. This is particularly interesting, since Jesus is in fact saying that He is the Taheb; for the woman did not ask Him if He was the Davidic Messiah, and probably the word Messiah itself is only used here because the author of the Fourth Gospel was a Jew. What is important is that in this chapter of John's Gospel we have the reference to Mount Gerizim, 'that mountain', followed by the reference to the Messiah, seemingly suggesting that the woman knew the Samaritan version of Exodus 20, with the reference to the Taheb following closely after the stress on Mount Gerizim as the place where God is to be worshipped. The question therefore arises whether the Samaritans had concocted the clever composition of their tenth Commandment, and then, after having done so, sought to cover their traces by harmonizing other events, etc., which, like the Decalogue, had their parallels in the early chapters of Deuteronomy. However, such a hypothesis can not stand scrutiny, for it puts the cart before the horse. We have seen that there is harmonization within Genesis, Exodus, and Deuteronomy themselves, not just a deuteronomizing of those parts of the Exodus and Numbers which were mentioned above; in any case, the apparent deuteronomizing was but part of the general harmonizing process which has taken place in the Samaritan Pentateuch in connection with parallel accounts in sources other than Deuteronomy. The fact that Deuteronomy, even in the final draft of the Jewish Pentateuch, stood out as a separate source which had not been interwoven into the other strands of the Pentateuchal narrative, gave the Samaritans more opportunity to carry on a process which they had not started on their own initiative (cf. Massoretic Num. 21:33f. and Deut. 3:1f.). This does not rule out the possibility of their having, in the case of the additional tenth Commandment and the epilogue thereto, seen the possibility of extending the method of harmonization to cases where the need for it was less obvious, but equally serviceable in support of their own claims.

(Exod. 20:1) And God spoke all these words saying, (v.2) I am the LORD your God, who brought you out of the land of Egypt out of the house of bondage.

(1) (v.3) You shall have no other gods before Me. (v.4) You shall not make for yourselves a graven image, or any likeness of anything that is in heaven above, or that is in the earth beneath, or that is in the water under the earth; (v.5) you shall not bow down to them or serve them; for I the LORD your God am a jealous God, visiting the iniquity of the fathers upon the children to the third and fourth generation of those who hate Me, (v.6) but showing steadfast love to thousands of those who love Me and keep My commandments.

(2) (v.7) You shall not take the name of the LORD your God in vain; for the LORD will not hold him guiltless who takes His name in vain.

(3) (v.8) Observe the Sabbath day, to keep it holy (v.9) Six days you shall labor, and do all your work; (v.10) but the seventh day is a Sabbath to the LORD your God; (in it) you shall not do any work, you, or your son, or your daughter, your manservant, or your maidservant, your cattle, or the sojourner who is within your gates; (v.11) for in six days the Lord made heaven and earth, the sea, and all that is in them, and rested the seventh day; therefore the LORD blessed the Sabbath day and hallowed it.

(4) (v.12) Honor your father and your mother, that your days may be long in the land which the LORD your God gives you.

(5) (v.13) You shall not kill.

(6) (v.14) You shall not commit adultery.

(7) (v.15) You shall not steal.

(8) (v.16) You shall not bear false witness against your neighbor.

(9) (v.17) You shall not covet your neighbor's house; you shall not covet your neighbor's wife, his field, his manservant, or his maidservant, his ox, or his ass, or anything that is your neighbor's.

(10) (Deut. 11:29) And when the LORD your God brings you into the land of the

Canaanites which you are entering to take possession of it, (Deut. 27:2) you shall set up these stones and plaster them with plaster, (v.3) and you shall write upon them all the words of the Law. And (v.4) when you have passed over the Jordan, you shall set up these stones, concerning which I command you this day, on Mount Gerizim. (v.5) And there you shall build an altar to the LORD your God, an altar of stones; you shall lift up no iron tool upon them. (v.6) You shall build an altar to the LORD your God of unhewn stones; and you shall offer burnt offerings on it to the LORD your God; (v.7) and you shall sacrifice peace offerings, and shall eat there; and you shall rejoice before the LORD your God. (Deut. 11:30) That mountain is beyond the Jordan, west of the road, toward the going down of the sun, in the land of the Canaanites who live in the Arabah, over against Gilgal, beside the oak of Moreh in front of Shechem. (Exod. 20:18) Now when all the people heard the thunderings and the sound of the trumpet and saw lightnings and the mountain smoking, all the people were afraid and trembled; and they stood afar off, and said to Moses (Deut. 5:24) Behold, the LORD our God has shown us His glory, and His greatness, and we have heard His voice out of the midst of the fire; we have this day seen God speak with man, and man still live. (v.25) Now therefore, why should we die? For this great fire will consume us; if we hear the voice of the LORD our God any more, we shall die. (v.26) For who is there of all flesh, that has heard the voice of the living God speaking out of the midst of the fire, as we have, and has still lived? (v.27) Go near, and hear all that the LORD our God will say; and speak to us all that the LORD our God will speak to you; and we will hear and do it, (Exod. 20:19) but let not God speak to us, lest we die. (v.20) And Moses said to the people, Do not fear; for God has come to prove you, and that the fear of Him may be before your eyes, that you may not sin. (v.21) And the people stood afar off, while Moses drew near to the thick cloud where God was. (v.22) And the LORD spoke to Moses saying, (Deut. 5:28) I have heard the words of this people, which they have spoken to you; they have rightly said all that they have spoken (v.29) Oh that they had such a mind as this always, to fear Me and to keep My commandments, that it might go well with them and with their children for ever! (Deut. 18:18) I will raise up for them a prophet like you from among their brethren; and I will put My words in his mouth, and he shall speak to them all that I command him. (v.19) And whoever will not give heed to his words while he shall speak in My name, I myself will require it of him. (v.20) But the prophet who presumes to speak in My name that which I have not commanded him to speak, or who speaks in the name of other gods, that same prophet shall die. (v.21) And if you say in your heart, How may we know the word which the LORD has not spoken? - when a prophet speaks in the name of the LORD, (v.22) if the word does not come to pass or come true, that is a word which the LORD has not spoken; the prophet has spoken it presumptuously, you need not be afraid of him. (Deut. 5:30) Go and say to them, return to your tents. (v.31) But you, stand here by Me, and I will tell you the commandments, the statutes, and the ordinances which you shall teach them, that they may do them in the land which I give them to possess.

Thereafter Exod. 20:22 is resumed.

ḲAṬAF OF THE TEN COMMANDMENTS RECITED ON THE SECOND SABBATH OF THE MONTH.

Exod. 20:1-17 in full, followed by:

And when the LORD, your God, brings you into the land of the Canaanites which you are entering to take possession of it (Deut. 11:29) you shall set up these

> stones, and plaster them with plaster (Deut. 27:3), and you shall write upon them all the words of the Law. And when you have passed over the Jordan, you shall set up these stones concerning which I command you this day, on Mount Gerizim (v.4). And there you shall build an altar to the LORD, your God, an altar of stones; you shall lift up no iron tool upon them. (v.5) You shall build an altar to the LORD your God of unhewn stones; and you shall offer burnt offerings thereon to the LORD your God (v.6). And you shall sacrifice peace offerings, and shall eat there; and you shall rejoice before the LORD your God (v.7). That mountain is beyond the Jordan, west of the road, toward the going down of the sun, in the land of the Canaanites who live in the Arabah over against Gilgal, beside the oak of Moreh in front of Shechem (Deut. 11:30).

On the other Sabbaths this is recited:

> And showing steadfast love to thousands of those who love Me and keep My commandments (Exod. 20:6). You shall not take the name of the LORD your God in vain; for the LORD will not hold him guiltless that takes His name in vain (v.7). Observe the Sabbath day, and the seventh day is a Sabbath, and He rested on the seventh day, therefore the LORD blessed the Sabbath day and hallowed it. (Ḳaṭaf of v.8-11). And you shall rejoice before the LORD your God; that mountain is beyond the Jordan (ḳaṭaf of Deut. 27:7 and 11:30).

On the last Sabbath of every month the following is recited: The Ten Commandments from Deuteronomy, read within the Deuteronomy ḳaṭaf, viz. (Deut. 5:4-5) 'Face to face, you did not go up into the mountain, saying'.

Then follows Deut. 5:6-21 in full.

The tenth Commandment is exactly as it is in the Exodus

reading of the Ten Commandments.

The contraction of the Ten Commandments read on other Sabbaths is the same as that in the Exodus ḳaṭaf.

THE ḲAṬAF OF GENESIS

The ḳaṭaf of Genesis is included here as an example of a literary form which, if not invented by the Samaritans, was at least used by them for a very long Time. We have already referred to the use of the ḳaṭaf in the Samaritan liturgy, and have suggested that it represented a Samaritan attempt to retain the all important place of the lessons from the Law as the main component of the liturgy; and that at one time readings from the Law presumably made up the whole liturgy. When prayers and hymns were subsequently added, the Samaritans were faced with the choice of either an interminably long service, with all the readings from the Law retained in full, or the omission of all such readings except the weekly parašah. The Samaritan solution to this dilemma was to select phrases from each of the little parašiyyot or ḳaṣim, and to string these phrases together into a fairly coherent digest of the Law, at the same time retaining at least in skeletal form the former place of the Law in their public worship.

Ḳĕṭafim are old. Ms. V3 and Ms. B.M. 5034, of the 14th and 13th centuries respectively, give the ḳeṭafim used in the weekday morning and evening services. In six days the whole Law was read in digest, or ḳaṭaf form. These weekday ḳĕṭafim were then combined, augmented with some of the references to the Sabbath occurring in the Law, and read again during the Sabbath morning service. Although the ḳeṭafim of Ms. V3 and Ms. B.M. 5034 were written down six or seven hundred years ago, they contain many snippets of verses which are exactly the same as those in the present-day Sabbath morning service.

The ḳeṭafim are indeed older than the thirteenth or

fourteenth century. Already in the Pirḳe dĕ-Rabbi 'Eli'ezer, (8th or 9th century A.D.), reference is made (ch. XXXVIII) to the Samaritan Law being written in Notariḳon - i.e. shorthand - an obvious but rather hostile reference to the ḳeṭafim; the Samaritans, after all, have the full text of the Law as well. An earlier reference is perhaps the statement in a Baraita,[16] that the *notarii* of the nations obtained the Law from the stones set up by Joshua (cf. Deut. 27:3-4 Josh. 8:32), and therefore their texts were defective. This may refer to the Samaritans and their abbreviated digests of the Law, i.e. the ḳĕṭafim. The ḳaṭaf form must therefore be very old, but the reading of the complete passages selected from the entire range of the Law is probably even older, since the custom was known to, and was approved by, both Jews and Samaritans; cf. on the one hand, the parašah of the King (M. Sot. 7:8), and on the other the Samaritan service for Sabbath eve, which is still made of selected complete parašiyyoṯ.

The ḳaṭaf is similar to some extent to the Latin and Greek cento of the Alexandrian period. With the cento as applied to Homer's and Virgil's epics, a half-line from one strophe was attached to a half-line from another strophe and the poem was thus reduced in length; the cento was still practised in the third or fourth century of this era. The Samaritan Decalogue inscriptions also contain a sort of ḳaṭaf of the full text of the Decalogue, and as was stated above, the four Decalogue inscriptions there translated are probably not later than the fourth century. The Samaritans could thus have adopted the general idea of the ḳaṭaf from the Latin and Greek epic usage, although in the application of the ḳaṭaf idea to the Law, other criteria for the selection of any particular phrase would be used than these which governed the centoists. It is of course possible that the Samaritan ḳaṭaf of the Law as a literary type is far older. It is not beyond the bounds of possibility that the ḳaṭaf form might have influenced the Alexandrians who might have modified it and applied it to making digests of classical epic poetry. After all, the Samaritan community was a large and influential one in Egypt from the time of the founding of Alexandria. Points of contact between Greeks and Samaritans were not restricted, so that either of the two could have become debtor to the other. Whether or not the ḳaṭaf form is older than the fourth century, it certainly was in the fourth century that the Samaritans were confronted with the problem of how to keep the liturgy as it had been, made up entirely of readings from the Law, and at the same time find space for the liturgical compositions of the great Amram Darah and Marḳah.

Cowley, in defining ḳaṭaf,[17] says that it is a series of similar words or phrases strung together. This is most misleading, for while there are such ḳeṭafim they are not representative of the ḳaṭaf form as a whole. It is unfortunate that Cowley did not, with one minor exception,[18] publish any ḳaṭaf in his monumental edition of the Samaritan liturgy. While we are indebted to him for gathering together the wealth of poetry and prayer of the Samaritan liturgy, the student of Samaritan literature would have appreciated a detailed exposition of just what a ḳaṭaf was and how ḳeṭafim were used in worship. In the Sabbath morning service the ḳeṭafim of the five books of the Law are not read in their entirety without a break. Rather, the pattern is as follows: first come two hymns, then a brief exclamation of praise; thereafter follows the ḳaṭaf of one of the five books, and in conclusion a *gloria* is sung. The process is repeated with each of the other four books of the Law.

The Sabbath ḳeṭafim, like the Sabbath service in general, are basic for all seasons and festivals of the Samaritan religious year. On such occasions, extra snippets of verses relating to particular aspects of worship, etc., are inserted in the basic ḳeṭafim of the five books of the Law. On festivals, the most important of such references to the particular day, although inserted in the ḳaṭaf, are read in full; indeed the ḳaṣim from which each phrase of the ḳaṭaf is drawn were presumably themselves once read in full. The ḳaṭaf is indeed a very useful method of reading the whole Law quickly, for undoubtedly the Samaritan who knows, as they all do, his Torah well can supply the rest of the sentences or paraš̆iyyot̲ from which the snippets of the ḳaṭaf have been taken. In short, the ḳaṭaf serves as a sort of mnemonic device for the entire Law. It is possible that there is more to the ḳaṭaf than this. In the first place a ḳaṭaf could hardly have been made until the Biblical text was rigidly fixed, otherwise the sometimes exceedingly short phrases which make up the ḳeṭafim could not have been chosen with any assurance of identification. It would seem therefore that the ḳaṭaf represents an attitude towards the Law involving belief in verbal inspiration. In the Samaritan *ḳeme'im*, or phylactries - not Tefillin, for the Samaritans have no Tefillin - the Law is written out in ḳaṭaf form in seven columns on a square of leather. The square is then folded into a strip of the required thickness and is worn over the arm or in the bosom, the idea being that of clothing one's self with God's word. In some Samaritan phylacteries the ḳaṭaf is partly a coherent digest of some passages of the Law, and partly an unintelligible Notariḳon; but to the devout Samaritan even the abracadabra was important, because it consisted of letters drawn from certain verses of the Law whose power and protection he believed he possessed when he wore the ḳame'a. It was the same with the ḳeṭafim. The reading of the ḳaṭaf of Genesis was as effective as the reading of the whole of Genesis, because the pieces selected were the best of the whole; and in any case, while it took a whole year to read the Pentateuch in the form of the weekly lessons of the Samaritan afternoon service, one could read the essence of the entire Law in the first part of the Sabbath morning service.

THE ḲAṬAF OF GENESIS

And the LORD God planted a garden, in Eden, in the east; and there He put the man whom He had formed. And out of the ground the LORD God made to grow every tree that is pleasant to the sight and good for food, the tree of life also in the midst of the garden and the tree of the knowledge of good and evil. A river flowed out of Eden to water the garden, and there it divided and became four rivers. The name of the first is Pishon (Gen. 2:8-11). The name of the second river is Gihon (Gen. 2:13). And the name of the third river is Hiddekel. And the fourth river is the Euphrates (Gen. 2:14). *Blessed be the LORD God, Praised be the LORD God.* The LORD God took the man and put him into the garden of Eden to till it and to keep it. And the LORD God commanded (Gen. 2:15-16). And they heard the voice of the LORD God (Gen. 3:8). To Seth also a son was born, and he called his name Enosh. At that time men began to call upon the name of the LORD.

This is the book of the generations of Adam. When God created man He made him in the likeness of God. Male and female created He them, and He blessed them and named them man when they were created (Gen. 4:26-5:2). Enoch walked with God (Gen. 5:24). And Noah found favor in the eyes of the LORD (Gen. 6:8). These are the generations of Noah. Noah was a righteous man and blameless in his generation; Noah walked with God (Gen. 6:9). Noah did this, he did all that God commanded him. (Gen. 6:22). And Noah did all that the LORD commanded him (Gen. 7:5). Only Noah was left, and those that were with him in the ark (Gen. 7:23). But God remembered Noah (Gen. 8:1). So Noah went forth and his son (Gen. 8:18); they went forth by families out of the ark (Gen. 8:19). Then Noah built an altar to the LORD, and took of every clean animal and of every clean bird, and offered burnt offerings on the altar. And the LORD smelled the pleasing odor (Gen. 8:20-21). While the earth remains, seedtime and harvest, cold and heat, summer and winter, day and night, shall not cease. And God blessed Noah and his sons, and said to them, Be fruitful and multiply (Gen. 8:22-9:1). And I will make of you a great nation, and I will bless you, and make your name great, so that you will be a blessing. And I will bless those who bless you (Gen. 12:2-3).

Abram passed through the land to the place at Shechem, to the oak of Moreh (Gen. 12:6). Then the Lord appeared to Abram and said, To your descendants will I give this land. So he built there an altar to the LORD who had appeared to him. Thence he removed to the mountain on the east of Bethel, and pitched his tent at Bethel (Gen. 12:7-8). Arise, walk through the length and the breadth of the land (Gen. 13:17). And Abram went up (Gen. 13:1). And he blessed Abram, and he said, Blessed be Abram (Gen. 14:19). I have sworn to the LORD God Most High, maker of heaven and earth (Gen. 14:22). Fear not, Abram, I am your shield; your reward shall be very great (Gen. 15:1). And He said, Look now toward heaven and number the stars (Gen. 15:5), and He said to him, so shall your seed be (Gen. 15:5). And he believed the LORD; and He reckoned it to him for righteousness (Gen. 15:6). On that day the LORD made a covenant with Abram, saying (Gen. 15:18), I am God Almighty; walk before Me, and be blameless. And I will make My covenant between Me and you (Gen. 17:1-2). And I will establish My covenant with Isaac (Gen. 17-21), so that they may keep the way of the LORD by doing righteousness and justice; so that the LORD may bring to Abraham what He has promised him (Gen. 18:19) *I am that I am* (Exod. 3:14). Behold your servant has found favor in your sight, and you have shown me great kindness (Gen. 19:19). He will pray for you, and you shall live (Gen. 20:7). Then Abraham prayed to God; and God healed (Gen. 20:17). *So may the LORD heal our wounds.*

God is with you in all that you do (Gen. 21:22) Abraham planted a tamarisk tree in Beer-sheba, and called there on the name of the LORD, the everlasting God (Gen. 21:33). God tested Abraham, and said to him, Abraham! (Gen. 22:1). Abraham lifted up his eyes, and saw the place afar off (Gen. 22:4). And we will worship and come back to you (Gen. 22:5). Abraham built an altar there, and laid the wood in order, and bound Isaac his son (Gen. 22:9). So Abraham called the name of that place, The LORD will provide, as it is said to this day, On the Mount of the LORD it shall be provided (Gen. 22:14). I will indeed bless you, and I will multiply your descendants (Gen. 22:17), and I will multiply your descendants (Gen. 26:24). And by your descendants shall all the nations of the earth bless themselves, because you have obeyed My voice (Gen. 22:18). The LORD the God of heaven, who took me (Gen. 24:7). O LORD, God of my master Abraham (Gen. 24:12). The LORD, before whom I walk, will send His angel with you and prosper your way, (Gen. 24:40). Then I bowed my head and worshipped the LORD, and blessed the LORD, the God of my master Abraham (Gen. 24:48).

And Isaac went out to meditate in the field in the evening (Gen. 24:63). God blessed Isaac his son, and Isaac dwelt (Gen. 25:11). And Isaac prayed to the LORD for his wife, and the LORD granted his prayer (Gen. 25:21). *So may the LORD grant our prayer, and have mercy upon us, and hear our requests, and ease our oppression, and relieve our suffering, and look upon us with His mercy and loving kindness, and fulfill for us.* And I will fulfill the oath which I swore to Abraham your father. I will multiply your descendants; and by your descendants all the nations of the earth shall bless themselves: because that Abraham obeyed My voice and kept My charge, My commandments, My statutes, and My laws (Gen. 26:3-5). And Isaac sowed in that land, and reaped in the same year a hundredfold. The LORD blessed him (Gen. 26:12). And he said, For now the LORD has made room for us (Gen. 26:22). You are now the blessed of the LORD (Gen. 26:29). *May the LORD fulfill that with which He blessed him.* May God give you of the dew of the heaven, and of the fatness of the earth, and plenty of grain and wine.

Let peoples serve you, and nations bow down to you. Be lord over your brothers, and let your mother's sons bow down to you. Cursed be every one who curses you and blessed be every one who blesses you (Gen. 27:28-29). *Fulfill for us this blessing, LORD, and for all our community.* God Almighty bless you and make you fruitful and multiply you, that you may become a company of peoples (Gen. 28:3). May He give the blessing of Abraham to you and to your descendants with you (Gen. 28:4). How awesome is this place! This is none other than the house of God, and this is the gate of heaven (Gen. 28:17).

Then Jacob made a vow, saying If God will be with me, (Gen. 28:20), of all that Thou givest me I will give the tenth to Thee (Gen. 28:22). *Praised be God. There is no God but One.* I am the God of Bethel (Gen. 31:13). Then the company which is left will escape (Gen. 32:8). And Jacob said, O God of my father Abraham and God of my father Isaac, O LORD, who didst say to me, Return to your country and to your kindred, and I will do you good. I am not worthy of the least of all the steadfast love, and of all the faithfulness which Thou hast shown to Thy servant (Gen. 32:10-11). But Thou didst say, I will do you good, and make your descendants as the sand of the sea (Gen. 32:13). And he encamped before the city (Gen. 33:18), and he bought the piece of land (Gen. 33:19). There he erected an altar and called it, El-Elohe-Israel (Gen. 33:20). And purify yourselves and change your garments; (Gen. 35:2) then let us arise and go up to Bethel (Gen. 35:3), because there God had revealed himself to him (Gen. 35:7). I am God Almighty: be fruitful and multiply (Gen. 35:11). Then God went up from him in the place (Gen. 35:13). And Jacob set up a pillar in the place (Gen. 35:14). This is the history of the family of Jacob-Joseph (Gen. 37:2). Now Israel loved Joseph (Gen. 37:3).

Now Joseph had a dream (Gen. 37:5). Meanwhile the Midianites had sold Joseph (Gen. 37:36). Now Joseph was brought down to Egypt (Gen. 39:1). The LORD was with Joseph (Gen. 39:2). May God Almighty grant you mercy (Gen. 43:14). God Almighty appeared to me at Luz in the land of Canaan and blessed me (Gen. 48:3). And he blessed Joseph, and said, The God before whom my fathers Abraham and Isaac have walked, the God who has led me all my life long to this day (Gen. 48:15). The Angel who has redeemed me from all evil (Gen. 48:16). I wait for Thy salvation, O LORD, (Gen. 49:18). By the God of your father who will help you, by the Almighty who will bless you (Gen. 49:25), beyond the bounties of the everlasting hills, they shall be on the head of Joseph (Gen. 49:26). But God will visit you, and bring you out of this land to the land which he swore to Abraham, to Isaac, and to Jacob (Gen. 50:24). Then Joseph took an oath of the sons of Israel (Gen. 50:25), and he was put in a coffin in Egypt (Gen. 50:26).

Moses commanded us the Torah, an inheritance of the congregation of Jacob. There is none like God, O Jeshurun. Praised be our God. The LORD, merciful and gracious God; forgive Thy people Israel who prostrate themselves towards Mount Gerizim, and whom Thou hast redeemed. O LORD, there is no God but One, there is no God but One.

FOOTNOTES

1. *Z.D.M.G.* XIV, p.622 and Montgomery *'The Samaritans'* Philadelphia, 1907, p.274.

2. *Ibid.*, plate facing p.272.

3. Pirke de-R. Eliezer, ed. Friedlander, Kegan Paul, London, 1916, p.299.

4. See Malef p.1f.

5. Cf. below p.31 Note the saying of Genesis in Kaṭaf starts with Gen. 2:8.

6. Cf. Sof. 1:18.

7. Cf. M. Ta'aniṯ 4:3 and M. Meg. 3:6.

8. See below p. 31-35 for the whole Ḳaṭaf of Genesis.

9. Cf. Neh. 8:8.

10. See the article on these four inscriptions by J. Bowman and S. Talmon, in the *Bulletin of the John Rylands Library*, XXXIII, No.2, (March, 1951), p.211-236.

11. *Ibid.* p.275.

12. For a discussion of the various traditions, Jewish, Protestant, Roman Catholic, and Samaritan, on the numbering of the Ten Commandments, cf. Bowman and Talmon, *ibid.*, pp.219-224.

13. Cf. *Origenis Hexaplorum*, Oxford 1875.

14. See Ben-Zebi, 'Eben-mĕzuzah Šomronit mik-kĕfar Bīlō, *Yĕdi'ot ha-Hebrah* le-Hakirat 'Ereṣ Yisra'el we-'atiḳoteha, XVIII (1954), pp.223-229.

15. I.C.C. pp.xl-xliii Numbers. T. & T. Clark, Edinburgh, 1912.

16. T. B. Sot. 35b.

17. *Samaritan Liturgy*, Oxford, 1909, II. p. xxii.

18. *Ibid.* Vol. I, p.7, line 4 up - p.9, line 14 down.

A photograph of the page in the Nablus Tolidah "Autograph" MS. with the famous reference to the Abisha Scroll in the Margin (and not in the text as it is in the laster MS. used by Neubauer). The translation of this marginal reference is on p. 46f.

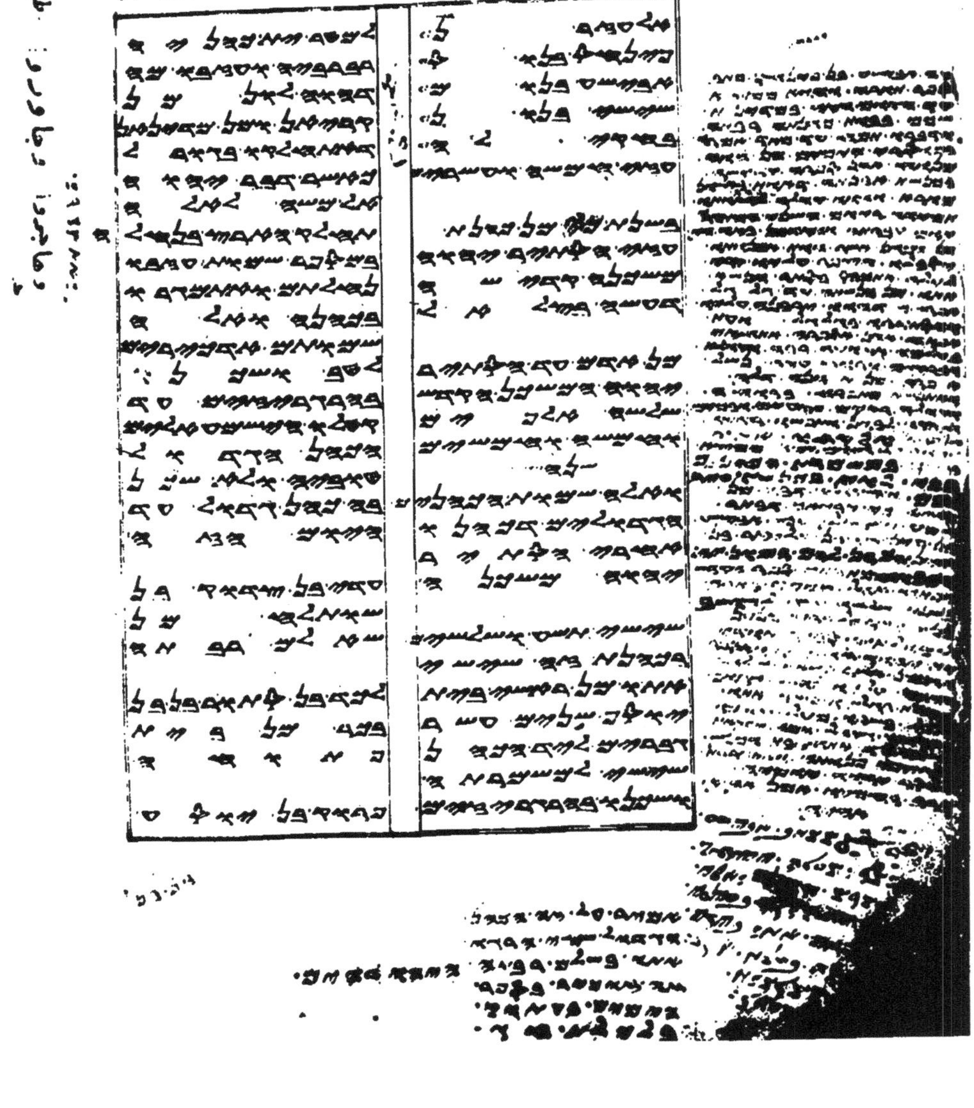

CHAPTER 2

THE SAMARITAN CHRONICLE TOLIDAH

The extract given here comprises the introduction to the Chronicle, setting out the Samaritan method of calendar calculation, followed by the text of the Tolidah itself from Adam to Abisha, the great grandson of Aaron. The latter portion is small, for the reason that while the chronicle is important, it hardly makes interesting reading, so that a small sample is sufficient to illustrate the general character of the work. The introduction, on the other hand, deserves to be given in its entirety, as it attempts to explain the basic principles of the Samaritan chronology which lies behind their annals in general.

There is some reason to believe that the introduction was written after the major part of the Chronicle itself. Pages 1-3 - the introduction - in the 'autograph' manuscript of the Tolidah kept in the High Priest's house in Nablus, are not as old as the part of the work copied by Jacob ben Ishmael in 747 A.H. = 1346/47 A.D. A note in this manuscript (page 11, margin), dealing with the discovery, or rather rediscovery, of the Abisha scroll (which is not mentioned in the main text), was probably written by the same hand as the introduction; in any case, it is certain that the introduction has incorporated a part of this note in its text (see below, p. 46f.), showing that the introduction in its present form is later than the major part of the Tolidah as copied by Jacob ben Ishmael in 747 A.H. (who followed, for the earlier part, Eleazar ben Amram's Tolidah written in 544 A.H. = 1149/50 A.D.). Successive priests after Jacob ben Ishmael's time added their bit to Jacob's manuscript which still survives in Nablus. It is not unlikely that the Samaritans had had genealogical lists of their high priestly succession long before Eleazar ben Amram wrote the proto-Tolidah. By that time the Samaritans had been reduced to a small community, but earlier they must have had a larger interest in stating their claims and counterclaims in their war of words against the Jews. By the twelfth century there were far fewer Samaritans and Jews in Palestine than there had been in the days of the Samaritan schism in the fourth century B.C., when Samaritan and Jew must have argued furiously as to who possessed a valid priesthood. R. H. Pfeiffer (*Introduction to the Old Testament*, London, 1952, p.806) is undoubtedly right in regarding the Biblical book of Chronicles as a Jewish apology against the Samaritans. If this is true of the main body of Chronicles, it applies all the more to a later addition like 1 Chron. 6 with its list of preexilic high priests. After the establishment of the Samaritan Temple on Mount Gerizim, the question of the validity of its priesthood was probably raised. The Samaritans knew that attack was the best method of defence. They knew that the Zadokite priesthood in Jerusalem had not always been dominant; at best, their supremacy went back no farther than the time of Solomon, when Abiathar, the descendant of Eli, the priest of Shiloh, had been ousted. The Samaritans knew also that Abiathar's line had eventually been to some extent reinstated. In any case, the fact that the Priestly God allows all priests of Aaronite lineage to officiate, free from Ezekiel's restriction of priestly functions to the sons of Zadok, meant that Abiathar's line had equal standing with Zadok's, because both claimed descent from Aaron. The Samaritans seized on the fact that Abiathar descended from Ithamar, Aaron's younger son, which made the Jews emphasize all the more their Zadokite priesthood, since it traced its lineage to Eleazar, Aaron's elder son and father of Phinehas, with whom the eternal covenant of the priesthood was made. Nevertheless, Aaronite priests who were not descendants of Phinehas had officiated, and still could officiate, in Judah. The Samaritans, eager to claim the validity of their own priestly orders, made no such mistake. Their priestly genealogy was traced back to Phinehas, Eleazar, and Aaron, and even a Zadok figured in it.

The Hebrew text of the Tolidah used for the following translation is that of the manuscript in the High Priest's house at Nablus, a transcript of which was published by the present writer, where the relationship of Neubauer's text (*Journal Asiatique*, 6e serie, XIV (1869) pp.385-470) based on the Bodleian manuscript of the Tolidah is discussed.

THE SAMARITAN CHRONICLE THE TOLIDAH

This is the Hebrew method of calculation by which we know the days, the months, and the years, and which we have inherited from Phinehas[1] the son of Eleazar the son of Aaron the priest - may the peace of God rest upon him, his forefathers, and his uncle - who learned it from Moses the prophet - the peace of God be upon him. It had been handed down by tradition from the three patriarchs: Jacob, Isaac, and Abraham - peace be upon them who acquired this knowledge from Eber, who received it successively from Shem, Noah, Seth, Adam, the angels and the LORD Himself.

Now our father Phinehas was the possessor of the covenant of the high priesthood,[2] which is our inheritance for ever, and after the children of Israel had entered the land of Canaan and were settled there securely, our father, Phinehas, tested this calculation on the side of the holy Mount Gerizim. With this calculation we determine[3] the course of the sun and of the moon, for God said at the time when He created them;[4] *Let them be for signs and for seasons, and for days, and for years.* We determine nothing by only one of them,[5] for the Lord has said;[6] *You shall therefore keep this ordinance at its appointed time from year to year.* For if we should calculate by only one[7] of them, we would not arrive at the month of Abib,[8] which must be Nisan[9] every year, seeing that the LORD has said, *Observe the month of Abib.*[10] Blessed be the LORD, our God, who has given us a right calculation[11] and a perfect Torah by the hand of a righteous and reliable prophet; in which He said, *The appointed feasts of the LORD which you shall proclaim as holy convocations, My appointed feasts are these.*[12] For this calculation was already in the hands of Noah in the ark, since we find it written in the Torah;[13] *In the second month, on the seventh day of the month, on that day all the fountains of the great deep burst forth;* and we read also,[14] *and the waters prevailed upon the earth a hundred and fifty days,* and so on, to[15] *And in the seventh month, on the seventeenth day of the month, the ark came to rest.* Now if we take the number of days and calculate them in months, we find them to be six. And it is said further,[16] *In the tenth month, on the first day of the month,*[16a] *the tops of the mountains were seen.*

We have inherited the tradition that God gave to our forefathers, from Adam to Moses, three books:[17] the Book of Wars, the Book of Astronomy, and the Book of Signs; and He informed Adam and his sons, the pure line of descent, as to who it was that created the two lights for seasons, for days, and for years. Nor was anything kept secret from Noah, for we read, *And the LORD spoke to his heart*[18] (Gen. 8:21), and informed him of the time for sowing and harvest, and of the time of cold and heat; and Noah taught this to his sons.

We find the same in the case of Jacob,[19] of whom it is said, *And he served with him seven years more and a month of days,* and we know therefore that this is true, for God has said to our forefathers:[20] *This month shall be for you the beginning of months,* thus vouchsafing them His goodness and mercy alone out of all peoples who are on the face of the earth, and they learned to know it (= the calendar), for He had hallowed the Sabbath. But the feasts and judgments, and the offerings He made known only to Moses,[21] His prophet, by His word, *And Moses told the feasts of God to the children of Israel* (Lev. 23:44).

And this calculation remained with our forefathers, for there is no way to derive it from the Torah,[22] so that we might have taken it therefrom; rather we have it from the high priests,[23] for it goes back to the house of Phinehas, who taught it to all the children of Israel.

And after our forefathers had come to the Holy Land, to the land of Canaan, and God had given them relief from all their enemies round about, and they were settled securely, Phinehas, our father, the son of Eleazar the priest - eternal peace be upon him, his forefathers, and his uncle[24] - tested it according to the length and breadth of the holy mountain, Mount Gerizim. And he revealed it in righteousness, and made known the correct courses of the sun and the moon, by which we know the seasons of the years, the months, and the days. He did this in the first month, which corresponds to the month of Nisan, in the year 2794 after the creation of the world. And this calculation remained with his descendants, who inherited the covenant,[25] being bequeathed to one after another in turn. For they are the holy chain,[26] and the calculation is a sacred teaching which they, and no one else, teach to all the children of Israel, as God has said with reference to the high priest,[27] *And Aaron shall take upon himself any guilt incurred in the holy offering which the people of Israel hallow,* and so forth, up to[28] *to distinguish between the holy and the common;* and also with reference to Joshua,[29] And he shall stand before the Priest Eleazar who shall inquire for him by the judgment of the Urim. And they[30] have kept it up to the present day. Magnified be the name of God!

We have investigated the Jubilees[31] which have elapsed since the settlement of the children of Israel in the land of Canaan, up to the present day, which is the month of Tammuz,[32] corresponding to the month of Rabī' I of the year 747[33] of the dominion of the children of Ishmael, and we have found them to be sixty Jubilees, the current year being the fourth year of the 5th period of release of the sixty-first Jubilee from the settlement of the children of Israel in the Holy Land, the land of Canaan, i.e. the year 5778 since the creation of the world, which is the year 714 of the Persian King Jezdegird.[34] This Jezdegird was one of the sons of Ptolemy[35] who was one of the foremost philosophers, supreme in the science of astronomy and in the courses of the stars, and composed many works on that subject. As Jezdegird looked into the works of the ancients and sought to comprehend the calculation which was in the hands of the Samaritans, and as he mastered their methods and the reckoning of days which was in their hands, their correctness became apparent to him. And he investigated it so that there should be mention of his testimony[36] as a witness to its truth.

As we said above, we have investigated the Jubilees[37] which have elapsed from the settlement of the children of Israel in the land of Canaan up to the present day, which is the month of Tammuz, corresponding to the month of Rabī' I of the year 747 of the dominion of the Ishmaelites. We have found them to be sixty Jubilees and four periods of release and four years of the fifth period of release,[38] of the sixty-first Jubilee from the settlement of the children of Israel in the Holy Land, the land of Canaan. During the first five Jubilees and two periods of release our fathers hallowed the fiftieth year by sounding the trumpets in the seventh month and proclaiming release throughout the land to all its inhabitants. But after the LORD had hidden[39] the Tabernacle, evil years came upon them, when the LORD scattered them over the face of the earth; yet despite all this they (still) kept this law.

Thus we have counted the number of the aforementioned Jubilees and periods of release, and have found them as it shall presently be written before you in this blessed recapitulation. And all the years from the day when God created man on the earth until the coming of the children of Israel into the land of Canaan are 2794 years; and from the settling of the children of Israel in the land of Canaan until the day in which this recital is being written, there are 2984 years, from the time when they began to observe periods of release, as God said,[40] *When you come into the land which I give you and reap its harvest,* etc. Between their coming into the land and their beginning the calculation, there passed six months, for the calculation of the years of release began with the onset of the seventh month, since the LORD has said in the holy Torah, *On the tenth day of the seventh month, on the Day of Atonement, you shall send abroad the trumpet throughout all your land.* If you investigate you will discover that in fact five Jubilees make 246 years,[42] namely, by summing up the five thus:

the	first	Jubilee	makes	50	years,
"	2nd	"	"	99	"
"	3rd	"	"	148	"
"	4th	"	"	197	"
"	5th	"	"	246	"
"	10th	"	"	492	"
"	20th	"	"	984	"
"	40th	"	"	1968	"
"	55th	"	"	2706	"
"	56th	"	"	2755	"
"	57th	"	"	2804	"
"	58th	"	"	2853	"
"	59th	"	"	2902	"
"	60th	"	"	2951	"
"	61st	"	"	3000	"
"	62nd	"	"	3049	"
"	63rd	"	"	3098	"
"	64th	"	"	3147	"
"	65th	"	"	3196	"

Should you endeavor to calculate the Jubilees that have

elapsed since the settlement of the children of Israel in the land of Canaan up to now, you will have to add six years to the years of the long calculation, for only in the seventh year did our father Phinehas test them according to the breadth of Mount Gerizim.

We have it by tradition from our forefathers upon whom be the favor (of God) - that they sojourned beyond the Jordan towards the wilderness of the Sea, seven years, until the LORD gave them relief from their enemies around them, and they could dwell securely; and the people began the calculation of the periods of release and of the Jubilees only at the time when they entered the land of Canaan, according to His word on Mount Sinai,[43] *When you come into the land which I give you, the land shall keep a Sabbath to the Lord. Six years you shall sow your field, and six years you shall prune your vineyard, and gather in its fruits.* And thus has He said;[44] *They ate the manna, till they came to the border of the land of Canaan.* And after that they sowed and reaped, and kept the periods of release and the Jubilees.

This, then, is the calculation which has been handed down to the present day, which is the month of Tammuz, corresponding to the month Rabī' I, of the year 747 of the dominion of the children of Ishmael, as mentioned above. And we have also received it from our forefathers of old, and famous are their words, that the children of Israel kept the Passover in Egypt on the fifteenth day of Nisan, and likewise celebrated the three feasts for forty years in the wilderness, until they entered the land of Canaan.

After the priest Eleazar the son of Aaron became high priest[45] in his father's stead, according to the command of the LORD, his son Phinehas[46] - peace be upon them all - established this calculation in the right way from the beginning, as the good and correct one according to the breadth of the holy Mount

Gerizim, in the thirteenth year of his father's (high) priesthood. And in the same year Abisha[47] the son of Phinehas, the son of Eleazar, the son of the great Aaron - peace be upon them - wrote the holy book which is to be found in the town of Shechem - may the Lord preserve it - where it is kept in the High Priest's house down to the present day. And this is the calculation by which we fix the feasts of the Lord; it neither ceases, nor changes, nor varies, forever, for we know from the holy Torah the reckoning from Adam down to the exodus of the children of Israel from Egypt, and this reckoning has remained with us. We preserve it just as we preserve our line of priesthood. And it is God who will preserve us and all our community until we shall reach the days of His grace.

And I - Jacob[48] son of Ishmael, the son of Abdel, the son of Jacob, the son of Phinehas, the son of Eleazar, the son of Nathanael, the son of Eleazar, the son of Nathanael, the son of Eleazar, the son of Amram, the son of Aaron, the son of Eleazar, the son of Levi, the high priest, may the glory and grace of God be upon them - wrote this recital in the aforementioned year for my son, Ishmael, the sun of knowledge and the treasure-house of learning and wisdom, who knows the secret of this calculation and all knowledge, and for his sons whom the **LORD** may vouchsafe to him, as well as for his younger brother Joseph and his sons whom he may beget, as well. And they shall be with the wise one who knows this calculation, I give thanks to the LORD my God.

I copied this recital from the recital written in the handwriting of my grandsire Eleazar[49] the son of Amram -- may his spirit rest in peace - in which he mentioned that he had written it in the year 544 of the dominion of the children of Ishmael. May our God make him blessed, Amen. And blessed be our God for ever, and blessed be His name for evermore.

The length of the hours at Mount Gerizim from the ascent

of Shechem is fourteen hours, one tenth of an hour and five ninths of an hour; the information about it was handed down from Phinehas the son of Eleazar, our forefather - praised be the name of the LORD our God who has singled us out with the holiness of his commandments, and has given us a holy rest,[50] a righteous and perfect Torah, and a trustworthy prophet.

If you wish to know the angle of the sun, i.e. the distance between the sun and the moon at the time of their conjunction,[51] you must find out the exact degree of its rising, and thus determine the degree of the middle of the sky from its rising until its setting. Then find out its Northern and Southern position,[52] and calculate the amount of declination in degrees and minutes. After that find out how many degrees and minutes the Dragon has at the same hour, and subtract them from the degrees and minutes of the middle of the sky. And when you have done that, take what is left as the angle of the moon[53] and find out its place. If the declination of the sun and the angle of the moon are in the same place, put them together; if they differ, subtract the lesser from the greater and note what is left. If they are both in the North, subtract them from the latitude of the earth; if they are both in the South, add them to the latitude of the earth. And from the result of this addition or subtraction you will find out the angle of the moon. Then subtract one sixth of this result, and what is left is the angle of the sun at that hour.

But God alone knows all secret things.

(54)	Adam	130 years
(55)	Seth	105 years
(56)	Enosh	90 years
(57)	Kenan	70 years
(58)	Mahalalel	65 years
(59)	Jared	62 years
(60)	Enoch	65 years
(61)	Methuselah	67 years
(62)	Lamech	53 years

From Adam to the birth of Noah there are thus 707 years,[63] and to the Flood, 1307 years.

(64)	Shem	100 years
(65)	Arpachshad	135 years
(66)	Shelah	130 years
(67)	Eber	134 years
(68)	Peleg	130 years
(69)	Reu	132 years
(70)	Serug	130 years
(71)	Nahor	79 years
(72)	Terah	70 years

From Arpachshad's[73] birth to Abram's birth there are 940 years. And from Adam to Abraham's birth there are 2247 years.

(74)	Abraham	100 years
(75)	Isaac	60 years
(76)	Jacob	87 years
(77)	Levi	52 years
(78)	Kohath	71 years
(79)	Amram	52 years
(80)	Aaron the Priest	40 years

Moses - peace be upon him - was a prophet for 40 years.[81]

The total number of years to the death of the prophet Moses are two thousand seven hundred and ninety-four years.[82] God is the *Everlasting* One into eternity.

(83)	Eleazar, son of Aaron the Priest	50 years
(84)	Phinehas, his son	60 years
(85)	Abisha, his son	40 years

This Abisha[86] the son of Phinehas wrote the Scroll of the Torah which is found to this day in the town of Shechem, in the High Priest's house, and its history is a most miraculous one. It is reported by the annalists thus: this holy book was preserved in the stone-built synagogue which was in Elon Moreh,[87] and the community used to view it every Monday,[88] which was called "the day of the procession". And it came to pass on this day that the priest whose charge was to carry the Scroll was overtaken early in the morning by a nocturnal pollution.[89] He washed himself secretly, and then carried the Scroll away from the synagogue to Gilgal in Ephraim,[90] where the people quarrelled with him about it; and as they arranged themselves in Gilgal, and the Scroll was opened, there occurred in the world a great earthquake and thunderings of lightning, and a mighty wind lifted the Scroll out of the ark wherein it lay, and it was carried up and whirled into the air by the wind, while the community was watching, trembling and weeping. But they strengthened their hearts and took hold of the end of the Scroll, and it happened that a fragment was torn off,[91] which is found in Shechem to this day; it goes from Num. 35:2 to Deut. 34:10, and the cryptogram which it includes is from Deut. 6:10, which is written after Deut. 6:4(-9); and it reads thus: I, Abisha, the son of Phinehas the son of Eleazar the priest - God's favor and glory be upon them - have written[92] the holy Scroll at the door of the Tent of Meeting on Mount Gerizim in the thirteenth year of the settlement of the children of Israel in the land of Canaan, within its borders roundabout. I praise the Lord. This is the history of the Scroll, and whosoever be the priest who has carried it away, against him may God send a fiery serpent beneath his feet, to bite him, and may his flesh fall from his bones, and may the community be defiled, and may his flesh fall from his bones, and may the community be defiled, and may the year not be concluded before the synagogue is destroyed, and may Panuta become more firmly established and prevail over all. May the LORD put an end to their days in the greatness of His mercy. Amen!

(The aforementioned cryptogram of Abisha's script is correct, sayeth Isaac,[93] son of Amram, the priest; I have seen the cryptogram with mine own eyes, and I have opened it with my own hand, and this was in the year ...).

(I have served (as guardian of) this holy Scroll for forty years, and I have seen its cryptogram as mentioned, seven times during the days of my priesthood. I, poor Jacob,[94] the son of Aaron, the priest).

(95)	Šiši, his son	50 years
(96)	Buhki	35 years
(97)	Uzzi	25 years

(98) In the twenty fifth year of Uzzi's priesthood the LORD hid the Holy Tabernacle made by Bezaleel.[99]

(100) From Adam to the time when the LORD hid the Tabernacle there were three thousand and fifty-five years.

NOTES ON THE TOLIDAH

1. Cf. Num. 25:10-13, where as a reward for his zeal, Phinehas and his descendants are granted the covenant of perpetual priesthood. 1 Chron. 5:30 (RSV.6:4) claims that the Jewish priesthood also goes back to Phinehas. It is still the function of the Samaritan priests to arrange the calendar; presumably this was also the case in old Israel as the calendar and religious festivals go hand in hand.

2. See above, note 1.

3. i.e. Mount Gerizim was the place from which the observations were made, as it was there (so the Samaritans allege) that the Tabernacle was set up on the entry into the land. According to Josh. 18:1 and 19:51 the Tabernacle was set up at Shiloh by Joshua in the time of Eleazar, the father of Phinehas, but Josh. 24:25-26 speaks of the sanctuary of the LORD at Shechem.

4. Gen. 1:14.

5. "By only one of them" i.e. the calendar is both solar and lunar.

6. Exod. 13:10.

7. i.e. with either the sun or the moon alone.

8. Abib is the first month of the ecclesiastical year with the Samaritans as with the Jews, and the seventh month of the civil year. However, among the Samaritans little notice is given to the first of Tishri, the Roš haš-šanah of the Jews; although the Samaritans regard it as a festival, but call it simply *Yom ha-tĕru'ah*, (cf. Lev. 23:24). The Samaritan, like the Jew, could not dispense with the lunar year, since the phases of the moon are essential for determining the duration

of months; but if he had relied only on the moon for the calculation of the year serious discrepancies would have developed between the months and the seasons; this does indeed happen with the Mohammedan month of Ramaḍān, when the Moslem has to fast from sunrise to sunset, which in the course of a period of several years goes round the year.

9. Nisan is mentioned in the Bible only in Neh. 2:1 and Esther 3:7, neither of which books the Samaritans are supposed to know, since they recognize only the Torah. However, the Samaritans lived in Jewish Palestine, and though the name Nisan is post-exilic, it was adopted by them, either prior to the Samaritan schism, or at some later date, before the final break between the two communities.

10. Deut. 16:1.

11. The secret method of calculation which Phinehas learned from Moses.

12. Lev. 23:2.

13. Gen. 7:11.

14. Gen. 7:24.

15. Gen. 8:4.

16. Gen. 8:5.

16a. The point here is that these Biblical quotations imply that five months comprised 150 days defining a month's duration as 30 days.

17. Further mention of these in the Malef and the Molad Mosheh (Birth Story of Moses).

18. The Samaritans dislike anthropomorphisms in speaking of the Deity. *The LORD said in his heart* (Gen. 8:21) means rather 'said to Himself', 'resolved' but the Samaritans could not take it thus; so the author here connects *His* with Noah, whose name occurs in the preceding verse, and interprets the sentence as 'God spoke to Noah's heart'.

19. Gen. 29:30. However, the reading in the Samaritan Pentateuch here is the same as in the Jewish Bible, *And served with him for another seven years.*

20. Exod. 12:2. The author appears to reason thus: the

fact that Jacob is said to have served several years plus a month is proof that he knew how to count months and years; and a later proof is the designation of Nisan as the first month -- showing by the way that previously the count may have begun with another month (Tishri?). Moreover, the ordinance of the Sabbath is anterior to the Ten Commandments, since it dates from the first week of Creation, when God rested on the seventh day -- if the patriarchs knew the count of weeks, they must have known also the count of months and years. The festivals, the mishpatim, and the laws of sacrifice, on the other hand, are Mosaic, since they were first revealed only to Moses. I am indebted to Professor Nemoy for this note.

21. Whereas the secret of the calendar was known to Adam and the Patriarchs antediluvian and postdeluvian, the feasts, the judgments, and the offerings were made known only to Moses. In this refusal to give pre-Mosaic knowledge of the feasts to the Patriarchs, the author differs markedly from the author of the Book of Jubilees (cf. Charles, *The Book of Jubilees*, 1902 p.L, and p.48f.

22. A candid admission that the calendar calculation is not in the Torah, although the author has tried to show earlier from references in the Torah, that the Patriarchs knew it and calculated the passage of time accordingly.

23. The God-given calendar was not revealed in the Torah in order to prevent the laity from learning it from the Torah; thus baulked, they had to come for it to the High Priest.

24. Moses.

25. Of the priesthood; see above note 1.

26. The complete name of the Tolidah is 'The Chain of the Priests from Adam until the Present'. The holy chain started with Adam, who passed on the drop of light of the first day which was finally incarnated in Moses. Cf. the Malef, and the Molad Mosheh extract and the notes thereto (below p.48f.). The chain does not stop with Moses as far as the priesthood is concerned.

27. Exod. 23:38.

28. Lev. 10:10.

29. Num. 27:21.

30. The Samaritan priests twice a year, at the Ṣimmuṯ

Pesaḥ and the Ṣimmut Sukkot, sell six months' calendars to the people. This must bring in a meager but steady income. The Ṣimmut falls sixty days before Passover and before Tabernacles respectively, and is a sort of semi-festival. There is a special liturgy for it. Ṣimmut Pesaḥ comes on the fifteenth of Shebat, and Ṣimmut Sukkot on the fifteenth of Ab. Megillat Ta'aniṭ lists both days on which there can be no mourning; while M. RH (1:1) knew of the fifteenth of Shebat as the new year for trees. In 4:8 Rabban Gamaliel states that the fifteenth of Ab (and Yom Kippur) had been at one time outstandingly joyous feasts. There is no Musaf for fifteenth Shebat and the fifteenth Ab in the Jewish liturgy.

31. This interest in the counting of the Jubilees as a method of calculating the passage of time is found also in Markah. One is reminded of the Book of Jubilees whose way of referring to such-and-such a thing happening in such-and-such a Jubilee is very similar to Markah's way of dating events; in both works the number of Jubilees are given in speaking of events in the pre-Mosaic epoch.

32. Again a Jewish month-name; but Tammuz does not occur in the Bible as the name of a month. The Samaritan calendar in designating months uses only the cardinal number along with the term month.

33. 747 A.H. was the date on which Jacob ben Ishmael copied Eleazar ben Amram's Tolidah (written in 544 A.H.).

34. Here we have three methods of dating used in Samaritan works: the Islamic, the year of creation, and the Persian era.

35. Ptolemy, the famous geographer and astronomer. That Jezdegird was a son of Ptolemy can only be understood as meaning that he was influenced by Ptolemy's work.

36. This is a delightful way of justifying their use of Ptolemy and Jezdegird.

37. For the Biblical law of the Jubilee cf. Lev. 25:10ff.

38. For the Biblical law of the year of release cf. Deut. 15:1f.

39. This happened, according to the Samaritans, when Eli built the rival Tabernacle at Shiloh. It marked the end of the period of divine grace which began with the revelation of the Law at Sinai. The Samaritans still observe the Jubilee, at least for chronological purposes. The Jews did not keep the

Jubilee for very long, as the Talmud admits (T.B. 'Ar. 32b). Modern scholars doubt if it was ever observed at all.

40. Lev. 23:10.

41. Lev. 25:9.

42. Five Jubilees do not make two hundred and fifty years, according to the Samaritan reckoning. The first Jubilee is on the fiftieth year, but thereafter each Jubilee falls in the forty-ninth year.

43. Lev. 25:2-3.

44. Exod. 16:35.

45. Cf. Deut. 10:5.

46. Cf. note 1. Since the covenant of perpetual priesthood had been made with Phinehas and his descendants after him, it was good policy to maintain that he was responsible for fixing the Samaritan calendar. The Samaritans doubtless believed that it would have been one of the earliest concerns of the Israelite priests on entering the Land to fix the calendar and thereby make sure that the feasts were celebrated at the proper times. Be that as it may, they were claiming impeccable authority for their calendar and their Festival celebrations.

47. If the calendar was arranged by the great Phinehas' son, the 'authorised version' of Scripture was fixed by his grandson. The author of the preface makes certain in this paragraph that none can say that while the Samaritans may know the time of the feasts year by year, they do not know the exact regulations regarding them as laid down in the Law. In short, the author would have us believe, that the Samaritans have everything, in valid priesthood (which nobody else has), the only correct calendar arranged by this valid priesthood, and the only correct copy of the Law issued by the same priesthood. Unfortunately for him, this paragraph owes much to the marginal note written beside Abisha's name in the Tolidah itself. When Eleazar ben Amram wrote the earlier part of the Tolidah in A.H. 544, Abisha's scroll had not yet been rediscovered, and the marginal note, saying that the scroll is in the High-Priest's house in Shechem is thus later than the actual discovery of the ancient scroll, but probably earlier than this paragraph in the introduction. The latter, even in the oldest known copy - the one in the High Priest's house in Nablus - is written in a wretched late cursive hand; while the main body of the Tolidah is in a fair *uncial*. Doubtless the Abisha of the fourteenth

century realized that if one could claim to have the ancient Abisha scroll written by a great-grandson of Aaron, one could also claim to have the only correct copy of the Law and the only reliable information on the festivals; it was only logical to suggest that another relative of Aaron, his grandson this time, had conferred on the Samaritans the only valid calendar to enable them to observe the Biblical feasts on the proper days. The fact that this calendar was geared to Mount Gerizim was also useful in support of this claim. It is of course possible that such claims had been made by the Samaritans long before the fourteenth century.

48. Jacob was a contemporary of Abisha ben Phinehas, the rediscoverer of the ancient Abisha scroll in the fourteenth century. If Jacob is the author of the introduction, he is surely too modest in saying that he wrote it for his son, Abisha, High Priest at that time, doubtless encouraged him to write it.

49. If Jacob knew of the rediscovery of the Abisha scroll, Eleazar, who compiled the early part of the Tolidah, did not. Even if Jacob did write the introduction he left Eleazar's bare entry regarding Abisha untouched. This would seem to indicate that the early part of the Tolidah was really written by Eleazar and was left as he wrote it.

50. i.e. the Sabbath.

51. The Samaritans do not watch for the new moon to observe its appearance and declare a new month. Instead, the priests issue calendars twice a year at Ṣimmuṯ Pesaḥ and Ṣimmuṯ Sukkoṯ, i.e. sixty days before Passover and Tabernacles (cf. above note 30). Ṣimmut means conjunction, i.e. the conjunction of the sun and the moon. Ṣimmut Pesaḥ is the conjunction of the sun and moon in the month of Shebat, and Ṣimmuṯ Sukkoṯ the conjunction of the sun and moon in the month of Ab. The conjunction of the sun and the moon could be calculated at the Ṣimmuṯ if not observed.

52. The northern and southern position and the decline in degree and minutes might be the same.

53. The courses of the moon and the sun cross each other at the so-called Dragon-point. This point moves as time goes on, and anyone who wanted to know the position of the Dragon at a certain time, probably consulted a table. It would appear that the information given in this paragraph assumes the existence of such tables. Professor Edward Robertson has indeed demonstrated (*John Rylands Library Bulletin*, 1939, p.461f.) that the Samaritans used al-Battani's tables for their calculation

of the calendar.

54. Cf. Gen. 5:5, which says that Adam lived nine hundred and thirty years. He was one hundred and thirty years old when he became the father of Seth, Gen. 5:3.

55. Cf. Gen. 5:5. According to Gen. 5:8, Seth lived in all nine hundred and twelve years, and was one hundred and five years old when he became the father of Enosh (Gen. 5:6).

56. Cf. Gen. 5:11, where it is stated that Enosh lived nine hundred and five years; the Samaritan Bible has eight hundred and fifteen years. Gen. 5:9 states that he was ninety years old when he became the father of Kenan.

57. Cf. Gen. 5:14; Kenan lived nine hundred and ten years, and was seventy years old when he became the father of Mahalel (Gen. 5:12).

58. Cf. Gen. 5:17; Mahalalel lived to the age of eight hundred and ninety-five years, and was sixty five when his son Jared was born (Gen. 5:15).

59. Cf. Gen. 5:20; Jared's lifespan was nine hundred and sixty-two years; the Samaritan Bible has eight hundred and forty seven. He was sixty-two when his son Enoch was born.

60. Cf. Gen. 5:23; Enoch's age at his assumption was three hundred and sixty five; he was sixty-five when his son Methuselah was born (Gen. 5:21).

61. Cf. Gen. 5:27; Methuselah's age at his death was nine hundred and sixty-nine years; the Samaritan Bible has seven hundred and twenty. Whereas in all the preceding cases the Tolidah's figures are each equivalent to the age of the respective patriarch at the birth of his eldest son, this does not apply in the case of Methuselah. According to Gen. 5:28, Methuselah was one hundred and eighty-seven years old when Lamech was born.

62. Cf. Gen. 5:31; Lamech lived for seven hundred and seventy-seven years. In the case of Lamech, as in that of Methuselah, the source of the Tolidah's figures is obscure. Lamech was one hundred and eighty two years old when Noah was born, Gen. 5:28. But cf. Charles (*ibid.*, Introd., p.lxxvii) for the striking similarity between the figures given in the Tolidah and those given in the Book of Jubilees.

63. The figure seven hundred and seven is the sum of the

figures opposite the names of the antediluvian patriarchs. Gen. 7:6 gives Noah's age at the Flood as six hundred years. Apparently the Tolidah adds this to the previous seven hundred and seven to arrive at the figure thirteen hundred and seven as the number of the years from Adam to the Flood. While there are three variations in the ages of the antediluvian patriarchs as given in the Masoretic Hebrew and in the Samaritan Hebrew text, they are insignificant compared with the variations in the Tolidah from both of them.

The life spans of Enosh and Methuselah are shorter by ninety and two hundred and forty-nine years, respectively, in the Samaritan than in the Masoretic Hebrew text. These are relatively minor discrepancies compared with those between the ages in the Samaritan Hebrew text and in the Tolidah; e.g. the Samaritan Bible figures yield 5876 years for the sum-total of the ages of the nine patriarchs from Adam to Lamech, as against the Tolidah's 707. We have noted above that the Tolidah's figures are equivalent, in all but two cases, to the number of years as given in the Bible that each patriarch lived prior to the birth of his eldest son and successor. It can hardly be argued that the Tolidah gives these years as the years of his priesthood, and not as the years of his life. At first sight it seems clear from Chronicle Adler (cf. *REJ*, XLIV-XLV (1902), p.191, note 1) that the numbers given in the Tolidah and adopted by Chronicle Adler were regarded as the complete lifespans of these antediluvian patriarchs. The matter, however, is not so simple, for Chronicle Adler (*ibid.*, p.193) gives the figure five hundred and two for Noah, but in the annalistic note on Noah quotes the Bible as saying that the Flood was in the six hundredth year of his life. The figure of five hundred and two was probably suggested by Gen. 5:32, where it is stated that Noah was five hundred years old when he became the father of his sons. It is noticeable that the Tolidah says nothing more regarding Noah, whereas Chronicle Adler devotes much space to him (*REJ*, *ibid.*, p.193-196).

64. Cf. Gen. 11:10-11. Shem's lifespan, according to the Bible, was six hundred years; he was one hundred years old when Arpachshad was born.

65. Cf. Gen. 11:12-13; Arpachshad lived four hundred and thirty-eight years; he was thirty-five when Shelah was born. The Tolidah adds one hundred years to his age at Shelah's birth, to obtain thereby the total length of his life.

66. Cf. Gen. 11:14-15; Shelah lived four hundred and thirty three years; he was thirty years old when Eber was born. Here also the Tolidah adds one hundred years to this thirty to obtain

his age at death.

67. Cf. Gen. 11:16-17. Eber's age at his death was four hundred and sixty four; he was thirty four when Peleg was born. Again, the Tolidah adds one hundred years to this thirty-four to arrive at Eber's total lifespan.

68. Cf. Gen. 11:18-19; Peleg lived two hundred and thirty nine years in all, being only thirty when Reu was born. Once more, the Tolidah adds one hundred years to his age at Reu's birth to arrive at his total life-span.

69. Cf. Gen. 11:20-21; Reu lived for two hundred and thirty-nine years, and was just thirty-two when Serug was born. One hundred added to Reu's age at Serug's birth yields the Tolidah's figure of one hundred and thirty-two.

70. Cf. Gen. 11:22-23. Serug lived two hundred and thirty years; he had fathered Nahor when he was thirty. The Tolidah therefore by adding one hundred years to his age at Nahor's birth discovers Serug's age at death.

71. Cf. Gen. 11:24-25; Nahor lived for one hundred and forty-eight years; he was only twenty-nine when his son Terah was born. The Tolidah adds fifty to his age at Terah's birth, and thus gives him seventy-nine years of life in all. This is an indication that here at least the Tolidah is scaling down these patriarchal life-spans proportionately, for Nahor lived after Terah's birth only half the time that Reu and Serug lived after the birth of their sons.

72. Cf. Gen. 11:26, 32; Terah lived for two hundred and five years; he was seventy years old when Abraham was born. The Tolidah takes his age at Abraham's birth as the limit of his life.

73. Arpachshad is surely a misreading for Shem, for the years given by the Tolidah to the patriarchs from Shem to Terah add up to just one thousand and forty. This last number added to the thirteen hundred and seven years from Adam to the birth of Noah gives the date of Abraham's birth as A.M. two thousand three hundred and forty-seven.

74. Cf. Gen. 21:5; 25:7; Abraham lived for one hundred and seventy years (Gen. 25:4). From Gen. 21:5 we learn that he was one hundred years old at the birth of Isaac. The Tolidah again takes his age at Isaac's birth as the total length of his life.

75. Cf. Gen. 25:26; 35:28; Isaac lived to be one hundred

and eighty, and was sixty years old when Jacob was born.

76. Cf. Gen. 47:28; Jacob lived for one hundred and forty-seven years.

77. Cf. Exod. 6:16; Levi lived to be one hundred and thirty-sen.

78. Cf. Exod. 6:18. Kohath lived to the age of one hundred and thirty-three.

79. Cf. Exod. 6:20; Amram died aged one hundred and thirty-seven years.

80. Exod. 7:7 says that Aaron was eighty-three when he and Moses spoke to Pharaoh. Aaron died one hundred and twenty-three years old (cf. Num. 33:39). Chronicle Adler reckons Aaron's priesthood not from the age of eighty-three but from his birth, so that Aaron is said to have served as priest for eighty three years, and not forty.

81. Exod. 7:7 states that Moses was eighty years old when he and Aaron spoke to Pharaoh. Deut. 34:7 says that Moses was one hundred and twenty years old when he died. The Tolidah reckons his service as a prophet from his eightieth year.

82. From Abraham to Moses there were, according to the Tolidah, five hundred and two years. This, when added to the period from Adam to Abraham's birth, gives the total of two thousand seven hundred and forty-nine years. The text, however, has two thousand seven hundred and ninety-four. What is certain is that in the case of both Aaron and Moses the Tolidah figures refer not to the length of their life, but to their service as priest and prophet respectively. In the case of Abraham, Isaac, Jacob, Levi, Kohath, and Amram it is impossible to see what criterion the Tolidah had used in scaling down the Biblical numbers given for their respective ages, as we have in the Bible only their age at death and not at the birth of their eldest son and successor. It should be noted, as providing some sort of criterion of the value of the Tolidah's calculations that to obtain 502 years from Abraham to Moses, Aaron and Moses are treated not as contemporaries but as one succeeding the other.

83. There are no Biblical data as to Eleazar's length of life.

84. There are no Biblical data as to the length of Phinehas' life.

85. There is no Biblical source from which the Tolidah might have drawn its information on the length of Abisha's life.

86. Cf. Above Note 47. The following paragraph is the famous account of the Abisha Scroll. In the Nablus manuscript of the Tolidah this account is in the margin; in the Bodleian library manuscript edited by Neubauer it appears in the text. Professor P. E. Kahle (*Festschrift Baudissin, Beihefte zu ZAW* 33 (1918) p.247-260) has already commented on the fact that the earliest manuscript of the Tolidah does not mention that Abisha wrote the Abisha scroll, nor does it know that it had been lost and was found again. See p.37b for Nablus Tolidah Ms evidence.

87. Cf. Gen. 12:6, Deut. 11:30.

88. The Abisha Scroll is now brought out only on the festivals. There are also pilgrimage processions up Mount Gerizim at Passover, Pentecost and Tabernacles.

89. i.e., he became a *ba'al keri* (one who had an involuntary emission of semen) and was therefore unclean, even after ablution, until nightfall of that day.

90. Cf. Deut. 11:30, 2 Kings 2:1; 4:38. Gilgal in Ephraim was in the neighborhood of Mount Gerizim and is to be distinguished from the Gilgal near Jericho which would be in the territory of Benjamin.

91. In the spring of 1952 the present writer, in a lecture before the Palestine Exploration Fund, pointed out that from this account it would appear that even at the time of the insertion of this note into the earliest copy of the Tolidah, only a portion of the ancient Scroll was in existence, covering only Num. 35:2 to Deut. 34:10. He went on to point out that at the present time the Abisha Scroll could therefore contain only this ancient portion, and that the rest of it must be of later origin. Professor Kahle, on the evidence of Professor Perez Castro's photograph of the complete Scroll (Cf. *Sefarad,* XIII, (1953), p.119ff.) has, I think, clearly vindicated this suggestion and established it as a fact, in his important article "The Abisha Scroll of the Samaritans", *Studia Orientalia Joanni Pederson dicata,* Copenhagen, 1953.

92. Cf. above, note 47.

93. Isaac ben Amram lived in the 19th century; cf. Cowley, *Samaritan Liturgy I,* p.xlvi.

94. Jacob ben Aaron also lived in the 19th century; cf. Cowley, *ibid.*

95. Šiši; cf. Chronicle Adler (*REJ* XLIV-XLV (1902), p.204). In the Biblical high priestly list, 1 Chron. 5:31,RSV, 6:5, Ezra 7:5, 1 Chron. 6:36 (RSV, 6:51), Šiši does not occur and Buḥḳi is the son of Abishua.

96. Cf. preceding note and also 1 Chron. 6:35-36 (RSV, 6:50-51). There is no evidence as to how long Bukki lived or officiated as high priest. Chronicle Adler (*ibid.*, p.204-205) states that Buḥḳi, like his predecessors Abisha and Šiši appointed the Judges to rule over Israel.

97. For Uzzi cf. 1 Chron. 5:31-32 (RSV, 6:5-6) 6:3b (RSV, 6:51), Ezra 7:4. The interesting thing is that none of these three priests appear in the Torah; the two who occur elsewhere in the Bible are mentioned in the high priestly lists of 1 Chron. 5 and Ezra 7. There seems to be some sort of interdependence between the Tolidah list and that in 1 Chron. 5. It is not necessary to assume that the borrowing has all been done by the Samaritans. Obviously, claims and counterclaims would have been made by both sides. It is perhaps significant that in Chronicles and Ezra, names had to be created of high priests who are not attested elsewhere in the Bible, but are found in the Samaritan high priestly geneaology.

98. Abu'l-Fath (Ed. Vilmar, p.38-39), the Book of Joshua (Ed. Juynboll) and Chronicle Adler (*ibid.*, p.205-206) all tell how Uzzi, the descendant of Phinehas, being a young boy, and Eli, the descendant of Ithamar, being a man of considerable age, the latter claimed the high priesthood for himself and the Ithamar line. Eli made a golden ark and put therein the copy of the Law written by Ithamar; he also set up a tabernacle at Shiloh; there the tribe of Judah joined with some of other tribes in the worship of God. Israel was divided into three groups: those who followed Uzzi and worshipped at Mount Gerizim; those who followed Eli; and those who followed the heathen and worshipped idols. It was at the end of Uzzi's pontificate that God hid the Tabernacle. Chronicle Adler and the Tolidah use the word *histīr* for God's hiding of the Tabernacle; it could also be rendered "God destroyed the Tabernacle".

99. Cf. Exod. 36:1, 38:21-22, etc.

100. From Adam until the death of Moses there were two thousand seven hundred and forty-nine years. From Eleazar to Uzzi there were only two hundred and sixty years. If however the period from Adam till the end of Uzzi's priesthood is to be three thousand and fifty-five years, the period from Adam to Moses must be 2795 years or two thousand seven hundred and ninety-four as in the Tolidah text. The Tolidah Chronicler has doctored his figures, and even so he is one year short. The

Adler Chronicler gives the date when the Tabernacle was hidden as A.M. three thousand and fifty-four; he at least was aware of the deficiency of one year. A further discrepancy in the Tolidah is the fact that in the introduction it is states that Phinehas announced the fixing of the calendar in the year A.M. two thousand seven hundred and ninety-four. This, according to the Tolidah (cf. above, note 82) was the year of the Moses' death. This again is proof that the introduction and the main text of the Tolidah were not composed by the same author.

THE SAMARITAN BOOK OF JOSHUA

It cannot be too strongly affirmed that the Samaritan Book of Joshua is in no wise canonical among the Samaritans - the Pentateuch is their whole Bible - it is rather one of the Samaritan chronicles. It differs however from the other chronicles, the Tolidah, Abu'l Fatḥ's Annals, and Chronicle Adler, in its make-up. The basis of the Samaritan Book of Joshua is not a list of high priests, such as the Tolidah provides, with short notes here and there about happenings in the Samaritan community (and very occasionally, outside of it) jotted down under a notice about the then reigning High Priest. This literary form provided by the Tolidah is retained even by Abu'l Fatḥ and by the Chronicle Adler. The Samaritan Book of Joshua on the other hand, is a regular Chronicle, and not a series of annalistic notes appended to a priestly genealogy. However, while it is true that the Samaritan Book of Joshua is a chronicle, it is a chronicle with much midrashic material appended to it. Montgomery[1] goes therefore too far when he says, "The work is actually a Midrash, not a chronicle". As it stands now; it is a chronicle with midrashic elements, but nevertheless very definitely a chronicle. The trouble is that too often scholars, having approached it and found therein what they wanted, failed to remember that the book is a composite one; what may justly apply to some part or element in it, does not apply to the whole. Thus it happens that one scholar would make extravagant claims for its historicity, while another would dismiss it as an example of the worst type of Samaritan mythologizing.

The Samaritan Book of Joshua is not new to the West: Scaliger is said to have obtained the Leyden manuscript from the Egyptian Samaritans in 1584. This manuscript is itself a composite; the earlier part of it[2] is dated A.D.1362, the latter part 1513. It is the earliest surviving manuscript of the Arabic text, and formed the basis of Juynboll's monumental edition,[3] which with the accompanying Latin translation and comprehensive introduction and commentary is still very important, although new material is now available in the Gaster collection of Samaritan manuscripts in the John Rylands Library in Manchester, and in the British Museum in London.

While it is true that the compiler of the Samaritan Book of Joshua claims at the beginning of the first chapter that it is a translation from the Hebrew, scholars are inclined to doubt that this Hebrew original has been preserved. To be sure, Hebrew texts of the Samaritan Joshua are indeed still in existence; but they are late, and it has yet to be demonstrated, beyond the shadow of a doubt that they are descended from an older Hebrew original and are not mere retranslations from the Arabic version. That is not to say that Hebrew originals, now lost, had never existed for parts of the Book of Joshua, but even so, it seems very unlikely that the whole of it was ever in Hebrew.

Juynboll was most probably right in thinking that the work, as we have it, was written not later than the thirteenth century, since the Leyden manuscript dates from the fourteenth century and there is no evidence that it is an autograph. Juynboll[4] is perhaps too emphatic in stating that the Samaritan Book of Joshua is the work of a single author; for he admits that the latter had used various earlier sources.[5] Had he seen some of the later manuscripts he would probably have modified his theory of a single author, even in the sense of a single compiler. Historiography, in so far as it existed among the Samaritans, did not mean so much the writing of new historical accounts, as the copying and recopying of old traditions and stories by scribe after scribe, each one adding a little to enhance the faded glories of the past, so that every Samaritan scribe copying a chronicle acts in a sense as a compiler.

Reland, on the other hand,[6] refused to concede that the Samaritan Book of Joshua had only one author, and argued that different parts of it had been written at different times. He was wrong in making too positive and definite conjectures as to the authorship of the individual parts and he erred likewise in believing that Koranic expressions in the Arabic text were introduced by the Arabic translator. Juynboll, as mentioned before, admits that the compiler had various earlier sources at his disposal. Not all of these need have been of the same date or of the same historical worth. The compiler probably had them not in Hebrew but in Arabic translation, or perhaps rather the Arabic originals.

Only chapters 1-25 of the Book of Joshua are about Joshua. In fact, chapter 9 is headed, "The beginning of the Book of Joshua the son of Nun", so that chapters 1-8 may be from a different source. While these chapters mention Joshua, they actually form an introduction telling how Moses appointed Joshua as his successor and invested him with royal power. Chapters 3-4 deal with Balaam and the Moabites. In chapter 5 Moses sends Joshua and Phinehas against the Midianites. Chapters 6-8 tell of Moses' death and of the mourning for him.

There is a considerable resemblance between chapters 9-24 and the Biblical Book of Joshua, but chapters 26-37 are quite different, although they too deal with Joshua; here we find a most fanciful midrashic account, put forward not as haggadah to illustrate a halachic point, but as actual history.

Chapters 9-12 are reminiscent of the first chapter of the

Biblical Book of Joshua. Chapter 13 tells of the despatching of the spies to Jericho; while it has some points of contact with the Biblical account, it is more in the nature of a Targumic Midrash on it. The crossing of the Jordan (Joshua 3) and the fall of Jericho are mentioned in chapters 14-17. Chapter 18 tells of the sin of Achan (cf. Joshua 7). Chapter 19, similar to the Biblical Joshua 9, gives the history of the Gibeonites. The conquest of Canaan and its division into ten parts is dealt with in chapters 20-23. There, too, we are told about Nabiḥ (Nobah of Num. 32:42) who was made King by Joshua over the two and one half tribes east of the Jordan. In chapter 24 the tribes are assigned their territory in Palestine by Joshua, who thereupon founds Samaria and builds the Temple on the summit of Mount Gerizim. Chapter 25 describes how the Israelites enjoyed prosperity and peace for twenty years.

Juynboll recognized that parts of chapters 9-25 not only echo the corresponding sections of the Biblical Book of Joshua, but in places seem to be close to the Septuagint version; this latter circumstance is supposedly an argument in favor of the Egyptian origin of the work. In itself this is hardly a strong piece of evidence for the origin of these chapters; at best it could indicate a relatively early date for the composition of this part of the work, and the Greek, Hebrew, or Aramaic prototype of this part of the Samaritan Book of Joshua could have formed part of the Samaritan Apologetic Literature of the Hellenistic period. Other examples of this literature are the drama of the Exodus written in Greek by Ezekiel, the Hellenistic dramatist who may have been a Samaritan, and an epic poem by Theodotus, who seems definitely to have been a Samaritan; both are cited by Eusebius.[7] Certainly, if these chapters show a familiarity with the Septuagint Joshua, their text in its original form must have originated in the pre-Muslim period. On the other hand, it may be that what the original writer knew was not the Septuagint Joshua, but the pre-massoretic Hebrew text of Joshua upon which the Septuagint was based.

Chapters 26-37 tell of the war between Joshua and Shaubak, king of Persia, and his allies. We are told that the Persian ambassador was amazed at the dignity and splendor of Joshua and his court. When Shaubak heard that Israel would fight if attacked, he consulted the Magi, and as a result Joshua and his army were trapped by seven magic walls which surrounded them as they besieged one of Shaubak's cities. Whereupon Joshua prayed for help, a dove appeared, and Joshua sent a letter by this pigeon post to Nabiḥ of Gilead, who forthwith came and defeated Shaubak. The walls that entrapped Joshua vanished as Nabiḥ and his men shouted at their victory. The Shaubak story probably originated from a Jewish source, (cf. T.B. Sot. 42b), but in Zacuto's *Sefer Yuḥasin* the version found in the Samaritan Joshua is inserted, with the explanation that it was found in a Samaritan chronicle. I am indebted to Prof. Nemoy for drawing my attention to the fact that the story was inserted in Sefer Yuḥasin in the Filipowski edition published Freimann F.A.M. 1924.

Chapters 38-44 tell of Joshua's death and burial, of his successors, and of the prosperity of Israel while the period of Divine grace lasted. Chapter 41 tells of the troubles which began after the death of Samson, the last of the kings of that period. Chapter 42 deals with the end of the period of Divine grace, the disappearance of the Tabernacle, and the hiding of the Temple vessels by Uzzi. In chapter 43 we hear of the disputes between the descendants of Phinehas and Eli, of Eli's tabernacle at Shiloh, and of the disgraceful conduct of his sons. Samuel, as a protege of Eli, comes in for his share of misrepresentation at the hands of our Samaritan author. Chapter 44 tells of the capture of the Ark that was in Shiloh; this of course was not the real Ark in Samaritan eyes.

So far the work is in some way connected with Joshua or with the early period of settlement in the Holy Land. Chapters

45-50 span the ages. In chapter 45 we hear of Nebuchadnezzar as king of Persia; he carries off all Israel, not Judah only, into captivity, which is in line with the Tolidah and Abu'l Fatḥ as the old chronicles did not know of the exile of Northern Israel by the Assyrians; obviously the Samaritans were dependent on Jewish sources when writing their history. The interesting thing about this account in the Book of Joshua is that it states, like 2 Kings 17, that new colonists were brought into the land. These colonists, we are told, complained about the blight which fell upon the land because they did not know how to worship God and how to offer sacrifices on Mount Gerizim, and as a result Nebuchadnezzar allowed 300,000 Israelites to return.

The rest of the chapter is devoted to the troubles of the post-exilic period. When the exiles came back, all Israel, excepting Judah, wanted to build a Temple on Mount Gerizim; Judah however, held out for Jerusalem. We are then told of the appeal which was made to the king, and this is followed by the well-known story of Sanballat and Zerubbabel throwing the Samaritan and the Jewish copies of the Law into the fire in front of the king. The Samaritan copy comes out three times unscathed, except where Zerubbabel spat upon it. Zerubbabel's copy of the Law is scorched whenever it is submitted to the test of fire. This edifying story ends with the declaration that Judah repented and all Israel worshipped on Mount Gerizim. It is unnecessary to comment on the historicity of all this.

Chapter 46 takes us forward to the reign of Alexander the Great. The most that can be said of this chapter is that it is part of the Alexander legend, and the fables it recounts are borrowed from Jewish accounts.

Chapter 46 tells how the Samaritans remained faithful to the Persians, so that as a result Alexander turned towards

Shechem in order to destroy it. He spared it, however, for he was impressed by the dignity of the Samaritan High Priest; this is an exact parallel to Josephus' account (*Ant.* XI.XIII.3), with the Samaritans substituted for the Jews, and the Samaritan High Priest replacing Jaddua the Jewish High Priest. We have in this chapter also the amazing tale of Alexander's journey to the land of darkness whose dust consisted of rubies and pearls, and the story of how Alexander soared up to the clouds in his chariot powered by eagles; chunks of flesh secured to a mast above the chariot urged on the eagles which were harnessed to it, and as the eagles bore the chariot aloft, the pieces of flesh were continuously pushed up out of their reach; when it was time to come down to land, the pieces of flesh were reversed below the chariot, and the eagles who had been bearing it upwards, dragged it downwards. We are told further of the clever stratagem by which the Samaritan High Priest circumvented Alexander's command to erect statues to him, in violation of the commandment prohibiting the erection of idols. The High Priest solved the dilemma in which he found himself, by naming all Samaritan male children born at that time Alexander.

These fables are found also in the Chronicle of Abu'l Fatḥ,[8] who may have derived them from the Book of Joshua or from its sources. A similar story of Alexander's visit to the land of darkness is known to the Babylonian Talmud (T.B. Tam. 32a), while the tale of Alexander's ascent to the clouds in a chariot drawn by eagles was known to the Palestinian Talmud (P.T. AZ 3:1). The stories of Alexander's journey to the land of darkness and of how the Samaritan High Priest named newly born boys Alexander were known to the author of the Yosippon.[9] It seems evident, therefore, that this chapter on Alexander, if not directly borrowed from Jewish sources, at least makes clear that the Samaritan compiler was not averse to adapting for his own use stories which were as much Jewish as Samaritan folklore.

Chapter 47 jumps ahead to the time of Hadrian. The claim is made that two Samaritan brothers, Ephraim and Manasseh, betrayed Jerusalem to the Romans - probably a confusion with the Samaritan betrayal of Bethar.[10]

The concluding chapters, 48-50, tell of the Samaritan High Priest 'Aḳbon, his son Nathanael, and grandson Baba Raba, all of whom lived in the times of Roman persecution. In chapter 48 we hear of the death of 'Aḳbon's two sons at the hands of the Romans and of the hanging of other loyal Samaritans on the walls of Nablus. Despite his personal loss 'Aḳbon kept the faith and told his young son Nathanael (born to him later) of the coming of Baba Raba. The whole chapter is found in Abu'l Fatḥ who probably took it from the Book of Joshua.

Chapter 49 deals with the high priesthood of Nathanael son of 'Aḳbon and tells how he managed to circumcise his son 'Aḳbon despite the Roman prohibition of the rite. The Roman Bishop German actually aided the Samaritan High Priest to conceal his violation of the prohibition of circumcision. Here again the material contained in this chapter is reproduced in Abu'l Fatḥ.

The last chapter of the Book of Joshua is likewise represented in Abu'l Fatḥ. It is not clear whether Abu'l Fatḥ actually found it in the Book of Joshua of his day, or whether he took it from a separate source later added at the end of the Book of Joshua. The latter is more likely to be the case, as Abu'l Fatḥ had obviously been using the Book of Joshua for the events immediately preceding his account of Baba Raba, but he does not introduce the information on these events in the same diffident way (cf. p. 151) as he does with the story of Baba Raba and his nephew Levi which he says he had found in an old Hebrew chronicle. This latter story, while it has much in common with chapter 50 of Joshua, actually covers much more of the life and doings of Baba Raba.

Chapter 50 tells us that the Romans forbade the Samaritans to ascend Mount Gerizim, and to make certain that this prohibition was not violated the Romans fitted up a talismanic bronze bird which would give the alarm by calling out "Ebraios" ("a Hebrew!"). Baba Raba decided to send his nephew Levi to Constantinople so that he might rise in the priesthood there as a sort of Marrano; and having attained power would come back and destroy the bird. For the story in all its improbability see Abu'l Fatḥ.[11]

From this brief survey of the Samaritan Book of Joshua it will be seen that it is not a single entity, but rather a late compilation of very uneven material, some of which may be early. As it stands now, the Book of Joshua is a chronicle which has exerted considerable influence upon the later Samaritan chronicles, and one must study it if one wishes to understand Samaritan historiography, for even their best historian, Abu'l Fatḥ made much use of it.

The controversy at the beginning of this century as to whether or not the original Hebrew text of the Samaritan Book of Joshua had been found by the late Dr. Gaster was perhaps complicated by the fact that the Samaritan Book of Joshua evokes different connotations in different minds. It is both much more and much less than the Biblical Book of Joshua. It is doubtful if all of it was ever available in Hebrew or Aramaic. Even if an original Hebrew text of it were found it would not tell us much more than does the Arabic text, and as we have seen from the summary of the contents of the work, much of it would have little relevance to the Biblical text of Joshua. But even those chapters which deal with the events mentioned to the Biblical Book of Joshua would hardly give us a better text than that of the Masoretic Bible. It might perhaps retain some early readings, but even in a larger measure than the Samaritan Pentateuch, the text of chapters 9-25 of the Samaritan

Joshua is a secondary recension. When one adds to that the fact that a Midrash has been worked into the text of these chapters, the result is that they are of interest only for what Samaritans of a later date had thought about Joshua and his period.

The following extract comprises chapters 38, 39 and 40 and the text used is that of the Juynboll edition.

FOOTNOTES

1. Ibid., p.301.
2. Cf. Nutt, *Samaritan Targum*, Introd., p.119, footnote 1.
3. *Chronicon Samaritanum cui titulus est liber Josuae*, Leyden 1848.
4. *Ibid.*, footnote 52-53.
5. Cf. *ibid.*, p.82f.
6. Quoted by Juynboll, *ibid.*, p.53.
7. *Praepar.* Evang. IX.
8. *Ibid.*, p.84-79.
9. Cf. *ibid.* ii, 16 - ii 17.
10. Cf. Nutt, *ibid.*, p.123.
11. Cf. below, p.151ff.

THE BOOK OF JOSHUA

(Juynboll, p.173, chapter 38.)

Account of the happenings in the time of the Divine grace.[1]

The extent of this period is 260 years. The period of Divine grace reached its zenith in the days of King Joshua and continued thereafter, until the end of this period, as I shall presently mention and set forth. During that time (Israel) observed the Sabbaths and the days of convocation, i.e. the New Moons and feasts. They let the land rest during the Sabbatical year,[2] one year in every seven from the date[3] of the kingship and onwards; during such a year there was neither sowing nor tilling of the ground, and yet every man had sufficient for his needs. Moreover, the Israelites paid the Levites[4] a tenth part of everything that they gained and came to possess out of crops, fruits, animals, etc., and of this the Levites in turn rendered a tenth part to the High Priest. The Israelites had also a second tithe[6] which they expended for themselves, for the Levites, and for the orphans and the poor. In addition, whenever they planted anything new in the land, its fruit was not eaten until the fourth year,[7] and then by none but the High Priest; in the fifth,[8] however, its consumption was permitted to everyone.

A Hebrew slave[9] who had completed seven years' servitude was set free and was removed from his master's possession. And if an Israelite grew needy and sold his son or even his own self,[10] his redemption price was always apportioned over his years of servitude, in the same way as wages.[11] (If he could not pay it himself), and if no redeemer, either closely or remotely related to him, could be found for this Israelite slave, he was (automatically) released in the Jubilee year. There was an analogous method of redeeming their land that had been sold.[12] Moreover, every seven years[13] the land was (re)-distributed among the tribe, together with any increase or decrease.

They always had officers, entrusted with the drawing up of calendars[14] and things brought to the (sacred) treasury. Firstlings[15] out of livestock, crops, and fruits, were rendered to the priest. One was not permitted to sacrifice goats, sheep, or cattle, save on the altar located on the sacred mountain, unless the animal was blemished;[16] likewise unfit for sacrifice (but fit for consumption) were animals of the following seven kinds: the hart,[17] the doe, the buffalo, the gazelle, the wild goat (oryx), and the antelope.

They also had judges[18] who at all times specified for them things commanded or prohibited, in order that they might observe them properly. None of them could commit a misdemeanor, such as denying God[19] or engaging in anything savoring of witchcraft,[20] without being detected forthwith. Before the author of a crime knew anything, he was seized, even if he had fled to the farthest region of the land. Crime was detected by means of the jewels[21] worn by the priest. The latter also administered the draught of water from the Temple to a woman who was suspected by her husband of adultery, and pronounced her accursed,[23] if she had been unfaithful to him and had defiled herself with another man. She was guiltless. This draught preserved her and she emerged unscathed; if guilty, she forthwith burst asunder and perished. Similarly, in the case of unintentional[24] homicide, once it was known that the author of the crime had acted involuntarily as a result of circumstances that overpowered him, his innocency was publicly declared. As for sins, omissions, and other reprehensible acts which a person might commit unintentionally, these the ordained priest would take upon himself on each Day of Fast,[25] which falls on the tenth day of the seventh month, whereon atonement is made for souls and spirits.[26] On the feast of unleavened bread[27] they used to remove the leaven. The Levites were divided into classes:[28] some of them prepared copies of the Law, others made copies of psalms, and still others made genealogies. Some were in charge of the sacred treasury[29] of Israel, others[30] attended to the continual and regular burnt sacrifice in the Temple and to the offerings which accompanied it; still others attended to the oil of anointing, the frankincense[31] of sweet odors, the sprinkling of the sacrifices, the flour-[32](offering), the olive oil and the candelabra; and some were entrusted with the Temple vessels, their arrangement, and the supervision of their use. Some selected the animals (fit for sacrifice), rejecting those that were blemished; some performed the slaughtering; some sprinkled the blood upon the altar; and some set up the sacrificial portions. Each group (of Levites) was organized for its particular functions, and it never strayed away from its appointed duties. The continual burnt offering was offered before sunrise[33] and after sunset. At the moment when the burnt-offering upon the altar was completed, the High Priest used to sound the trumpet[34] from the summit of the blessed mountain; whereupon the call was taken up by the rest of the priests wherever they were, so that it took but a twinkling of an eye before all Israelites knew that the sacrifices had been offered on the altar, and forthwith rose to pray. In those days prayer was accepted, blessings were effective, grace was vouchsafed in fullest measure, mercy was all-embracing, circumstances were in a good state, all matters were known and understood in full light and with happy consequences, and withal an intimate relationship prevailed between them and their Lord.

This is a synopsis of all (their institutions). The children of Israel used to pray to God and address their requests to Him who in His mercy leads men in the right way. He is our sufficiency, and He is the best Protector.

Chapter 39.

History of the days of Divine grace until the onset of the error.[35]

Joshua the son of Nun reigned for forty-five[36] years. At the approach of his death he assembled[37] the Israelites and made a covenant with them[38] to observe the laws which Moses the Prophet, upon whom be peace, had codified. He then offered sacrifices[39] on his own behalf and on theirs and bid them farewell, and in general did approximately the same things as those done by our master Moses the Prophet, upon him be peace, when he bade (the people) farewell. He moreover chose twelve[40] chieftains from all the nine and a half tribes, for whom he drew lots in the presence of the entire assembly of Israel in the meadow of al-Bahā,[41] after having tested their knowledge and ability. The lot of kingship fell to a certain 'Abīl,[42] the son of the brother of Caleb, of the tribe of Judah. Joshua consequently girded him with the royal and judicial authority, invested him with the crown, and called upon the assembly to obey his commands. 'Abīl himself he bade render obedience to the Priest, keep him informed about all his affairs, and set no undertaking in motion without letting him know of it first. Thereupon Joshua the son of Nun, upon whom be peace, died and was buried[43] in Kafr Ghuwaira. When Caleb, his companion, also died, he was buried next to him.

This new King 'Abīl now took charge of the government of the people and conducted it in the best possible manner. Now when the King of Moab learned of Joshua's death, he sent out envoys to muster his forces and marched towards 'Abīl's territory. But 'Abīl, too, assembled his people, and God granted him victory over the invaders,[44] so that fear of him overtook the rest of his enemies also, and he conquered them and annexed portions of their territory. He reigned for nine years,[45] and then died.

He was succeeded by Tarfī'[46] of the tribe of Ephraim. After he had assumed royal power the King of Ammon[47] advanced against him, but God granted him victory. He continued to rule for the length of time allotted to him by God, upon the completion of which he died.

Thereafter, until the close of this period which we have mentioned above, namely two hundred and sixty years, nine[48] kings ruled in succession, drawn from all tribes, who occupied the throne for a total of two hundred and fifteen years, the balance of forty-five falling within the reign of Joshua the son of Nun. The last of these kings was Samson: he was unique amongst them, and none was seen to be fairer than he, or greater in affording help against their enemy. But strength, and beauty, and success, and perfection will be adjudged to such as follow them provided that they follow hard in the footsteps of their predecessors, and act as they acted, and offer sacrifices to the ones offered by them.

Chapter 40.

History of the priests of the Lord who served Him in the time of the Divine grace during the aforementioned period.

When Eleazar[49] the Priest, upon whom be peace, knew that death was approaching, he acted in the same manner as did Joshua the son of Nun. He summoned the chiefs of Israel,[50] made a covenant with them, and impressed upon them the duty of obedience to God. He then bade farewell to them and to the Temple, made his devotions to God, and set out walking while the fragrance of his holiness was wafted from every side. Thereafter he set forth to Kafr Ghuwaira, where he removed[51] the sacred vestments wherewith he was robed, and clothed his son Phinehas with them. He then died and was buried in Kafr Ghuwaira; and the whole people of Israel wept[52] for him in the manner of the Patriarchs.

His son[53] assumed the high-priestly office after him and conducted himself in the same manner as his forefathers had done. He, too, at the approach of death,[54] made a covenant with the people, brought an offering, bade his farewell and betook himself to Kafr Ghuwaira, where he removed the sacred vestments with which he was robed and invested his successor, who was of his own issue, with them. He then died and was buried in the same place.

He was succeeded by five[55] priests of the Lord who served him with the proper service. They, too, acted as did their predecessors, until the conclusion of the aforementioned period. Its days were days of good order, interlaced with light and felicity, both heavenly and earthly, which lasted until the priestly office devolved upon Uzzi, the last of the priests of the Lord in the period of the Divine grace, who was but a youth.[56] The King who ruled at that time had also died, and no other king succeeded him.

From the time of Adam until the end of this time[57] three thousand and fifty-four years passed over the earth. Up to King Samson's death the Israelites had amassed such great wealth that had it been spread over the earth it would have filled the world, such was the profusion of that wherewith God had blessed them and increased their possessions. But then there occurred that which Moses the Prophet - upon whom be peace - had said in his sermon:[58] *Jacob did eat and was satisfied, Israel waxed fat, and kicked,* and so forth, to the end of the Pericope in the Great Song. Then indeed they strayed from the way which God had commanded them to keep and act accordingly. For us sufficeth God, the Mighty, the Beneficient, who shows forbearance to the forward.

(Notes on the selections from *Chronicon Samaritanum cui titulus est liber Josuae*).

1. The period of *riḍwān*. The first period of Divine grace had been in Paradise up to man's fall. The time from the fall until the Exodus and the revelation at Mount Sinai was a period of *fanuta,* or Divine disfavor. After that came the second period of Divine grace which by the time of Joshua was at its zenith; for although it had commenced in the wilderness it was fully established only with the invasion and conquest of Canaan. It lasted until the time of Eli, which marks the beginning of the second period of Divine disfavor which will last until the coming of the Taheb. The length of the first period of grace, two hundred and sixty years, is given also by Abu'l Fatḥ (p.33).

2. Cf. Exod. 23:10.

3. This would imply that Joshua did not become king until after the entry into Canaan, for there the year of release was first kept by Israel.

4. Cf. Num. 18:24.

5. Cf. Num. 18:26-28.

6. Cf. Deut. 14:22-29. The Rabbis knew of three tithes: (1) the *ma'ăśer rišon*, given to the Levites as laid down in Num. 18:21ff., (2) the *ma'ăśer šeni*, which was to be taken to Jerusalem and there consumed by the owner and his family, and which was levied from what remained after the first tithe had been deducted; (3) the *ma'ăśer 'ani*, the tithe given to the poor. In each year, except the seventh, a man paid two tithes, one of which was always the first tithe. The other tithe was in the first, second, fourth, and fifth years of the *ma'ăśer šeni*, and in the third and sixth years the *ma'ăśer 'ani*. The second tithe mentioned here is not the *ma'ăśer šeni* but the *ma'ăśer 'ani* paid on the produce of the sixth year, since in this section what the author has in mind is what would happen in the sixth year in preparation for the year of release.

7. Cf. Lev. 19:23-24; that it could be eaten in the fourth year only by the High Priest is a non-Biblical addition.

8. Cf. Lev. 19:25.

9. Exod. 21:2; cf. Deut. 15:12.

10. Lev. 25:39.

11. Cf. Lev. 25:50-52.

12. Cf. Lev. 25:23-28.

13. This goes further than the Pentateuchal legislation for the seventh year or even than that which governs the redemption of land in the year of Jubilee, Lev. 25.

14. Presumably the officers who drew up the calendars were priests, as even now.

15. Cf. Deut. 18:1, 4.

16. Cf. Lev. 22:22f.

17. Cf. Deut. 14:5.

18. Cf. Exod. 18:21-22; cf. also Deut. 1:13-17.

19. Cf. Exod. 20:3.

20. Cf. Exod. 22:18 also Deut. 18:10-12.

21. Either the Urim and Thummim are referred to (cf. Exod. 28:30 and Lev. 8:8) or the stones of the Ephod and the breastpiece of Exod. 25:7. It is more likely to mean the former. While we do not learn specifically from the Pentateuch of their use in the detection of crime, it might be possible to infer from Deut. 17:8-11, 21:5 that some such method was used. However, in 1 Sam. 14:41, 42 we have Saul seeking a judgment from God through the Urim and Thummim as to whether he and Jonathan or the people of Israel had been guilty. Joshua 7:14 is an example of direct appeal to divine judgment in case of guilt, but the method used to ascertain God's will is not mentioned. In the Samaritan Book of Joshua (cf. ch. 18 which deals with the same event as Joshua 7:14) the gem in the high priest's breastplate which bore the name of Judah grew dim; and it thus became known that one of that tribe had sinned. But Deut. 33:8 shows that the Urim and Thummim were the insignia *par excellence* of the priesthood.

22. Cf. Num. 5:16-22, which, however, does not suggest that it was the High Priest who administered the bitter waters.

23. Cf. Num. 5:20b.

24. Cf. Num. 35:13, 24-25. But in the Bible the congregation is the judge between the manslayer and the avenger of blood, and restore him to the city of refuge whither he had fled; there he must stay till the reigning High Priest die.

25. Cf. Lev. 23:27f. and Lev. 16:29-34.

26. This is wider than atonement for the crimes of error and negligence referred to by the writer of this section as taken upon himself by the High Priest and for which he makes atonement. True it could be argued that it is for the souls and spirits of those who committed them that he makes atonement; but on the other hand it is within the scope of Samaritan thought that prayers can be offered for the dead. It is possible that the Samaritan writer does feel that on the Day of Atonement the High Priest, at least in the period of Divine grace, did make atonement for souls and spirits in the widest sense, whether of those who were alive or dead.

27. Cf. Lev. 23:6, Deut. 16:3-4.

28. In Num. 1:50-51 the duties of the Levites are listed, but they are not as extensive or detailed as here, nor are we told there that the Levites were divided into classes. One might argue that the Samaritan writer here has been influenced at least in part by extra-Pentateuchal Biblical information as

to the organisation of the Levites, but one should remember that our Samaritan writer would not differentiate between priests and Levites; the priests were "the Levitic priests". The section on the duties of the Levites is important not only as reflecting what the writer regarded as the duties of the Levitic priests in the time of Divine grace, i.e. when the Samaritans had a Temple on Mount Gerizim prior to its destruction by John Hyrcanus, but as in some measure describing the duties of the Samaritan priesthood of his own day. Of course most of the duties had gone with the disappearance of the sanctuary, but they still prepared copies of the Law, psalms, and pedigrees: even today, the inspection of animals for sacrifice has not been entirely discontinued - there are still the paschal lambs.

The question remains, to what extent is this picture of the priestly Levitical duties derivative, and whence was it taken? Not all of this by any means can be derived from the Pentateuch. Is our writer indebted to the Book of Chronicles and to the Mishnah, or did he have material belonging to his own community on how the Samaritan Temple was organised?

29. Cf. the *gizbarim* and the *'amarkalim*, treasurers and accountants of Jerusalem Temple property, mentioned in Rabbinic sources, e.g. M. Shek. 5:2.

30. For the continual burnt offering cf. Exod. 29:42, Num. 28:6, 10, 15. As to the various duties of the priests in connection with sacrifices, cf. e.g. Lev. 1:3-9.

Note that the Samaritan writer depicts a more highly organised corps of Levitical priests, with closely defined duties, than does even the Priestly Code. But the latter makes a distinction between the priests who were the sons of Aaron, and the Levites; the Samaritans do not, and yet according to our writer specific duties were assigned to each group of the Levitical priests, some of which appear to have been those performed in the Jewish sanctuary by the Levites and not by the priests.

31. Cf. Num. 2:1, 2, 14, 16.

32. Cf. Num. 2:1, 2, 14, 16 and Num. 6:14-15. While the cereal offerings were undoubtedly made in the Jewish post-exilic Temple by the priests, and not by the Levites, Neh. 13:4 shows that the Levites kept in their charge the cereal, the frankincense, and other supplies which were to be used in the appropriate offerings by the priests. When our writer speaks of the oil of anointing, etc., being attended to by others, does he mean to refer to their storage before their use by the priest, or is he actually speaking of the priestly use of them?

33. The *tamid* in the Jerusalem Temple was offered not *before* sunrise, but *in the morning* (Num. 28:4).

34. We know of no parallel practice at Jerusalem in connection with the tamid.

35. i.e. Until the time of Eli, who according to the Samaritans set up a tabernacle at Shiloh. The Samaritans could not accept the statement in Joshua 19:51 that the tent of meeting was set up at Shiloh in the time of Joshua.

36. Abu'l Fatḥ (p.33) declares that Joshua reigned for twenty-five years, but adds 'some say fortyfive years'.

Chronicle Adler (*REJ*, XLIV/XLV (1902) 201) says that Joshua died aged 110; he had been twenty-five years in Egypt, forty years in the desert, and forty-five years as king in the land of Canaan.

37. Joshua 24:1; note that all the tribes of Israel were summoned to Shechem.

38. Joshua 24:25. The Samaritan writer says nothing of Joshua making statutes and ordinances for them at Shechem and (cf. Joshua 24:26) writing them down in the book of the law of God. It was Moses who had set the laws down in writing.

39. Joshua 24:25 says nothing of offering sacrifices, but adds that Joshua *took a great stone, and set it up there under the oak in the sanctuary of the LORD*. It is interesting that the Biblical book of Joshua admits that there was a 'sanctuary of the LORD' at Shechem, important enough to have the stone of witness to the covenant stored in it.

40. There is nothing parallel to this in the Biblical book of Joshua. It is just possible that this is an erroneous adaptation of the story of the allotment of the land to the nine and one-half tribes mentioned in Joshua 14:1-2.

41. Cf. Abu'l Fatḥ (p.34) for the assembly convened by Joshua before his death. The meadow of al-Bahā seems to be the meadow of Nablus (cf. Abu'l Fatḥ, *ibid.*).

42. According to Chronicle Adler, Joshua's successor was Nathanael; so also Abu'l Fatḥ (p.33). This Nathanael is likewise said to have been a nephew of Caleb. In neither source is it stated that Joshua's successor was appointed while Joshua was still living. Chronicle Adler (p.202) says also that Nathanael was appointed at the instance of Eleazar, the priest.

Interestingly enough, the Tolidah mentions neither Joshua nor any of the Judges. Of course, the Tolidah was interested only in giving the priestly chain; but perhaps because it represented the priestly point of view, it preferred to forget anything which seemed to intrude on the high priest's power and sphere of influence.

43. According to Chronicle Adler (p.201), Joshua was buried on the hill facing Mount Gerizim at Timnath Saraḥ. Abu'l Fatḥ (p.34) says that Joshua "was buried at Timnah, which is 'Awarta", the latter name being obviously a variant of Ghuwaira.

44. Chronicle Adler ibid. p.2 says that Nathanael warred against Kushan-rish'athaim, the king of Mesopotamia, cf. Othniel's exploit against the same king, Judges 3:8-10.

45. Chronicle Adler (p.202) and Abu'l Fatḥ (p.33) agree that Joshua's successor, Nathanael, reigned nine years.

46. Abu'l Fatḥ (p.33) says that Yāwut of the tribe of Ephraim succeeded Nathanael and reigned eighteen years; Chronicle Adler (p.202) says that it was Ehud the son of Gera of the tribe of Benuamin, who reigned eighteen years. In hasty Arabic writing the names Yawut and Ehud look very much the same, and Abu'l Fatḥ's Arabic form may be based on the Samaritan pronunciation of Ehud. Abu'l Fatḥ adds that Yāwut made war with Gal'ūn king of Moab.

47. Chronicle Adler (p.202) says that Ehud made war with the Amalekites.

48. Both Abu'l Fatḥ and Chronicle Adler give thirteen kings, but even so not all the tribes were represented, as our writer maintains was the case with his nine rulers. It seems worth while to set out the lists given by Abu'l Fatḥ and Chronicle Adler and to put alongside of them the Judges mentioned in the Biblical Book of Judges.

It will be seen from the table on p.82 that according to Chronicle Adler four of the thirteen Judges were from the tribe of Judah. Abu'l Fatḥ does not always give the tribes from which his judges were drawn, but two out of them were from Judah. According to Abu'l Fatḥ the thirteen Judges covered a period of either 260 or 233 years: the total of Chronicle Adler (excluding Samson for whom no figures are given) is 205 years. Assuming that Samson reigned for twenty years, we reach a total of 225, which with the forty-five years' reign of Joshua would exceed the required total of 260 years for the period of Divine grace. The whole concept of thirteen kings in the period of the Judges is quite artificial. It is to be noted that the writer here has not developed the artificiality to the same extent as did Abu'l Fatḥ and Chronicle Adler. Our writer merely tells us that there were nine kings, whom he must fit into the period of 215 years; of these kings he gives us the name of three. He at least shows his originality in not drawing the names of two of these kings from the Book of Judges, whereas Abu'l Fatḥ and even more so Chronicle Adler are deeply indebted to it. Even the Book of Judges does not claim that all these Judges actually reigned; Othniel, Ehud, Shamgar, Deborah, and Barak did not rule for the rest of their lives, but were rather called up at intervals when they were needed. The Book of Judges has however its own chronological scheme different from that of the Samaritans: cf., e.g., Judges 11:26, where the period between the division of the land and Jephthah is 300 years. Nevertheless, Abu'l Fatḥ and Chronicle Adler bring forward thirteen kings modelled on the thirteen Judges mentioned in the Book of Judges.

49. Third son of Aaron by Elisheba daughter of Amminadab, and therefore descendant of Judah through Pharez (cf. Exod. 6:23, Ruth 4:19-20). His elder brothers Nadab and Abihu were eliminated (Num. 3:4) when they offered unholy fire before the LORD. Eleazar succeeded to Aaron's office (cf. Deut. 10:6). According to Num. 34:16, Eleazar and Joshua were jointly to divide the land, and according to Joshua 14:1, they indeed did so.

50. This is not in the Biblical Book of Joshua, but is modelled on what Joshua did before his death (cf. Joshua 24). Since Eleazar and Joshua had been associated in much of what they did, the Samaritans presumably felt that Eleazar must have an end similar to Joshua's. Note also that only three verses after the statement about Joshua's death (Joshua 24:29) we are told of the death of Eleazar (v.35). Abu'l Fatḥ (p.34-35) makes Eleazar call all Israel to the meadow of Nablus opposite God's House (on Mount Gerizim) and adjure the people, as Joshua had done there also, to serve God loyally on Mount Gerizim.

51. Abu'l Fatḥ (p.35) says nothing of Eleazar paying his devotions to God in the Temple and then setting out for the place where he was to be buried, but states only that he divested himself of the sacred garments and invested Phinehas with them. Chronicle Adler (p.202-203) says that Eleazar died and was buried at Kiriath 'Amratha facing *Mount Gerizim Bethel*. The Tolidah (p.398) notes only that Eleazar was high priest for fifty years. So also Abu'l Fatḥ (p.35), who adds that he was buried in the *Kal'a* which is opposite the Sacred Mount. Abu'l Fatḥ (p.34) gives also a tradition that Joshua was buried

at 'Kafr Ḥarith in the *Kal'a* which is opposite the Mount'. It would thus seem that Eleazar was buried in the same place as Joshua.

52. Abu'l Fatḥ (p.35) notes that the people wept for Eleazar thirty days; the same is said with regard to the death of Joshua (*ibid.*, p.34).

53. Phinehas (cf. Judges 20:28).

54. Abu'l Fatḥ (p.35) says that Phinehas was high priest for sixty years, but does not make him go through the formal leavetaking and the removal of his priestly vestments before his death; at least this is not explicitly detailed by him. However, Abu'l Fatḥ tells us (p.35) of Phinehas' calculations, basic for the fixing of the Samaritan calendar, referred to above (p. 38). This, according to Abu'l Fatḥ, was apparently done in the same year - the thirteenth after the entrance of Israel into Canaan - in which Phinehas' son wrote the copy of the Law. (cf. above, p.46).

55. Five is not what one would expect, but rather four: Abisha, Šiši, Buḥḳi, and Uzzi (so Tolidah, p.399; above, p.46, 48; Chronicle Adler, p.203-206).

56. Abu'l Fatḥ (p.38) says that Eli was fifty years old at this time. Eli led the schism and set up the rival altar and tabernacle at Shiloh (cf. Chronicle Adler, p.205; and Joshua 41-44). Note that the Tolidah (p.398; above, p.48) merely says that Uzzi was high priest for twenty-five years, and that it was in the twenty-fifth year of his office that God destroyed or concealed the Holy Tabernacle made by Bezaleel; it adds nothing about Eli. Chronicle Adler obtained this information from Abu'l Fatḥ, who enlarges on the split between the sons of Phinehas and those of Ithamar; it was from the latter that Eli was descended.

57. The Tolidah (ibid.) notes that the period from Adam to the destruction of the Holy Tabernacle amounted to three thousand and fifty years. Abu'l Fatḥ (p.37) agrees with the Samaritan Book of Joshua that three thousand and fifty years had elapsed.

58. This is part of Deut. 32:15 in the Samaritan version, which inserts at the beginning of the verse 'Jacob did eat and was satisfied'. However, the Samaritan version reads next not *Israel*, but *Jeshurun*.

59. Presumably Deut. 32:15b-18 is meant, especially the last part of v.15 and all of v.18.

Judges	Chronicle Adler, p.202-205
1. Othniel, Caleb's nephew; as a result of the deliverance wrought by him the land had rest for forty years; cf. Judges 3:11.	1. Nathanael, Caleb's nephew reigned 9 years
2. Ehud, son of Gera the Benjaminite; as a result of his leadership the land had rest for eighty years; cf. Judges 3:30.	2. Ehud reigned 18 years
3. Shamgar, son of Anath; cf. Judges 3:31.	3. Gomer son of Anath reigned 20 years
4. Deborah and Barak; cf. Judges 4-5; Barak the son of Abinoam from Kedesh in Naphtali, Judges 4:6.	4. Parak reigned 30 years
5. Gideon of Manasseh; And the land had rest forty years (Judges 8:28 in the time of Gideon).	5. Gideon reigned 7 years
6. Abimelech, son of Gideon, made king of Shechem, ruled over Israel for three years, Judges 9:6, 9:22.	6. Abimelech son of Gideon reigned 3 years
7. Tola, son of Puah of Issachar; judged Israel for twenty-three years, Judges 10:1.	7. Tola son of Puah reigned 13 years
8. Jair the Gileadite judged Israel for twenty-two years, Judges 10:3.	8. Jair son of Gilead reigned 27 years
9. Jephthah the Gileadite, judged Israel for six years, Judges 12:7	9. Jephtah reigned 10 years
10. Ibzan of Bethlehem, judged Israel for seven years, Judges 12:8.	10. Abida' reigned 10 years
11. Elou the Zebulunite judged Israel for ten years, Judges 12:11.	11. Ibn tal reigned 18 years

12. Abdon son of Hillel of the tribe of Ephraim, judged Israel for eight years, Judges 12:14.	12. Anithal reigned 40 years
13. Samson son of Manoah of the tribe of Dan, judged Israel for twenty years, Judges 16:31.	13. Samson

	Abu'l Fatḥ p. 33-34	
of the tribe of Judah	1. Nathanael nephew of Caleb reigned 9 years	
of the tribe of Benjamin	2. Yawut reigned 18 years	of the tribe of Ephraim
	3. Gomer reigned 20 years	
of the tribe of Naphtali	4. Faraḳ son of Naphtali reigned 30 years	
of the tribe of Manasseh	5. Gideon reigned 7 years	
	6. Abimelech son of Gideon reigned 30 years, but the more likely figure is 3 years	
of the tribe Issachar	7. Tola reigned 23 years	
of the tribe of Manasseh	8. Jair son of Gilead reigned 28 years	of the house of Manasseh
of the tribe of Judah	9. Yūftaḥ (Jephthah) reigned 7 years	of the tribe of Judah
of the tribe of Judah	10. Abūdham reigned 10 years	of the tribe of Ephraim from Sailun
of the tribe Zebulon	11. Ibn Lail reigned 18 years	of Ephraim
of the tribe of Judah	12. 'Antiyal reigned 40 years	of Judah
of the tribe Dan	13. Samson reigned 20 years	of the tribe Dan

CHRONICLE ADLER

The Chronicle Adler was published by E. N. Adler and M. Seligsohn, with a French translation, in *Revue des Etudes Juives*, XLIV-XLVI (1902-3), Adler (ibid. XLIV, p.188) tells us that in April 1901 he was not permitted to see the original. The text which he published had been transcribed from the Samaritan script into Hebrew cursive by a German Jew resident in Jerusalem; who had seen the original at Nablus and had transcribed it there. Adler says that the Chronicle extends from Adam to 1889, the year of the World Exposition in Paris. But it goes in fact even further (cf. ibid., XLVI, p.145), since the chronicler's colophon states that the year of writing was 6179 of the Creation (Samaritan reckoning), 3385 since the Hebrews crossed the Jordan (Samaritan reckoning) to enter Canaan, 1900 A.D., 1616 of the Diocletian Era, or 1317 A.H.

The fact alone that the Chronicle comes down to the end of the nineteenth century need not necessarily mean that the whole of it was composed in the nineteenth century. Samaritan chronicles were added to from time to time, as for example, the Tolidah which, though written in the 14th century, has been extended by each successive high priest. Nevertheless there is every reason to think that the Chronicle Adler is recent,[1] for its text is a derivative. The basic source for all Samaritan chronicles is the Tolidah list of the high priests. This was used by Abu'l Fatḥ, and both the Tolidah and Abu'l Fatḥ have been used by the compiler of the Chronicle Adler. The Book of Joshua, also used by Abu'l Fatḥ, does not seem to have been used independently by Chronicle Adler, while Abu'l Fatḥ's Annals seem to have been used as the main source of information, doubtless supplemented by occasional reference to the "autograph" text of the Tolidah in the High Priest's house at Nablus. But although the compiler of Chronicle Adler keeps to the system established by the Tolidah and expanded by Abu'l Fatḥ of arranging events of interest within the high priestly framework of history, he uses his own discretion to a considerable extent as to what is to be included and what is to be excluded, and under what high priest each significant event is to be noted. Even more than Abu'l Fatḥ, Chronicle Adler seeks to note matters of interest outside the immediate Samaritan field of reference, e.g. matters referring to early Roman history. There again, the Tolidah had set a precedent, for though in it the priestly list is the main thing, references, though meager and relatively infrequent, are made to world history in general.

It would hardly be fair to Abu'l Fatḥ to say that the writer of the Chronicle Adler had materially improved on him. Some of Abu'l Fatḥ's more glaringly unhistorical passages have been curtailed, and some systematization of the material retained is noticeable. One can perhaps say with some justification that Chronicle Adler shows that the Samaritans have learned nothing more about historiography since the 14th century. This is particularly evident in the way in which the author handles the period after Abu'l Fatḥ's Annals stop. Seligsohn's criticism (ibid., XLIV, 189-191) is still perhaps valid. It may be, as he suggests, that the Book of Chronicles to which the compiler refers for legends and events of universal history was the immediate parent of the Chronicle itself. But even if we had it, it would have added little to our knowledge of Samaritan historiography, for it seems to have been based upon the Tolidah and Abu'l Fatḥ, with the addition of some other material, all of which the Chronicle Adler has abridged. Seligsohn is probably right also in assuming that the Chronicle of Ṣadaḳah, referred to by Abu'l Fatḥ only to be rejected, was not used by our Chronicler, although Adler thought that it was. The Chronicle of Ṣadaḳah whatever its nature may have been, did not agree with Abu'l Fatḥ's priestly lists, as Abu'l Fatḥ himself notes; whereas the Chronicle Adler does on the whole, agree with them.

Seligsohn's remark about the language of the Chronicle Adler, that its Hebrew if full of arabisms is quite justified. The compiler, though writing in Hebrew, was more accustomed to Arabic.

The notes to the French translation of the Chronicle Adler are helpful, though meager, and I have made use of them in the notes accompanying the present translation.

FOOTNOTE

1. Professor Paul Kahle has told me that at Nablus, at the end of the 19th century, "there was a manufactory of chronicles" to supply the demand then current.

ADLER

Uzzi the son of Buḥḳi,[0] *25 years.*

In the days of his priesthood, the head of the house of Ithmar[1] was Eli the son of Yafni, of the sons of Ithamar, the son of Aaron the priest. He was an old man[2] far gone in days, while Uzzi[3] the son of Buḥḳi was a little lad; yet he sought to be installed in the high priesthood[4] instead of Uzzi. Now in those days the prince over Israel was Samson, of the tribe of Dan, who was a mighty man in the land; he was the last of the kings of the period of Divine grace,[5] for in his days the LORD hid[6] the holy Tabernacle from the eyes of Israel. And so at that time Eli the son of Yafni went and made for himself an ark of gold, wherein he placed the books written in the handwriting[7] of his ancestor, our lord Ithamar. He also made for himself a tent and pitched it at Shiloh,[8] because the children of Israel who were at that time in Shechem and in other cities of Palestine, had driven him from Mount Gerizim, together with those who joined him. There in Shiloh he built an altar and offered sacrifices upon it, and all the men of the tribe of

Judah joined him, as well as many men from the other tribes. And all the things which Eli had done, are they not written down in the Book of Chronicles?[9]

And the children of Israel in his days were divided into three groups: one did according to the abominations of the Gentiles and served other gods; another followed Eli the son of Yafni, although many of them turned away from him after he had revealed his intentions; and the third remained with the High Priest Uzzi the son of Buḥḳi, in the chosen place, Mount Gerizim Bethel, in the holy city of Shechem, and in all the (other) cities. Then the LORD hid[10] from the eyes of all Israel the holy Tabernacle which Moses had made by the command of the LORD in the wilderness. This happened at the end of the priesthood of the aforementioned Uzzi.

Šiši[11] *the son of Uzzi, 37 years.*

In the days of his priesthood Eli the son of Yafni died, and Samuel the son of Elkanah arose in his stead to attend[12] the Ark which Eli had made at Shiloh; it is said that he was of the sons of Korah[13] the son of Izhar. He appointed as king over his community Saul the son of Kish,[14] the son of Abiel, the son of Seror, the son of Bechorath, the son of Afiah, of the sons of Benjamin. And there was great enmity between Saul and his community on the one hand, and the community of the observant Israelites on the other, who were of the sons of Phinehas[15] and of the sons of Joseph, with a few men from among the sons of Benjamin. And so there was great war between them and the community of Saul and Samuel. Now the High Priest Šiši had his residence in the chosen place, Mount Gerizim Bethel,[16] and twelve men from among the princes of the community settled there with him, their names being these: the first, Eli the son of Zadok the son of Shuthelah of Salem the Great;[17] the second, Lakhed the son of Ṣethur, of Beth-Pethuaḥ; the third

Paruḳ the son of Joseph the son of Taḥam, of the town Shinthah Garithah; the fourth, Na'ăneh the son of Nathanael the son of Shuthelah, of the town of Ḥilanah Ṭabah, the fifth, Abnabi the son of Eden, of the holy city of Shechem; the sixth, Garmi the son of Geber the son of Taḥam, of the town of Timnath Seraḥ; the seventh, Eglon the son of ha-'Ayuḏ the son of Perath, of the town of Beth Pe'or; the eighth, Zayith the son of Sachar the son of Becher, of the town of Yiskor; the ninth, Sĕgi'an the son of Sa'ud the son of Nun, of the town of Luzah,[18] which is Samaria, built by Joshua the son of Nun in the days of Divine grace around the holy Tabernacle; the tenth, Eber the son of Semekh the son of Machir, of the town of Kefar-Yahebeth; the eleventh, Uri the son of Gamar the son of Jair, of the town of Ḳa'athah; the twelfth, Meshabbeah the son of 'Omed the son of Nobah of the city of Nobah; in all twelve men, established to attend[20] the high priests. May the Lord reward their deserts with good. They dwelt[21] on Mount Gerizim until they died.

Buḥḳi the son of Šiši served for 23 years, Šabaṭ the son of Buḥḳi served for 28 years, Šallum the son of Šabat served for 25 years, Hezekiah the son of Šallum served for 20 years, and Jonathan the son of Hezekiah served for 28 years. In the days of the latter's priesthood King Saul died, and the community of Shiloh made David the son of Jesse king in his stead, he being thirty[22] years old at the time when they made him king. Jair the son of Jonathan served for 25 years, and Delaiah the son of Jair for 25 years. In the days of his priesthood King David the son of Jesse died. The duration of his reign was forty years[23] seven in Hebron and thirty-three in the city of Jebus.

Jair the son of Delaiah, 19 years.

In the days of his priesthood,[24] King Solomon the son of David built the Temple which his father had founded at the threshing-floor of the Jebusite;[25] he built it four hundred and eighty years after the crossing of the children of Israel into the land of Canaan, and two hundred and twenty years after the concealment of the holy Tabernacle which had been made by the command of the LORD in the wilderness. Solomon reigned over all the tribes of Israel, even as David his father had done, for forty[26] years in the city of Jebus. He had many foreign wives,[27] including the daughter of Pharaoh, as well as Moabite, Ammonite, Edomite, Sidonian, and Hittite women. Moreover, he had seven hundred wives (who were) princesses, and three hundred concubines, and his wives turned his heart. And so it came to pass that in his old age his wives inclined his heart towards other gods, and he worshipped them, and thus did what was evil in the eyes of the LORD, and did not fear Him, nor keep His commandments and His statutes. The name of Solomon's viceroy was Abisaph[28] the son of Berechiah, who was born four hundred and ninety years after the crossing of the children of Israel into the land of Canaan.

Jonathan, 28 years.

In the days of his priesthood King Solomon the son of David died, and his son Rehoboam was made king in his stead. He was brought to the city of Shechem to be crowned[29] there, for it was the custom of the kings of Israel to be invested with the crown of the kingdom in Shechem, below the chosen place on Mount Gerizim Bethel, that is to say, the Sanctuary of the LORD. And at that time the tribes of Israel separated themselves from the jurisdiction of the kings of Judah, so that Rehoboam the son of Solomon ruled only[30] over the tribe of Judah, while Jeroboam the son of Nebat ruled over the rest of the tribes of Israel for twenty-two years;[31] Rehoboam ruled over the tribe of Judah for eighteen years.[32] During that time the tribes of Israel were divided into four groups.[33] The first was the community of the Observers[34] who remained true to the truth, and they were the sons of Joseph, the sons of Phinehas, and a few of the sons of Levi and Benjamin, who maintained the sanctity of Mount Gerizim Bethel. The second group consisted of the sons of Judah and the sons of Benjamin who maintained the sanctity of the city of Jebus. The third group belonged to one of the tribes dwelling in the town of Faratha who worshipped Baal. And the fourth group were those who followed Jeroboam the son of Nebat. And Jeroboam removed to the city of Samaria[35] and dwelt there.

Ishmael, 26 years.

In the days of his priesthood Jeroboam the son of Nebat died, and Nadab[36] reigned in his stead for two years; then he too died, and was succeeded by Baasha[37] the son of Ahijah. And likewise in the days of his priesthood, Rehoboam the son of Solomon died and there reigned in his stead over the tribe of Judah Abijam,[38] his son, for two years. He was succeeded by his son Asa,[39] who ruled over the tribe of Judah for forty one years. And in those days a man[40] from the sons of Ephraim the son of Joseph went and bought the (site of the) city of Samaria from a man whose name was Shomer; and it and the cities which were round about it were called the cities of Samaria, and those of the children of Israel who dwelt in it were called Samaritans[41] down to this day.

Tobiah the son of Ishmael, 28 years.

In the days of his priesthood Baasha the son of Ahijah died; and Elah[42] his son reigned in his stead for two years. His successor Zimri[43] reigned for only seven days, whereupon Omri became king in his place. It is said that it was Omri[44] who bought the hill of Samaria from Shomer for two talents of silver. And in the final year of the priesthood of Tobiah, the

Ishmaelites came and waged war against the children of Israel who were Observers, and slew the High Priest Tobiah on Mount Gerizim. From that time and for a long period thereafter no high priest was able to dwell on Mount Gerizim.[45]

Zadok[46] the son of Tobiah, 20 years.

He dwelt during his office as priest in the town of 'Aḳrabah within the limits of the chosen place, Mount Gerizim Bethel, and twelve princely men of renown, of the sons of Joseph the righteous - may they be remembered for good - dwelt with him, their names being these: the first Zaith the son of Sachar the son of Becher, of Yiskor; the second, Sĕḡi'an the son of Sĕgiel, the son of Shomeron, of Luzah, which is the city in the environs of Mount Gerizim Bethel. These two men were with Rabbi Zadok continually; never leaving the place of his dwelling, while the other ten would meet with him when required;[47] and these were their names: the first, Eber the son of Machir, who dwelt in the town of Ephratha;[48] the second, Shelah the son of Hori, who dwelt at Birtah and its suburbs; the third, 'Omed the son of Nobah, who lived in the town of Liban[49] these three men were of the tribe of Manasseh the son of Joseph the righteous; the fourth, Zadok the son of Shuthelah, who went back and dwelt in his native city which is Salem the Great; the fifth, Becher the son of Ishmael, who dwelt in the town of Miṣpah;[50] the sixth, Taḥam the son of Abraham, who dwelt in the town of Mardah; the seventh, 'Aḳḳub the son of Na'aneh, who dwelt in Tirath Nim'arah; the eighth, was Eden the son of Ab, who dwelt in Beth-Porek; the ninth, Geber the son of Karmi, who dwelt in the town of Ḥagga; the tenth Porath the son of Ahihud, who dwelt in the town of Socho.[51] And in those days Omri died and there reigned in his stead his son Ahab.[52] Asa the king of Judah likewise died, and was succeeded by his son Jehoshaphat,[53] who reigned for twenty-five years.

Amram the son of Zadok, 28 years.

In the days of his priesthood died Ahab the son of Omri, who had married Jezebel[54] the daughter of Ethbaal the king of Sidon. Ahab's son Ahaziah[55] reigned in his stead for two years; and was succeeded by his brother Jehoram,[56] who reigned for twelve years. Jehoshaphat the king of Judah also died, and his son Jehoram[57] reigned in his stead for seven years. After him Ahaziah[58] reigned for one year, being replaced by Jehoash[59] who reigned for forty years.

Hilkiah, 24 years.

In the days of his priesthood, Jehoram the king of Israel died,[60] and there reigned in his stead Jehu[61] the son of Jehoshaphat the son of Nimshi, for twenty-eight years. He was succeeded by his son Jehoahaz, who reigned for seventeen years.

Amram, 38 years.

In the days of his priesthood Jehoahaz the king of Israel died, and his son Joash[63] reigned in his stead for sixteen years. Jehoash the king of Judah likewise died and was succeeded by his son Amaziah[64] who reigned for twenty-nine years.

'Aḳḳub, 36 years.

In the days of his priesthood Joash[65] the king of Israel died, and there reigned in his stead his Jeroboam[66] for forty-one years. In those days appeared Hosea, Joel and Amos who called themselves prophets, but the community of the Observers did not hearken unto them, in obedience to the command of the LORD in the Torah, *You shall not utter a false report.*[67] After Jeroboam died, his son Zechariah reigned in his stead for six months,[68] being succeeded by Šallum[69] the son of Jabesh, who reigned for one month. Amaziah[70] the king of Judah likewise died, and Uzziah[71] reigned in his stead for fifty-two years.[72]

And in those days also there appeared a man of the sons of Edom[73] whose name was Romulus; he founded the city of Rome, and reigned in it for thirty-seven years. At that time Romulus made a census of his men, and their number came to three thousand footmen and three hundred horsemen. He divided them into three divisions[74] and set a captain over each division.

'Aḳabyah,[75] *39 years.*

In the days of his priesthood Menahem[76] the son of Gadi reigned over Israel for ten years; during his reign Pul[77] the king of Assyria came over, and Menahem gave him a thousand talents of silver so that he might help him to strengthen his hold upon the kingdom. And Menahem[78] exacted the money from the wealthy men, fifty shekels of silver from every man to give to the King of Assyria, whereupon the King of Assyria turned back to his own land, and did not stay in the Land of Israel. Then Menahem died, and there reigned in his stead his son Pekahiah[79] for two years, being succeeded by Pekah[80] the son of Remaliah, his officer, who with fifty men of Gilead, slew his master Pekahiah.

In his time there came Tiglath-Pileser[81] the king of Assyria, and carried captive thither all the inhabitants of the land of Naphtali. Likewise in his days, Jotham[82] the son of Uzziah reigned over Judah for sixteen years, the while Isaiah, Hosea, and Micah were acting as prophets[83] among the sons of Judah and Israel. Jotham's son Ahaz[84] reigned in his stead, also for sixteen years, like his father, so that Isaiah, Hosea, and Micah were active during his reign as well. At the same time Hoshea[85] the son of Elah reigned over Israel, and in his days Shalmaneser[86] the king of Assyria came and imprisoned him. Thereupon the King of Assyria besieged the cities of Samaria[87] for three years, and then carried Israel[88] captive to Assyria. And these were the names of the princes[89] exiled to Assyria with the High Priest 'Aḳabyah, who were left of the tribe of Ephraim and of the tribe of Manasseh, of the sons of Joseph the righteous; the sons of Ephraim: Joseph, Pamur, Ḥarfīf, Šallem, and Zarwand; the sons of Shuthelah; Karim, 'Ayin and Haroham (Jeroham); the sons of Machir: Hamṣiṯ, Ḥako, Sa'ad, and Gideon; the sons of Manasseh: Sarbah and Sar of the Machir family, Suf the son of Sered of the Gilead family, and Er and Dahag likewise of the Gilead family; these were the princes of the tribe of Joseph. In those days Tullus[90] was king of Rome and reigned for thirty-two years. After him Phanus Marsius[91] reigned for fifteen years; and was succeeded by Tarquinius Priscus who reigned for forty-eight years.

Ḥalal,[92] *45 years.*

In the days of his priesthood Hezekiah[93] was king over the sons of Judah for twenty-nine years; while Isaiah, Hosea, and Micah were active as prophets.[94] After him Manasseh[95] reigned for fifty-five years. In those days a new king reigned in Rome, whose name was Numa,[96] a native of Sabinia. Towards the end of his days Numa retired to the wilderness and dwelt in caves all alone, no man being with him. And so two men of the princes of his people went to him to bring him back to the throne of his kingdom, but he refused to hearken to them. Afterwards, however, he went and sat once again on the throne of his kingdom, until he completed forty-two years of rule. And his people wept for him like orphans for their father.

Seraiah,[97] *50 years.*

In the twenty-first year of his priesthood the children of Israel returned to the land of Canaan. In those days lived the wise man Salus[98] the philosopher.

Levi[99] *the son of Seraiah, 50 years.*

In the days of his priesthood, Amon[100] reigned over Judah for two years, and was succeeded by Josiah who reigned eleven[101] years. At this time lived also Zephaniah and Jeremiah the son of Hilkiah, of the priests of the Jews, who acted as prophets. The next king was Jehoahaz,[102] who reigned for three months, after which the king of Egypt carried him away to his city where he dwelt until he died. And there reigned for eleven years in his stead Eliakim,[103] whose name was changed to Jehoiakim by the command of Pharaoh the king of Egypt. He was succeeded by Jehoiachin[104] who reigned for eight years, being replaced by Zedekiah[105] the brother of Jehoiakim. In those days the king of Rome was Serpius Tullius,[106] who reigned for forty-four years.

Nathanael, 52 years.

In his days Nebuchadnezzar king of Assyria came up against the city of Jerusalem,[107] which is Jebus, encamped over against it, built a wall around it, and besieged it. And[108] the Chaldeans pursued the king of Judah and overtook him after all his army had scattered away from him. They captured him and brought him up to the King of Babylon at Riblah, where they first slew his sons before his eyes, and then put his eyes out. Thereupon the King ordered him to be bound in fetters and brought to Babylon. This Nebuchadnezzar ascended to royal throne in the fourth year of Jehoiakim king of Judah, and in the nineteenth year of his reign he[109] sent his servant Nebuzaradan, the captain of the bodyguard, to the city of Jebus which is called Jerusalem. And Nebazaradan[110] burnt the house of the golden ark, which is the Tabernacle made by King Solomon the son of David, and the king's house, and all the houses of the city; every great house he burnt down, and the walls around the city they demolished, while the rest of the people who were left were exiled to the cities of Babylon. As for the doors of the Tabernacle and all its furnishings, they broke them and carried them to Babylon. The king of Rome in those days was Tarquinius the second,[111] who reigned for twenty-four years, after which the kingdom of Rome became a consulate, that is to say the men of Rome put two men over them who were called consuls and served as judges for twenty-one years, extending into the days of the priesthood of Azariah. Three years after the consulate was set up over Rome a great civil war took place in it, accompanied by exceedingly heavy famine.

Azariah, 35 years.

This Azariah, together with his entire community of Observers, was carried off by the king of the Chaldeans[112] from the land of Canaan to a distant land in the East. This took place in the tenth year of his priesthood, so that their stay in the Holy Land between the first captivity and the second came to one hundred and thirty one years.[113] In those days the army of Nebuchadnezzar[114] came and besieged Tyre for thirteen years, that city being then built upon a wall; before that it had been built in an open field. Thus the land at that time became desolate of all (its inhabitants) the children of Israel, the children of Judah, and the community of Jehoiakim. And the king of Assyria[115] brought in foreigners[116] and settled them in the land of Canaan in place of the children of Israel. And at that time Ezekiel, Nahum, and Daniel were acting as prophets; they were scattered in the land of Babylon.

Abdiel[117] the son of Azariah, 40 years.

In the thirty-fifth year of his priesthood he returned from captivity to the Holy Land, and with him three hundred thousand men of the children of Israel, fifty-five years having elapsed from the beginning of the captivity till their return to the Land of Canaan. The prince of the sons of Joseph at that time was Uzzi[118] the son of Simeon. Also at that time the princes of the tribe of Judah came to Abdiel the priest at Haran - having come from the cities of Kush - and likewise the inhabitants of Galilee, the children of Hananiah, the children of Benjamin, the children of Zechariah, and the children of Tobiah. A great number of people came also from Babylon - namely, the children of Merari - and they wrote to other men who likewise came, making a great multitude which arrived at Harran. With them was also Zerubbabel[119] the son of Šaršar, the prince of the sons of Judah. And they said to Abdiel the High Priest and to Uzzi the son of Simeon, the prince of the children of Joseph, "Come, let us all go together to Jebus, the city of King David". And Abdiel the High Priest and Uzzi the son of Simeon, the prince of the sons of Joseph the righteous, rebuked them, saying, "Why should we do this thing? Go ye rather and your seed with us to Mount Gerizim, the holy House of God, which the LORD has chosen to make His name dwell therein, and let us all return to the LORD our God, perchance He will then return to us and deliver us from the wrath of the judgment of our enemies; for the thing which you have spoken is an abomination and unacceptable. How long will you cling to this evil thing and fail to be persuaded by all the misfortunes which have befallen all of us of the community of Israel?" And when Zerubbabel heard their words he waxed wroth, and a fierce quarrel broke out between the princes of the sons of Joseph and the princes of the sons of Judah, until the Babylonians heard of it, as did also the king's household who thereupon reported it to him. And the king sent after them to summon them to his chamber of assembly, and asked them about the things which he had heard; and Abdiel the high priest recounted to him what had taken place between them and the sons of Judah. Then the King bade them to assemble before him and requested each party to reveal the testimonies which it claimed in the Holy Torah, in order that he might search after the truth between them. And the community of the Observers, i.e., the sons of Joseph, brought the Scroll of the Torah and recounted before the King the testimony contained therein in favor of Mount Gerizim and in proof that it was the chosen place. The sons of Judah likewise brought a book which they said was the book of King David, and Zerubbabel approached to speak before the King, saying, "King David commanded us to the effect that the threshing floor of the Jebusite[120] which is in the city of Jebus is the chosen place". The King, seeing that the truth was not with Zerubbabel and his community, but clearly with the sons of Joseph, waxed wroth with Zerubbabel[121] and commanded that sacrifices be brought on Mount Gerizim, and not in Jebus. He thereupon imprisoned Zerubbabel and all his followers in the cities of Babylonia, while letting Abdiel the High Priest and the princes of the sons of Joseph and all their followers go to the Holy Land. And they went and came to Mount Gerizim Bethel and worshipped the LORD their God upon it with joy and gladness. The number of those from all the tribes of Israel who came back at that time was three hundred thousand men. And it came to pass after these events, that the king of Babylon died, and his son reigned in his stead for thirty-six years, and all that time there was exceedingly great enmity between the sons of Joseph and the sons of Judah by reason of the aforementioned matters. And in those days[122] a war broke out between the (Tar)-quins and the men of Rome.

Hezekiah[123] the son of Abdiel, 30 years.

In the days of his priesthood Zerubbabel, Nehemiah[124] the priest, and Ezra the priest came and gave to the king of Babylon a large bribe and petitioned him for an edict to rebuild the House which Solomon the son of King David had built in the city of Jebus. The king issued such an edict, and they came and built the house of the Ark, the house of the king, and all the city. Likewise in his days there lived in the land of Greece a wise philosopher named Hippocrates,[125] and also another wise man of the community of the children of Israel who were Observers in the cities of Babylonia, named the wise Aaron.[126] There was yet a third philosopher named Democritus,[127] and also a fourth named Lazan. The priest Ezra, after his coming to the city of Jebus, which is called also Jerusalem, sought for a Scroll of the Law, but could not find any among the men of his community, for the king of Assyria had burned all the books of the sons of Judah. Whereupon Ezra used deceit to obtain an ancient torn Torah from a man who was one of the community of the children of Israel who were Observers of the Truth. At that time the Jews no longer knew the holy tongue, nor the holy letters therof, indeed all of them knew no language save that of the Assyrians in whose cities they had dwelt for seventy years in captivity. Therefore Ezra the priest assembled his friend Nehemiah[128] and all the princes of his community, and they wrote the book of the Holy Torah in the tongue of the Assyrians and in their letters, and he altered many things in the text of the Holy Torah out of hatred for the community of the children of Israel who are Observers of the Truth, that is to say, the children of Joseph the righteous, adding some things and subtracting many others; for he did not keep that which the LORD had commanded by the hand of His servant Moses: *All this word which I command you today, you shall not add to it nor diminish from it.*[129] Moreover many errors were made by him in the book of the Torah; which neither he nor his people perceived or understood. In addition to this he gathered many sayings and writings composed by former authors and prophets, such as suited his aims and desires, and he and his colleague Nehemiah commanded his community to keep them all. And Ezra said to all his community; "Thus did the LORD My God command me to do"; but He whose Name is to be blessed, commanded him nothing, rather did he do all these things of his own design. And all the words of Ezra and what he had done, are written in the Book of Chronicles.[130] But the LORD knows best.

Hananiah,[131] *24 years.*

In the days of his priesthood, there were two men, princes of the sons of Joseph, which is the community of the Observers. The name of one was Jomakim[132] and the name of the other was Jehozadok;[133] both were possessed of very great wisdom and understanding. And the community of the Observers sent the two aforementioned princes, by the command of the High Priest Hananiah, to serve the king of Babylonia. Accordingly, they went and served him, and he delighted in them, and his heart was inclined towards them. In those days, Esther, one of the daughters of Judah, became the wife of the king of Assyria who loved her very dearly. He also had for his viceroy a man of the community of the Jews whose name was Mordecai, Esther, the wife of the king at that time, being his niece. They did many favors to the community of the Jews who resided in the land of Canaan.[134]

NOTES ON CHRONICLE ADLER

0. *REJ*, XLIV, 205 ff.

1. Ithamar, the youngest son of Aaron; cf. Exod. 6:23.

2. Eli at the time of his death was ninety-eight years old; cf. 1 Sam. 4:15. Abu'l Fatḥ and the Book of Joshua say that Eli was fifty years old (cf. above, p.86, note 56).

3. Cf. 1 Chr. 6:5, 51.

4. In the list of 1 Chr. 6, Eli is not mentioned, as he was a scion of Ithamar and not of Eleazar. The Samaritans maintain that Eli was a schismatic and set up a rival tabernacle

at Shiloh. The Bible gives us to understand that in the days of Joshua, immediately after the entry into the Land, the Tabernacle was set up at Shiloh, not at Mount Gerizim, as the Samaritans maintain. However, it is noteworthy that by the time of Solomon the house of Eli, or rather of Ithamar, was, according to the Biblical account, superseded by that of Zadok. In the post-exilic period, the Jewish priestly lists stress the descent from Eleazar. Yet the story of Eli as priest in charge of the first sanctuary, the Tabernacle at Shiloh, has remained. The Samaritans were not slow to seize upon this ascendancy, temporary though it appears to have been, of the Ithamar priesthood, and to claim that their priesthood has always been descended from Eleazar.

5. This agrees with the Samaritan Book of Joshua in making Samson the last of the kings of the period of Divine grace and the contemporary of Eli; cf. above, p. 84.

6. This hiding of the Tabernacle marks the end of the period of Divine Grace. The Biblical basis of this concept is the verse Deut. 32:20, *I will hide my face from them:* since the Tabernacle was the place where the Shekinah dwelt, the Shekinah, too, was withdrawn with the withdrawal of the Tabernacle. The root used in Deut. 32:20 for hiding, *str*, may have also had in Samaritan usage the meaning of 'to destroy', and is indeed used in the Tolidah for the destruction of the Tabernacle, although it is possible that the destruction originally referred to the Samaritan Temple demolished by John Hyrcanus. The one and only Tabernacle they knew was thus presumably projected back to an earlier period. There is moreover every likelihood that the Samaritan scheme of the following six world periods is artificial and late:

grace (Ridwan): from the Creation to the Fall
Displeasure (Panuta) : from the Fall to the Exodus
grace (Ridwan): from Sinai to Eli
Displeasure (Panuta) : from Eli to the coming of the Taheb
grace (Ridwan): from the coming of the Taheb to the end of the millenium.
Displeasure (Panuta) : from the end of the millenium to the Day of Judgment.

If that is so, it is possible that the Tolidah statement concerning the destruction of the Tabernacle was later reinterpreted to refer to the hiding of the Tabernacle, and that the verse Deut. 32:20 was used as a proof-text.

7. i.e., not the copy of the Torah written by Abisha, which the Samaritans claim they now have. Abisha was a descendant of Eleazar.

8. Shiloh, according to official Samaritan history, was since the time of Eli a center of Israelite worship only. According to the Jewish Bible, Shiloh was the first site of the Ark, and remained so until the time of Eli. If the references to Shiloh in Joshua, Judges, and Samuel are historically accurate, the Samaritans have turned history upside down: instead of being a rival sanctuary founded at the end of the period of the Judges, Shiloh had been the true sanctuary since the entry into Canaan. All the things which, according to the Samaritans, mark that period as the age of Divine grace, happened not at Mount Gerizim, but at Shiloh. The fall of Shiloh must have seemed to the early Israelites to signify the end of the age of Divine grace, especially as the Ark of the Covenant was lost. But the full effect of it was to come later, when David took the Ark to Jerusalem and therefore entirely out of the Northern Israelite orbit. There is also the possibility that Shiloh was not the first sanctuary founded after the entry into the Land.

9. Probably a reference to Abu'l Fatḥ.

10. The Tabernacle is supposed to be hidden on Mount Gerizim with all its furnishings, including the Ark of the Covenant. When the Taheb comes he will discover it and set it up again. There is a parallel story about what Jeremiah had done with the Ark, etc., of the Jerusalem Temple, prior to its fall in B.C. 586 (cf. II Macc. 2:5-7).

11. Šiši is not named in the Bible.

12. This account overlooks the fall of Shiloh and the capture of the Ark by the Philistines at the battle of Aphek. (cf. 1 Sam. 4:11). The Ark was subsequently returned to Israel, not to Shiloh but to Kiriath-Jearim (cf. 1 Sam. 7:1-2) where it remained for twenty years. David (2 Sam. 6:2) brought it up from Baale-Judah. Samuel did not attend the Ark himself, but charged Eleazar the son of Abinadab with this duty.

13. Korah the son of Izhar the grandson of Levi conspired with Dathan and Abiram against Moses and Aaron (cf. Num. 16:1ff). 1 Sam. 1:1 however states that Elkanah was not of levitical stock, but an Ephraimite. The author of the Chronicle Adler seized the opportunity to condemn Samuel as a product of the bad stock of the rebellious Korah, by identifying his father, Elkanah, with a son of Korah who was also called Elkanah (Exod. 6:24).

14. 1 Sam. 9:1.

15. i.e. Levites of the right stock.

16. The Samaritans identify Bethel with Mount Gerizim on the ground that it was there that Jacob saw the ladder which reached up to heaven.

17. A small village near Shechem on Mount Gerizim. Some thought that this was the city of Melchizedek, Gen. 14:18.

18. i.e. Luz, afterwards called Bethel; cf. Gen. 28:19.

19. The Tolidah gives Gamal instead of Gamar: the confusion of resh and lamed is not an uncommon phenomenon.

20. Abu'l Fatḥ understands that these twelve men were to guard Šiši.

21. Tolidah (ed. Neubauer, p.399) and Abu'l Fatḥ say that the high priests dwelt on Mount Gerizim until the Arabs slew the high priest Tobiah. As the sentence stands in Chronicle Adler, 'they' refers to the priestly bodyguard. Abu'l Fatḥ has copied the Tolidah statement faithfully, although it does not make as much good sense, while Chronicle Adler has emended it. The Tolidah margin (Nablus Ms., fol. 12b) reads 'Jews' instead of 'Arabs'. The Tolidah statement thus refers to the high priests of the Samaritan Temple built on Mount Gerizim in the time of Alexander and destroyed by John Hyrcanus, and is significant as an indication of how this Temple was projected back into the past to form the story of the Tabernacle on Mount Gerizim in which, according to the Samaritans, their ancestors had worshipped in the days of Divine grace before Eli's schism. Although Samaritan history is often fictitious as far as early Biblical times are concerned, the possibility remains that once we recognize how later events had been projected into the past, we may be able to reconstruct the original information about these later events.

22. Abu'l Fatḥ (p.46) says that David was 18 years old at his accession.

23. Abu'l Fath (*ibid.*) gives the figure of 40 years for David's reign at Jerusalem.

24. Abu'l Fatḥ (p.51) dates the building of the Temple at Jerusalem in the time of the aforementioned Jair son of Jonathan, while the Tolidah does not mention the building of the Temple at all. In addition, Abu'l Fatḥ (p.55) inserts four priests between Jair and Delaiah. The Chronicle Adler agrees with the Tolidah as far as the priestly genealogy is concerned.

25. Cf. 2 Sam. 24:24-25.

26. Cf. 1 Kings 11:42.

27. Cf. 1 Kings 11:1-3.

28. Cf. 1 Chron. 15:17: Asaph the son of Berechiah. The interesting thing is that the Samaritan priestly list has taken Zadok, the priest of David's and Solomon's time, for their own (although they have put him a few generations later), and in his stead have elevated a mere Levite, Asaph, to be Solomon's high priest. It may seem a clumsy way of covering up the traces of their indebtedness to Jewish priestly lists, but there is more to it than that. With Samaritan history one has to work backwards, for that is how it was written. Manasseh, son-in-law of Sanballat, was of the Jerusalemite high priestly line, which was Zadokite. Ezra had opened the priestly ranks of the second Temple to include all Aaronides, so that Ezekiel's view that only Aaronides of Zadok's line should be priests at Jerusalem had been pushed aside. However, Ezra had offended the high priestly family at Jerusalem by his ban on mixed marriages, and Manasseh himself had had to flee to Shechem. Manasseh thus established the Samaritan priesthood as a Zadokite one, and the Samaritans therefore insisted that they had the legitimate priesthood; and that the priestly line of the Jews, being not wholly Zadokite, but including all Aaronides, was invalid. This was Manasseh's reply to Ezra's rejection of him because of his mixed marriage. There is reason to believe that Manasseh and the Samaritans stressed not only Ezekiel's insistance upon a Zadokite priesthood, but also his prophecy and plan for the reunion of north and south; for with the only legitimate priesthood - according to Ezekiel - in their hands, and with administrative power in the Persian period centered in Shechem, the future looked hopeful for them. In a Samaritan chronicle it was essential for the Samaritans to deny Zadok's Jewish origin.

29. Cf. 1 Kings 12:1.

30. Cf. 1 Kings 12:17, 20.

31. Cf. 1 Kings 14:20.

32. Cf. 1 Kings 15:1 Abu'l Fatḥ (p.51) says that Rehoboam reigned for 17 years.

33. Cf. Abu'l Fatḥ, p.53.

34. i.e. the Samaritans, who call themselves *Šomrim*, 'the

keepers' or 'the Observers' (of the Law). It is significant that the Samaritan chronicler felt obliged to repudiate Jeroboam and his following, even though it meant making the Samaritans a group in northern Israel. In other words, the Samaritan chronicler knew the Biblical story (1 Kings 12:28ff.) of the making of the golden calves, and having no northern Israelite source of information to draw on, denied any connection with Jeroboam and postulated the Samaritans as having existed in Jeroboam's time. To be sure, 1 Kings 16:21 shows that northern Israel was divided at the beginning of Omri's reign.

35. According to 1 Kings 12:25, Jeroboam built Shechem, but the city had really been in existence since patriarchal times. The text here reads *Šomron*, Samaria, but this city was built later on by Omri; cf. 1 Kings 16:24 and see below.

36. Cf. 1 Kings 15:25.

37. Cf. 1 Kings 15:27-28.

38. Cf. 1 Kings 15:1 ff.

39. Cf. 1 Kings 15:8-10.

40. According to 1 Kings 16:24 the buyer was Omri King of Israel.

41. The chronicler implies that the Hebrew term *Šomronim*, 'Samarians, Samaritans', as applied to Samaritans, is not their original name, but a later appellation.

42. Cf. 1 Kings 16:6, 8.

43. Cf. 1 Kings 16:9-15.

44. Cf. 1 Kings 16:23-24.

45. But cf. above, note 21. The Tolidah's 'until this day' has been softened.

46. The Tolidah (p.400) calls him Zaddik the priest and gives the name of his place of residence as 'Aḳrabith.

47. The Tolidah (*ibid.*) says that they themselves chose the towns of their residence.

48. Tolidah (*ibid.*): Aphrah.

49. Tolidah (*ibid.*): La'an.

50. Tolidah (*ibid.*): Yispah.

51. The Tolidah (*ibid.*) makes it clear that the aforementioned twelve men were the chiefs of the tribes of Israel at that time.

52. Cf. 1 Kings 16:28f.

53. Cf. 1 Kings 22:41-42.

54. Cf. 1 Kings 16:31.

55. Cf. 1 Kings 22:40, 51.

56. Cf. 2 Kings 1:17; 2:1.

57. Cf. 1 Kings 22:50.

58. Cf. 2 Kings 8:25-26.

59. Cf. 2 Kings 11:2; 12:1.

60. Cf. 2 Kings 9:24 ff. The odd thing is that Ahaziah and Jehoram died at the same time, according to the Biblical account to which Chronicle Adler is indebted, yet here Jehoram is made to die in the time of the Samaritan High Priest who was the successor of the one during whose period of office Ahaziah is supposed to have died.

61. Cf. 2 Kings 10:36.

63. Cf. 2 Kings 10:35; 13:1 (seventeen years).

64. Cf. 2 Kings 14:2.

65. Cf. 2 Kings 14:16.

66. Cf. 2 Kings 14:23.

67. Exod. 23:1.

68. Cf. 2 Kings 14:29; 15:8.

69. Cf. 2 Kings 15:10, 13.

70. Cf. 2 Kings 14:17, 22.

71. Cf. 2 Kings 14:21 (Azariah - Uzziah).

72. Cf. 2 Kings 15:27.

73. Edom = Rome, as in Rabbinic usage. Rome was founded in B.C.753.

74. The three tribes bore the names of Ramnes, Tities, and Luceres. The people were divided into three tribes and 30 *curiae* all of which mustered 3,000 footmen and 300 horsemen called *celeres*, Chronicle Adler is somewhat confused on these points.

75. 'Aḳabyah. Tolidah p.401, 39 years.

76. Cf. 2 Kings 15:14, 17.

77. Cf. 2 Kings 15:19-20.

78. This and the following sentence with very few variants is practically an exact quotation of 2 Kings 15:20.

79. Cf. 2 Kings 15:22-23.

80. Cf. 2 Kings 15:25.

81. Cf. 2 Kings 15:29.

82. Cf. 2 Kings 15:32-33.

83. Literally 'were giving themselves out to be prophets'; the Hebrew original uses the reflexive of the root *nb'*. The Samaritans did not believe in the inspiration of any prophet after Moses.

84. Cf. 2 Kings 16:1-2.

85. Cf. 2 Kings 17:1.

86. Cf. 2 Kings 17:3-4; the Tolidah (p.401; cf. Abu'l Fatḥ, p.55ff.) knows only of the Babylonian exile. 'Aḳabyah was therefore, according to them, carried captive to Babylon by Nebuchadnezzar.

87. Cf. 2 Kings 17:5; Samaria is used here in the sense of the land of Northern Israel; in the Biblical verse Samaria is the name of the capital only.

88. Cf. 2 Kings 17:6.

89. The Tolidah mentions no names, apart from 'Aḳabyah.

90. Tullus Hostilius.

91. Adler suggests that Phanus Marsius is a copyist's mistake for Ancus Martius, who was the fourth king of Rome and reigned in B.C. 640-616; he is said to have been the son of Numa's daughter. Tarquinius was the name of a family in early Roman history to which the fifth and seventh kings of Rome belonged. L. Tarquinius, the fifth king, is given by Livy the further name Priscus.

92. Tolidah (p.401) states that 'Akabyah and Halal both died in Babylon, but the next High Priest Seraiah returned to Mount Gerizim.

93. Cf. 2 Kings 18:1-2.

94. Cf. above, note 83.

95. Cf. 2 Kings 21:1.

96. The reference seems to be to Numa Pompilius, the second king of Rome. Livy gives the length of his reign as 43 years.

97. Cf. above, note 92. Seraiah was also the name of the chief priest at Jerusalem when Nebuchadnezzar captured it (2 Kings 25:18). Another Seraiah, the son of Hilkiah, dwelt in Jerusalem after the exile, and was called *the ruler of the house of God* (Neh. 11:11). Either personage may have suggested a likely name for our Samaritan chronicler to insert here. It is, however, given also in the Tolidah.

98. Perhaps Thales is meant, the Ionic philosopher born at Miletus (ca. B.C.636-546).

99. Tolidah p.401, 50 years.

100. Cf. 2 Kings 21:19.

101. Cf. 2 Kings 22:1, where Josiah is said to have reigned for thirty-one years.

102. Cf. 2 Kings 23:30, 31, 34.

103. Cf. 2 Kings 23:34, 36.

104. Cf. 2 Kings 24:6, 8, 12.

105. Cf. 2 Kings 24:17-18.

106. i.e. Servius Tullius, the sixth king of Rome, whose mother was a slave of Tanaquil wife of Tarquinius Priscus.

107. Cf. 2 Kings 25:1f.

108. For this sentence and the following cf. 2 Kings 25:5-7; the chronicler has adopted these verses with very slight changes.

109. Cf. 2 Kings 25:8.

110. This and the next two sentences are, with few omissions, slavish paraphrases of 2 Kings 25:9-11.

111. Tarquinius Superbus. The usual date for the first consulate is A.U.C.245 = B.C.509. The first consuls were L. Junius Brutus and L. Tarquinius Collatinus. The former served less than a year.

112. The Tolidah (p.401; cf. also Abu'l Fatḥ) says that he was carried off by the King of the Greeks.

113. Chronicle Adler, while using the material provided by the Tolidah and Abu'l Fatḥ, attempts to get rid of the telltale fact that the first exile known to the Samaritans is the Babylonian. It attempts to identify the first exile with the Assyrian exile of the Northern Kingdom, while the second exile, placed by its predecessors in the Greek period, is assigned to the Babylonian period. But then Chronicle Adler obviously did not have the same qualms as its predecessors in using the Jewish Bible. As an explanation of how the figure of 131 years was arrived at by our Chronicler we have to note the Samaritans returned to the Holy Land in the 21st year of Seraiah; hence we have 19 years of Seraiah and 102 years of Levi and Nathanael and 10 years of Azariah = 131.

114. Cf. Ezek. 26:7, etc.

115. The King of Assyria is none other than Nebuchadnezzar!

116. This is obviously a clumsy attempt to apply 2 Kings 17:24 to Judah and the Babylonian exile.

117. The Tolidah (p.401) and Abu'l Fatḥ (p.61) add that Abdiel (and his father, i.e. Azariah, so Tolidah) returned together with young people, children, women, servants, and strangers (i.e. proselytes). The Tolidah then states that on his return to Mount Gerizim, the High Priest Abdiel built an altar there and offered sacrifices, and the Bodleian Ms. of the Tolidah (p.401) - but not the "autograph" Ms. (p.14b) -

specifically states further that Sanballat, the chief of the tribe of Levi, shared the government with the High Priest. Th-rest of the story of events under the high priesthood of Abdiel given here is not derived from the Tolidah, which has nothing more to add to the bare mention of the return. For this additional material Chronicle Adler is indebted to Abu'l Fatḥ (p. 64f.) who gives a long narrative of the alleged events, but the fact is that the chronicler has borrowed his information from Abu'l Fatḥ with considerable restraint; the grosser fictional stories, like the one about the throwing of the books of David and of the Samaritan Torah into the fire in order to see which would survive (Abu'l Fatḥ, p.70) have been omitted.

118. Tolidah (p.401) says nothing about him; cf. above, note 117.

119. Zerubbabel was the son of Shealtiel and the grandson of King Jehoiakim of Judah. He led back the first band of exiles in B.C. 536.

120. Cf. 2 Sam. 24:24-25.

121. Cf. Abu'l Fatḥ (p.71), who says that the king was angry with Zerubbabel and the Jews and slew thirty-six of their chief men. Sanballat and the Samaritans, on the other hand, were at the king's command given aid and royal gifts.

122. This again is confused chronologically. The *regifugium* was established before the institution of the consulate.

123. The Tolidah gives merely Hezekiah's name and the length of his tenure of office.

124. Cf. Abu'l Fatḥ (p.73) where only Zerubbabel and Ezra supplicate the king.

125. Hippocrates, (B.C. 460-357) the famous Greek physician, mentioned also by Abu'l Fatḥ (p.77), who says that Artaxerxes asked him to come to his court.

126. Cf. Abu'l Fatḥ (p.77), where Aaron is specifically stated to have been a physician.

127. The celebrated contemporary of Hippocrates, born about B.C. 460.

128. Cf. Abu'l Fatḥ (p.84) where Ezra and Zerubbabel are the ones who altered the Law.

129. Deut. 13:1 (R.S.V. 12:32).

130. i.e., in Abu'l Fatḥ's Annals. If however "the Book of Chronicles" is understood to refer in the wider sense to the Biblical chronicler, the books of Ezra and Nehemiah might be meant; but this is unlikely.

131. The Tolidah (p.401) merely gives the length of Hananiah's tenure of office.

132. i.e., Joíakim (cf. Neh. 12:10).

133. Jehozadok was the Jewish high priest at the time of exile; cf. 1 Chron. 6:15. It is characteristic of Samaritan historical methods that the Samaritans should claim the credit of sending Jehozadak to Babylon!

134. One might imagine that the Jews in Palestine benefited from Esther's influence at the Persian court; cf. Esther 9:2.

THE CHRONICLE OF ABU'L FATḤ

The text used is that of the edition of E. Vilmar. *Abulfathi annales Samaritani,* Gothae, 1865. Abu'l Fatḥ was commanded in 1352 by the High Priest Phineas to write a history of the Samaritans. Abu'l Fatḥ, himself a Samaritan, tried to compile, as he himself claimed, an authentic narrative. He wrote in a rather vulgar Arabic, but he did succeed in producing something which is of value for the study of the history of the Samaritans. Abu'l Fatḥ lived in the fourteenth century when the Samaritan community was but a shadow of its former self; yet it was an important century for the Samaritans, as certain not unsuccessful attempts by masterful high priests were made in that century to halt the process of disintegration and to consolidate the religious inheritance of a more glorious past. Abu'l Fatḥ's history was to promote a pride in the past. It is not history written for its own sake; it is apologetic and didactic, but it has more right to the name of history than any other Samaritan annals. For Abu'l Fatḥ's treatment of his source material, reference should be made to Vilmar's

Prolegomena,[1] and also to Montgomery.[2] Montgomery is right in stating,[3] that Abu'l Fatḥ 'intended to recover the history of his people in a day when the traditions of the sect seemed in danger of disappearing, and he evidently made an honest effort to procure all reliable written material at his command.'. That Abu'l Fatḥ was unfitted as a critic, and very disproportionate in his use of material, as Montgomery (*ibid.*) avers, may be true if one looks at his work from a modern western standpoint. He at least tells us at the outset regarding the sources he was going to use in his history; furthermore, he is not without occasional flashes of an incipient critical faculty, e.g., when he gives the story of Baba Raba and his nephew Levi.[4] True, a more critical historian would have ignored it; Abu'l Fatḥ includes it, with the apologetic remark, 'I decided that I should set it down in this history, lest someone who might happen to come across it would think that I had overlooked it'. Since the work was commissioned by the High Priest, it is primarily apologetic, a popular Samaritan church history, rather than the product of scholarly research. Abu'l Fatḥ's basic source was the Tolidah chronicle with its priestly lists; on that ecclesiastical skeleton Abu'l Fatḥ built his edifice. Another source which has survived for us independently is the Book of Joshua, the midrashic material of which was undoubtedly drawn upon by our author. Other sources used by Abu'l Fatḥ have since disappeared.

I am not as certain as Vilmar and Montgomery were that Abu'l Fatḥ, in inserting items of information about universal history, did not draw from original Samaritan chronicles or traditions, 'but', as Montgomery says 'ignorantly and ineptly borrows from various late chronicles of Jews, Christians, and Moslems'. This seems to me too sweeping a judgment, more applicable to the Chronicle Adler, where the author's knowledge of Roman history seems to have been borrowed from a nineteenth century school primer; but even in the Chronicle Adler there are snippets of information which are derived neither from Abu'l Fatḥ nor from non-Samaritan works, and which may represent an old Samaritan tradition concerning outside events.

Josephus (I believe it was the Greek Josephus, and not the late pseudo-Josephus, i.e. the Hebrew Yosippon) was indeed used by Abu'l Fatḥ as the source of much of Jewish history, especially for the Maccabean period. Abu'l Fatḥ is not always consistent in his narrative, e.g. in some cases simply because he is using different sources, without attempting to reconcile and blend his source material, so that the inconsistencies in his narrative are quite apparent. Examples of such inconsistencies will be seen in the excerpts given in the following pages. Suffice it to mention here that Abu'l Fatḥ gives two accounts of the Dustan heresy, and apparently two very different dates for its rise. It may be, however, that the second reference to this heresy, coming as it does in a lengthy excursus on the Samaritan sects, is not to be taken as an indication as to when the sect arose. This excursus, which is given further on, is one of the most valuable sections in Abu'l Fatḥ's work; his source is not identifiable, but seems to have been a Hebrew one, from the use of the term *ha-Mašiaḥ* in reference to Jesus. One would surely be justified in regarding this section as an example of independent Samaritan traditions preserved by Abu'l Fatḥ and containing *inter alia* information on Judaeo-Christian sects. The fact that the digression comes in the discussion of the period of the High Priest Akḅon (fourth century A.D.) does not mean that the material on the sects given in the digression refers necessarily to that period; at the most, the information about Dusis seems to have been regarded by Abu'l Fatḥ as belonging to that period, and in that he may have been wrong. What is certain is that he inserted a lengthy excerpt on schismatic Samaritan sects in the account of the high priesthood of Akbon with the sole introductory remark: 'And after that came Dusis the son of Fufali'. The section that follows reads as if it had been translated in its entirety from some separate source; the Arabic of this section is not quite the same as in the narrative portion into which it is inserted.

Abu'l Fatḥ's Chronicle treats of a lengthy period, from Adam to 756 A.D., i.e. from man's beginnings till the early period of the Muslim empire. Additions have subsequently been made to the original Chronicle, as well as the original Tolidah, bringing it down to the nineteenth century.

The section of Abu'l Fatḥ's Chronicle translated here may serve as a characteristic sample of Abu'l Fatḥ's work. It begins with the basic framework of high priestly information. Thereafter follows the fanciful story about Darius' daughter. The Tolidah also knew of the son of a Samaritan high priest who married the daughter of Darius, but it devotes to him only a laconic reference in passing. In the Tolidah he appears to have been the son of the High Priest Amram, and not of the High Priest Hezekiah.[6]

The fate that befell the daughter of Darius and her Samaritan husband at the hands of the Samaritans led, so Abu'l Fatḥ tells us, to Darius helping the Jews rebuild their sanctuary at Jerusalem where Simeon was king. Simeon took punitive measures against the Samaritan sanctuary; and the Samaritans in turn destroyed the Jerusalem sanctuary. This resulted in Darius helping the Jews and punishing the Samaritans. Many Samaritans then left Nablus for Babylon, while some went to Wadi Kutha. All eventually returned, including those from Wadi Kutha, and, says Abu'l Fatḥ, 'it is because of this that the Jews called them Kutheans'. Thereafter Abu'l Fatḥ mentions the death of Simeon, the king of the Jews, who was succeeded by his son

'Arkiya (i.e. Hyrcanus). The Jews, says Abu'l Fatḥ, were dealt with by the kings (unspecified); Jerusalem was invested and laid waste and the Jewish community scattered abroad. It was at the time when the Jewish dispersion began that the Samaritans were restored to Nablus from beyond the sea and from Kutha, and at the command of the king (of Babylon) they returned to Mount Gerizim.

This is a curious hodgepodge. The didactic purpose, if somewhat meretricious, is at least obvious. Here we have a deliberate attempt to explain away the Jewish name for the Samaritans, Kuthim, known in Mishnah and Talmud, and based originally on 2 Kings 17:24.

There might be a grain of fact in King Darius helping the Jews to rebuild their sanctuary and the Samaritans later destroying it, or rather hampering the building of it. But did Abu'l Fatḥ derive this information from the Jewish Bible, namely from Ezra 6:1ff., where Darius' decree in favor of the rebuilding of the Jewish Temple is referred to? Josephus' *Antiquities* (XI, III, 8 and IV, 1-9) seem quite clearly to have been used here by Abu'l Fatḥ, freely and none too faithfully, but the story explaining away the Jewish appellation of the Samaritans as Kutheans might have been inserted in answer to the *Antiquities* (XI, IV, 3-4, beginning) where the origin of the Samaritans is set forth.

But Josephus tells us only of Darius' decree in favor of the rebuilding of the Temple, of the Samaritan opposition to it, and of the crushing of that opposition by Darius. He says nothing about Simeon, nor would we expect it, for here Abu'l Fatḥ projects the Maccabean kings back into the Persian period, and brings in also the destruction of Jerusalem by the kings (of Rome, Vespasian and Titus). And he does all this before telling us of the coming of Alexander. It must be added, however, that Hyrcanus and the Maccabees are dealt with, albeit inadequately in their proper historical sequence later on in Abu'l Fatḥ's work.

It would appear that Abu'l Fatḥ knew only too well of what John Hyrcanus had done to the Samaritan Temple, built thanks to Alexander the Great on Mount Gerizim. The memory was a painful one for the Samaritans. It was the first temple that the Samaritans as a sect had known. As we shall see in our second translated excerpt from Abu'l Fatḥ, Hyrcanus' treatment of this temple has been altered there to one of reverent regard. But the fact remained that this temple had been destroyed by the Jews, and that it was probably Alexander who had allowed them to build it (cf. Josephus, *Antiq.* XIII, III, 4). But true Israel (meaning, in Samaritan eyes, themselves) had a temple there before the time of Alexander. And so its building and its destruction are pushed back to a time before Alexander. The Jews under Simeon (Simeon Maccabeus, and not John Hyrcanus) destroy the temple which had been built in the time of 'Abdel. True, Abu'l Fatḥ does not designate Simeon as a Maccabee, but he shows his hand in mentioning his son 'Arḳiya. History has given way to apologetics, when a Maccabee, although not designated as such, destroys a temple several hundred years before the birth of the first Maccabee. In the Tolidah, 'Abdel is a high priest, the fifth Samaritan high priest from the Babylonian exile, who had been exiled and carried far to the east by the king of the Greeks; on his return with his people he built an altar on Mount Gerizim and offered sacrifices upon it - no mention is made of his having built a temple. Significantly enough, the Tolidah does not know of Alexander having helped the Samaritans build a temple, as Josephus maintains; but Abdel's building of an altar after the king of the Greeks had exiled him may be a tacit Samaritan admission that their first temple and the coming of Alexander had something in common. Here in Abu'l Fatḥ's work the hagiology of the temple is carried a stage further. It had been built and destroyed before the coming of the Greeks; it was Darius who had given them permission to build their temple, just as he had done for the Jews.

The sect of Dustan is said by Abu'l Fatḥ to have originated in this early post-exilic period, or at least before the time of Alexander. For a useful summary of the tenets of the Dustan sect and its possible relation to that of Dusis (placed by Abu'l Fatḥ in the 4th century A.D.), as well as the relation of both to the Dositheans, see Montgomery's summary of the Samaritan sects (ibid., p.252-264).[7]

FOOTNOTES

1. p.85ff.

2. *The Samaritans*, p.305-310.

3. *Ibid.*, p.305.

4. Ed. Vilmar, p.139.

5. *Ibid.* p.310.

6. Cf. *Chronique Samaritaine*, p.401-402, Neubauer, J.A. 1869.

7. This section of Abu'l Fatḥ on the Dustan sect had already been translated by De Sacy in his *Chrestomathie arabe* i. 342f.

FIRST EXCERPT FROM ABU'L FATḤ pp. 78-83.

We shall now return to the topic of the high priests, the favor of God be upon them! We have already mentioned the rule of Hezekiah,[1] what happened in his days, and how long he held office. He thereupon died, and passed to the mercy of God. Hananiah[2] assumed office after him, and continued in the high priesthood for twenty-four years; and there reigned after him

Amram,[3] who held the priesthood for thirty-two years. This Amram is the one whose son King Darius[4] took as a husband for his daughter. The reason for this being that Darius' daughter had seen in her sleep a lad, a goodly youth, standing before her, while someone kept saying to her, "This shall be your husband". She awakened from her sleep with her mind perturbed and her breast anguished, and when her father saw her, she was overcome with passionate love. Now since he loved her greatly he said to her "What is the matter, my little daughter?" So she told him the story and recounted her dream, whereupon he summoned painters who painted many pictures and brought them to her. And she said: "He resembles this picture". The King then supplied that picture to several men who were to go round to various countries searching for anyone who looked like it. And they went round until they came to Nablus. Now it happened that the son of Chief Priest Amram had just then come out, and they found that he resembled that picture; whereupon they seized him and took him to the King. And when the King's daughter saw him, she said: "This is the very person whom I saw in my dream". She forthwith was married to him and had three children by him, two sons and a daughter. Some time later he said to the King, "I have a longing to see my father, my mother, and my family", to which the King replied: "Go wheresoever you wish". So he departed, together with his wife and children, and reached Bādhān. When the Samaritans heard of his coming they were disturbed, and said: "Why did he not expose himself to death by remaining steadfast in his faith? Instead he has sinned and brought grievous shame upon himself and upon the nation". Some of them were of the opinion that he should be slain, while others thought otherwise. The final resolve was to slay him, and so they slew him, his wife, his children, and his accompanying servants. When King Darius heard about the slaying of his daughter and her husband and children and those who were with them, it affected him most grievously, and he assembled troops in order to slay all the Samaritans. Now those who had slain the King's daughter and her companions fled to Babel and dwelt in safety, while those who had been of the opinion that these persons should not be slain remained in Nablus,[5] where a countless number of them were killed, and the rest were taken to be punished by the King. When they were asked: "Why have you done what you have done?" they replied: "We have done nothing. Those who did the slaying told us that they had done it out of zeal for their faith. Now all of them have fled to Babel and are safe. Yet it is we who are about to perish." So the King commanded that the sword be withdrawn from them, and that none be slain thereafter.

And the King who loved the Jews, set up over them a king from among them named Simeon;[6] who commanded them to build the sanctuary.[7] And when they had finished building it they manifested joy and gladness, saying, "There is no sanctuary but ours, no priesthood[8] but our priesthood, and no Levites except those who are around us." They prevailed over the Samaritans and forbade them to go up to Mount Gerizim;[9] they demolished the altar and the Temple which 'Abdel had built, and they remained upon the mountain for forty days, laying it waste and defiling it. They set watchmen over the Samaritans to prevent them from worshipping towards Mount Gerizim, observing their festivals and gathering in their holy places; and they severely oppressed them.[10] When this became too much for the Samaritans, they wrote to those who had gone to Babel, and they came over, so that they all joined together to form an army and set out with raging fury in their hearts. First they killed the Jewish watchmen which were placed over them, then they turned on the Jews and killed an incalculable number of them. Thereupon they went up to Jerusalem and killed all who were in it; but Simeon, the King of the Jews, fled, and they did not get hold of him.

They then demolished the structure which the Jews had constructed, and razed the wall of the sanctuary[11] from its foundation. When King Darius heard of this,[12] he stood by Those Who Went Astray (i.e. the Jews) and helped them; he subdued the Observant Ones (i.e. the Samaritans) and did not allow them to ascend the mountain; he rebuilt the wall of the sanctuary once again; and he gave the Jews authority over the Samaritans, so that they reduced them to nought, until the Samaritans could not bear to continue to remain under their rule. The Samaritans thereupon assembled in the Synagogue, and as they pondered over their plight they found their spirits broken, overwhelmed, and subdued, and themselves left with no strength or power; and they agreed to depart from under the rule of the Jews and to look for relief from them and their tyranny. They took out the Law of God and deposited it in a place (p.81) which they knew, while they wept and wailed so bitterly that they were nearly undone because of the intensity of their tears and their moaning. Afterwards they embarked in ships; some of them reached the outlying regions of the earth, some went to Babel, and some to Wadi al-Kutha.[13] That is why the Jews call the Samaritans Kutheans, and go so far as to deny them the name of Israel.[14] Some of the Samaritans went (eastward) toward the rising of the sun, others remained in Nablus as they were, and suffered such calamities and afflictions as cannot be described. Those who remained were not permitted to observe anything pertaining to their faith, either Sabbath, or festival, or New Moon's Day, or reading[15] in the Law of Moses, the son of Amram - upon him be the most bountiful peace - until they forgot it.

After this Simeon, the King of the Jews, died - may God have no mercy upon him - and there reigned after him 'Arḳiya,[16] his son. In his reign there arose a quarrel[17] between the house of Ithamar[18] and the house of Manasseh.[19] The latter said to the family of Ithamar: "Let us have a portion of the Meadow of al-Bahā[20] (Splendor)". An adjudicator then arose who thought that he could satisfy them, but he did not succeed at all, for he said: "Mount Gerizim belongs to you, and to them, and to all Israel; Nablus belongs to the house of Ephraim alone; the Meadow of al-Bahā belongs to all the tribes; and the Roll of the Law belongs to all Israel".[21]

And the Jews increased in unbelief and error, and the nations were troubled by their tyranny and their error. Thereupon the kings[22] assembled against them, slew an incalculable number of them, and finally besieged them in Jerusalem until they perished. The kings then took possession of Jerusalem and laid it waste. Thus the community of the Jews was scattered among the various countries, and woe and disaster overtook them. At that time the Samaritans were gathered together from beyond the sea, from Babel, from Wadi Kutha, and from every place, (p.82) and they came back to Mount Gerizim, rejoicing in their return; this was done by command of the King. And the ten stones were returned to their places in the mountain, in order that the Roll of the Law might be read there.

About that time[23] a sect split off from the community of the Samaritans, and adopted a teaching of its own; they were called the Dustān,[24] because of their abolition of the legitimate festivals and of all that they had received by tradition from their fathers and their grandfathers. They differ from the Samaritans in some things, e.g., every water-spring in which is found a creeping thing they found unclean; and when a woman begins to menstruate they do not commence counting (the period of her impurity) until the morrow of that day,[25] on the analogy of the festivals which run from sunset to sunset.[26] They banned the eating of eggs,[27] except those found when birds are slaughtered. They likewise declared unclean the unborn foetus of animals[28] after their death. They also declared that the overshadowing of tombs causes uncleanness, and that consequently anyone whose shadow fell on a tomb must remain unclean seven days.[29] They banned the benediction, "Blessed be our God for ever"; they forbade pronouncing the name *YHWH* as the Samaritans do, and pronounced it instead *ELOHIM*.[30] They claimed that in the book which they had and which was written by the children of the Messenger[31] (of God), it was stated that God shall be worshipped in the land of Zawila[32] until the time when He shall be worshipped on Mount Gerizim. They renounced the use of astronomical tables,[33] and they made the number of days in every month thirty[33a] days, without exception. They abolished the true festivals,[34] as well as the commandment of fasting and mortification; and they used to reckon the fifty days[35] from the morrow of the Passover, as do the Jews. They allowed (p.83) their priests to enter a house suspected of uncleanness, in order to see what was in it, but without saying anything, so that when they came forth outside they would be clean, even though the house was suspected of uncleanness; this on the analogy of a house known to be clean. And when a house was attached to the unclean house and they wanted to know whether it was clean or unclean, a man would sit down facing it and watch it, and if a clean bird alighted on it, they declared it clean, but if an unclean bird alighted on it, they declared it unclean.[36] On the Sabbath day they[37] considered it unlawful to eat or drink from vessels made of copper or glass, or of anything capable of becoming unclean and then being cleansed, but only from earthen vessels, which, if they became unclean, cannot be cleansed.[38] They would not feed or water their cattle[39] on the Sabbath day, but would instead place before the cattle on Friday whatever was needed for them. They differed from the Samaritans also in many things other than matters of belief and law, and for this reason they separated from them and made for themselves synagogues[40] and a priesthood of their own. The son of the (Samaritan) High Priest became their spiritual leader, and this is how it happened: the (Samaritan) community brought irrefutable evidence against him to the effect that they had found him with a loose woman; they therefore shunned him and placed him under a ban. His name was Zur'a.[41] When he saw that there was no hope for him in the (Samaritan) community, he inclined to the Dustān, who accepted him and made him their High Priest. He composed a book in which he satirized all the (Samaritan) high priests, and he did it in a most skillful manner. There was no one in his time more learned than he, and that is why they called him Zur'a.

SECOND EXCERPT FROM ABU'L FATḤ pp. 94-104.

The following section from Abu'l Fatḥ's Chronicle is of interest as giving the Samaritan version of the making of the Septuagint translation of the Law, and also of John Hyrcanus' attitude to the Samaritans. In connection with John Hyrcanus it is worth noting the Samaritan version of his quarrel with the Pharisees; here, as in the account of the Septuagint translation, Abu'l Fatḥ's dependence on Josephus is quite clearly apparent; to some extent Abu'l Fatḥ seems to show also some knowledge of the letter of Aristeas.

In the day of this above-mentioned (High) Priest Dalyah,[42] there arose a king whose name was Faltama (Ptolemy).[43] He loved learning and wisdom, was diligent in gathering books containing them, eagerly occupied himself with them, and exerted himself in making himself familiar with them. Now when the Egyptians saw that he pursued the way of justice and travelled in the path of truth, they chose him to be king over them; they thereupon sent a message to him asking him to come to them, so that they might set him up to reign over them. So he went out and came to them, and they made him king over them; and when he learned that the cause of his election was his love of knowledge, his eagerness for it, and his travelling (in the way) of justice, his desire for wisdom increased all the more, he searched for it ever more diligently, and he intensified his efforts to gather books dealing with it. So he assembled[44] books and searched for them in every country and place that he might become known for his learning.

Now in the tenth year of his reign he became acquainted with the disagreement which existed between the Samaritans and the Jews regarding the Torah,[45] and with the refusal of the Samaritans to accept any book other than the Torah which was reputedly handed down by a prophet. In his desire to become acquainted with this matter, he sent to the Jews asking them for a number of their elders,[46] and addressed a similar request to the Samaritans also. And so there came from the Samaritans a man called Aaron, and with him a company of Samaritans among whom was the scholar Symmachus,[47] and Jahudṭa. From the Jews there came a man called Eleazar,[48] and with him a company also.

Now when Ptolemy learned of their arrival at Alexandria, which was at that time a seat of knowledge, he commanded that lodgings[49] be assigned to them according to their number, in the place which is called al-Ruwāḳ, and that each one of them be kept separated from his fellow. Then He commanded also that there should be with everyone of them a Greek scribe to write down what everyone of them translated. And so the Samaritans translated the Torah, while the Jews translated both the Torah and the other books which they had; and it is said that the world was darkened for three days.[50] When the King learned of this, he looked in the Torah which was in the hands of the Samaritans and saw there some things which were not in the Torah of the Jews; and he found that for the most part the sacred text possessed by us was more perfect[51] than that possessed by them. He thereupon inquired about the cause of this disagreement, whether it concerned things indispensable to the Law, or whether the Law was perfect without them and could dispense with them. To this the Samaritans replied: The *Ḳibla*[53] is one of the principles of the Law and one of its pillars. It is utterly impossible that Moses the Lawgiver should have died without informing the people of the Ḳibla. With us it (the Ḳibla) is the last of the Ten Commandments; for the first[54] of them prohibits the worshipping of anyone other than God; this is followed by commands and prohibitions, and after this God concluded[55] the Ten Commandments with the commandment appointing the Ḳibla (towards Mount Gerizim), because the marks of His majesty and dignity appear upon it. For this (i.e. the Ḳibla) the Jews have no explicit commandment. Rather according to them, Moses died[56] without informing (the people) of the place,[57] yet he has commanded both us and them to offer a sacrifice at that very place, as it is written, *year by year;* nor did the (High) Priest (Aaron) inquire[58] whither this sacrifice should be brought. Now in the past did the High Priests offer sacrifice or did they not? If they did, it must have been in an accustomed place. And if they did not offer it, they transgressed the command of God Most High. This despite the fact that they agree that the Tabernacle[59] stood on the Mount for many years, and that the people every year offered what He had prescribed for them. Moreover, the Creator Most High has stringently commanded us in His Divine Scripture that we should not offer burnt sacrifices in any place[60] we may see, but only in the place which God has chosen: *There thou shalt offer thy burnt offerings, and there thou shalt do all that I command*[61] *thee,* today. He has thus prohibited us from offering sacrifices anywhere else, and ordered us to offer His burnt offerings in that specific place[62] alone and to bring there the tokens of our worship for Him. Indeed, He (Himself) has mentioned, both in our text (of the Law) and in theirs, that this place is a high and lofty mountain (and not the low hills of Jerusalem), by saying *upon one*[63] *of the mountains*, at the place where Isaac was offered as a sacrifice, *in*[64] *the mountain of Thine inheritance, the place which Thou hast made for Thee to dwell in.* Then He called it the ancient mountain[65] as He said in the Blessing of Joseph. "With the finest produce of the ancient mountains and the abundance of the everlasting hill(s)." And because of this, Joseph considered specially the dignity which is in it - this majestic mountain, the home of God's might; for Joseph when he was the cause of the life of his father ailing,[66] inherited the place which was the place of everlasting life.[67] And it belonged especially to him,[68] and in the Torah there are many proofs of this. And it is the place of Return[69] (to the life to come) also; and it is one of the great roots of religion, and one of its supports because if one does not know that there certainly is reckoning and requital, he would follow his own passion and go to extremes therein, and would be less interested in, and glad about his religion and its works, and have neglected obedience if there is no promise of reward for obedience, nor threat of retribution for disobedience; and one would also take the road of passion and neglect his obligations and duties. And it has come about in a number of places that we and they agree upon some of it, and differ on others; but what we disagree about is the section which more rightly concerns the life to come, which says in our Book:[70] 'To the Day of Vengeance and Recompense', but with them 'Vengeance is Mine, and recompense'. And the difference between His saying: 'Vengeance is Mine and recompense' and His saying that their deeds are with Me and stored up in My storehouse until the Day of Vengeance, is great. And there is a great distinction between them, because according to their wording, He could take vengeance at this hour, or tomorrow, before and after, and it might be in this world or it might be in the next world; but with us it is when He describes the multitude who have neglected to obey Him and have become accustomed to do and to praise what is not to be done, as the sting of snakes[71] and the poison of malevolent serpents His saying being: 'Their grapes[72] are grapes of poison, their clusters are bitter'. But, of course the grapes in this context were not pôison, nor their clusters bitter, and by that He only meant to what evil he who used it wrongly would come in the next world. And so later on He said by the way of predestination: "Is not this laid up in store with me, sealed up in my treasuries until the Day of Vengeance and Recompense?"[73] And there is in this world no day of such description. Then He said in this section "I kill[74] and I make alive". But He does not put any to death except one who is alive, and He does not make alive except one who is dead. Then He said at the end of the threat, "Praise His people, O you nations",[75] Tidings to His people who know His Law, that He avenges their blood for their oppression. And He said after this section "And I repay those who disobey Me with Vengeance"[76] meaning He gives a surfeit of retribution to His opponents who forsook knowledge and the doing of what was laid down in His Law. And He said: "Cleanse[77] the land of My people", and the hidden meaning in it is that the Most High compelled one who touches a grave (to be unclean) seven days;[78] and one was not purified except after the making of atonement on the third day[79] and the seventh, and then one was completely free of uncleanness. Then one went to the ritual of cleansing, as the obedient do, for their obedience completely frees them from the impurities with which they were mixed and the touching of their tomb does not cause impurity because of them, for the world has become pure just as the tombs of the apostate are defiled. And there comes in one of our songs: "People will leave this world with what they have obtained for the next world, or with what they have lost. And when Death comes to them, they go out of this world, and nothing followed them from it to the Next World, except their deeds and what their souls had acquired. With good, they are rewarded in it, or with bad they are requited therein. Of the things of this world we have not mentioned many, and have not bothered with (them) since this is not the place for them". And when the king reflected[80] on what they had said, and meditated on their arguments, he knew that the truth was in their hands, and that the complete, perfect Torah was that which they had, and he said to them: "What do you say about those whom the Jews call prophets[81] and these books which they have?" And they said: "As to these, verily, we do not recognise their prophecy nor their books because they (the books), O King, either have come down by the hand of prophets or by other than prophets; and if they were by the hand of prophets, the Mosaic Law has forbidden that after Moses there should be a prophet for He says:

[82]"And there has not arisen a prophet since in Israel like Moses." If we demanded from them the substance of their claim, although that sort of thing is not accepted by us, then either it will bring something like what is in the Torah - either (their argument is the same as the Torah) - and in that case there is no need of it; or it falls short of what is in the Torah; then to follow the more complete thing is more necessary, or their argument contains an increase on what is in the Torah, and in that case the religious law both with us and with them has prohibited the acceptance of that sort of thing according to His saying:[83] "You shall not add to it or take from it" meaning that the Law is complete, nor to annul what is in it, for that would be abrogation. Abrogation[84] is not allowed with us. And he said: "O he who is present with the King, the argument of the Greeks in favour of abrogation is that which was banned at a later time, and what was bad at one time, may become acceptable at another time: and that follows the aim of

the Lawgiver, and the character of those on whom it was imposed. And these things are not of that which the law pertains to, in so much that the quality (ought to) adhere to it as long as that thing endures. And they said: "Consider this answer; had what you mentioned of characters and circumstances been right, considering these things, differences at the same time would have been possible as the characters of people of one period are not equal nor similar throughout, but are different and disagree. But as for your saying that it is not one of the things on which a judgment depends, whereas the quality adheres to it as long as that particular thing endures; but our short-coming and our inability would not realise its cause and its means, and it is not that if minds could not grasp the knowledge of something, that thing would be impossible in itself. And when the Creator Most High, knew by His foreknowledge, of our in-ability, and the shortcoming of our intelligences to comprehend the knowledge of the reasons of this and its causes, He dis-closed it to us by religious law and He indicated to us its rules and its qualities, with a complete indication, and some He indicated in detail; but we must not assume that the rule follows therefrom, as He forbade to us the camel, since it lacks certain of the marks of purity, and the pig as well, and others, even though these marks are there, and this is the cause of the rule; and the rule follows the cause and the cause is lasting as long as the species endures, for the Law lasts as long as Creation lasts. And sufficient for us is what Tradition has to say about its being eternal, and the mention of its causes in general, such as the permitted animals and the for-bidden animals similarly. And regarding the being eternal, we know that the necessity of rule(s) about it is everlasting, and that is that one should follow its prescriptions; and it is not right to follow the honour of the worshippers over dispositions nor their customs, and only follow the substance of it, and the essence of it particularly, but the impressive prescriptions concerning the rule(s) and the exclusive adherence to rule always openly."

As he was pleased with their answer and their arguments pleased him, so their status was raised in his eyes and their weight became preponderant with him, and they continued like that. May God have mercy on them. They had clear arguments and eloquent and incisive proofs and sound and weighty reasons. And he honoured them, and raised their names amongst men, after Aaron came to King Ptolemy. And he (Aaron) said to him (King Ptolemy); "We have received from the seventy elders[85] (God have mercy on them) who bear the marks of the Prophet, and who receive this Law from him, that he prohibited them from accepting anything other than it, because the Creator, Most High is He, when He taught by his foreknowledge how mankind can be reformed and its affairs be set aright, sent down by the hand of His prophet (the most trustworthy of His world), a Law comprising the manner of the road to righteousness for mankind[86] and keeping to that righteousness, and its following it in this world. If they do not approach in pilgrimage[87] to a place in which He is, then He would grow anxious about their word; but the pilgrimage is made now by their command to the place in which He is, and whosoever does not do that, He kills him; and the Jews prevented them from pilgrimage to the Blessed Mount, and when they prevented them, three sects[88] branched off. One of them was called the Pharisees and the meaning of that is those who separate themselves; and this priest[89] was from this sect. And another sect was called the Saddducees, and they were only called by this name because they disliked to behave other than justly; and they quote only[90] the Torah and what the Scriptures indicate by analogy,[91] and they do not allow anything other than it, of that which the Pharisees' sect allows of books,[92] wishing to remain in accordance with the views of the ancestors.

And their dwelling was in villages which are around Aelia.[93] The other sect was called the Hasidim,[94] and the meaning of that is the righteous ones, and this sect is the one which is nearest to the Samaritans;[95] and they hold their belief, and dwell in the villages[96] which are in the neighbourhood of the Blessed Mountain[97] for the purpose of devoting themselves to worship. And there was between the Sadducees and the Pharisees, violent enmity, and each party allowed shedding the blood of the other. And the cause of that was the secession of the elders[98] who separated in the time of John (Hyrcanus) that they might have a book of religious law,[99] for it was agreed that that would bring benefit on them. And his commander-in-chief and his chief men came and the seceding elders were present with him; and they passed judgment on his intelligence and got the mastery over him; and when they ate and drank out of respect to him, and he said joyfully to them:[100] "Indeed I am a disciple of yours and shall have recourse in what I do, to what you say, and what you see fitting. And I have accepted what you have said and I ask you if you have known sin and error in me; (if so) bring me back from that and prevent me from (committing) it." And they said to him:[101] "May God bring you back from error and sin, and may you be virtuous and straightforward in all your doings." But among them was a man called Eleazar,[102] and he was great among them. He wanted to stop him (John Hyrcanus) from appointing to the priesthood any of his relatives.[103] And he said[104] to him: "If you want to be virtuous and to give up sin as you have mentioned, then it is up to you to remove yourself from the priesthood, and to be satisfied with kingship, because you are not fit for it (the priesthood); and that is because your mother was a prisoner in the days of Antiochus". And he said to him:[105] "As for my mother, when she was captive, she and my father were routed and hid in a cave of the mountain. So what is the reason for depriving me of this right and handing over His (God's)[106] service to the elders of the seceding group (the Pharisaic party)?" So he brought them and he[107] said: "What do you say about a man who reviles a man about something of which he was never guilty?" And the elders[108] said: "We want to know the sentence". So he told it to them. And they said: "He ought to seek pardon by an offering[109] or he should be struck forty (times)".[110] (And he said) "Verily (I say) that he should make an offering and be struck forty (times)". Then (verily) from that time he (John Hyrcanus) transferred to the sect of the Sadducees. And he forsook[111] the Pharisaic party and treated them as enemies. And he said: "These truly are the Pharisees,[112] i.e. seceders from the Law of God". And he killed[113] a great company of them and he burnt their books, and proclaimed in his kingdom that one should prevent people from teaching about Pharisaism and he killed many of those who disobeyed him; the Sadducees and the Samaritans[114] were permitted to kill them. And this king had before this[115] come down to Sebaste, which is a town of the Samaritans, and has besieged it closely and had conquered it, and slaughtered many of the Samaritans. Then he came to Nablus,[116] and waged a mighty battle, and killed a great number of the two parties, but was not able to enter it as he had been able to do at Sebaste. But when John (Hyrcanus) transferred to the Sadducees and did to the Pharisaic party what he did and burnt their books, and prohibited the children from learning from them, (then) he returned to seek (to make) the pilgrimage to Nablus,[117] to the Blessed Mountain, and confirmed that it was the House of God. But the Samaritans refused to make it possible for him to go (up) to it. And they were vigilant to prevent him, and overcame his pride by the greatness of their God. So when he despaired of that, he began sending offerings and tithes, free-will offerings, and alms, and gifts to it, and he continued (doing) that and the Jews who were called Pharisees went away to Aelia.

THIRD EXCERPT FROM ABU'L FATḤ pp.212ff.

"Bring 'Aḳbon[118] their High Priest as he is their example and compel him to prostrate himself and all follow him." Now the High Priest 'Aḳbon was possessed of very great wealth, and they sought the High Priest 'Aḳbon, and he was afraid, and he concealed himself; and they searched for him in the mountains and the caves and in every place, but they did not find him. So the King[119] said to his servants: "Plunder all his wealth and burn his house".[120] And they did that and burned his house, and there was burned in it the prayers and ascriptions of praise and the songs which were said on Sabbaths and Festivals and which had been handed down from the days of Divine Grace.[121] And it was said to the High Priest 'Aḳbon: "All that is yours has been taken and your house is burnt down". And he answered and said: "All is from God and it belongs to God, and if they have obtained mastery over me and my abode,I submit myself to affliction and destruction but I will not disavow God nor Moses, His prophet, nor His Law".

So they seized his two sons and the King said to them: "Worship idols". And they said: "We will die, but we will not worship other than God the Merciful". And they inserted sticks under their nails and they flayed them alive and they put them to death with all torture and they cast their corpses to the dogs;[122] and they hanged on the walls of Nablus thirty-six priests and they did not take down their corpses until they fell of themselves. And in the days of this King Commodus (may God curse him) none taught his son the Torah,[123] except one out of a thousand and two out of a myriad secretly. And Commodus reigned thirty two years[124] and he died (may God not have mercy on him). And in the tenth year of his reign the Persians appeared, and Ardashir[125] the son of Babaka the son of Sasan was victorious over the Romans; and he was the first of the Kings of the Persians in the second dynasty; and it is said

that Ardashir means 'with the long arms', but he was only nick-
named that because of his being a bold fighter (or treacherous
murderer) and of the greatness of his rule. And his (Ardashir's)
appearance was five hundred and forty five years after Alexander.
He was a violent killer. Now the High Priest 'Aḳbon feared for
the Samaritans, so he sent to him Ahirod[126] and Joseph who were
possessed of learning and understanding. And they found him in
Iraq and went in to him and said: "O King, the King is a tree
of which justice is its fruit, and if you do justly, God will
establish the foundations of your glory, and He will be pleased
with what you desire". So the King was pleased with their
speech and he showed good cheer in his face, and kindness on
his expression; and Joseph said to him: "O King you know at
this hour, the nobility of your self and the excellence of your
power". And he said: "And how did you know?" So he said, "O
King the noble soul is known by its acceptance of the truth,
and when it has accepted the truth, it reveals signs of its
acceptance in the body". And He became more pleased at his
speech, and he inferred from that the source of his excellence;
and he asked him about himself, the object of his worship, and
his religion; and he answered him regarding all that. And he
approved of that in him, and wrote for him protection for himself and the people of his religion, and their pious foundations
and their houses of worship. And the two of them bade the King
farewell and returned thankful.

Now the High Priest 'Aḳbon was blessed with a male[127]
child, and he said: "God has blessed me compensating me for
the loss of my wealth and my sons". So he called him Nathanel.
And there remained to the High Priest 'Aḳbon some of his wealth
and he built for himself a beautiful house in Namara, and it is
a village west of Nablus, and he dwelt in it. And Suyaris[128]
(i.e. Severus) the King sent to the High Priest 'Aḳbon saying
to him: "I desire that you go to worship the idols and the

pictures as we do; I will make you my deputy in the Kingdom and I will entrust you with all that is in my store houses of treasures and clothes, and I will restore to you all your possessions". But he returned answer: "This is the thing which I will not do, and I will not deny God my God for the goods of this world, that has little to do with truth, and much with falsehood". And the chiefs of his kingdom advised him to compel the Samaritans to worship their idols, and if they refused, to kill them. And Suyaris said to them: "What advantage will it be to our idols if we kill the people? And how is it lawful for us to kill him who chooses death rather than worship other than his God? And they say that the Lord whom they worship, He is the Lord of Lords, and God of Gods, and He is, so they pretend, creator of the Heavens and the earth; and how can we prevent them from worshipping Him if they do not admire our God? Nay, let us leave them in their error, and if they wish to worship our idols, let it be by their choice; but if they do not wish we will not compel them". And his servants said to him: "If you do not kill them, act severely towards them and set watchmen over them to prevent them from practising circumcision and purification; and we ourselves will make for our God altars in every place." So the King did that and he imposed also a tax on the children of Israel for keeping the Sabbath. And when 'Aḳbon drew near to death - it was towards the beginning of the reign of King Alexander[129] - he ('Aḳbon) sought his boy, Nathanel, and gave him his last charge and said to him: "Pay no heed to these times and these calamities nor to the strength of the enemies of God, whereby in their rebellious conduct they have rebelled; but know and be sure in your heart, my boy, that these calamities are a trial from God to us to make clear that we should have afflicted our spirits, and devoted ourselves to the service of God, exalted by He; be patient my lad; the calamities and the difficulties will be altered and cease, and one will arise from us[130] and save us and will remove from us this violent hand and put it far from us". And his boy Nathanel and the company with him answered him and said to him: "May God your redemption act on our behalf". And the High Priest 'Akbon said to them: "This is not he who will arise from us to establish the age of Divine grace in its entirety, but this violent hand he will break and make it cease from us by the power of God exalted be He". So the High Priest 'Akbon died and his period of office as High Priest was twenty three years. And there reigned after him his son Nathanel[131] thirty two years; and there befell the Samaritans in his days, calamities and distresses such as no tongue can describe. This was in the reign of Alexander[132] (God curse him!) for he was more tyrannical than Commodus. And in his days there were calamities and excess. He killed and ordered that everyone in the neighbourhood of any village not worshipping his God,[133] should be killed, and he who killed him have weighed out for himself a reward of twenty bronze coins.[134] So it happened that every one of the people when there was enmity in his heart for an Israelite would sit in the neighbourhood of the village until he met him, then he would kill him and have weighed out for him twenty bronze coins as the King ordered. And he killed many scholars and he devastated synagogues and burnt teachers and imprisoned[135] little children and crucified wise men and killed young men for no offence; and he burned them in caves and ruined many girls and thereby defiled their fathers the priests while they plundered them. And he set over them in the villages some Romans to prevent[136] them circumcising. And they, when it was morning, would say: [137]"Would that it were evening." And when it was evening, they were saying "Would that it were morning". Out of doors the sword was bringing bereavement, within the house was dread and fear. And Nathanel begat three sons: Baba, the firstborn,[138] 'Akbon, the second, and Phinehas the third. Now Phinehas' home was in Mahana, but Baba was a strong man of dignified and stern bearing and he had zeal and sanctified spirituality. When he saw what had befallen his tribe and the people of his religion because of Rome, he reflected, and thought earnestly and deeply about it, and said: "I want to be zealous for religion. Misbelief has become prevalent and certain truth is made void. Remind the body (of the people) of the word of sincerity and unity". And he said to his brothers and to the community: "How long will these uncircumcised nations that be against God treat us harshly; they intend to ruin us and they prevent us from keeping God's way and commands; however we of the children of Israel and we of the tribe of Levi, we be not like them in zeal; we will be zealous for the truth and bring up Israel from this affliction in which it stands because of the enemies of God. And has anyone been zealous for God with zeal like this, and not succeeded in it? For Levi[139] and Simeon were blessed; they had no anxiety or fear for the villages which were around them in the disaster which befell Nablus (Shechem). And the tribe of Levi when they killed[140] the worshippers of the calf, how it resulted in blessing to them and dignity for them. And Phinehas our Father when he alone was zealous[141] for God, apart from the community, how it resulted in responsibility and steady dignity acquired for him alone of his tribe, and his offspring for ever. And now let us show courage for the sake of the nation and the commands of God our God; and nothing remains to us apart from crying to God and seeking His Gate with prayer and fasting, and humility and repentance and abasement and earnest prayer; so we will abase ourselves in obedience to Him, and ask help of His power and His strength against our enemies; for He has assisted us by His Grace and His Bounty, and if He has withheld His mercy from us, then we will have to abase ourselves in pleasing Him, and obeying Him and be zealous for the pure Law; and we should strive to renew the learning of the Law which has perished, and we should be eager to raise the standards of truth which have disappeared and been obliterated, and we should imitate our predecessors among those who longed to meet God, and seek His reward; and we should purify our hearts of the stains of sins, and we should banish them from evil inclination. And if we do, then God knows the sincerity of our intentions and the purity of our thoughts and the sincerity of our hearts; He will help us and supply us with strength, and success in repelling these uncircumcised impure ones; so we will drive them out from this pure holy land and set fire to their wily and filthy followers. Then he arose and performed ablutions and prayed and fasted, and went up the sacred[142] mountain and made supplication to God, and made humble entreaties to Him and humbled himself and abased himself. And summing up his call for help he said at the end of his prayers: I beseech Thee O He who by His power has created all that exists, O He who has set it in order by His wisdom, and O He who has made it move at His will and when He wishes make it rest. And O He who has chosen this people by His Grace and His Bounty to obey Him, so that He render victorious this nation which does not flee for protection for itself except to Thee, and not relying on, nor trusting in any save Thee. Nor is there a helper for it save Thee, and Thou knowest what has befallen that nation from those kings who do not believe in Thee, who deny the need to obey Thee, who worship what Thy Law has declared abominable, who stray from Thy guidance, who are remote from Thy Favor, who worship idols that are deaf and dumb, the work of their own hands, and make their fancies their God; and if our sins have made us deserving of destruction, do Thou take our souls to Thyself, and if our misdemeanours preclude Thy help and Thy succor to us, do not let our enemies get Thy mercy, and we deserve thereby the dominion of our enemies over us, do not charge us with what we are not able to do, because of our enemies at the pain of submitting to the worship of their idols and to rebel against Thee, and their preventing us from commemorating Thy name and explaining Thine attributes. And Thou hast promised us that Thou wilt not cast us off from Thy mercy if we were in the lands of our enemies. Our eye is upon what we resolved upon in pleasing Thee. And we have determined completely to follow the ways of Thy Unity and Thou art the Powerful, Victorious One; so accomplish for us what Thou didst swear to us in Thy gracious Favour and look upon us in Thy mercy, and deal with us according to Thy Favour and Thy Liberality as Thou didst with our Fathers in releasing them from the hand of the Egyptians, when Thou didst manifest Thy miracles in the land of Egypt, and didst divide the sea that the Israelites might cross, and didst destroy the unbelieving Pharaohs and didst assist Thy people and made them to reign in the land of the obstinate Giants. When he had finished his supplication, he returned to his brethren and his congregation and said to them: "What do you think?" And they answered him and said: "Good is all that you have said. And right is it; whithersoever you command us to go, we will go". And Baba Raba went out and his brothers and his associates, and they passed through all the places of Israel. And they opened the synagogues[143] which their enemies had shut up; and he and his brethren gathered in them first, and read the scroll[144] of the Law in the hearing of all the people, and ascribed much praise and glory to God with uplifted voices. And Baba sent and brought all the scholars of the Law and the priests from every place;[145] yet he could only find out few of the elders of Israel, and Sages, because they had perished in the period of Roman (domination) since they had not sacrificed to their gods. So Baba Raba said to them: "Go every man (of you) to his place, and persevere and reflect and strive to instruct all Israel, men, women, and children in the Law of God that they may keep it, and follow the commandments and laws as did your fathers. And guard the correct reading of the Law, and see to the soundness of the service of the Synagogues and the Blessing. And every man who does not keep and does not fulfil this charge wherewith I charge you, I will kill him. Now it was a hard thing which was on Israel from Baba Raba, for he compelled young and old, and the elders to teach, and it was because of that difficult for them. But the children of Israel removed their cares, and they drew a good omen for their freedom and rejoiced exceedingly at this speech. And Baba Raba took seven[146] men from the best of Israel, men who were wealthy and experts in the Law, and he honored them by calling them Sages.[147] For the priestly community were not called Sages. And of the seven above-mentioned Sages, three were priests and four were Israelites; and as to the priests, before that whoever was greatest in power among them was called in Israel the High Priest. Then Baba came and called the priesthood, Sages, for the sake of honoring those of them who were called thus, and the naming of the priests was their prerogative and for them to hand down after them, because that when he entered Beisan the priests did not meet him, and they did not do what they should by way of honoring him; but when he entered the City they came greeting him according as their custom was. However he removed them from their offices in which they were, and they did not meet him when he went out from the city; so he put Israelites[148] in their places doing all their tasks, except the carying of the sacred Book;[149] and the children of Israel (i.e. Israelites) were to perform the commandment of circumcision[150] though it had not been theirs before that to do it; and they were saying in the synagogue: "Full of Glory,[151] and full of Pardon". And all the service[152] of the synagogue they carry out until this day. And there the genealogy[153] of the priesthood was missing. So he made them claim descent from them that preceded them for none of them any longer was concerned to preserve his lineage as Baba Raba would not confer the name Sages except on honoured scholars whether they were priests or Israelites; and as for the body of the priests he did not confer on them either the name sage or priest. And Baba Raba honoured the seven sages, and he clad them in a robe of honour, and he created for every one of them a special rank as an honour to him and his posterity after him, which should not be annulled nor terminated; and he made them sit[154] before him, every man according to his rank, until every man knew his place. And the seven abovementioned were heads over all the people; every man was to keep watch on his limit and guide his people to the laws and distinguish for them between unclean and pure, and make them acquainted with the reading of the Law; and the first Sage[155] was Arūb'ī a descendant of Ithamar and he was the Haftawi,[156] and his limit (of his jurisdiction) was from Bait Ḳabiḥa[157] in the great plain; and he had the first rank so that he should interpret before him first. The second was Jose an Israelite[158] from Kefar Sabla and he had the second position and the interpreting at the end;[159] and the third Al-Yanah[160] from Sarafin had the second reading, while the fourth was a Kahin Levi from Zaita[161] and he had the reading at the beginning and commemorated[162] the names of those who were honoured with dignities and gifts at any time; the fifth was an Israelite from Kefar Maruth[163] interpreting fifth,[164] and the sixth was Amram Ḍarir,[165] a priest from Kefar Safasah and he held the place of giving the second interpretation. It is recorded that this is the father of Marḳah (the Favor of God be upon him). And the seventh was an Israelite.[166] In this manner Baba Raba organised the seven men,[167] priests and Israelites and said to them: [168]"You shall command and prohibit and shall be set in precedence over all Israel great and small and be Sages over them; and everyone who stands before you and who disobeys you in anything which you command him, I will sue him. And among the body of seven men, Baba set up four called overseers;[169] now this management and organisation was not from the time of Divine Grace; but there were in the time of Divine Grace, seventy Elders chosen, and scholars of the multitude, Israelites, and twelve[170] from them were heads over all the multitude of Israel. He was called Judge along with the High Priest, but he did not have full control over the priests and he was judged by them. But in the tribe of Levi, for any offence, either the High Priest (judged) or one of the High Priesthood deputized for him (the High Priest) in the presence of the elders, until it was said that they were too cautious in judgment; and likewise (did) the elders in the presence of the priests. The office of elder was not inherited from father to his son nor from the son to his father, but if one of them died another was put instead of him from among the scholars of the nation; then the choice was in the hand of the High Priest and in that of the Elders. This was the organisation of the (the period of) Divine Grace. However the Sabu'ai[171] did not obey Baba Raba and had not heard of the choice of him, and they did not accept the Sages whom he organised; but their priests were judging in their villages. And the seven Sages whom Baba Raba set over them were going round the rest of the villages, and they kept the Sabbath[172] in them, making known and disclosing whether there was there any priest to whom unmindfulness had happened in an injunction or in a law or judgment among the priesthood of the Sabu'ai; (then) they would raise their matter with the chief who was friendly to them. But in every war they would assist Baba Raba and show for him at all times concern and regard. And Baba Raba said to the Sages: "Consider and reflect on all you do, and beware of unmindfulness and mistake, and feel concern for the reading of the Law and the teachers". And Baba Raba built in the confines of the sacred mountain a cistern[173] of water for purifying oneself therewith at the time of prayer,[174] and it was before the rising of the sun and at sunset. And he built a house[175] for prayer that the people might pray in it, facing the sacred mount; and they remained until the time of the Kingdom of the Franks (may God curse Them). And the house of prayer which Baba Raba built, was on the site[176] of the house of prayer which was built in the eyes of all in the days of Divine Grace; and he made it resemble it and made its floor, a piece of land (such) as one could see clearly. And he took seven stones from the stones of the Temple which the men of Saul[177] destroyed, and he made them benches for the seven sages, and he took also a big stone and he put it for himself to sit on. And Baba Raba built eight[178] synagogues in the villages with no wood in any of them; and there was the synagogue at 'Awarta,[179] and the synagogue at Salem[180] and the synagogue at Namara,[181] and the synagogue at Kirya Hajja[182] and the synagogue at Ḳarawa[183] and the synagogue at Ṭira Luza[184] and the synagogue at Dabarin,[185] and the synagogue at Bait Gan,[186] and he built a place[187] for the order of the reading and the interpretation, and the hearing of those with questions, before the house of prayer, so that every one in whose mind there was a question could ask the Sages about it, and they might answer him rightly: and he who wanted[188] to be called a sage should present himself at the times of Festivals and New Moons and present himself before the High Priest and the Sages; and if they found him sound, they called him Sage. And Baba Raba said that the reason for the building[189] of a house of prayer and a place of knowledge was so that the kings of the earth should not think that he showed regard to anything of the states of the kings and their countries which departed thereby from the worship of God and the doing of His commandments, nor that they might think that he showed regard to anything frivolous, anything after the nature of jesting. And Baba Raba distributed[190] the priests over the heads of the people, as he found them and he gave them an inheritance.[191] And Baba Raba said to the Sages: Depart in peace and be strong and be brave and be afraid of none and tremble not in fear all the days of my life. So the Sages went out from his presence with great strength and joy of heart, and there was great joy in all Israel: and when the Sages entered into the villages they manifested joy and praise to God, and they appeared in judgment, and the people did as the Sages did. But the overseers[192] arose preventing them, so they killed them and they burnt them with fire on the eve of the beginning[193] of the seventh month; and thereby came about the Samaritan custom until now of the boys of the cities and villages burning the notorious ones as a memorial of that night on which they burnt the overseers who prevented Israel from serving God. And when the advisers of the King[194] heard that the chief ones of Israel had killed the overseers, they sent condemning the chief ones of Israel. And Baba Raba heard and went out to meet them and put them to flight and killed them; and they who had been put to flight returned in a very bad state. Now Baba Raba knew that they would muster and come to him, so he chose for himself men from the best of Israel, men of war, and he prepared them and gathered them, also a mighty company. And they came to Baba Raba with a strong hand, and Baba Raba went out to meet them, and God gave him strength and victory; and he killed them and obliterated them and filled Mount 'Askar[195] with their corpses. But those who were safe, fled to the king and informed him about what had happened to them, and the king magnified himself and acted insolently, and his power became strong against Baba Raba. And he gathered and mustered against him tens of thousands. Now when Baba Raba heard, he sent word to all the places of Israel that all the men of war should come to him; and they came from the coast of the sea, and from the mountain and from the south, and from meadowland and from the lowland, 10,000 men of them advancing, ready for war; and their warriors with swords and spears and the bow and arrows ready for their enemies. And Baba Raba saw that the men were many and they needed much expense and provisions, so he went out with a strong hand and took all the villages which the unbelievers of the enemies had prepared against them, and which they had taken from the children of Israel; and the men took food from them as would be enough for them day by day. And he ordered that no one should pay tax to the King nor carry provisions or victuals to his (the King's) army. Baba Raba loved the inhabitants of 'Awarta since therein were buried the Fathers, the glorious and blameless High Priests. Eleazar, and Ithamar and Phinehas, the peace of God, Most High is He, be upon them; and Baba Raba dwelt there. And he was informed that the enemy had arrived and were in great number and a numerous company. Then Baba Raba and the company stood before God, Blessed is He, and Most High is He. And they betook themselves to Him in sincere worship, and the horns sounded and they cried with a loud cry: "O God look from Thy Holy Dwelling from heaven and redeem Thy people Israel from the hand of Thine enemies, for the war is not ours but Thine, O our LORD". And Baba Raba went out to war[196] with his enemies and God saved Israel on that day with a mighty salvation, and they killed their enemies and they fled from their presence. So Baba Raba pursued swiftly after them and overtook them and slaughtered many of them, and destroyed of them men and beasts in the mountain[197] which is opposite Nablus, and the place is unclean because of their corpses until this day. And God made Israel rejoice greatly and they knew that it was the power of God, Most High is He, that delivered them. And God put it in the soul of the King who was at Mosul that he should fight with Alexander and take the lands from him; and the war was great and violent with Alexander, and God put into the souls of the Arabs, the Ishmaelites, that they should come to the dwellings and plunder and smite them. And Baba Raba heard and went out to meet them and pursued after them swiftly to the valley of the Jordan, and smashed them and slaughtered many of them and took great booty from them sheep and cattle and camels and riding-beasts and very many garments. And when the kings of the earth heard that Baba Raba had gone out and fought with the Ishmaelites and smashed them, they sent food and provisions for 10,000 men, and sent to him wealth and robes of honour. And Baba Raba said after that: "God has been good to us and to all Israel and delivered us with this great deliverance and put our enemies into our hands and we have taken their wealth; and these (enemies) are those who came to take us and to take our children into captivity. God put them into our hands and it was a great deliverance for our other enemies; because of that they have shown this great generosity to us, and He has proved to us what God Most High has shown in the Holy Law[198] that your enemies shall incite you but you shall tread on their skulls; and now go in faith and of right, every man to his place until I need you to come to me; but there shall remain with me, 3,000 men accompanying me always. And I shall put them in villages around the village of 'Awarta in which I am dwelling so that they may be near me". So they did that and Baba Raba called them and blessed them, and every man returned peacefully to his place. And it happened that on every Saturday night the foremost of Israel from every place, and the nobles of Nablus, would come to the priest Baba Raba with horses and men, greeting him. And the King would at no time take a place which was within his power, except when the priest ordered it in his own handwriting. Then Alexander died and he had not been able to take tax from Israel; so when the Kings were unable to take tax from the children of Israel they said to the Jews: "If you are able to kill Baba Raba, you shall be enabled to build the sanctuary".[199] And many Jews were dwelling in the village of Namara and when Baba Raba went to keep the Sabbath there, the Jews determined that they should go in to Baba Raba and his brothers on the eve of the Sabbath to kill him, for they at the standing for prayer were unable to carry a sword; but that was not accomplished, for God in His mercy was kind, and their affair was revealed on the Thursday, and that was because that a Jewish woman learned of their plan. She had a friend a Samaritan woman to whom she had become attached, and she said to her: "I wish you not to enter the Samaritan synagogue on the eve of the Sabbath". And the Samaritan woman said to her. "Why is that?" And she said to her, "I fear that you will mention me". So she swore to her that she would not mention her. Then she said to her: "The Jews want to kill Baba in the synagogue on the eve of the Sabbath". So the woman came and informed Baba, and he made it clear on the Friday that he would keep the Sabbath in the synagogue. And he entered the synagogue clad in his clothes but when it was dark, he changed his robe and he went out of the synagogue and no one knew about his going out; and when night came on the Jews gathered together and they were many people, and they entered the synagogue searching for Baba Raba; and they held the doors and lit the fires in it, thinking that Baba Raba was inside. And when Baba Raba saw what they had done he cried out against them, he and his company. Then when they heard his voice they threw down their weapons and came to him and they said to him: "We are your servants, and we have sinned because we sought your blood". And he held them all and he detained them until day appeared; then he killed them all and burnt them and took the fort which was opposite the castle and drove them from it, except the woman who had informed them; for her he took and was good to her and made her a Samaritan woman, for she remained afraid of the Jews. And a company of the Jews came and burnt many crops in the fields, and Baba went out and killed a numerous company of them. Then Gordianus[200] the King ordered them to build a sanctuary and they gathered material for the building and wanted to turn their hands to the building. But God manifested a wonder from heaven and winds came and carried off all that had been gathered and all was destroyed and the building stopped. So until now they have not again proposed to build it.

Now I came across an ancient Hebrew[201] history, and in it was mentioned a story concerning Baba Raba, and I decided that I should set it down in this history, so that no one who might happen to come across it would think that I had not observed it. And it is that Baba Raba said to the congregation of the children of Israel: "It has seemed good to me that the son of my brother should betake himself to Rome[202] and busy himself in their law, then he will return in the garb of a monk, a priest; they will not know where he is and he will go up to Mount Gerizim and cross to the synagogue, and by using guile break the bird Talisman;[203] and when he has done that we will be able to go up to Mount Gerizim, and petition God on it, and He will give us victory over our enemies". And all the people said: "O our lord do what seems good to you". So he said: "Give me your signature so that after he has gone, you will not change your mind". So they did so, and Baba Raba brought Levi his nephew before him in the presence of the company, and he said to him: "See how it will be, and apply your mind to learning everything, and take care lest you stop reading the Torah night and day, and God aid you in all your deeds". So Baba Raba sent his nephew Levi, and he went making for Constantinople. Now this Levi was a clever man, worthy and expert in the Law, pious and chaste, in him was all excellence; and he spent seventeen years on his travels and when he came to Constantinople he sought instruction, and strove successfully to obtain what he sought and remained occupied ten years, and there was not in all Rome one more knowledgeable than he. And he increased in knowledge until the Romans all of them would come to serve him; and because of the greatness of his knowledge they made him the greatest bishop;[204] and he was exalted to highest position with them until all the kings began coming to his door. At that time the king could not rule except by his command and he directed the king's crown itself. However when the thirteen years of his journeying were completed he said to the king: "I wish to visit the churches which are at Nablus". So all the troops were brought forth, and the king went and the forces in his service; and when they came near Nablus the command of the king was conveyed to all the peoples that they should come out to meet the great archbishop. And when Baba Raba heard about that he was greatly afraid and gathered all the people and said to them: "We are deeply worried about Levi; we sent him off, but no news of him has arrived, and there is no doubt that he had perished; and this great archbishop who is coming, I have heard is the chief of the nation of Rome, and their model, and I have heard that he is fargone in misbelief.[205] So we can be certain of our complete destruction if we do not go out to meet him, and we shall not be safe from him if he is displeased with us. And all the troops of Rome are before him, and he may command them to kill us, so what can we do to him without enmity and without war in the face of their multitude". And when they heard that, they were greatly afraid, and they said: "We rely on God and Him do we obey". After that, he arrived at Nablus and all the crowd went out, and Baba Raba and his people went out, and when they drew near the great Archbishop then he lifted up his eyes and saw his uncle. And all the body of Israel, the Samaritans, were great in fear and were calling out to him with a very great din, and with that, tears appeared in his eyes. But his uncle and the Samaritans did not know him, for they had sent him off when he was a beardless youth and now he returned thirty years old, fully bearded, and in this great majesty. And Levi turned to the king and he said to him: "These people what are they?" And the king said to him: "O our lord and our master, these are infidels who are called the Samaritans"; and he said: "What do they know and worship?" And he said: "They worship a god who is not seen, and who has no form". And he said: "How do they not worship idols and images?" and the king said to him: "We are wearied with these, but they have never done so". And he said: "If they do not, then they shall not be allowed to live". And the news of the speech of the great Archbishop spread abroad regarding the duty of the Samaritans, and their fear increased. Then Levi and the king in his attendance went up to Mount Gerizim, and when he was on the top of the mountain the bronze bird cried out "Ebraios", and he said: "What is this?" And he said: "This Talisman does not let a Samaritan come up the mountain without this bird calling out 'Ebraios'". And he said to them: "I perceive it cries out, but see if there is a Samaritan upon the mountain and kill him". So they went round upon the mountain and they did not meet any. So Levi went over to the church and he sat down and all the kings before him, and the brazen bird was calling out and would not cease screeching. And Levi said: "What is the matter with that bird? It has wearied us with its crying, and yet there is no Samaritan on the mountain, and without doubt it has become weakminded and there is no need for us to have a headache by its remaining". And the king said: "You have said rightly O my Lord, what do you want us to do with it?" And he said: "Smash it". So they smashed it, and threw it down, and that was the eve of the beginning of the seventh month. And when four hours had passed of the night, while all the kings and the priests and the monks were asleep, Levi arose, took his sword in his hand and went down to his uncle Baba Raba. And it happened that on that night the Samaritans had assembled with him and they were afraid, perplexed as to what they should do about this great Archbishop who had ordered their killing. And while they were thus, lo, there was a light knocking at the door and they were afraid. And Baba Raba arose and the heads of the people looked at who was knocking at the door, and when they opened the door they saw. And behold it was the great Archbishop, and they were surprised to see him; and Levi prostrated himself before his uncle Baba Raba, and embraced him and fell on his neck and wept and said: "Now let me die, since I have seen your face and know that you are still alive".[206] (Gen. 46:30). So Baba Raba knew that he was Levi his nephew, and never was greater joy in the heart of Baba Raba and his communnity; and Levi began describing to his uncle and to the people all that had happened to him, and they were rejoicing and joyful about him and at what he was saying. And he said to his uncle: "When tomorrow night is a thing of the past, we shall describe that night as the unsheathing by young warriors of their swords, and they shall be with me; and while the people are sleeping, I will get up and smite their watchmen and will apply the sword among them and wipe them out". And when they were agreed on that, Levi arose, went up to his place, and found them all sleeping. And they did not know of his having gone down, nor of his coming up. And when the beginning of the seventh month was drawing to a close, Baba Raba sent to all the villages in which were the Samaritans and he said to them: "Be ready for the coming of the night, and when you see fire on a dome, at the right moment, kill the supervisors who are over you, and do not spare of those around you a single man of the Romans, but kill and strike out with the sword, until you all meet together in the meadow of Bahā". And when the night came, all the people were mustered and ascended Mount Gerizim and Baba Raba was in the van of the troops; and Levi arose with the might and power of God Most High, and smote the guards of the king, and the monks, and the priests, and cried out in a loud voice:[207] "The LORD is a man of war: The LORD is His name" And when Baba Raba heard the voice of Levi his nephew, they all raised their voices saying as he has said, and they unsheathed their swords and killed many of the Romans. And they did not cease until they had wiped out everyone who was on Mount Gerizim. Then they kindled the fire on the top of the Dome,[208] and all the Samaritans arose and killed all the overseers who were over them, and there did not remain one of them. And they continued throughout the whole night burning the churches of the Romans, and destroying them until they had effaced their name from Mount Gerizim and round about. There has remained a memorial of that to our own day, for at the beginning of the seventh month the children of the Samaritans gather together wood, and they burn it on the night of the outgoing[209] of the beginning of the seventh month. When the Romans who were on the coastal areas heard what had befallen their companions at the hands of Baba Raba, they gathered together a very large body of men and came seeking Baba Raba until they came to near Nablus. Then Baba Raba came out to them and smashed them and killed most of them. Then the news reached King Alexander[210] at Rome; now he was the great king, and he gathered many troops, men of war and he sent them against Baba Raba. But God helped Baba Raba against them and he smashed them; and the war between them was over by the village of 'Askar[211] and he killed them leaving only a few of them so they asked for a sally of troops against Baba Raba and he equipped tens of thousands against him. When Baba Raba heard of that he wrote letters to all the Samaritans to present themselves. And there presented themselves to him from every place, ten thousand horsemen, warlike youths with their weapons and their military equipment. And Baba Raba delivered to them the villages in fee; and the news came to Baba Raba that his enemies were coming in number like the sand of the seashore, and Baba Raba stood before God Most High, and prostrated himself and sought help from God. And he spent a long time praising and glorifying God, and he made for himself ambushes in burial grounds and he said to them: "When you see battle has taken place between us and when I cry out at the top of my voice 'O people of the graves assist me' then emerge from the graves". And the number of the ambushes was five thousand and when Baba Raba drew near his enemies the priests sounded the trumpets and all the people lifted up their voices saying: "God is a mighty man in war, God is His name". And the earth was rent by their voices and the battle was joined between them. No battle in this world was ever like it, and Baba Raba cried out in the middle of the battle and said: "O people of the graves aid me against the enemies of God". And the soldiers of Rome were astonished. When he spoke thus the men who were lurking, came out saying: "Fear not, fear not, all of us will strengthen you and the rest of the dead are coming after us; on every side they will strengthen you". And when the Romans saw that, they thought that it was genuine, and their hearts were broken and they lost courage and they turned back fleeing and some of them fell over others. And God came to Israel on that day with a mighty victory. This is what I found in the copy which I have described, and God knows best about the unseen; but there remains information about Baba Raba in the copies (of the Mss.) and even if it occurs later, it will be given for it deals with the same topic. [212]And after all that, Philippus[213] sent messengers to Baba Raba with a letter in his own handwriting, saying to him: "It is desired by our ruler and our lord the great King, that he may grant a favor to the slave, that he should come to him at Constantinople where he will stay with him a few days;[214] and when we are satisfied at having seen him then he will return here". Baba Raba gathered together his people and his son and his family, and informed them that he must go on the journey. And his father and the heads of his people said to him: "How is your cheerfulness possible seeing that the people will be left alone and we would have found comfort at your hand? So do not do that, lest we return to humiliation and degradation and be reduced to nought, for your enemies were grievously disappointed at your victories". And he said to them: "Know that I have submitted my command to God Mighty and Glorious, and perhaps this enmity will cease and this fire be extinguished which is between us and the nations. And if God will, I shall not tarry, but shortly I shall return to you; and if it be not so, then the matter is finished as far as I am concerned, and I bequeath you my son, Levi". Now this Levi was his son, and not his brother's son. And they said to him: "Let a company of us go with you; they will serve you". But he said: "I will not have that, but I charge you not to turn aside from keeping the commands of God and His ways. And fear not nor grow anxious, but be strong and be of good courage for God is with you and will not forsake you". Then he took the hand of his son Levi and delivered him to Nathanel his father and said: "This is my charge to you, and my command to you is that you will keep him in it; may your happiness continue and the trust of all the people likewise . And he went in company with the messenger of the king, and when he drew near Constantinople King Philip summoned the crowd to go out to meet Baba Raba; and all the people went out with crosses and images and in prayer. All the kings walked alongside Baba Raba's camel; and he alone continued riding. And it was a great day for him when he entered Constantinople with great ponp. No other king had so entered. And when he was in the fortress, the King said to the great ones of his kingdom: "Baba has come into our power, so what do you think we should do with him?" And some of them there were who said: "Have him killed". Others said: "That is not possible, for he is a great king and we have sworn to him that we shall not harm him; if then we were to do so, it would cause the destruction of all Rome and of their survival". So the King said: "Truly have you spoken. It is our duty that we serve him and we should consider his opinion, but we shall not let him again go from this country all his life". Now formerly he had had gold and silver, so the king ordered its return to him, and he charged all the watchmen of the gates about him. But Baba said to the king: "I want to return to my family". And he said to him: "Stay with us some time and be at ease". And he knew that he had got hold of him. So when the father of Baba saw that his son did not come, he married his son Levi to Rebecca, daughter of his uncle 'Akbon. Then Nathanel[215] the father of Baba Raba died. And after his death Levi went to be with his father at Constantinople and he stayed with his father a few days. And Baba Raba was sick with a mortal sickness; and when the sickness increased in him, he sought a man, a Jew,[216] a true friend of his, and he handed over to him his son Levi and said to him: "I want you to bring him to his people and his relatives, but do not hand him over to uncleanness, but guard him like your son". And he bound him by oath to that. And Baba Raba died in Constantinople by the mercy of God Most High, and the day of his death was a momentous day; and he was buried in a beautiful tomb, and that Romans built a beautiful church over it. And after his death the King brought his son Levi and released him and restored to him all that had been his father's, of gold, silver and raiment and sent him off. And he sent in his service on the journey, men to bring him to his people; and the Jewish man went with him, and did as Baba Raba had charged him, and he served him until he brought him to his relatives. When the people heard of the arrival of Levi the son of Baba Raba, they rejoiced greatly for him, and all the community of Israel came to Namara. They greeted him and they filled the earth and the wadis and the river-beds and the fields; and they brought their companions many and good, and they made for him a festival with the ceremony of eating in the wadis and the mountains and meadows and fields. And all the people wanted Levi to come and go down and bless them; so throughout the length of that day he remained abiding with the Samaritans and would go round among them. And all the Samaritans were rejoicing and being happy with him until the evening came, the time of prayer. He crossed to his house, he prayed, and laid down his head to take rest. Now no food had entered his mouth that day; and they brought to him food, but they thought that he was sleeping and they would have roused him. But he could not be roused, and they drew near him and discovered what was the matter with him for they found that he was dead (God Most High have mercy on him). And joy was turned to violent grief, the like of it there had never been; and they buried him in the grave which his uncle 'Aḳbon had prepared for himself in the village of Namara, and he was the first to be buried in it. And when Rebecca his wife saw that her cousin was dead she swore by her soul not to eat nor drink until she died; and she died on the seventh day[217] after the death of her cousin, and she was buried beside him in the above-mentioned tomb.

So the priest 'Aḳbon was invested with the high priesthood after the death of his nephew. But there were men powerful, stern in judgement, vigorous in affairs who all spoke against him and said that the (high) priest 'Aḳbon was acting unfairly in judging, and that he was speedy in carrying out an order if it affected those not related to him, but if it affected his relatives, he did not do that. And some of them agreed that they should testify against the daughter of the priest 'Aḳbon, whose name was Maryam, that they found her with a Samaritan man. And those who cast suspicion on her agreed together that he should flee until the priest had decided what should happen in the case of his own daughter; and thus he would make it plain whether he was acting wrongfully in judgement or not. So they came before him and they testified with false testimony against his daughter to wit that they had found her with a certain person (and) not on the road.[218] So he sent seeking that person, and he found he had fled, and the affair seemed to him to be certain by the flight of the accused; so he took his daughter and burnt her as God said in passing sentence in His revelation:[219] "And the daughter of any priest, if she profanes herself by playing the harlot, profanes her father, she shall be burned with fire". But in that night he saw her likeness in a dream saying to him: "In the place where you burned me, O my Father, kill not until you have examined and searched out; for me you killed unjustly". And on the second night, and on the third he saw this dream exactly the same; and he arose on the morning of the fourth day for judgement, and he brought the witnesses and he disputed with them. Then they acknowledged that they had wronged his daughter, and had witnessed falsely to try the high priest's judging of his relatives. So he burned them as God said:[220] "Then you shall do to him as he had meant to do to his brother".

And at that time Philippus the king[221] took from 'Akbon all the wealth which Baba Raba had left, in the presence of the companions of Levi his son. And there reigned after him Dahikhus[222] and he was worse than Alexander at his worst; and he sent to the land men and among them a wicked man called Rākūs. Now it came to pass during his term in Caesarea that he found a woman praying and her son with her in her room. He repaired frequently to it for one year and two months, then he commanded his servant to bring her to him. When she came before him, he said to her: "To whom are you praying?" She said "I am praying to the God of the Heavens and the Earth". He said to her: "Do you see him when you pray to him?" And she said to him: "I do not see Him, nor can any see Him". And he said to her: "Why do you not pray to one you can see" And she said to him: "That is hateful to us". So he said: "Punish her so that she will worship the idols". So his youths took her and beat her, but she could not be made to worship. So he said: "Bring fire and burn her". So they brought fire and he said to her: "If you do not worship the idols I will burn you and your son in the fire". But she refused to worship, so they took her son and threw him into the middle of the fire. And when she saw her son in the fire, she hurled herself into the fire upon him. So the two of them were burnt completely. When Dahiḳhus the King heard, that seemed good to him, and he said: "The like of this should be done in every place". But God did not spare him a year, and he was killed (May God not have mercy on him). And there reigned after him Tahus,[223] and he ill-treated the Samaritans and he set over them agents to prevent them saying their prayers and sacred readings and from doing the commandments.[224] And the name of the agent who was over the house of the High Priest was Germon[225] and he sat at the door of the High Priest, night and day. Now he was possessed of great dignity and they feared him greatly. Then the High Priest 'Aḳbon was blessed with a male child, and he and his family and the heads of the Samaritans were gathered together and he said: "How can the act of circumcision of the child take place?" And he (Germon) remained with him and with them continuously. When it was the morning of the eighth day, the High Priest took a basket and wrapped up the little one in wool and put him in it (the basket) and covered him with wool and he said to the woman: "Take this basket and go out. Wait for me at Ras al-'Ain. And the woman took the basket out and Germon was at the door. When Germon saw the basket he knew that the baby was in it, and he said to the woman: "Do your business joyfully". So she went out with 'Aḳbon and she told him the saying of Germon, and he was violently afraid but he said: "The affair belongs to God. Let Him do as He thinks best". So he entered the cave and circumcised the boy, and handed him in the basket to the woman as he was, with the wool over him. And after a short time

'Aḳbon went home, and Germon stood up and said in Hebrew (for he knew Hebrew better than ten Samaritans) *Rabbi, rabbi hadi,* which being explained is "O my master rejoice greatly". Now when the High Priest heard that, he was violently afraid and went into the house and said: "Who gave Germon information about us?" And he filled his hand with gold and said to Germon: "Take this little in exchange for much". But he said: "Far be it from me that I should sell my obedience to God[226] today for the lucre of this world". And the High Priest's fear increased when he refused to take the gold. But when Germon saw the High Priest's fear he said to him: "Your heart is good. Do not fear, for I for the sake of God have treated you haughtily: But for the sake of your good pleasure I will take from all this, three dinars and it will be as if I had taken it all. So rejoice in your son. My God spare him to you". So in that hour did the joy of the High Priest 'Aḳbon increase in his son, and the community was gathered with him, and they greatly praised and glorified God (Praise be to Him the Most High). And 'Aḳbon said to the Community: "This event shall be commemorated by us for ever and we shall implore mercy on this overseer Germon at the times of festivals and holy convocations (as follows) *D^{e}kir l^{e}tob ad l^{e}Olam Germon 'Asora Roma'a*, i.e. may Germon the Roman overseer be remembered for good for ever.[227]

After that came Dūsīs the son of Fufali.[228] Now he had committed[229] adultery with the wife of one of the chief ones of the Jews in one of the villages of the Jews; and the leaders of the Jews sought to kill him. But he said: "Do not kill me and I will go to Nablus and I will restore in the house of Ephraim the two golden (bulls),[230] and I will make them causes of dissension and I will compensate you for all the shedding of blood they have caused you". So they let him live[231] because of that. And this is written[232] among the Jews, that they released him from condemnation because of what he would do in

Nablus. Now the origin of Dūsīs was from the mixed rabble[233] who went out with the children of Israel from the land of Egypt to Nablus. And Dūsīs went to the village of Askar, and there was there a person called Yaḥdu a very learned man, who was unique in his time in knowledge and in law. And Dūsīs followed him closely and gave him generous alms;[234] and he went into him one day and found him eating firstlings. So Dūsīs said to him: "How is it lawful for you to eat firstlings when its blood has not been sprinkled on the altar as it says:[235] 'You shall sprinkle their blood upon the altar' and so on". Yaḥdu said to him: "And it is like the bread of which God said: 'And you shall eat neither bread nor grain parched or fresh'[236] and so on". And they stopped eating bread and firstlings for a period of two years; when they had finished being ascetic, after two years they entered Nablus and ate and drank and got drunk. Now Yaḥdu got drunk and slept in his place; so Dūsīs took Yaḥdu's mantle, and went and gave it to a prostitute and said to her: "Take this mantle and when it is the day after tomorrow, go up the mountain and all the Samaritans will be on it. And seize hold of the elder who will be next to the High Priest; his name is Yaḥdu. And say that he has committed adultery with you, and that he left his mantle in pledge with you in lieu of your due; and that you need not fear, for you are known for this, so take this your reward, SIX dinars". Now when Yaḥdu awoke and sought his mantle he could not find it. So he went to the people of the town asking them about it, and they swore to him that they had not taken it, so he sought Dūsīs and he could not find him. And when it was the third day - now it was the Day of Atonement[237] - the prostitute went up to the mountain, and found the elder whom Dūsīs had described to her beside the High Priest; she accosted him and asked for help and said: "O my lord High Priest take my due from the elder who stands beside you". He said: "What have you to do with him?" She said "He spent the night with me and gave me this mantle in pledge, and I lost him until today". And they said to Yaḥdu: "Is this your mantle?" He said: "Yes, this mantle is mine". And the High Priest said: "Take him to be burned". But Yaḥdu said: "Do not act hastily as to my case. Those with whom Dūsīs and I were drinking know it, so let them and Dūsīs be bound by oath as to it, as to what opinion is to be held; but if you neither hold me nor them trustworthy, then burn me, me and this whore". Then the High Priest 'Aḳbon called the whore and said: "Tell me the truth, and if not, I will burn you, and I will burn this man with you". So she confessed the truth and said: "O my Lord, Dūsīs gave me six dinars and this mantle and said to me: 'Do this deed'".

And the High Priest 'Aḳbon searched for Dūsīs but could not find him. For Dūsīs, because of his fear of the High Priest 'Aḳbon and the violence of his strength and the swiftness of his resolve, fled to Suwaika,[238] and lodged with a woman whose name was Amantu the widow, and said to her: "I am the son of the High Priest". So she served him and he spent many days with her writing. And when he had finished his task, he knew that the High Priest 'Aḳbon would not pardon him, but sought him; so he arose and departed from that place to another. And he charged the woman and said to her: "I know that behind me is one who seeks me and wants to kill me, so I asked of you the right of entry to your lodging; you shall say to him who comes seeking me that he stayed with me a short space of time writing on these pieces of paper and went out and departed but I do not know whither he has betaken himself. However he charged me that no one was to come near these pieces of paper until after that person had gone down into this pool and dipped himself in it, and that nothing should soil you after you have cleansed yourself of the stains of the road". Dūsīs went to 'Anbata[239] and went up the mountain and concealed himself in a cave and died in it from hunger, and dogs came in, and ate him. This was what happened to Dūsīs, cursed be his name. And as for the High Priest 'Aḳbon, he did not cease pursuing him until he heard that he had come to Suwaika and that for a long space of time, he had been with Amantu the widow. So he sent Levi[240] the son of Phinehas his brother; now he was a man bold in religion. And he sent along with him seven men to bring in Dūsīs and to kill him as he had intended to do to Yaḥdu. So Levi went, accompanied by the men, and they came to Suwaika and entered the house of Amantu the widow, and said to her: "Is not my friend Dūsīs with you, who deserves to be killed? And she said: "I know not that he deserves to be killed, but I was exceedingly generous to him when he said to me 'I am the son of the High Priest'. And I found him continually busy and writing on these pieces of paper and when he wanted to set off on a journey, he said to me: 'No one is allowed to approach them until he has dipped himself in this pool'.[241] And he went away from me and I know not where he has gone". Then Levi said to the company: "What is against our dipping in this pool and purifying ourselves from the stains of the road, before we venture to read the names of God Most High is He". So one of the men who accompanied Levi went down to the pool and dipped and came up and said: "My faith is in Thee LORD, and in Dūsīs Thy servant, and in his prophecy". Levi called out against him and struck[242] him and said to another: "Go down", and he went down, dipped himself and said the same as had the one who had preceded him. And they went on dipping, until not one of them remained undipped. And they were repeating this saying, and testifying regarding Dūsīs in prophecy. Levi was perplexed in his mind and said: "By God, now I will dip and see the wickedness of these men and their blasphemy and I will oppose them if God, Most High is He, will". Then Levi went down and dipped and came up and said: "My faith is in Thee LORD, and in Dūsīs Thy prophet. Woe to us who pursue after the prophet of God, Dūsīs". They took the books[243] of Dūsīs, and they found that he had altered much of the Law, e.g. punishment (prescribed) and more. But they all preserved what he had written and altered. Then they returned to Nablus, and they said to the High Priest that they had not lighted on him, and that he had gone from the woman and she did not know whither he had gone. Now when it was the first Festival Day of the Feast of the Passover the Samaritans were gathered together and the High Priest 'Akbon said to the son of his brother Levi the son of Phinehas: "Rise read:[244] 'Then Moses called all the elders of Israel'". And Levi arose and read until he reached:[245] 'Take a bunch of hyssop'. He read instead of hyssop, thyme, as Dūsīs had altered it, and the Samaritans refuted him. But Levi said: "No, the correct (reading) is what God said by the hand of Dūsīs (upon him be peace), 'thyme', and verily you, all of you are shamelessly ignorant of the prophecy of Dūsīs; you alter[246] the festivals and make a substitute[247] for the greatest name Yahwah, and send chasing after the second prophet whom God had first signified from Mount Sinai. Woe to you from God". Thereupon they said: "The scholar has blasphemed". And his uncle the High Priest cried out against him and said: "Kill him". And Levi fled and the Samaritans followed him to a point near the field of Joseph and they vied with one another as to the number of stones they threw at him. And they went on stoning him until he died; and they made a cairn of stones over him, and is called Levi's monument until this our day. And when the men who were with Levi saw what happened to Levi, they concealed their affair, and led astray along with them a company of people who believed in Dūsīs; and when they became numerous[248] they turned towards a village beside Jerusalem out of fear of the Samaritans. When Levi had been stoned these took palm leaves[249] and smeared them with Levi's blood and said: "This is he concerning whom God said:[250] 'lest innocent blood be shed in your land'. And what was the sin of Levi that he was stoned? When he testified that Dūsīs was a prophet - he was a prophet - he was killed". They took the sinful books and put in them the palm leaves, and agreed among themselves that whoever wanted to see the palm leaves of Levi and read Dūsīs' own writing, should fast seven days during the nights thereof before he should see them. They said that the dead would rise soon, also that Dusis had prophesied that he would die aged twenty eight of hunger and thirst, and dogs would eat him after his death. So Levi, his first martyr, was stoned in the field of Joseph. They cut their hair and made all their prayers while in water; and when they bathed in the water they used to veil their bodies when they went down into it. And they did not go out on the Sabbath day from house to house. And they kept no Festival but the Sabbath day, and if it were shifted from its proper time to another time, they would not even put out their hands from their sleeves. Also when one of them died they would gird him with a strong girdle and put in his hand a staff, and on his feet sandals, and they would say: "When we arise from the graves we will arise in readiness". It is said that they believed firmly that as soon as the dead were buried, he would rise from the grave and go away to Paradise. Now all these rulings were drawn up by Dūsīs,[251] (may God curse him). And these followers continued in hiding until the Samaritans left off trying to kill them. Then the High Priest 'Aḳbon died (God Most High have mercy on him) and his son Nathanel[252] succeeded him in office, and he continued in the High Priesthood thirty one years. Now Nathanel had a son whose name was Yah'am[253] who had a serving girl called Sul. She was greatly enamored of the aforesaid Yah'am and fell more and more in love with him and became obsessed with him, but he would not devote himself to her. But when she knew that he would not fall in with her, and that we would not get any response from him, nay, that he would not heed her, nor give heed to anything but prayer and worship and occupying himself with learning, she despaired of him, but the passion kept working in her. She went to Simon the wizard from 'Alin[254] and said to him: "My lord the High Priest salutes you and desires that you kill his son, for he is disobedient to him, and has disappointed his parents. He desires that he be killed in secret, and these twelve dinars he has furnished for you". Simon thought that her words were true,[255] so he said to her: "Whatever he had commanded us we will do". And he said to the greatest of the Jinn:[256] "Go to the son of the High Priest and take his soul, but do not cause his spirit to pass until his father regrets his killing, and wishes the keeping of our power over his life". So the Jinn went forthwith to the son of the High Priest but he was not able to have power over him because he was eating firstlings.[257] He returned and said to Simon: "I have no power over him because he has sanctified himself and is eating holy things". Simon said to him: "Go to him, and when he has finished the food seize him". So he went and he returned to him the next day and said: "I have no power over him because when he finished the food, he prayed again until morning". Simon said to him: "Follow him until the rule of the night overtakes him and you have power over him". And he continued with him until the rule of the night[258] befell him. And he became impure and he was nearby him and seized his soul until he swooned and became like one dead. Then his father and mother and his relatives arose and cried for help and much was their crying and much their uproar; and the Samaritans came and wept mightily, and the father was unable to bear his grief for him. The Samaritans tried to console him but he refused to be consoled and he lost patience. Now Simon was present in the assembled company of the mourners, and when he saw the High Priest in great grief and sorrow over his son, he was astonished at him, and came to his side and said: "I see you in this great grief, and yet you sent your serving girl to me in order to have him killed. But if you want him to live, let me know". And he said to him: "Earn the reward from God, Mighty and glorious". So Simon drew near to him and exorcised him, and he arose at once but knew nothing of what his condition had been. Then the High Priest brought his serving girl and tortured her; and she confessed that she had done that because she had not obtained what she longed for from him. So he put her to death in the presence of the people. Simon was confounded before the High Priest, and went away immediately and betook himself to 'Armiya.[259] And he and the disciples of the Messiah[260] vied in witchcraft, but he gained the mastery over them.[261] Then he found a Jewish philosopher whose name was Philo from Alexandria and he (Simon) said: "Strengthen me and I will stop the sect of the Messiah". But Philo said to him: "Rest thy soul, for if this matter is from God,[262] no one has power to stop it". So Simon returned and came to Bait 'Alin, and died and was buried in the Wadi which is situated opposite the house of the disciple who testified to the Messiah first, and his name was Saftanah.[263] The disciples of the Messiah were fifteen[264] persons, the last of whom became a Jew[265] and to him were attached the circumcised disciples. And after that[266] they did not accept the circumcised, but all of them were uncircumcised. And men called Ba'unaī[267] (Ebionites) seceded according to the opinion of Dūsīs and his disciples. And they came to Beisan and they made for themselves a place in the market of the beasts of burden; but the seven men who were disciples of Dūsīs all perished.[268] Then arose one called Ansma[269] who began leading men astray, and attempting to annul the festivals. Now a man of the Samaritans saw in sleep Abraham, Isaac and Jacob. They were saying to him: "Go to Ansma and say to him: 'Refrain from causing our children to err, and destroying them; and if you refrain not, then you shall perish and everyone who listens to you'". But when it was told him, he increased in rebellion, and began to make them err more than before. And he said: "You do not know the festivals except in dreams". And on a certain Sabbath night he was at a house and the seven with him, and lo in the house an accident befell him and them, and they perished to the last of them. So none remained of the Ba'unaī except one man. And another sect arose from them who they called Ḳīlṭāi[270] (but I found in a Hebrew version Ḳaṭiṭaī) and they said: "Do not keep any commandments, for all the commandments are annulled". And they went up to Mount Gerizim[271] and said before God: "O God, what Dūsīs Thy prophet said we will do here; we have annulled all the commandments and you are the One who is able to reveal the Tabernacle". And God afflicted them and they went down from the mountain barking[272] like dogs and they continued like that till they died. When men saw what had befallen them, they turned from believing firmly in them. And there arose another sect[273] from these, the company of Ba'unaī, who caused to sin by their saying that the world shall endure because Dūsīs died his shameful death, and Levi was stoned because Dūsīs[274] had died and all the righteousness of the world had died. These believed firmly that the winged dragon[275] should rule the creatures till the day of resurrection. And they bound men to silence,[276] and the inner secret of their way of acting they did not disclose to anyone. They used to practise in a village whose name is Mālūf,[277] and they were called Ṣadūḳaī. They lasted seven years, and when their secret was revealed, the place where they were fell upon them,[278] and they perished to the last of them. And there arose after this Abiya and Dusa.[279] One hundred and twenty persons inclined towards them and said: "All the commandments have not been annulled,[280] so let us go out to the wilderness as Dūsīs[281] said, for what we experience is neither security nor Divine Grace.

So they went out from Nablus on a Sabbath day, and passed the graves and crossed the Jordan on the Sabbath day[282] and went out to the wilderness. And snakes set on them and killed them, and only two of them were saved. And they narrated how they met their death, and this sect passed away also. And there arose an insolent man called Šalyah[283] the son of Ṭairun the son of Nīn, and he sought advancement in the synagogue. The people of the city did not enable him to do so, so he went out and came to the Samaritans[284] and began making them err and said: "Come up with me and see how the Tabernacle[285] will appear". And they made for him a large tent and he began teaching in it; and he said from this tent: "Let us go up to Mount Gerizim". And a hundred and eighteen men were gathered to him. Now he stipulated for them asceticism[286] for each one, and no woman should come to them, nor a boy, as Dūsīs said. And Ba'unaī came back and they said: "Bad is what they said,[287] that the dead will shortly arise, and no one need fast[288] if he wants to see the palm leaves of Levi, and the handwriting of Dūsīs, nor need one pray[289] in water". So he began changing the festivals[290] and making this error among the Samaritans; and he called Mount Gerizim a substitute,[291] similar to the everlasting mountain. Further he said that he who prays towards Mount Gerizim[292] is like one who prays toward a grave. He divided the unclean practices into two: one was called primary and the other intermediate. He declared permitted marriage with the Gentiles[293] and the touching of woman in the menses.[294] He said that there is no uncleanness in dead animals except that which is prohibited[295] for eating. As for all the pearls which they used, and the clothing which they wore, and the rest of the fine garments which are the root cause of it, it is the business of the Gentiles, not the business of Israel; it does not make unclean.[296] He permitted also the touching of the dead, and said: "Wherever he wished, he might pass provided it is not contiguous to it; and it is not incumbent on him to be purified except the first day only".[297] He said that a child acquires what his mother acquires of uncleanness. And he said: "There is no holiness in the time of error", and he prohibited the continuous immersing[298] of oneself and baptising on the Sabbath day. And he called the name of his soul 'The Measurer'. He made the prayer like the reading be from a sitting position.[299] He said that the synagogues were like houses of idols, so he who paid anything to the Synagogue, it was as if he paid (it) to the house of idols. And he made vessels in which were the (manuscript) scrolls in the synagogue like the prostitute when she passes with pomp. He made every man when he read or prayed, cover his head;[300] and he who did not do what he said, deserved the curse. He ordained that the teachers of the Samaritans should be those concerning whom God said:[301] "You shall make for yourselves no idols". And he it is who established the reading Qinah. He said concerning himself that he was the father of all who listened to him, and they were the Dustān (Friends)[302] calling him: "O our father", while his disciples were saying: "May God cause[303] the spirit of our father Šalyah to pour forth but grant that he die not on the Sabbath". And he changed the reading of the greatest Name and he said one should only read "Blessed is He".[304] He put a stop to the ascending of the noble mountain, and said that one does not fling away what one repairs to frequently, following the words of Dūsīs (God curse him). And he made women read with the men in the meeting place. Then he died (May God not have mercy on him) on the Sabbath day. Now he had never gone up Mount Gerizim in his life.[305]

Five brothers arose from Taira Luza. They were called the sons of Joṣadaḳ;[306] and another was called Ṣadoḳ the great from Bait Fara. And they differed from Šalyah[307] and his companions for they said that Mount Gerizim was sanctified as was the House on it, and that it was incumbent that one do what was written, and one should not do what is not allowed upon it. He who came near to a dead man should bathe, and on the first day he should cleanse himself before touching anything. But they called him by the abovementioned name "the Measurer", and they agreed with him on annulling:[308] "And Blessed is His Name for Ever". They organised the making of a distinction in relation to all Sabbaths, and annulled the saying of (Deut. XXXIII[4]) [309]'Moses commanded us a law'. After that Ūliānah went out who was living in Alexandria,[310] and there was gathered together to him a company and he said: "Receive from me the Divine Grace,[311] it will appear and we have no power to act straight since we read all together; but let the men be set apart[312] from the women and the women from the men, and the sons be set apar- along with their fathers, and let none take anything from anyone; but he who wants to have a measure of anything in itself, let him say: "holiness belongs to God". So he removed the men from the women, and the sons from their mothers, and the men divorced their wives and left their possessions. And Bustunus[313] went out against them from the sea, and destroyed of them many people, and threw a company of them into ships. And Ūliānah died; and he died an unclean death. Those who remained of his sect thought they were under Divine Grace[314] but they were mistaken for a number of trials befell them; yet they did not change nor take warning therefrom; and there arose after that others who were called Fasḳuṭai,[315] and they said: "Here there is no Garden and no Resurrection but there is only trial, and the woman is the strength of the trial". So they said: "A man ought to sleep with a different woman six nights, and they should be clothed". But when it was the seventh night, they shunned them for they were now free from whoring and they had reached the limit of temptation.[316] And when they had done that, all of them had contaminated themselves by whoring. So they arose and gelded themselves and said: "He who has gelded himself, filthiness has passed away from him". All those divisions came from the books of Dūsīs; and there came upon the Samaritans because of them, much error and great sin and vice and enmities from which no profit came; but God is the rewarder of every man according to his act.

NOTES ON ABU'L FATḤ, pp.78-87 VILMAR'S EDITION

1. P.78 Hezekiah according to both the Tolidah and Abu'l Fatḥ, was the successor of 'Abdel; both agree that the length of his term as high priest was thirty years.

2. Hananiah the successor to Hezekiah: so too the Tolidah which also agrees as to his term of office having been twenty-four years. Note that the Tolidah, too, has no additional information on Hananiah, other than his name and length of service. But it would be wrong to draw the conclusion that Abu'l Fatḥ merely expanded the list of high priests into a chronicle where the Tolidah had some note appended to a high priest's name. In the case of Hezekiah, for example, Abu'l Fatḥ devotes to him some five and a half pages (p.73-78, Vilmar's edition), whereas the Tolidah gives only his name and length of service.

3. Amram: the Tolidah agrees with Abu'l Fatḥ that Amram held office for thirty two years, and states that his son married the daughter of Darius King of Assyria. The source of Abu'l Fatḥ's further story is not known; it is not the Book of Joshua.

4. From the support given by this Darius to the Jews it is to be inferred that Abu'l Fatḥ meant the Darius mentioned in Ezra 6:1; cf. also Josephus, *Antiq.* XI, III-IV, which has been utilised by Abu'l Fatḥ in a desultory manner.

5. Nablus: i.e., Neapolis, founded by the Emperor Vespasian west of the older Shechem. But here Abu'l Fatḥ uses the current Arab term Nablus for the Biblical Shechem.

6. Simeon, obviously Simeon Maccabee; but Simeon Maccabee, though he was leader and governor of the Jewish people (cf. Josephus, *Antiq.*, XIII, VI, 4), never assumed the title of king. He was (*ibid.*, 7) made high priest by the multitude. True, he was called ethnarch of the Jews, (*ibid.*, 7).

7. In no sense could Simeon Maccabee be regarded as the builder of the sanctuary, even in his own true period. One

might say that Abu'l Fatḥ confuses him with Zerubbabel, were it not for the fact that in dealing with the high priesthood of 'Abdel, he had already mentioned Zerubbabel.

8. This is in effect what did happen, if not at the time of the building of the second Temple in Jerusalem, then at least later. Pfeiffer has very rightly called the Biblical book of Chronicles the first Jewish apologetic and noted that it was directed against the Samaritans. 1 Chron. 6:1-15 attempts to show that the Jews have the genuine Aaronide and Zadokite priesthood. The Samaritans in their Tolidah are trying to claim the same for themselves. The dispute must be old, indeed as old as the Samaritan Jewish schism.

9. While Mount Gerizim was undoubtedly an ancient holy place in Israel, it is unlikely that the Samaritans had already a Temple there at that time.

10. It is possible that there was some dispute among the inhabitants of the land and the returned Jews from Babylon, as to where the sanctuary was to be built. But unless Ezra's attitude to mixed marriages, (cf. Ezra, ch.9-10) represents a later stage when attempts at conformity had broken down, it is unlikely that the Jews wanted to force the Samaritans to fall into line with them. Actually Ezra 4:1-3 tells how the adversaries, i.e. the Samaritans, wanted to help rebuild the Temple.

11. True enough, Ezra 5:16 admits that from the time of Sheshbazzar until that of Zechariah and Haggai the Temple had not progressed beyond the foundations.

12. Cf. perhaps Josephus, *Antiq.*, XI, IV, 9. According to Josephus, the Samaritans were told to refrain from obstructing the building of the Temple, and to supply money for the Jerusalem sacrifices. We hear nothing there of repression of the Samaritans by Darius.

13. Cf. 2 Kings 1:24 where it is stated that some of the settlers transferred into depopulated Israel after the destruction of the Northern Kingdom in 721 were from Kutha.

14. The Samaritans to this day call themselves Israel. Among the Jews, certainly since the Mishnaic period, Kuthim has been the usual name for the Samaritans; cf., e.g., the minor Talmudic tractate Kuthim. Cf. also Josephus *Antiq.*, IX, XIV, 3.

15. There is reason to believe that readings from the Law, interspersed with brief blessings and prostrations, constituted originally the whole liturgy of the Samaritans. The present day

Sabbath liturgy of the Samaritans is much the same as it was in the time of Amram Darah and Markah, in the fourth century; with the introduction of their hymns the readings from the Law were condensed into digests; but still on a Sabbath morning the whole Law is read in the form of a digest, in the first part of the service. For a picture of what the old Samaritan service would have been like, compare Nehemiah 8:6-8, though there the service is Jewish and conducted by Ezra. Much as they hate Ezra, the Samaritans unconsciously testify to the work which he achieved, prior to their enforced separation.

16. 'Arkiya must refer to John Hyrcanus, son of Simeon Maccabee. Abu'l Fath does refer to John Hyrcanus later, but only as John; cf. the second extract from Abu'l Fath, below. Already Vilmar (Prolegomena, p.lix) suggested this identification.

17. This quarrel, which takes place in 'Arkiya's lifetime, may be a projection back into the past of Hyrcanus' part in the dispute between the Pharisees and the Sadducees, just as Hyrcanus' part in the overthrow of the Samaritan temple, here ascribed to his father, has been pushed back to the time of the rebuilding of the Jerusalem Temple after the return from the Babylonian exile. If so, Abu'l Fath has used his material loosely and for his own ends. What makes it feasible for Abu'l Fath in this case also to reinterpret Hyrcanus' reign and antedate it, is the nature of the quarrel between the house of Ithamar and the house of Manasseh. Note the emphasis by the adjudicator of the dispute that "the Roll of the Law belongs to all Israel". True, this is not the only point under dispute, but it is a significant one. At the bottom of Hyrcanus' dispute with the Pharisees lay the question of their interpretation of what constituted the Law of Moses, the Oral Law as well as the Written Law, as the Pharisees asserted, or the Written Law alone, as the Sadducees held (cf. Josephus, *Antiq.*, XIII, X, 6). But Abu'l Fath is rewriting history, and he is trying to gloss over the Samaritan schism. Hyrcanus the Samaritans knew. He provided the central fact in Samaritan history, the destruction of their temple and the end of the period of Divine Grace. History is therefore rewritten; in fact, a lengthy history must be found for the sect. The Tabernacle was destroyed in the time of Eli, and it was then that the period of Divine Grace came to an end; that is one version of the story. Another version is the one given here, namely that the temple, admittedly a temple built only after the Babylonian Exile, was destroyed by Simeon, when the Jews were building their second Temple. Hyrcanus could be used also to explain the schism between Jews and Samaritans, for after all he was associated with a religious schism; this it would appear is how Abu'l Fath was reasoning.

18. Ithamar - a significant name. Ithamar was the youngest son of Aaron, and Eli was descended from him. True, in the time of Solomon the Zadokite priesthood supplanted the house of Ithamar. As 1 Chron. 6:1-15 (Eng.) shows the Zadokite priesthood were supposed to have descended from Eleazar, Aaron's elder son. The Samaritans claimed that the Jewish priesthood was descended from Ithamar, while theirs traced its origin to Eleazar.

19. Manasseh. This name reminds one of the Manasseh who was made high priest among the Samaritans (Josephus, *Antiq.*, XII, IV, I; cf. also *ibid.*, XI, VII, 2: Manasseh, the son of Jaddua, high priest of the Jews, who married Sanballat's daughter. Cf. also Neh. 13:28). It would appear that Abu'l Fatḥ is here being remarkably honest as to the origin of the Samaritan priesthood. Josephus says that Sanballat gave his daughter in marriage to Manasseh in an attempt to get the goodwill of the Jews, while Neh. 13:29 shows how this attempt failed. It is significant that Abu'l Fatḥ admits the failure of the adjudicator and that he said, among other things, that "Mount Gerizim belongs to you, and to them, and to all Israel". The Jews could not accept any other sacred site for the sanctuary but Zion.

20. The meadow of al-Bahā: meadow at Nablus (cf. note 41 on Sam. Joshua ch. 39 p.73 of this present work, but the reference must be to a territorial dispute between Samaritans and Jews). Cf. Josephus, *Antiq.*, XII, IV, 1. Josephus, speaking of the Ptolemaic period, admits that the Samaritans were in a flourishing condition and much distressed the Jews, cutting off parts of their land and carrying off slaves.

21. This much was accepted by both Jew and Samaritan.

22. Probably a reference in advance to the destruction of Jerusalem by the Roman Emperors Vespanian and Titus in 70 A.D., or even to the Hadrianic war of the third decade of the second century A.D. This latter is preferable, for it was then that the Samaritans rebuilt their temple. Just as Abu'l Fatḥ antedated the events of Hyrcanus' reign, so he now antedates on an even greater scale the events of the first and second centuries A.D.

23. In the Chronicle Adler (*REJ*, XLV (1902), 72-73) the appearance of the Dustān sect is placed in the high priesthoods of Hanan and Hezekiah, the immediate successors of Amram III.

Patristic writers know of a Dositheus who was an early Samaritan heresiarch (cf. Montgomery, *ibid.*, p.255ff.). A Dosithean sect was in existence far into the Arab period.

The name, according to Photius, was Dosthes or Dositheos. Epiphanius (*Haeres*, I, 13) calls the leader of the sect Dositheus, but is obviously speaking of the same person as is Abu'l Fatḥ when dealing with Dūsīs. It is therefore not impossible that the founder of the Dustān and Dūsīs sects are the same person, and that the Dustān mentioned as having arisen before the time of Alexander and the various Dūsīs sects which are mentioned in the discussion of the events of the fourth century A.D. are, if not identical with, then variants of, the same sect. While it is possible that a Dosithean sect existed at an early date among the Samaritans, Montgomery's attempt, (*ibid.*, p.260-262) to harmonize the great discrepancy in date between the Dustān sect and the followers of Dūsīs according to Abu'l Fatḥ's chronology, is indeed brilliant. One may agree with his conclusion (ibid., p.262) that there were two sects founded by and named after different persons called Dositheus. But we are faced with the fact that only in connection with the rise of the Dūsīs sect is a heresiarch mentioned; while the Dustān sect is described as a sect, we are told nothing of the heresiarch who founded it. While it is true that the tenets and practices of the Dustān sect and those of the Dūsīs heresy are in a considerable measure different, they are hardly as different as those of the various heresies cited by Abu'l Fatḥ immediately after the Dūsīs heresy which all stemmed from that heresy. Montgomery took Abu'l Fatḥ's chronology too seriously. The fact that the Dustān sect is mentioned in the Persian period is not necessarily of any value chronologically, any more than the mention of the Maccabees as active in the Persian period. Abu'l Fatḥ is concerned with apologetics. The Pirḳe de R. Eliezer, late though it is, was certainly written some hundreds of years before Abu'l Fatḥ's Chronicle. It is not impossible that the Samaritans knew the Pirḳe de R. Eliezer or at least the material from which the Pirḳe de R. Eliezer was compiled (cf. e.g., the resemblances between material in the Memra Marḳah and that in Pirḳe de R. Eliezer; and Marḳah lived in the 4th century A.D.).

Pirke de R. Eliezer mentions Dosethai or Dostai as coming to the Kutheans settled in Northern Israelite territory, and teaching them what knowledge of the Law the Samaritans have. Abu'l Fatḥ mentions the Dustān sect not long after he has been discussing the reason for the opprobrious term "Kutheans", but he carefully makes it clear that the Dustān were heretics. The introduction of the Dustān sect here can hardly be accidental - its apologetic value is patent.

The Tolidah mentions only the heretic of the time of the High Priest 'Aḳbon, i.e., of the fourth century. Instead of calling him Dūsīs the son of Fufali, the Tolidah says Dustis ben Philphuli came to Shechem. As in Abu'l Fatḥ, he is not of

Samaritan origin, but a scion of the mixed rabble who went out with the Israelites from Egypt. No mention is made of his pact with the Jews to cause trouble in Nablus. It would be foolhardy to maintain that the sect of Dustān and that of Dūsīs are different, when the form of the name Dūsīs can also be given as Dustis by a Samaritan source. Was the Dustān story inserted here by Abu'l Fatḥ to blanket the Jewish allegation of general Samaritan heterodoxy?

24. Al-Dustān. De Sacy (*op. cit.*) tried to explain the name as originally Darastān, from the Arabic *darasa*, "to efface", taking this as a reference to their abolition of the festivals and traditions. Abu'l Fatḥ p.161-2 refers to the tenets of a Samaritan sect led by Šalyah the son of Ṭairūn the son of Nīn, which was based on the teaching of Dūsīs, at least in its origin. On p.162 we are told that Šalyah said that he was the father of all who accepted his teaching, and that the Dustān addressed him as 'our father'. Abu'l Fatḥ tells us also that his disciples used to say:"May God cause the spirit of our father Šalyah to pour forth". The name Dustān probably means Friends, Colleagues, and if so is derived from a Persian expression. The Jewish Pharisees used to call themselves *haberim* = colleagues. Whether this be the case or not, the fact that Dustān is used again in connection with a sect at least inspired by that of Dūsīs, points to a connection between the sect of Dustān here mentioned, and that of Dūsīs (see below in our third extract). It is possible that Abu'l Fatḥ has altered the word form, in order to give an intelligible meaning (or what would appear to him as such) to the name. In Pirke de R. Eliezer (ed. G. Friedlander p.299) it is asserted that when the Israelites were exiled from Samaria (cf. 2 Kings 17) and the inhabitants of various nations were brought in, the King at the request of the new inhabitants sent Rabbi Dosethai and Rabbi Micaiah to them. It might be unsafe to put too much weight on this evidence, but it is interesting that Abu'l Fatḥ mentions the Dustān sect after a section in which he has been trying to explain away the designation of the Samaritans as Kutheans (a libel based on 2 Kings 17).

25. According to the Rabbis (M. Nid. 1:1-3) even from the most lenient point of view a woman was considered unclean from the moment she noticed the flow.

26. "From sunset to sunset" - cf. perhaps Lev. 23:32, the Day of Atonement: *from evening to evening*. Clearly they thought that the count should begin at sunset of the day in which the blood was first noticed, i.e. at the legal beginning of the next day, the "morrow" (i.e. for example, if the blood first appeared Monday morning, they thought the count should begin Monday evening at sunset, which is legally the beginning of Tuesday).

27. While it might be argued that this ban on the eating of eggs,except those found in slaughtered birds, was inspired by regard for the preservation of young life and the perpetuation of the species, it is more likely that they felt that eggs, in as much as they contain the germ of life, could not be eaten unless sacrificially slaughtered. This of course could not be done; but if the hen were slaughtered sacrificially, the eggs within her body would be included in the sacrifice.

28. It is not clear whether or not this refers merely to unclean beasts, but cf. M. Hul. 4:3, where the question of the young of a beast dying in its mother's womb is discussed as to whether it conveys uncleanness or not. The prevailing rule is that the herdsman who touched it is clean, whether it is a clean or unclean beast. R. Jose the Galilean thought that he would be unclean if it were an unclean beast. Does the Dustān ruling show a tendency towards vegetarianism? It is interesting that Šalyah ben Ṭairun ben Nīn (see below in the second translated extract; or Ṡaktu ben Ṭabrin ben Nin, as Chron. Adler calls him, leader of one of the sects stemming from Dūsīs, apparently insisted on vegetarianism, though he did not regard any animals as unclean. But here the meaning of Abu'l Fatḥ's text is: "they forbade the eating of an unborn foetus found inside the womb of a dead animal". This rule in itself shows no tendency towards vegetarianism - the question is simply, should the foetus be regarded as live flesh, and therefore permitted, or dead flesh, and therefore forbidden.

29. Šalyah, leader of one of the sects stemming from that of Dūsīs, minimized corpse uncleanness; proximity to a tomb or corpse did not convey uncleanness, but only actual contact conveyed it; purification in such cases was only for one day. The sect of the sons of Joṣadaḳ or the sons of Ṣadoḳ (Adler, *op. cit.*), while agreeing with much of Šalyah's teaching, insisted that corpse uncleanness was conveyed without contact, and that a man must purify himself by bathing on the first day of being near a corpse. But in such a case the Rabbis would have said that the man had contracted a seven day uncleanness (cf. M. 'Oh. 15:8, 10).

30. This probably was a parallel development to what happened in Judaism with the perpetual *ḳĕre, Adonai,* for the Tetragrammaton. It is interesting that Šalyah and his sect likewise refused to pronounce the Tetragrammaton; he read instead, "Blessed be He".

31. This on the face of it refers to some book said to have belonged to the children of Moses, unless "children of the Messenger of God" is a reference to themselves as the disciples

of the Dustān heresiarch. (Cf. below p172) 'the sons of Jozadak', for a possible similar use of the term 'sons' for disciples.

32. The land of Zawīla is unknown. It would mean that they held, like at least some of the sects deriving from Dūsīs (e.g. that of Šalyah), that Gerizim was but the substitute for the everlasting mountain. The name Zawīla itself is certainly not unknown. Yākūt (*Ma'jam al-buldān*, ed. Wustenfeld II 961ff.) names two towns called Zawīla, one in the Sudan, the other in the province of Africa (Ifriḳiya); there is also a district in Cairo, so called. I am indebted to Prof. Nemoy for this information on the occurrences of the name Zawīla. It is probable that the land of Zawīla is Egypt. Could the book referred to, in which it was stated that God shall be worshipped in the land of Zawīla, be a version of Isaiah or at least have contained Isa. 19:18-22?

33. According to the introduction to the Tolidah, the true calculation of the calendar was a secret in the possession of the Samaritan high priests, handed down from Adam who received it from God. Professor Edward Robertson, in the *John Rylands Bulletin*, XXIII (1939) p.461f., shows convincingly that the Samaritans of the Middle Ages and later used al-Battānī's tables. It is interesting that Abu'l Fatḥ, or his source, admits that as early as the time of the Dustān sect (thought by Abu'l Fatḥ to belong in the fifth century B.C.) astronomical tables were used.

33a. This making the months uniformly of 30 days duration is based on Gen. 7:11, 24; 8:3-4 from which it appears that 150 days constituted 5 months, or 30 days per month. According to al-Ḳirḳisānī (cf. *HUCA*, VII (1930), p.363) the same thing was adopted by the Sadducees.

34. This abolition of festivals and of the commandment to fast and mortify oneself is something that finds echoes in quite a number of the sects stemming from that of Dūsīs. In the Dūsīs sect itself all festivals were abolished, and only the Sabbath was kept. Ansma's sect (if indeed it be another sect separate from the Ba'unai, and not a second account given by Abu'l Fatḥ of the Ba'unai) attempted to abolish the festivals and Ansma denied the authority for keeping them. Šalyah changed the festivals. While the sons of Joṣadak ascribed special sanctity to all the Sabbaths, nothing is said of their attitude to the festivals, but it is not unlikely that it was different from that of the other Dūsīs sects. The fact that the Dustān sect and the Dūsīs sect abolished the festivals is a pointer toward the possible common origin of the Dustān and Dūsīs

heresies. As to the Dustān's abolition of the commandment of fasting and mortification, one may not be entirely wrong in seeing in this not only a decided attempt to tamper with the dictates of the Law, but as in the case of some of the sects, though not all, a reaction against asceticism. What is more important to observe is the freedom which the sectaries claimed in abolishing some commandments of the Law. The followers of Dūsīs, we are told, had to fast seven nights before seeing the palm leaves of Levi and before reading Dūsīs' manuscripts. They said that not all the commandments had been abolished, implying that some had. We are told by Abu'l Fatḥ that the sons of Jozadak, a sect stemming from the Dūsīs sect proper, differed from Šalyah's sect, which was also derived eventually from that of Dūsīs, in holding on to the positive and negative commandments of the Law, whereas the Ḳilṭai sect, also inspired by Dūsīs, abolished the commandments.

35. The fifty days between Passover and Pentecost. Samaritans, Ḳaraites, Christians, and Sadducees, all counted the fifty days from the morrow of the first Sabbath following the Passover; the Pharisees and their Rabbinic successors interpreted the Sabbath in question, mentioned in Lev. 23:15, as meaning the Passover.

35a. They thought that unless uncleanness is certain, a house is presumed to be clean and that the inspecting priest therefore cannot contract uncleanness, so long as he *says nothing* until he has left the suspected house - i.e. so long as he waits until he is outside before confirming the suspicion.

36. Cf. perhaps the dictum of R. Eliezer when he had seen a starling go beside a raven: "Not without cause does the starling consort with the raven, for he is of its kind". (T.B. B.Ḳ. 92b) But the attraction of one kindred bird to another is not the same thing as the attraction (supposed) of an unclean bird to a temporarily unclean house.

37. Cf. J. Bowman, "A Megillat Setarim (?)", *Journal of Jewish Studies*, II (1950/51), p.31ff. Obviously this sect were strict Sabbatarians. This seems to have been the strong point of the Dūsīs sect. The latter did not walk from house to house on the Sabbath Day, i.e. from one domain to another. It follows *a fortiori* that if they did not walk from one house to another on the Sabbath, neither did they carry anything from one house to another, and so had no *'erub*, as indeed neither have the Samaritans of today. The Dūsīs sect, if in doubt as to whether a given day was the Sabbath, would not take their hands out of their sleeves on that day. The sons of Jozadak, a sect inspired by Dūsīs, gave special sanctity to all Sabbaths.

38. In this use of earthen vessels on the Sabbath which, if they became ritually unclean, would offer no temptation to clean them (as earthenware cannot be purified when defiled), the Dustān sects reminds us of the strict Sabbatarianism of the Damascus sectaries.

39. This goes beyond even the strictness of the Damascus sectaries, who did allow a man to walk not over two thousand cubits in order to pasture his animals; cf. C. Rabin, *The Zadokite Documents*, Oxford, 1954, p.54, XIV, 28.

40. Abu'l Fatḥ mentions that in the time of Baba Raba (see below p.145) the Sabua'i refused to obey him and had their own ecclesiastical organisation.

41. *zr'h* in Vilman's text, *zara'ahu* ("he sowed him"), by slight emendation can be read *Zur'a* which is a recognised Arab name. Sura is obviously not the priest's real name. Doubtless some Hebrew name either lies behind it or is hinted by it. Could it have been 'Ezra? Certainly Zur'a and 'Ezra have the three consonants *'zr* in common though in different order. One wonders if Abu'l Fatḥ brought in this story of the High Priest's son becoming the leader of the Dustān sect, as a sort of parallel to what happened in the Jewish community when Jaddua's son Manasseh married Sanballat's daughter and thereby disqualified himself in the eyes of Ezra's followers. Is he rebutting the story in Neh. 13:28 by explaining that a Samaritan High Priest's son did misbehave and became the head of a sect, that this is the true story, and that of course it is unthinkable that a Jewish High Priest's son could have become High Priest of the Samaritan community?

NOTES ON SECTION pp.94-104 OF ABU'L FATḤ VILMAR's EDITION.

42. The Tolidah mentions Hezekiah (a later Hezekiah than the one mentioned in the preceding extract) and adds: "at this time there came Alexander, the king of Macedonia, and conquered all the earth". It thereupon proceeds to mention Dalyah, but the sole information it gives about him is that he was High Priest for forty-two years.

The Chronicle Adler (*REJ* XLV (1902) p.74-75) is clearly dependent on Abu'l Fatḥ for the period covered by the section which we have here translated; in fact when Chronicle Adler mentions in passing the *apologia* of the Samaritans for their beliefs, it points out that they are given in full in the Book of Chronicles (meaning Abu'l Fatḥ).

43. Faltama: for the identification with Ptolemy see Vilmar's Prolegomena, p.LXII. But Adler (*ibid.*, p.74) in a note thinks "Phaltama" is a corruption of Philometor, confused with Philadephus. Ptolemy Philadelphus was the Ptolemy in whose reign the translation was made; cf. Josephus, *Antiq.*, XII, II, I.

44. Cf. Josephus, *ibid.*

45. According to Josephus (*ibid.*), Ptolemy simply wanted a translation of the "many books of laws among the Jews worthy of inquiring after, and worthy of the king's library". Josephus gives no hint of Ptolemy's wanting a translation of the Torah in order to adjudicate upon the Samaritan and Jewish claims regarding it. There were of course numerous Samaritans as well as Jews in Egypt at that time.

46. Josephus (*ibid.*, 4) states that Demetrius, Ptolemy's librarian, asked for six elders out of every tribe. (cf. also *ibid.*, 5, Ptolemy's letter to the Jewish High Priest), but mentions no request for a similar deputation from the Samaritans.

47. That this is the well known Symmachus, the Greek translator of the Bible, seem unlikely, since the discrepancy in dating would rule out the identification. What is more likely is that Abu'l Fatḥ is claiming Symmachus as a Samaritan, and projecting him back into the alleged period of the origin of the Septuagint.

48. Josephus tells us that Eleazar was the name of the Jewish High Priest who was approached with the request to supply the seventy-two translators.

49. Cf. Josephus (*ibid.*, 11, end) who says that Ptolemy ordered that excellent lodgings be provided for them in the upper part of the city.

50. Cf. T.B. Meg. 3a, where the same is said to have happened when Jonathan ben Uzziel translated the Prophets into Aramaic. Cf. also Josephus (*Antiq.*, XII, II, 14) where Ptolemy is told by Demetrius, his librarian, that Theopompus and Theodectes had been stricken with madness and blindness, respectively, when they attempted to make reference to what was in the sacred books. In Josephus this is given as an answer to Ptolemy's question why non-Hebrew writers had not made reference to the Law; it is part of Josephus' apologetic. In Abu'l Fatḥ and in the Talmud it is rather the fear that the Law, the special revelation to Israel, might be misunderstood by the Gentiles.

51. This account of the comparison of the two recensions by Ptolemy is of course not in Josephus, but is part of Abu'l Fatḥ's defense of the superiority of the Samaritan version. The arguments may be older than he, it was a well-worn theme. That there was a Samaritan Greek recension is not unlikely, since there was a large Samaritan community in Hellenistic Egypt. It is not impossible that such a disputation indeed took place; cf. Josephus's account (*Antiq.* XIII, III, 4) of a similar dispute before Ptolemy Philometor, in which Sabbeus and Theodosius were to manage the argument for the Samaritans and Andronicus for the Jews. The dispute was about their temples, the one at Gerizim and the one at Jerusalem, "the Jews saying that according to the Law of Moses the Temple was to be built at Jerusalem, and the Samaritans saying that it was to be built at Gerizim". Note the part that the place which God has chosen (see the next note) would occupy in such a disputation. It is interesting that the demonstration of each side's case was to be made according to the Law. Andronicus, the Jewish spokesman, spoke first, according to Josephus, and was apparently so successful that the Samaritans were adjudged the losers, without even stating their case.

52. Reference presumably here is to the special Samaritan Tenth Commandment (see above), in which reference is explicitly made to the altar which is to be built on Mount Gerizim; it is based on the Samaritan reading of Deut. 27:4, and the Samaritan reading of 'the place which God has chosen' instead of 'which God shall choose' as in the Jewish Bible, cf. Deut. 12:11, 14, 18, 21, 26; 14:23, 24, 25; 15:20; 16:2, 6, 7, 11, 15, 16; 17:8, 10; 18:6; 23:16; 31:11.

53. The Samaritan faces towards Mount Gerizim when praying. Mount Gerizim is the place which God had chosen, while Jerusalem in any case did not become the site of the Jewish sanctuary till the time of David and Solomon. Samaritans would say that God had chosen Gerizim from the beginning of the world as His sanctuary. The Jewish *reading* would justify the future choice of Jerusalem.

54. Cf. Exod. 20:3.

55. A reference to the special Samaritan tenth commandment. "The marks of His majesty and His dignity" refer not only to the command to worship God on Mount Gerizim but to the much enlarged ending to Ex. 20 found in the Samaritan version incorporating Deut. 5:24-27 after 'and said to Moses' of Ex. 20:19 and before Ex. 20:21. After Ex. 20:21 both Deut. 18:18-22 and Deut. 5:28-31 are inserted between the beginning and the rest of Ex. 20:22. Thereafter the ending is the same as Ex. 20,

Jewish version, except that in verse 24 instead of 'in every place' but merely 'in the place' is read.

56. This allegation that Moses died without informing (the people) of "the place" possibly refers to Deut. 31:11 the last reference in the Torah to "the place which God will choose", coming as it does shortly before the death of Moses, Deut. 34:5 notification of which impending event is given to him in Deut. 31:14.

57. Mount Gerizim understood as the place which God has chosen. The reference to offering a sacrifice must be a loose reference to the offerings detailed in Deut. 12, 14 and 16 as to be made at the Place which God had chosen. The quotation "year by year" apparently is from Deut. 14:22 referring to the annual tithe; but used by Abu'l Fatḥ to cover all offerings.

58. This argument is of force in the eyes of the Samaritans who accepted all the Law as Mosaic and given at Sinai; God they argued must have chosen a Place for His worship and made it known to Israel. Where could the offerings, if already commanded, be offered by Israel before the Jerusalem sanctuary was instituted?. In any case did not Joshua and the tribes act in accordance with Moses' injunction, Deut. 27:4 to set up the stones on Mount Gerizim (Sam. reading instead of Ebal)? So a Samaritan would argue.

59. The Samaritans held that the Tabernacle stood on Mount Gerizim from the time of the entry into the Land until Eli set up his schismatic (in their eyes) Tabernacle at Shiloh.

60. Abu'l Fatḥ paraphrases Deut. 12:13, 14 here.

61. Deut. 12:14 end is quoted verbatim except 'today' is added.

62. i.e. in the Place which He had chosen. See the commands in Deut. 12:14; 14:23 and 16:6 as to other offerings. See especially Deut. 12:5-7.

63. Gen. 22:2. Cf. Memar Marḳah Book Two as the twelfth of the thirteen names of Mount Gerizim mentioned in scripture.

64. Exod. 15:17: Marḳah does not give 'the mountain of thine inheritance' (RSV 'thy own mountain') as one of the names of Mount Gerizim, but quotes Exod. 15:17, 18 as referring to a proof of Gerizim being the *Har haḳadim* which he gives as the first name of Mount Gerizim.

65. See previous note. Markah does not cite Deut. 33:15 as a proof text for this name of Mount Gerizim.

66. Reference to Gen. 37:34-35.

67. The Samaritan belief is that Eden was situated on Gerizim, and Paradise will be revealed on the Day of Resurrection there too.

68. Gerizim was in Ephraimite territory. The Samaritans claim descent from Joseph.

69. Cf. note (25). From the site of the resurrection and Paradise being at Mount Gerizim, Abu'l Fatḥ passes on to show how that being so, Mount Gerizim is a witness to a Day of Judgement, and belief in such he argues keeps men moral.

70. Deut. 32:35. The LXX has the Samaritan reading here in Deut. 32:35. The reading of the Day of Vengeance and Recompense seems to have been known to the Jewish Targumists, cf. Pseudo-Jonathan op. cit. which has both readings in mind.

71. Cf. Deut. 32:33.

72. Ibid. v.32.

73. Ibid. vv. 34-35.

74. Ibid. v.39.

75. Ibid. v.43a.

76. Cf. ibid. v.43b.

77. Cf. ibid. v.43 end.

78. Cf. Num. 19:16.

79. Cf. Ibid. v.19.

80. Ptolemy Philadelphus, but cf. Josephus *Antiq.* XII, II, 13. Ptolemy there adores the Jewish version and ordered that it should be uncorrupted. Abu'l Fatḥ admitted that there was a Jewish verion; that was more than Josephus did, vis-a-vis the Samaritans and their version.

81. The Samaritans have only the Law as canonical. The patriarchs ante-deluvian and post-deluvian were prophets, but Moses is the greatest and last of the prophets.

82. Deut. 34:10a.

83. Deut. 12:32b.

84. True, the Samaritans have been very conservative. Abrogation was not impossible in Rabbinic Judaism, e.g. cf. the work of John Hyrcanus and his alteration of Tithe Law, cf. M. Sota 9:10, T.B. Sota 48a, or Hillel and the Prozbol which in effect abrogated one aspect of the Šemittah year. (cf. M.Sheb. 10:3).

85. Cf. Num. 11:16, 24, 25. In the Jewish story of the seventy men who translated the Law into Greek, it may have been not without deliberate intention that the number was fixed at seventy as offering a parallel to the seventy elders who in Num. 11:25 received some of the spirit that was on Moses. Does Abu'l Fatḥ here intend to give a parallel to M. Aboth 1:1, but implying that the Samaritans are nearer the fountain head than the Jews?

86. A clever touch in an address to a heathen King, for Samaritanism now, if not then, offers hope only for its own community of Samaritans.

87. The Samaritans as even their present customs show, took Ex. 23:14-17 (cf. also Deut. 16), seriously. Thrice a year they made pilgrimage to Mount Gerizim, in their eyes the place which God chose.

88. Cf. also Chronicle Adler (*REJ* XLV (1902), 73): "After these events, all the children of Israel were divided into three sects, the Sadducees, the Pharisees and the Hasidim. The last sect was composed of the Samaritans, who are the children of Joseph and Phinehas and some who joined themselves to them from the other tribes. Apart from the statement in Josephus *Antiq.* XIII, V, 9 (beginning) that there were three sects among the Jews, one can hardly find resemblance in Abu'l Fatḥ to anything Josephus says here or elsewhere on the three sects.

89. The Eleazar who was according to Abu'l Fatḥ the head of the Jewish contingent of Bible translators at Alexandria.

90. Cf. Josephus *Antiq.* XIII, X, 6, Abu'l Fatḥ is probably referring to the Sadducees' refusal to accept anything as obligatory unless it was in the Written Law. The traditions of the Pharisees and Rabbis as to observances not stated in the Law, they could not accept. It may be that the concept of the Oral Law as also itself having been given at Sinai was (cf. Lauterbach *JQR* 1915, Midrash and Mishnah, v.503-27, vi.23-95,

303-23) an attempt by the Pharisees to bring under the aegis of the Law, observances which had become customary and for which no clear basis in Scripture could be found. Then in the second century C.E. a deliberate attempt was made by Akiba and his school to find an *Asmakta* for them by the use of the complicated system of *Ribbui u miut.*

91. Analogy was also used by the Rabbis.

92. This cannot be a reference, unless mistaken, to Mishnah and Talmudim because they were not compiled in the time of the Sadducees, let alone written. It may be that Abu'l Fatḥ is arguing that the Sadducees refused not only to accept the "Traditions of the Elders" cf. Mark 7:5 but the rest of the Bible apart from the Law i.e. the *N^{e}bi'im and k^{e}tubim.*

93. Jerusalem, called Aelia Capitolana when rebuilt by Hadrian.

94. If Abu'l Fatḥ is indebted to Josephs *op. cit.* for mention of the three Jewish sects, then it would appear that he means by Hasidim, the Essenes.

95. If Abu'l Fatḥ means by the Hasidim, Essenes, then it might be that it was because of the Essenes' special honouring of Moses (cf. Josephus *War* II, VIII, 9) and their strict Sabbatarianism (*ibid.*) that Abu'l Fatḥ could say they are nearest to the Samaritans. It might not be without significance that Josephus *War* II, VII, 2 says of the Essenes: "These last are Jews by birth".

96. Cf. Josephus *War* II, VIII, 4 'They have no certain city, but many of them dwell in every city'. Presumably even in those near the Samaritans.

97. Mount Gerizim. They may have devoted themselves to worship in villages near Mount Gerizim, as they would have done anywhere else; Abu'l Fatḥ is surely wrong in suggesting that their worship was in any way connected with the proximity of Mount Gerizim.

98. The elders who separated must be the Pharisees. Cf. Josephus *Antiq.* XIII, X, 5.

99. Cf. Josephus *ibid.* (towards end). 'Book of religious law must refer to the "great many observances by succession from their fathers which are not written in the Law of Moses", i.e. the Oral Law.

100. This short speech of John Hyrcanus is clearly dependent on the speech in Josephus' account *Antiq.* XIII, X, 5.

101. There is no exact parallel to this in Josephus' account according to which the Pharisees attested to his being entirely virtuous.

102. Eleazar is also mentioned by Josephus *ibid.* Abu'l Fatḥ omits Josephus' strictures on the character and conduct of Eleazar.

103. This is a detail not in Josephus.

104. Eleazar's speech as recorded by Abu'l Fatḥ is a practically exact parallel of that in Josephus. Josephus however gives the last accusation as a separate speech by Eleazar in answer to Hyrcanus' query why he should give up the priesthood; in Abu'l Fatḥ, Eleazar's demand for Hyrcanus to give up the high priesthood and his allegation of his unfitness for the office are delivered together in one speech. The insinuation was that Hyrcanus was a *Mamzer* (i.e. bastard) and unfit to be a priest.

105. i.e. Hyrcanus. This reported speech by Hyrcanus is not in Josephus. Josephus merely states that Eleazar's story was false. Abu'l Fatḥ's report of Hyrcanus' speech is feasible, and the additional information that Simeon (John's father and his wife had actually hid in a mountain cave is of some interest).

106. This presents difficulties for had Hyrcanus given up the High Priesthood, there would have been other Sadducean priestly leaders. Pharisaic priests there may have been, though the party was predominantly lay.

107. Cf. Josephus *ibid.* where Jonathan instigates John Hyrcanus to put the question.

108. i.e. The Pharisees. According to Josephus, Jonathan tells Hyrcanus that the Pharisees by advocating a light sentence would show that they all were implicated in Eleazar's demand for him to give up the High Priesthood and that they likewise were associated in his libellous insinuation. In Abu'l Fatḥ this is not implied. It may be that when the elders said to him: "We want to know the sentence", that they want to know the Sadducean sentence. Abu'l Fatḥ does not tell us at once what John demanded, nor does Josephus, though we get a hint of what Josephus thought it was in, "but it did not seem right to punish reproaches with death". From Abu'l Fatḥ we see that this was not what John demanded, but that he should make an

offering and be struck forty times.

109. There is no mention in Josephus *ibid.*, of the Pharisees demanding as punishment that Eleazar as a false witness should either make an offering *or* be struck forty times. There in Josephus we are told that he deserved stripes to bonds.

110. Josephus does not say how many stripes the false witness Eleazar should get according to the view of his fellow-Pharisees. Abu'l Fatḥ is more exact in this respect. The Biblical legislation on the false witness was Deut. 19:19 'you should do to him as he had meant to do to his brother'; Deut. 25:1ff. was applied by T.B.Makk. 2b to false witnesses. But as M. Makk. 1:1 said (If they had said of a Priest) 'We testify that such-a-one is the son of a divorced woman or the son of a woman that performed halitzah, we cannot say: 'Let him be made in his stead the son of a divorced woman or the son of a woman that performed halitzah but he must suffer the Forty Stripes'. (Danby's translation). From Deut. 25:3 the sentence of the 40 stripes was derived. The case is parallel to that set the Pharisees by Hyrcanus. Josephus is unfair to the Sadducees in suggesting that they would have demanded the death penalty. We do not have evidence of the Sadducean ruling on this point, but it is unlikely that in view of Deut. 19:19 they could have demanded the death penalty, as that bore no relation to Eleazar's false testimony. It may be that they would have demanded a sacrifice as well as the stripes since the honour of a high priest was at stake.

111. Cf. Josephus *ibid.*

112. Abu'l Fatḥ's explanation of when the Pharisees received their name and from whom, is quite plausible.

113. Josephus does not tell this of John Hyrcanus; it reminds one of the charges that are brought against Jannai in rabbinic sources.

114. This seems most unlikely.

115. Abu'l Fatḥ is on the whole right here in his chronology cf. Josephus *Antiq.* XIII, IX, 1, *War* I, II, 6 and *Antiq.* XIII, X, 2 in that this that he is now going to relate happened before Hyrcanus' dispute with the Pharisees; but Hyrcanus according to Josephus dealt with Sebaṣte after Shechem (Nablus).

116. According to Josephus *Antiq.* XIII, IX, 1. Hyrcanus did take Shechem and Gerizim and left the temple devastated.

117. It is to say the least highly improbable that Hyrcanus made a pilgrimage to Shechem and Gerizim other than to destroy. The Samaritans could not stop Hyrcanus and his forces. Abu'l Fatḥ wants to associate the hostility of Jew to Samaritan with the Pharisee; in this little haggada he tells of how Hyrcanus was a changed man, better disposed to the Samaritans when he became a Sadducee and left the Pharisees. Actually Abu'l Fatḥ knew the truth about Hyrcanus, cf. above the story of Simeon and 'Arkiya and what they did to the temple on Gerizim.

NOTES ON THE THIRD TRANSLATED EXCERPT FROM ABU'L FATḤ

pp. 121-

118. 'Aḳbon: according to the Tolidah 'Aḳbon was the fourth high priest from the time of Hadrian. The Tolidah gives no other details about 'Aḳbon except that he was high priest for twenty three years.

119. The emperor Commodus (180-192), cf. "Chronicle Adler", *REJ*, XLV (1902), pp. 85-86, gives details largely derived from Abu'l Fatḥ of the persecution of the Samaritans by Commodus during the high priesthood of 'Aḳbon. Cf. Montgomery *ibid.* pp.93-94 who suggests that as nothing is known from classical sources of persecution by Commodus of Israelites that it may be Verus Commodus, successor of Marcus Aurelius who is referred to.

120. Cf. also Chronicle Adler *ibid.* p.86.

121. According to the Samaritan Book of Joshua this loss had been incurred in the days of Hadrian. Book of Joshua XLVII Juynboll's edition.

122. Cf. Chronicle Adler op. cit. which says they were flayed in front of their father's eyes.

123. Cf. Chronicle Adler *ibid.* p.85 which says that he prohibited them from reading the sacred Torah.

124. So also Chronicle Adler.

125. Chronicle Adler: Ardashir the son of Babel. This marks the rise of the Sassanid Kingdom of Persia. The date given is remarkably almost exact cf. Montgomery *ibid.* p.96.

126. Cf. also Chronicle Adler *ibid.* p.86 where the embassy is mentioned: according to that source Ahirod and Joseph were

sent to ask help against the Romans. Abu'l Fatḥ states that Ardashir had been victorious against the Romans, and speaks as if the Samaritans were afraid of Ardashir.

127. There is no mention of the birth of Nathanel in Chronicle Adler. Nathanel was the next high priest but neither in Tolidah nor Chronicle Adler is his relationship to 'Aḳbon stated.

128. Severus i.e. Septimus Severus (193-211). The Samaritans had apparently helped Niger Pescennius, Severus' rival, as a result Severus "took away the right of citizenship from the people of Neapolis in Palestine because they had for a long time been in arms for Niger's cause". (cf. Spartianus, Severus quoted by Montgomery *ibid.* p.94). Eventually Severus pardoned the Palestinians for having supported Niger, and restored them civic rights; but he in 202 took repressive action against Jews and Christians, and presumably the Samaritans suffered too, as Montgomery surmises (*ibid.* p.95). We can agree with Montgomery that Abu'l Fatḥ 'preserves a fairly accurate reflection of this reign' (ibid. p.95).

129. Alexander Severus (222-235).

130. Either an expression of his trust in God, or a dramatic touch by Abu'l Fatḥ making the dying 'Aḳbon prophesy the coming of Baba Raba.

131. The Tolidah also gives the period of office of Nathanel as thirty two years. The Tolidah furnishes us with no information as to the events of his high priesthood.

132. Alexander Severus (cf. note 129). Chronicle Adler agrees with Abu'l Fatḥ in saying that Alexander (Severus) persecuted the Samaritans worse than Commodus. We note that Chronicle Adler does not mention Septimus Severus (193-211) and regards Commodus as having been the immediate predecessor of Alexander Severus. Montgomery *ibid.* pp.95-96 points out the difficulty of Alexander Severus being portrayed as a persecutor, since he is noted for his humanity and liberality. Montgomery's suggestion (*ibid.* p.96) is feasible that Carcalla (211-217) who dubbed himself Alexander may have been confused by Abu'l Fatḥ with Alexander Severus.

133. Cf. Chronicle Adler *ibid.* p.86 which says that any man found prostrating himself before another god than ours is to be put to death. This gives the sense more clearly than Abu'l Fatḥ; presumably the Samaritans had to withdraw outside the city to worship in their own way and towards Mount Gerizim.

134. Chronicler Adler *ibid.* p.86-87 makes it clear that the coins were Shekels. The reward may have been paid out of the dead man's effects (cf. Chronicle Adler *ibid.* p.87 note 1).

135. Chronicle Adler *ibid.* p.87 is briefer and does not specify the imprisonment of little children, crucifixion of wise men, killing of young men, and the burning of them in caves, or the rape of girls. But it does mention that the same treatment was meted out to Jews as well as to Samaritans.

136. Cf. also Chronicle Adler *ibid.* p.87.

137. Cf. Deut. 28:66, 67.

138. The Tolidah (*ibid.* p.442) only mentions Baba as successor in the high priesthood to Nathanel. Later on p. 442 it mentions that 'Aḳbon the brother of Baba succeeded Baba as high priest. Phinehas is not mentioned in the Tolidah. Chronicle Adler *ibid.* p.87 mentions Nathanel's three sons and adds a valuable topographical note that Mahana 'the place of Phinehas' home was a township at the foot of Mount Gerizim.

139. Cf. Gen. 34:25, 26.

140. Cf. Exod. 32:26-29.

141. Cf. Num. 25:7-12.

142. Cf. Chronicle Adler *ibid.* p.87-89 for Baba's going up the mountain and supplicating God; the text of the prayers in Chronicle Adler shows some slight points of contact with that in Abu'l Fatḥ particularly at the beginning and end.

143. So also Chronicle Adler p.89. Tolidah *ibid.* p.403 says he built synagogues. Neubauer translates wrongly in the singular, *ibid.* p.440.

144. So also Chronicle Adler p.89. Tolidah informs us that he taught the reading of the Law and established schools (*Batte Alpana*).

145. Cf. Chronicle Adler *ibid.* p.89.

146. Cf. Chronicle Adler *ibid.* p.90.

147. *Hahamim* Cf. the title *Haham* given to Rabbis among the Sephardim.

148. Chronicle Adler *ibid.* p.90 is not explicit about the

change which Baba introduced. True in detailing the seven sages, Chronicle Adler mentions in the main whether one of them was lay or priestly; but it does not state Baba's manifest plan to weaken the power of the priesthood. Baba did not succeed. The Samaritans are conservative and the priests to this day have kept both learning, and ecclesiastical and judicial power in their hands.

149. The scroll of the Law, which is brought out to be adored and kissed at the Sabbath morning; it is similarly brought out and adored at the Sabbath noon service and then the weekly Parashah in the yearly cycle of the Law is read from it. On Festivals the Abisha Scroll is brought out instead of the ordinary sacred scroll, but the Abisha Scroll was already lost in the time of Baba.

150. Actually circumcision should be done by the Samaritan priest. In Nablus today only priests would circumcise, but in Jaffa where there is no priest among the Samaritans a layman would circumcise.

151. This liturgical response apparently before this had only been said by the priest.

152. It is possible for the Samaritan layman to carry out all the service of the synagogue; it was done in the little Samaritan community in Israel (before 1967), but it would not have been done by them if they had had priests. There is no opposition on the part of the laity to the priests. The Samaritans, despite Baba, never advanced to the state the Jews reached with the emergence of the Pharisees in the second century B.C., and certainly not to the non-priestly religion of Judaism of the post 70 A.D. epoch. The Samaritans had no temple in the time of Baba and they have not had since, but they have never liberated themselves from the hereditary priesthood. It is not merely the question of Cohens' "dukaning"; the Cohens of the Samaritans see to it that they are an integral part of Samaritanism. Yet thanks to Baba, what is done at Jaffa is possible and has a respectable precedent.

153. The Tolidah gives the list of the high priests from Adam down! In fairness to the Tolidah one should point out that we are not told that the genealogy of the high priests was missing; but even so this is a frank admission of the break in priestly genealogies as a result of the confused years of persecution. The Tolidah like Abu'l Fath's history is like the curate's egg, good in parts.

154. This reminds one of the haggada about the ordering of

the Beth Din with carefulprecedence given to *Nasi, Ab Beth Din* etc. on which Gamaliel II insisted in order to give greater standing to his Beth Din. cf. T.B. Hor. 13b.

155. The name of the first sage is given in Chronicle Adler *ibid.* p.90 as Arubaī.

156. Interpreter, presumably Meturgeman, among whose duties would be the giving of the Aramaic translation of the Torah. Chronicle Adler *op. cit.* first scribe.

157. From the oak of Moreh to Mahana, so Chronicle Adler *op. cit.*

158. Chronicle Adler, *op. cit.*, has Jacubu from Kefar Sila (Shiloh?). Chronicle Adler does not note that he was an Israelite, i.e. a layman.

159. Chronicle Adler *op. cit.* calls him second scribe.

160. Chronicle Adler *op. cit.* gives his name as Elinaa. Neither Abu'l Faṭh nor Chronicle Adler say whether he was lay or priestly; probably he was the former.

161. Chronicle Adler *op. cit.* makes it clear that 'from Zaita' means that he was from the inhabitants of Zaita.

162. This extra duty that was his is not recorded in Chronicle Adler.

163. Chronicle Adler *op. cit.* 'of the inhabitants of K^e^far Maruth.

164. Chronicle Adler *op. cit.* 'he was the fifth scribe'.

165. Chronicle Adler: Amram Kohen Levi of the inhabitants of K^e^far Safasa. Chronicle Adler agrees with Abu'l Faṭh here in saying that Amram held the office of making the comment (obviously on the scripture). Chronicle Adler though it talks of the second comment has not told us who makes the first comment, whereas Abu'l Faṭh has mentioned Arub'i as interpreting first; the interpretation need not have been *peshat* like the Samaritan Targum which has come down to us; it may have been a sort of midrash. Chronicle Adler calls him second scribe. Abu'l Fath adds with regard to Amram that this Amram was the father of Markah (i.e. the great Samaritan liturgiologist and theologian). Actually Amram is probably Amram Ḍarah of the liturgy (Ḍarir of Abu'l Faṭh may be the same as Ḍarah). Amram's hymns are used oftener than Markah's; with

Markah's hymns they make up the bulk of the ordinary Sabbath liturgy even of the present day.

166. Chronicle Adler is candid in saying that he does not know either his name or where he lived.

167. The Tolidah *op. cit.* knows nothing of these seven sages, but tells us that he apportioned out the priests the sons of Aaron over the provinces of the Samaritans and in their towns and villages during his forty years' high priesthood. The Tolidah gives lists of Samaritans who, like the tribes in the Biblical Book of Joshua, were to have sections of the land to possess. It is doubtful if they actually could take possession of such tracts of land in reality. Cf. also Chronicle Adler p.91ff. for similar division of land to possess.

168. Cf. also Chronicle Adler *op. cit.*

169. The four overseers are not mentioned either by the Tolidah or Chronicle Adler.

170. The seven sages with the addition of the four overseers and the inclusion of Baba himself would make twelve. It is just possible that Abu'l Fatḥ is imagining what would have been in the time of Baba, whose period of office was the most similar to the period of Divine Grace which the Samaritans had ever experienced. Therefore he might feel that the community might have had a similar organisation under Baba to that which it had been in the Period of Divine Grace. In the time of Divine Grace some of the elders had not been priests, likewise it must have been so in Baba's time too, like as it was to the Period of Divine Grace. Is Abu'l Fatḥ tacitly criticising priestly autocracy of his own day?

171. A Samaritan sect, probably the Sebuaeans one of the four Samaritan sects mentioned in Epiphanius. Probably called Sabu'ai because they kept the Passover celebration in the seventh month. So Joynboll and Montgomery explain the name, cf. Montgomery *ibid.* p.253.

172. Presumably then it was only on Festivals that the seven sages exercised their offices of first interpreter or first commentator etc. at the mother synagogue at Shechem.

173. It is noteworthy that only two times of prayer are mentioned. This is of course still the case for weekday prayers, morning and evening. Sabbath has as its main service the noonday prayers. Before praying the Samaritan ritually washes

himself and recites the Samaritan Creed.

175. This synagogue lasted, says Chronicle Adler, till the time of the Crusades.

176. This site would be on top of the mountain, cf. the site of the Tabernacle or the Temple destroyed by Hyrcanus; but Chronicle Adler says it was below the mountain.

177. Is this Hyrcanus' work being further projected into the past?

178. So also Chronicle Adler *ibid.* p.91.

179. Chronicle Adler: the town of Amratha where the early high priests were interred, the children of Eleazar and Ithamar the seventy elders, our lord Abisha the son of Phinehas and many others descended from Aaron.

180. Chronicle Adler *ibid.* p.91 lists this as the sixth synagogue Baba built. Salem, of which the original name, Chronicle Adler tells us, was Ai, was to the east of Mount Gerizim.

181. According to Chronicle Adler the synagogue at Beth Namara was the third he built.

182. Cf. Chronicle Adler *ibid.* p.91 where it is the second of the eight synagogues which he built.

183. This name does not come in Chronicle Adler's list.

184. Cf. Chronicle Adler where the synagogue at Tira is the fourth of the synagogues built by Baba.

185. This is probably the same as the synagogue built at Dabarin (Chronicle Adler *op. cit.*). It is the fifth in that list.

186. This is probably the same as the seventh synagogue built by Baba, that at Beth Dagan (cf. Chronicle Adler *op. cit.* p.91).

187. In Chronicle Adler *op. cit.* p.91 we are told that Baba built in front of the synagogue at Abantha (the eight synagogue Baba built according to that Chronicle) a big gathering place which he established for the reading and study of the Law. The French translation of Chronicle Adler *op. cit.* p.91 gives the wrong idea by translating Miqweh by *école*. Before the eve of

sabbath service to this day there is a service which is basically all readings from the Law, which is said in the courtyard of the synagogue about half an hour before the service proper begins. Doubtless this was a courtyard or vestibule where in addition to such a service being read, comments on the Law and *Teshuboṯ* to *She'eloṯ* could be given by the Sages.

188. This is not in Chronicle Adler.

189. This is Baba's reason for building synagogues: it does not refer to any one specific synagogue.

190. This occurs in Tolidah. It is hard to harmonise this with the statements earlier in Abu'l Fatḥ of how Baba curtailed the power and privileges of the hereditary priesthood, and set up instead his system of seven Sages. As we saw above, there is trace of artificiality in this account of the seven sages. Further (cf. note 54 and the text to which note 73 refers) it would appear that the number of Sages was not necessarily only seven. Had Abu'l Fatḥ made up his mind on the matter? Then occurs this statement that Baba Raba distributed the priests over the heads of the people as he found them and gave them an inheritance. This surely is what did happen with respect to the priesthood; he left them alone more or less as he found them. The giving to them of an inheritance is somewhat more putative, being linked up with his actual power to give Samaritan chiefs tracts of territory, covering among them most of Palestine.

191. Here follows in Abu'l Fatḥ a list of Samaritans who were given such and such a tract of country, and 'with him was the priest so and so' is added in each case. The list in Abu'l Fatḥ like that in the Chronicle Adler is based on that in the Tolidah. In this list Chronicle Adler and Abu'l Fatḥ sometimes disagree with each other and sometimes both disagree with the Tolidah. The differences are largely due to textual corruption. It was thought advisable not to include this list here; if anyone desires to see it reference can be made to *REJ*, XLV, pp.92-93 where the Chronicle Adler text is given with Tolidah and Abu'l Fatḥ variants.

192. The overseers here are not Baba's four overseers who with the seven sages and Baba himself, Abu'l Fatḥ supposes acted as a Samaritan Cabinet. The overseers in our text are Roman overseers. But as Montgomery rightly points out ("*The Samaritans*" p.102): 'Despite the arrangement of the Samaritan chronicles, which assign Baba Raba to the IIIrd Century, specifically to the reigns of Severus and Phillip, all the sure data refer his life to the middle of the IVth Century; probably

he flourished under the eastern co-emperor Constantius'. If so the overseers could be Christian Bishops. Cf. later the story of Germanus.

193. But see below for another explanation of this custom. The parallel to this burning of the overseers is found in Chronicle Adler pp.93-94 and is explicit as to what the overseers prevented them from doing - the statutes and commandments of the Sacred Law. Chronicle Adler does not say the custom of burning effigies on the first of the seventh month arose from the burning of the overseers.

194. Alexander cf. Chronicle Adler *op. cit.*

195. For this victory on Mt. Askar cf. also Chronicle Adler p.94-95 which explains that Mount Askar faces Mount Gerizim.

196. Chronicle Adler p.94-95 merely says that Baba made wars against the kings; all his wars are written in the Chronicles (presumably those of Abu'l Fatḥ).

197. Is this a doublet of the battle of Mount Askar? In any case the battle seems to have been on the same mountain. As a result of each battle in turn the mountain was rendered unclean. If Mount Askar 'the Mountain which is opposite Nablus' is Mount Ebal, the mount of the cursing according to even the Jewish version Deut. 27:13, one wonders if both stories of the victories there are not mere fabrications. Ebal is unclean; a reason had to be found for this uncleanness. It is a measure of the greatness of Baba and the size of his victories, if he could make Mount Ebal unclean from the corpses of his enemies.

198. Cf. perhaps Deut. 33:29 end.

199. Cf. Chronicle Adler p.94-95 for a similar account of the promise to the Jews to allow them to rebuild the Jerusalem Temple if they killed Baba Raba. The story of the plan to kill him at the Samaritan Synagogue at Namara on the eve of Sabbath, and how this was foiled by the Jewish maidservant passing on the information is given very similarly in Chronicle Adler.

200. Gordianus (238-244) this story of his giving permission to the Jews to rebuild the temple at Jerusalem, but how their efforts were frustrated by storm and portents, is a parallel to the Christian legend assigned to Julian's reign (see Montgomery *ibid.* p.96).

201. This 'ancient Hebrew history' may be the Book of Joshua. Cf. Ch. L of Juynboll's *Chronicon Samaritanum qui Titulus est*

Liber Josuae, Leyden 1848 where part of this story is given, but breaks off at the point where the Samaritans hear of the Archbishop's intended visit to Nablus. The Book of Joshua edited by Juynboll is in Arabic. It is still a matter of controversy as to whether there was a Hebrew original to the Samaritan Book of Joshua. One might however ask whether Abu'l Fatḥ means a history written in the Hebrew language or merely a Hebrew or Samaritan history. The Book of Joshua (the Samaritan chronicle of that name) was one of Abu'l Fatḥ's sources.

What is more likely is that Abu'l Fatḥ knew this story from some old Hebrew narrative, later added to Joshua as a supplement, though it had not been added at that time, cf. Montgomery *ibid.* pp.304, 305. Though it could be argued from Abu'l Fatḥ's reference to a manuscript containing "the Book of Joshua and other material" that it had already been added and that Abu'l Fatḥ did not refer to this story as from the Book of Joshua because he knew it was merely supplementary being from the 'other material'. The story of Baba Raba sending Levi to Constantinople that he might become a monk, bishop or Christian priest so as to come back and go up Mount Gerizim to break the Talismanic Bird which cried out "Hebrew" when a Samaritan approached, is not in Chronicle Adler.

202. Rome in the Arabic sense of Constantinople.

203. The Book of Joshua ch. L has two explanatory paragraphs prefacing Baba's suggestion of sending Levi to Rome (Constantinople). The first paragraph admits that the Romans were then oppressing the Samaritans. This is important, because it in effect gives a candid admission of their difficulties even when they had the great Baba. If Abu'l Fatḥ took his account from the same prototype as the Book of Joshua, perhaps he omitted this paragraph because it would not have read well with the previous great victories ascribed to Baba. The second paragraph explains what the Talismanic bird did. Abu'l Fath starts *in media res*. The Samaritans at this time were forbidden to go up the sacred mountain. The Romans had set up a brazen bird (eagle) at the top of the Mountain and when a Samaritan approached it declared his presence by calling out 'Hebrew'. One wonders how Baba could, when he first rallied the people, have gone up the mountain and there addressed them (see above).

204. This story definitly puts Baba in the fourth century after the Empire had become Christian.

205. The Book of Joshua account ends here in Juynboll's edition *ibid.* p.193.

206. Jacob's words on finding his son Joseph still alive, whom he had thought dead Gen. 46:30.

207. Ex. 15:3.

208. Probably of the church on the top of Mount Gerizim.

209. Cf. note 78 where the same custom is kept because of the rising against the 'overseers' and the burning of them in the fire. In that earlier account Baba had only just finished his ecclesiastical reformation and the overseers interfered with the work of the Sages. The burning of the overseers, led to the successful battles against the Romans. It is hopeless to try to harmonise these accounts or to do more than recognise that the chronological order of events in Baba's life is no more trustworthy than much of Samaritan chronology in general. Abu'l Fatḥ, however, gave this second account with obvious mental reservations.

210. Alexander Severus does not fit in with the Christian Roman Empire in which the story is set; he was decidedly before its time.

211. We have here one battle, the battle of the Graves, whereas in the earlier account of the burning of the overseers, we have two battles.

212. Abu'l Fatḥ means that he is aware that there is a gulf of time between what he has just recounted about Baba, and what he is now going to tell.

213. Philip the Arab (244-249).

214. We are to imagine that, according to Abu'l Fatḥ and his sources, the Roman Emperor by trickery got Baba to Constantinople as a guest and then imprisoned him. Baba was High Priest and according to the Tolidah High Priest for forty years; further the High Priest could *not* leave the Holy Land. We must understand that Baba was taken prisoner to Constantinople.

215. If Nathanel were still alive up till then, Baba had not been High Priest and could perhaps have gone to Constantinople on a journey voluntarily; but how can we explain the Tolidah's statement that Baba was high priest for forty years? If his father died when he (Baba) was in Constantinople, Baba could never have become high priest.

216. This friendly relation with a Jew may point to the

origin of some of Baba's ideas ascribed to him by Abu'l Fath e.g. the laicising of the Samaritan Sanhedrin by the bringing in of lay Haḥamim. However it is pleasant to find twice in the story of the life of Baba friendly relations with Jews, and the historian admitting such.

217. The Samaritans keep full mourning seven days.

218. For a single woman to be seen with a man was bad enough, though allowable if they were on the road; but beside the road (not on the road) was incriminating.

219. Lev. 21:9.

220. Deut. 19:19.

221. So also Chronicle Adler *ibid.* 223.

222. Decius (249-252).

223. Vilmar *ibid.* Prolegomena p.LXX suggests that Taḥus was Constantius 337-361. Note that Chronicle Adler *ibid.* p.223 ignores Taḥus and ascribes the story of Germanus to the reign of Decius.

224. Among the commandments interdicted, would be circumcision. Chronicle Adler says that Decius was worse than Philip, and we know of the rigor of the law against Samaritan circumcision in his reign: on this latter cf. Origen C. Celsum ii 13, and Eusebius Hist. Eccles. 6 cc. 34, 36 referred by Montgomery *ibid.* p.97.

225. Germanus. To Montgomery *ibid.* pp.101-102 belongs the credit of having identified Germanus with the Bishop of Neapolis who was present at the councils of Ancyra and Neo-Caesarea (314) and of Nicea (325).

226. As Montgomery *ibid.* p.102 says: "We may assume that the stringency of official measures against the Samaritan religion depended much upon the zeal of the ecclesiastics; in this case we have a rare and noble instance of the Christian charity of a bishop of that age to the enemies of his Church".

227. Chronicle Adler *ibid.* p.223-4 mentions merely that "Germanus did a favour to the Samaritans contrary to the order of the king, in not preventing the practice of circumcision" (in general). Then Chronicle Adler states that the Samaritans make an act of remembrance of him in the prayers of circumcision, in a hymn in the language of the Targum composed by Markah who

lived then. The sentence quoted is the last hemistiche of the hymn. The 'for ever', is not in the usual text, and in any case would make the half line too long.

228. The Tolidah and Chronicle Adler put the rise of Dūsīs in the high priesthood of 'Aḳbon. The Tolidah *ibid.* p.405 says "'Aḳbon succeeded his brother Baba Raba as high priest and functioned as such twenty six years. During his high priesthood there came to Shechem Dūsethīs or Dūstīs the son of Falfūlī; he was not of the Samaritans but of the mixed rabble which came out of Egypt." Chronicle Adler merely calls him Dūsīs. Montgomery suggests with a query that Fūlfili (in Abu'l Fatḥ *ibid.*) may be Philip. This however does not explain Falfūli. There is every chance that this form given in the Tolidah is earlier than Abu'l Fatḥ's Fūlfili. The first vowel 'a' is merely conjectural, it could be 'i', in which case the word could be Pilpulī (though as said by a Samaritan the 'peh' would be aspirated. *Pilpul* in Mishnaic Hebrew is discussion, debate. In T.B. B.B. 1456 *Ba'al Pilpul* is 'master in dialectics'. It might be that the cognomen, ben Pilpuli is a reference ironical or otherwise to Dūsīs' deductive powers.

229. Neither Chronicler Adler *ibid.* p.225 nor the Tolidah *ibid.* p.405 tell of the adventures of Dūsīs before his coming to Nablus.

230. Cf. 1 Kings 12:28.

231. It was more likely that those dissatisfied with Jerusalem voluntarily left for Shechem, than that the Jews sent them to cause trouble.

232. The source is unknown, unless Abu'l Fatḥ means the reference in Pirḳe de R. Eliezer (*ibid.* p.299) to Rabbi Dosethai who was sent by the King of Assyria to teach law to the Kutheans etc. that had been settled in depopulated Northern Israel after 721 B.C.; but it is not the Jews who send Dosethai and the only condemnation he would have been released from was exile.

233. Cf. Exod. 12:38.

234. Still the way to the Samaritans' hearts; at least to the hearts of those in Shechem. The Samaritans in Jaffa are generous, never ask for gifts; but as they say we are *Po'alim* not *Kohanim*.

235. Num. 18:17.

236. Lev. 23:14.

237. On the Day of Atonement as on all the great Festivals, the Samaritan Community, then as now, would go to the sacred mountain, Mount Gerixim.

238. Chronicle Adler *ibid.* p.225 having said that all the acts of Dūsīs are written in the Annals of Abu'l Fatḥ, states merely that the high priest 'Akbon wished to put him to death. Dūsīs, it says, fled to the town of Suca where he lodged with the widow Amantù.

239. Chronicle Adler *ibid.* p.225 omits description of what Dūsīs did at Amantu's house and his instructions to her, but proceeds to say after stating that he went there, that he left for Anbata. Chronicle Adler does however tell what befell him at the cave at Anbata.

240. Chronicle Adler *ibid.* p.225 states that this Levi was the Levi who had been sent by his uncle Baba Raba to the country of the Romans and who had come back and broken the brazen bird on Mount Gerizim. It is perhaps significant that Levi had been instructed in Christianity at Constantinople.

241. A similar account of Dūsīs and his instructions is given by the widow Amantu in Chronicle Adler *ibid.* p.226 in answer to Levi's inquiry. In that source however it is stated that Dūsīs had charged the woman to swear to fulfil his request, swearing by the name of God and his servant Moses.

242. Chronicle Adler's account is similar except that it says Levi killed with his sword each of his seven companions who plunged into the pool before him, and who came us saying 'My faith is in Thee, LORD, and in Dūsīs Thy servant and in his prophecy'.

243. Chronicle Adler *ibid.* p.229 says that he (Levi) took the book which Dūsīs had written and he saw that it was the Torah, in which he had changed many words just as Ezra the priest of the Jewish community had done in his time. In Chronicle Adler *ibid.* p.227 Levi takes back with him to Shechem some men of Suca who had been guarding the book of Dūsīs. This sounds as if there had been a community established there by Dūsīs.

244. Exod. 12:21.

245. Exod. 12:22.

246. Levi is here saying that the orthodox Samaritan community have altered the Festivals presumably from their (to him) pristine purity, which he following Dūsīs will restore. Dūsīs

in short altered the Festivals, but see below. It is said that Dūsīs' followers kept no Festival but Sabbath and that Dūsīs like Dustān annulled the Feasts. However it may be that Dūsīs changed the calendar; by his reckoning, the feasts fell at different times from those kept by the rest of the community. If so, he would be liable to the charge of annulling the feasts, as his celebrations would not be held to be regular festival celebrations. The same thing may have applied to the Dustān sect.

247. This was what Dustān was said to have done; here the follower of Dūsīs is blaming the orthodox Samaritans for having done this. Neither this nor the charge of altering the Festivals is reported to have been made by Levi in the Chronicle Adler version *op. cit.*

248. 'They enticed many men'. Chronicle Adler *op. cit.*

249. This information about the palm leaves of Levi is not here given in Chronicle Adler, nor is the information regarding the tenets and practices of the Dūsīs sect.

250. Deut. 19:10a.

251. For discussion of these tenets and practices in relation to those of Dustān see the notes on the first translated extract from Abu'l Fatḥ in which the Dustān sect is discussed. Vilmar *ibid.* Prolegomena p.LXXII f. says that the name of the sect of Dositheans, the Dustān sect must have been re-attached to the name of Dūsīs. Above in connection with the Dustān story I have argued that it is the other way round; the Dūsīs sect of the Dositheans has been projected back by Abu'l Fatḥ to before the time of Alexander. Vilmar *op. cit.* says 'Accedit quod ritus ac dogmata a Dusi prolata pag. 157 sqq. simillima sunt eorum, quae Dositheis pag. 83 tribuuntur . With this I agree, but feel that Abu'l Fatḥ has made these appear to have been two sects where there was only one. As I have shown above Abu'l Fatḥ considered it necessary to scotch the Dosethai story of Pirḳe de R. Eliezer by making it appear that orthodox Samaritanism was not derived from his teaching. As with the Hyrcanus story so with the Dūsīs story we have doublets; in both cases later events are projected back in one of two versions of the same event.

252. The Tolidah (*ibid.* 405) merely states that Nathanel was high priest for thirty one years. The story of Sul is not given; the story, however, is found in Chronicle Adler *q.v. ibid.* p.228-230.

253. Chronicle Adler p.228 the priests's son is given as Baha'am.

254. Chronicle Adler p.228 Tablin. Simon Magus cf. New Testament: Acts 8:9ff.

255. In Chronicle Adler, Simon does not believe the servant.

256. Chronicle Adler. *Nasi' ha-'Ob*.

257. He would be in a state of ritual purity to do this (cf. Num. 18:10).

258. *Q^e re ha-Lailah*. i.e. seminal emission. cf. M. Ber. 3:4.

259. Cf. Chronicle Adler *ibid.* also note 1 where it is suggested it might be Rome. That Simon went to Rome is also the Christian tradition as old as Justin. Cf. Montgomery *ibid.* p.266.

260. Jesus. In Chronicle Adler *ibid.* he is not called the Messiah, but Jesus son of Mary, of Nazareth.

261. Cf. Acts 8:24 for the Christian version of this. Simon comes off worse.

262. This is what Gamaliel the Pharisee is reported as having said in Acts 5:39.

263 The disciple who testified first to Jesus being the Messiah was Peter, Mark 8:29. The meaning of Saftanah is uncertain, and the connection of this name with Peter, if any connection there be, is unknown. This and the next sentence are not in Chronicle Adler.

264. It is not clear how the disciples of the Messiah are reckoned as fifteen instead of twelve. Yet the twelve were not all the disciples cf. Luke 10:1 for seventy disciples over and above the twelve in Jesus' lifetime; cf. also Acts 6:2 'And the twelve summoned the body of the disciples'. 'Disciple' could be applied to others beside the twelve. But the problem remains why Abu'l Fatḥ chose the number fifteen.

265. There is the Toledoth Yeshu'a story of how Peter became a Jew; this might be in Abu'l Fatḥ's mind or in that of his source, but Peter was not the last of the disciples. The reference to the circumcised disciples recalls Peter's advocacy of Circumcision.

266. Probably a rather obscure reference to the Council of Jerusalem, Acts 15.

267. In Chronicle Adler *ibid.* p.230 they are called the 'Ab'ūnaī. One thinks of the Ebionites, coming as they do after reference to circumcised disciples; but the root is different. Actually 'Ab'unaī of Chronicle Adler and Ba'unaī of Abu'l Fatḥ are the same word. The aleph 'a' of 'Ab'unai may well be the prosthetic aleph usually said in Samaritan pronunciation and not written. It sometimes slips into the written form cf. 'Armiya for Rome note 141. The Ba'unaī may be those who make a request from Ba'a to ask, pray, search.

268. Chronicle Adler establishes them at Basan and leaves them there. No word is given of their perishing.

269. Ansma and his sect may be a doublet of Abu'l Fatḥ's story of the Ba'ūnaī. Note that Ansma and his seven disciples perished in the same way as the seven Ba'ūnaī. Note also that at the end of the Ansma narrative Abu'l Fatḥ says 'none remained of the Ba'unaī except one man'. Ansma attempted to annul the festivals. We know nothing of the tenets of the Ba'unai, but annulling the festivals was one of the practices of the Dustān sect and Dūsīs and his disciples. Here again 'annul' may mean merely to refuse to celebrate them on the same dates as the rest of the community,cf. note 246 above.

Chronicle Adler gives as the second sect, the one called Abiya, the leader of which was Anthami, one would think of equating this with Abu'l Fatḥ's sect (mentioned later) headed by Abiya and Dusa, had it not been that in Chronicle Adler the Abiya sect die like that of the Ba'unaī and Ansma's sect, whereas according to Abu'l Fatḥ, Abiya and Dusa and 120 followers go out into the wilderness beyond Jordan. However since Ansma and Anthami may be the same name, it may be safer to identify the second sect of Abu'l Fatḥ with the second sect of Chronicle Adler.

270. In Chronicle Adler *ibid.* p.23-Ḳaṭiṭaī. With Montgomery *ibid.* p.264,we may connect the Ḳaṭiṭaī with the Encratites; if so the sect would be libertine; we may see this hinted at in their antinomian attitude referred to by Abu'l Fatḥ. They were probably Messianic in outlook as well. It may be because of their messianism that they considered the commandments no longer valid.

271. Their going up Mount Gerizim and expecting God to reveal the Tabernacle points to their expecting the Taheb (Samaritan Messiah) to come and discover the Tabernacle, cf. Josephus, Antiq. XVIII IV 1 of a man who incited the Samaritans to go up Mount Gerizim, and assured them that he would show them those sacred vessels which were laid under that place,

because Moses put them there. This man mentioned in Josephus was a Messianic claimant. Only when the Tabernacle and altar of incense were rediscovered could the Samaritan priests, the true descendants of Eleazar and Aaron make proper atonement for Israel, and *Panutha* (end), and *Ridwan* (return).

272. Barking - this is probably a pun on prophesying.
'naḥaḥa' in Arabic / *'nabah'* in Hebrew is to bark: *naba* in Arabic / *nab̲a* in Hebrew is to prophesy.
The Samaritans do not pronounce the gutturals in Hebrew and so bark and prophesy sound the same to them in Hebrew. The barking/prophesying reminds one of prophecy as a gift of the spirit in the early Christian Church which Paul tried to control, cf. 1 Cor. 13:2. Chronicle Adler merely says of the Ḳaṭiṭaī that God smote them. The Ḳaṭiṭaī sect obviously were Dūsīs inspired, so also were the Ba'unaī from whom the Ḳaṭiṭaī seem to have arisen. Note how the next sect listed by Abu'l Fatḥ, the Ṣadūḳaī are said to arise (likewise) from the Ba'unaī.

273. i.e. The Ṣadūḳaī. Chronicle Adler *ibid.* p.230 mentions here instead the sect of Ṣaḳtu b. Ṭabrin b. Nin, which is identical with the sect of Šalyah b. Tairun b. Nin that Abu'l Fatḥ mentions later. There seems no parallel in Chronicle Adler to the Ṣaduḳaī. It is important to note that this sect arose from the company of the Ba'unaī and belief in Dūsīs is central.

274. This approaches Dūsīs soteriology in the Christian sense.

275. Cf. the Pauline concept of mankind not having to contend against flesh and blood, but against principalities, against the powers, against the world rulers of this present darkness, against the spiritual hosts of wickedness in the heavenly places. Ephesians 6:12.

276. One thinks of the Haša'im mentioned in Rabbinic sources. If the Haša'im were Essenes it may be that such a mystic sect as the Samaritan Ṣaduḳaī were in sympathy with them.

277. The name Mālūf looks artificial, as if they had called their settlement 'the place of teaching'.

278. This mode of winding up a sect becomes a bit artificial.

279. There is no exact parallel to them in Chronicle Adler, though the second sect in Chronicle Adler is called Abiya, its chief Anthami who may be the same as Ansma the leader of the second sect of Abu'l Fatḥ (see above).

280. Abiya and Dusa do not go so far as Kaṭiṭaī.

281. Their going out to the wilderness as they claimed Dūsīs commanded is probably modelled on Dūsīs going to a mountain cave and fasting to death.

282. The fact that they went on a journey on the Sabbath day would imply that their Sabbatarianism had been modified. It may be noteworthy that they went across the Jordan to the wilderness. The discontented of Nablus may have found contact with the Essenes and as far as Nablus was concerned "this sect passed away also". In dealing with these sects one has to bear in mind that we do not know the dates of their origin. Though earlier I have argued for the Dustān sect in Abu'l Fatḥ's Annals being deliberately antedated by him in the late Persian period, it must be remembered that in this section dealing with the Samaritan sects he has probably along with the Tolidah inserted the rise of Dūsīs at an equally arbitrary date. We know that Simon Magus was not of the period of 'Aḳbon but of the first century. With the Ba'unaī etc. we have no means of dating their rise, but we know that they are all to some extent influenced by Dūsīs. The dating of the rise of Dūsīs in the high priesthood of 'Aḳbon is largely due quite probably to identifying Levi, Dūsīs' first martyr, with Levi the nephew of Baba as does Chronicle Adler *op. cit.*; the real emergence of Dūsīs may be earlier. It would appear that the Dūsīs sect was already known in the first century A.D., so much so that Josephus *Antiq.* XIII III 4 can make the heresiarch one of the two protagonists for the Samaritan Version of the Pentateuch before Ptolemy; for so we must understand Theodosius which is but another form of the name Dositheus. It is not by accident that the other protagonist of the Samaritans on that occasion was Sabbeus; presumably the actual or imaginary leader of the Saba'ian heresy is intended. We would hardly be wrong in thinking that to Josephus the Jew Samaritanism meant either the Dosithean heresy or the Saba'ian.

283. Šalyah b. Tairim b. Nin appears as the leader of Chronicle Adler's fourth sect. Apart from telling us that Saktu b. Tabrin b. Nin had eighteen disciples Chronicle Adler tells us nothing of him and his sect.

284. Apparently Abu'l Fatḥ would have us believe that he was Jewish in origin. It is possible that Jewish malcontent or deviationists came to Nablus.

285. The old Messianic claim, cf. note (271).

286. While there is here a Puritanical trait in his earlier

phase, it is quite wrong to compare him with the Karaites as Montgomery does, *ibid.* 264. Montgomery does not give an adequate picture of him. He does point out that Šalyah argued against the going up of Mount Gerizim; this is from his second phase after the Ba'unaī came back and criticised. But to be consistent Montgomery should have cited Šalyah's legislation from this second phase too. What Karaite would e.g. have permitted marriage with the Gentiles, or the touching of a woman in the menses? In any case if we stick to the first phase, that of asceticism, his authority for it is Dūsīs.

287. 'they' must refer to the Dūsīs sect, for it was that sect that taught that the dead rise soon.

288. Another practice of the Dūsīs sect.

289. Another practice of the Dūsīs sect.

290. This was the charge brought against Dūsīs and which Levi nephew of Baba had tried to rebut; the attitude of the Dūsīs sect towards the Festivals was like that of the Dustān.

291. Cf. the Dustān teaching that in some books belonging to the children of Moses, one read that God was served in the land of Zawīla until he was served on Mount Gerizim. Orthodox Samaritan belief was that Mount Gerizim was the eternal mountain. Is Zawīla - Zion?

292. Since the Ḳiblah was towards Gerizim this would seem an outrageous thing to say as graves were unclean.

293. Gentiles were unclean. Marriage with Gentiles is unthinkable even today for the dwindling Samaritan community.

294. Orthodox Samaritans have always been stricter on the laws of Niddah than even Jews. (M. Nid. 4:1).

295. This was not necessarily undermining the Biblical laws of uncleanness as had his previous ruling (note 176). He may have been merely restating a Dustān ruling q.v. that some animals were unclean after their death.

296. Gentiles were not unclean.

297. This again modifies the Biblical Law.

298. This was a mark of the Dūsīs sect (see above) in which they were like the Essenes and Hemerobaptists.

299. The Samaritan like the Jew stands for prayer.

300. With the Tallith.

301. Lev. 26:1.

302. The Dustān - Friends, a Persian word in Arabic.

303. Obviously Šalyah made Messianic claims; probably because of the way in which he altered the Law he claimed to be Moses rededivus. Moses in the flesh like the Johannine Jesus was bound by the flesh. John 7:39: "Now this he said about the spirit, which those who believed in him were to receive; for as yet the spirit had not been given, because Jesus was not yet glorified". After death Šalyah's spirit, the spirit of Moses, which was the spirit of God, would be released to intercede for Israel. Or was the request that God should pour forth on the Dustān some of the spirit of Šalyah just as some of the spirit of Moses in his life-time came upon the Seventy elders.

304. Dustān banned the pronouncing of YHWH by the people, making them say Elohim.

305. In his earlier phase he had called a meeting in a large tent and had said he would go up Mount Gerizim presumably to find the Tabernacle; but it is not said that he did carry out the ascent of Mount Gerizim even for this purpose.

306. This sect is mentioned by Chronicle Adler *ibid.* p.231 as the sons of Ṣadōḳ. He adds that they were five brothers.

307. Though they differed from Šạlyah, they had much in common with his teaching. Cf. below their calling him "the Measurer" cf. perhaps John 3:34.

308. This may have been because of Sadducean leanings. On the other hand it may have been that like the Rabbis they did not wish it to be deduced that there was only one world. The Rabbis countered this suggestion by saying; From everlasting to everlasting. M. Ber. 9:5.

309. Deut. 33:4 a common response even in the present day liturgy. Did they deny it was for them? After all they taught that commandments and prohibitions of the Law were still valid.

310. Chronicle Adler names a sixth sect that of Aulia at Alexandria; this sect is obviously the same as Abu'l Fath's Ūliānah.

311. Obviously this Ūliānah was making Messianic claims. Divine Grace came only after the Taheb's coming.

312. The setting of men and women apart would not only be a reversal of Šalyah's practice of letting men and women worship together, but shows that he considered sex as sin. It has a monastic rather than communistic basis.

313. Bustunus, as to his identity we have no clue.

314. It almost sounds like a comment on the early Christian Church.

315. Fasḳūṭāi: Montgomery *ibid.* p.265 sees this name as connected with the Greek *physikos* or *psychikos* and "the sect [as] another specimen of encrative delusion". This sect is the only Samaritan sect which denies the resurrection.

316. They were not so much licentious as endeavouring by this method to conquer the flesh. The flesh is the ultimate enemy.

CHAPTER 3

SELECTIONS FROM THE COMMENTARY OF IBRAHIM IBN YA'ḲUB

Ibrahim ibn Ya'ḳub the well-known Samaritan Bible commentator lived either in the 15th century as Klumel thinks, or not before the 16th century. Meier Klumel (*Mischpatim: Ein samaritanischer-arabischer Commentar zu Ex. 21-22. 15 von Ibrahim ibn Jakub.* Berlin 1902 p.6) points out that Ibrahim cannot have lived before the 14th century because he quotes in his Commentary on Exodus the Samaritan poet Abisha b. Phinehas who lived at the end of the 14th century. Klumel however proceeds to date Ibrahim the commentator in the 15th century because he identifies him with Ibrahim the hymn writer whom he believes lived in that century.

However, S. Hanover (*'Das Festgesetz der Samaritaner nach Ibrahim ibn Ja'ḳub,* Berlin 1904, pp.6-7) shows that Ibrahim commenting on Ex. 12:16 knew of coffee and tobacco. Coffee was not known in the Muslim East before the middle of the sixteenth century, while tobacco was not introduced there till the beginning of the seventeenth century. Therefore Hanover argues that Klumel's dating is too early, and he would date the commentary not before the sixteenth century.

But both datings are too early. Klumel was right in identifying Ibrahim the Commentator with Ibrahim the hymn writer, but he, following Heidenheim, was wrong in his dating of Ibrahim in the fifteenth century. Ibrahim lived in the mid-eighteenth century. The commentary is therefore not more than two hundred years old. It is nevertheless a very important commentary as it consists of 3288 manuscript quarto pages (cf. Montgomery *ibid.* p.295), treating the first four books of the Pentateuch. Petermann, last century, had a copy made in Nablus; his manuscript copy is now in Berlin, and it is from this Ms.

that M. Klumel and S. Hanover published selections of the text. I believe that Ibrahim's commentary once covered the whole Torah. When in Nablus in 1950 I had a portion of a Samaritan Arabic Commentary microfilmed; it was Ibrahim ibn Ya'kub on Deuteronomy 32.

Ibrahim's Commentary, as Montgomery rightly says, contains 'but a minimum of haggadic material and is predominantly Halachic'. One must however qualify this be stressing that Ibrahim's commentary gives scarcely any more halakah than haggada if we understand halakah in its usual rabbinic connotation. Ibrahim's Commentary is relatively *Peshat*; he first translates each verse on which he is commenting into Arabic, then adds a grammatical or more usually an exegetical note. One would not go to Ibrahim's Commentary for information on Samaritan *Hilluk* e.g. one would not learn from Ibrahim the customary rules relating to the celebration of any of the Festivals. Ibrahim's comments on the verses of Lev. ch. 23 however do show the Samaritans attempting to explain the Bible text literally, just as they try to carry out as much as they can of it literally. But it tells us too little of what the Samaritans really do (as in the case of Passover) and what else they do not do.

Belief has always been important in Samaritanism. Whereas practice could not exceed what was laid down in the Torah, there was no limit to developing a system of belief. I would say that Ibrahim's Commentary, interesting as it is as an example of the literalness of Samaritan exegesis, is more interesting for its few pieces of haggadic midrash. Even his discussions of the laws of slavery testify more to Samaritan haggadic conceptions than to halakic practice.

Below I set out translations from Ibrahim ibn Ya'kub on Exod.21:1-3 and on Lev. 23:1-32. The texts used are those prepared by Klumel and Hanover. For notes on the half vulgar

Arabic cf. Klumel *ibid.* p.7f. and Hanover *ibid.* p.7-13. For the relation of Ibrahim's Arabic translation of the Bible verses to that of Abu Sa'id,cf. Hanover *ibid.* p.17. Ibrahim is much more literal than Abu Sa'id; even at the cost of his Arabic he does try to preserve the nuances of the original Hebrew.

In this present work there are some small chapters of the *Kitab al-Tabbaḥ* of Abu'l Hasan as-Suri (who lived in the eleventh century), which are in the nature of commentary on Deut. 34:1ff. Comparison between the work of a commentator of the eleventh century and one of the eighteenth (i.e. Ibrahim ibn Ya'kub) should illustrate the conservative approach of the Samaritans to the Law.

"These are the ordinances":[1] the expression "ordinances" is sometimes to be explained as "custom" or "manner of action", sometimes as "regimen". The best known meaning of the word is "judgment" and this is how it is to be taken here. They are in three sections.[2] The first one of them is (made up of) statements of what it is lawful to do according to His saying "When[3] a man leaves a pit open" and His saying "If[4] a man delivers to his neighbor" and similar statements. The second section gives judgment where an action has been omitted by one commanded to do it, according to His saying:[5] "And if he does not do these three things for her", and His saying[6] "and its owner had not kept it in". And the third section is about an evil deed which is prohibited, as in the case of his saying:[7] "Whoever strikes a man so that he dies", and similar cases.

His saying:[8] "Which you shall set before them" i.e. write them down and read them out to them according to His saying later on:[9] "Then he took the book of the covenant and read it in the hearing of the people". The end of "the ordinances", is[10] "Behold, I" and some say,[11] "If you lend money." His saying:[12] "When you buy a Hebrew slave", if you acquire, i.e. if you purchase a Hebrew slave, since the possession of a slave is an evil thing according to reason, and therefore it is necessary to indicate its permissibility by a statement; but it is probable that it originated in the time of our lord Abraham[13] (upon him be peace). He starts off with that[14] kind of slave, as some say, because they were[15] slaves in Egypt, and knew the tyranny of the Egyptians towards them, and what benefits were bestowed upon them (by God) for that reason, intending thereby to lead them to good conduct towards their slaves. And by this slave, as some say, is meant the righteous[16] proselyte, not the (Hebrew) of pure[17] stock; because God, exalted is He, made the legal limit of his acquisition and service six years, not more and not less, according to His saying: "He shall serve you six years, and in the seventh he shall go out". But if the slave wanted to remain with his master, he shall continue in his slavery permanently, his life long.[19] However the man who is of pure stock may sell himself for less than that, and go out at the Jubilee according to his saying:[20] "He shall serve with you until the year of the Jubilee". And this statement expressly concerns him who is of pure stock and not strangers, according to His saying:[21] "and return to the possession of his fathers. For they are My servants". But the proselyte has no possession, and God did not bring his father out of Egypt.[22] The (fact of) the going out of the rabble[23] with them from Egypt does not imply that they are included in the statement[24] "whom I brought forth". Because the rabble was neither commanded nor invited to go out with Israel, but they wanted to go out from fear of what would overtake the Egyptians; and because He had specified concerning those who went out from Egypt that they are those of pure stock according to his saying:[25] "For the children of Israel are not slaves;[26] they are My servants whom I brought forth out of the land of Egypt".[27] "They shall not be sold as bondsmen", i.e. the children of Israel were not "slaves", My servants were they, whom I brought out from the land of Egypt; they shall not be sold as a slave is sold, and the name of servant of other than God must not be given them, as it is given to the above-mentioned individual here.[28] On the contrary he made it plain that he (the pure Hebrew) should be with his purchaser as a hired servant, and as a sojourner according to his saying:[29] "he shall be with you as a hired servant and as a sojourner. He shall serve with you until the year of the Jubilee". And he made a distinction also between the two (categories) of them in the going out (at the Jubilee) of the man of pure stock and his children from his purchaser, according to his saying:[30] "Then he shall go out from you, he and his children with him"; and the remaining behind of the children of the above-mentioned (slave), who shall remain as a possession of his master according to His saying Exalted is he;[31] "The wife and her children shall be his[32] master's, and he shall go out alone". And to this slave he draws attention in the book of recapitulation of the laws:[33] "If your brother, a Hebrew man, is sold to you". Thus the appellation 'Hebrew'[34] becomes something like a mark of his being other than of pure stock, because he does not restrict Himself to saying: "If your brother is sold to you" in His saying:[35] "but to your brother you shall not lend upon interest". With all this He makes it probable that this slave is a righteous proselyte and not of pure stock, but God knows best. His saying "six years"[36] is said if the Jubilee happened to take place after the year of purchase; he serves in it without going out as has been said before. These are not natural years (calendar years), but years of service to be served from a certain date to a certain date. Like the year (applicable) for the (redemption) of a dwelling house.[37] His saying: "he shall serve you"[38] means the continuity of his service the whole of the six years in service, acting as a servant, inside and outside.[39] Different is he of pure stock.

Of him it is said:[40] "you shall not make him serve as a slave". And His saying:[41] "and in the seventh (year)": He means that he starts the seventh (year) in distinction from what is before it, by going out from service. As to His saying: "free"[42] either the *lamed* (of *le hophši*) should drop out and it should be *hophsī*, an adjective referring to man as if 'and your servant is free'. Or the *yodh* should fall out, then *l'phš*[43] would be a verbal noun, meaning he goes out to freedom. Regarding His saying "for nothing"[44] after his saying "free", it is said He means, for nothing, without anything which he (need) pay him; for sometimes a slave becomes free by money which is paid to his owner, before the period passes; I mean the period of his being owned (i.e. 6 years). If he wanted freedom for himself, then he had power to purchase a certain period from his master. His saying "single"[45] is explained as being celibate i.e. without a wife and without children; and it is explained as bodily, being an emphatic expression for 'alone'. But his meaning is that he, just as he enters without a wife and child, should go out similarly, because it is explained afterwards:[46] "if he comes in married, then his wife shall go out with him" i.e. but if he had a wife, then his wife shall go out with him. It is said to inform us that his wife[47] had sold herself also. If that had been otherwise there would be no sense in His saying[48] "And his wife shall go out" which is parallel to his saying about him: "And he shall go out". For her sale could not have been completed except with her agreement and that of her husband. Lo, that would be impossible, at the desire of one of the two of them without the other.

NOTES ON IBRAHIM IBN YAK'UB COMMENTARY ON EXODUS 21:1-3

1. Ex. 21:1. The judgments or ordinances are expressed hypothetically and occur in 21:1 - 22:17, 22:25a, 26; 23:4f.

2. Ibrahim's classification is largely formal and is based on the first clause of the ordinances.

3. Exod. 2:33.

4. Exod.22:6 (RSV 7). The shallow nature of Ibrahim's classification is seen in the way he cites these two quite disparate cases as belonging to the same category. Neither it is true belong to the two other categories, sins of omission and commission.

5. Exod. 21:11.

6. Exod. 21:36.

7. Exod. 21:13.

8. Exod.21: Ibrahim dealing with the extent of the Book of the Covenant.

9. Exod. 24:7.

10. Exod. 23:20.

11. Exod. 22:24 (RSV 25).

12. Exod.21:2. Ibrahim is torn between his dislike of the institution of slavery and his reverence for the Law which permits it.

13. The earliest references in the Pentateuch to someone actually having servants or slaves are in the stories connected with Abraham: cf. Gen. 14:5; 21:25; 24:2, 5, 9, 52, 53. But as Gen. 21:25 shows he was not the only one who had servants.

14. i.e. Hebrew slave. Ibrahim finds it difficult to accept that Hebrews could be slaves to other Hebrews; further he has to explain the prominence given to this fact.

15. Cf. Deut. 5:15.

16. The expression 'righteous proselyte' sounds like a debt on Ibrahim's part to Judaism. Samaritanism never proselytised. In Judaism the *Ger ha-zedek* (righteous proselyte) was the technical term for the proselyte who had submitted to circumcision, whereas the *Ger Toshab* was the half proselyte.

17. Ibrahim in this emphasis on pure stock is typically Samaritan. Ibrahim does not allow that Exod.21:2 really applies to Hebrews of pure stock, but only to proselytes. The law of Lev. 25:39, 40 and that only applies to impoverished Israelites; there it is envisaged that a Hebrew might sell himself but he

is not to be treated as a slave, but as a hired servant and to be manumitted at the Jubilee even if this is less than six years ahead.

18. The Samaritan of proselyte stock however cannot serve less than six years and so cannot claim the benefit of the Jubilee for manumission if it falls before his six years are completed.

19. Cf. Exod. 21:5, 6.

20. Lev. 25:40.

21. Lev. 25:41, 2.

22. Cf. Lev. 25:41.

23. Cf. Exod. 12:38.

24. Lev. 25:42.

25. Lev. 25:55. Ibrahim's proposition is that Israelites are of pure stock and are not slaves. The universal conversive is: slaves are not pure Israelites. Therefore if there is mention of real slavery in Exod. 21:2 etc. it cannot apply to real Israelites but only to proselytes. It is a clever attempt to harmonize the differences between the laws of slavery in the Book of the Covenant and the Holiness Code, and to explain away the difficulties of having both the system of the seventh year of Release and that of the Jubilee in operation together.

26. M.T. reads *li* instead of *lo* giving "my servants" in-staed of "not servants" of the Samaritan.

27. Exod. 25:42.

28. Exod. 21:2.

29. Lev. 25:40.

30. Lev. 25:41.

31. Exod. 21:4.

32. M.T. has "her".

33. Deut.15:12. In Lev. 25:39 the Hebrew who sells himself into servitude is referred to as 'your brother', but in Deut. 15:12 as 'your brother, a Hebrew man, etc.' In Ibrahim's view

a Hebrew of pure stock cannot be sold into slavery, but only become a hired servant; therefore Deut.15:12 like Exod.21:2 cannot refer to a Hebrew of pure stock, but to a proselyte.

34. Ibrahim ignores the fact that in both Deut.15:12 and in Lev. 25:39 the unfortunate man is called 'your brother'. Deut. 15:12 and Exod.21:2 speak of actual selling into actual slavery, and the name Hebrew is applied to such a one. Since Hebrews of pure stock cannot become slaves, these so-called Hebrews of Exod. 21:2 cannot be actual Hebrews.

35. Deut. 3:20.

36. Exod. 21:2.

37. Lev. 25:29 where a dwelling house in a walled city does not come under the law of the Jubilee; likewise the Hebrew slave of proselyte stock whom Ibrahim regards as referred to in Exod. 21:2 is unaffected by the Jubilee.

38. So Samaritan reading of Exod.21:2.

39. Ibrahim wishes to underline the fact that the slave of Exod.21:2 is quite at his master's disposal for all kinds of work.

40. Lev. 25:39.

41. Exod. 21:2.

42. Exod. 21:2.

43. An aleph is written as the first radical. One would have expected a heth. But aleph and heth are confused as Samaritan gutturals are not sounded.

44. Exod. 21:2.

45. Exod. 21:3 '*begappo*' lit. with his body i.e. by himself.

46. Exod. 21:3.

47. Deut.15:12 where both the case of a man and a woman selling themselves into slavery are envisaged. It does not say that the woman is the man's wife. One wonders if the wife sold herself into slavery or did not rather go with her husband. Ibrahim's idea that the woman had sold herself into slavery is based on the slender fact that whereas it is explicitly stated that if a man sells himself into slavery and that at the end of

six years he goes out, in the case of the wife we have a similar statement that she goes out, but nothing about her having sold herself into slavery. To his tidy mind, it is clear that this last must be implied.

48. Exod. 21:3 'then his wife shall go out with him' Ibrahim merely cites the verb to give better parallelism.

49. With 'and he shall go out' (ibid).

50. Ibrahim's comment testifies to the Samaritan's high regard for women, but probably underrates the power of the ancient Israelite husband.

THE CHAPTER ON THE PRESCRIBED FEASTS

The LORD spoke to Moses,[1] "Say to the people of Israel, The appointed feasts of the LORD which you shall proclaim as holy convocations, My appointed feasts are these". Verily they return every year at their set times. *Al-'id* 'the feast' is a name for something, which returns at its (appropriate) time. Every (point of) time can be called (in Hebrew) *Mo'ud*.[2] This expression occurs in His saying: "At the time you came out of Egypt,"[3] and also in the speech to the Patriarch Abraham the phrase runs as follows: "At the appointed time I will return to you, in the spring".[4] Differentiation is made between the prescribed time and the unprescribed, because he designates the prescribed as *Mo'īd* i.e., feast,[5] the unprescribed as *Mo'ud*[6] i.e., a time at which something is promised. The pronunciation of the first word is in Hebrew with an 'I' sound, that of the latter with an 'u' sound. But the spelling of the consonants is the same in both words. Here He names them now Mo'Īd i.e., feasts and He means the prescribed times, and the feasts which are known and fixed in number.

The mention of the Sabbath[6a] comes before the mention of the feasts, because of its perfect holiness, and the following is the word of God:[7] "Six days shall work be done, but on the seventh day is a Sabbath of solemn rest, a holy convocation;

you shall do no work." The explanation regarding the ordinance of the Sabbath, the reason for it, and its individual prescriptions have already been given in this book[8] in the first and second volumes, to wit that after the Creator had completed the creation of Heaven and Earth in six days, He revealed Himself to His creations on the seventh day,[9] and they stopped their movements through the power of God, from fear of Him; and God announced on that day, the creation of Adam. That is made clear in His saying: "Thus the[10] heavens and the earth were finished, and all the host of them," down to - "And he rested[11] on the seventh day", etc. Then He says further:[12] "These are the generations of the heavens and the earth", down to the end of His statement:[13] "For the Lord God had not caused it to rain upon the earth, and there was no man", and down to His statement:[14] "And the LORD God formed man." Hereby it is certain, that the creation of Adam was in the second week,[15] and that it was after the revelation and proclamation of the (news of) the creation of Adam had taken place on the seventh day. At His command, all created things rested, and forbore from all motion on this day. And He commanded that no people rest on that day, and to forbear from work, so that they might draw nearer to Him (God) so that He might lead them in the straight way. But some scholars[16] say that the reason is because of the relation of the Sabbath day to Saturn; but Saturn means misfortune: therefore work on the Sabbath does not bring success. Therefore God commanded this people to observe a cessation of work on this day. Nevertheless the explanation which we have given first is the correct one, it is clear and unmistakably proved. But God knows best.

After the Lawgiver had given here the command regarding rest on the Sabbath day, and had finished it (the command) God said:[17] "These are the appointed feasts of the LORD, the holy convocations, which you shall proclaim at the time appointed for them." With His expression: "holy convocations" he means those days, on which you shall dedicate sacred things, freewill offerings vows, tithes, and firstfruits. The Creator had ordered this people, to dedicate holy gifts and this is meant to be restitution on their part for the many benefits which God had given to them, which cannot be described, and which had not befallen any other people.

The first of these benefits was their liberation from Egypt from vulgar slavery wrought by the noble messenger (of God) from their midst; and God carried out through him signs and wonders. Never had the like happened before, nor will the like take place hereafter. Their Exodus from Egypt was on the night of the fifteenth[18] of the first month. God ordained that this month should be for them the first of the months of the year, and this year should be the first of the years according to chronological reckoning[19] (starting with) their Exodus from Egypt. He commanded them to slay a passover offering to God on that night; that is already mentioned in the second volume of this Torah.

After God had imposed on them the slaying of the passover offering as a constant command, which should be carried out in its due season, God says here:[20] "In the first month, on the fourteenth of the month at even is the LORD'S passover." The passover became thus the first of the feasts in the series of the feasts. He had already given the command in another place, that the passover offering should be offered only at the chosen place Gerizim, and in fact only after they had entered the country, and after they had conquered it, might it be sacrificed. This is also the cause of His statement:[21] "You may not offer the passover sacrifice within any of your towns," and further:[22] "But at the place," and this is Mount Gerizim.

The Second prescription is the appointed time of the offering on the fourteenth day of the month towards evening.

The reason why the passover should be celebrated at the time of the Exodus from Egypt, and that it is called passover, is that therewith the word of God should find confirmation:[23] "You shall remember that you were a slave in Egypt". The law about the individual prescriptions about the passover offering, how it should be, how it should be prepared and how it should be eaten, this is all explained in its proper place. Here the Law-giver mentioned it only, because it is the first of the feasts, and He mentions also its date, but the command as to its preparation, He does not repeat for the sake of brevity.[24]

The second feast is the feast of unleavened bread. Its set time is the following: On the fifteenth of the abovementioned month after the offering of passover is its beginning, and on the twenty-first of the month is its end, so it lasts full seven days; its beginning is the night of passover and its end is a pilgrimage feast.[25] To the commands of these days belong the eating of unleavened bread during the length of the seven days, and the bringing of burnt offerings to God during the duration of the seven; the first of these days is the passover feast, their last a pilgrimage. The first is called the passover feast, the last the feast of unleavened bread. The reason for His command to eat unleavened bread during the space of seven days is in agreement with what happened to them on their Exodus from Egypt, according to His statement:[26] "And they baked unleavened cakes of the dough which they brought out of Egypt". God enjoined on them this command as a reminder at its season; the significance of this act of remembrance has already been explained in its place. Here God says:[27] "And on the fifteenth day of the same month is the feast of unleavened bread to the LORD." He mentions the prescriptions for this day at the end of His statement:[28] "Seven days shall you eat unleavened bread". This is the first requirement. The second is:[29] "On the first day you shall have a holy convocation; you shall do no laborious work". The third requirement is:[30] "But you shall present an offering by fire to the LORD seven days; the fourth requirement is:[31] "On the seventh day is an holy convocation; you shall do no laborious work".

As to the command of the Omer, it is valid on the seven days of the abovementioned feast of unleavened bread. This is explained in the word of God:[32] When you come into the land which I give you and reap its harvest". This command is enjoined them after their entry into the Holy Land and their subjugation thereof, and after they have sowed crops in the Land. It is to be at the time when the crop is ripening and good to eat husked; but it not allowed to cut any of the standing corn until after fulfilling the command relating to the Omer, i.e. the sheaf, corresponding to His word:[33] "You shall bring the sheaf of the first fruits of your harvest of the priest". This ripening sheaf of the corn they shall cut and bring to the priest and the priest shall take it and wave it before God in the tabernacle, after the Passover offering, namely on the Sunday in fulfilment of the word of God:[34] "And he shall wave the sheaf before the LORD, that you may find acceptance; on the morrow after the Sabbath the priest shall wave it". Then they shall bring after the waving of the sheaf, on the same day a burnt offering and it is to be a ram of the flock one year old, perfect, free from blemishes, in fulfilment of His statement:[35] "And on the day when you wave the sheaf, you shall offer a male lamb a year old without blemish as a burnt offering to the Lord".

Then they shall bring a cereal offering in addition to the abovementioned lamb, and in fact two-tenth parts of the finest flour, mixed with oil, as fire offering of sweet savor for God, i.e. they shall let them dissolve in smoke on the altar together with the lamb, after they have sprinkled all with the required measure of wine, and indeed with a quarter of a Kist which is the recognised measure. This corresponds to the divine word:[36] "And the cereal offering thereof shall be two-tenth parts of an ephah of fine flour, mixed with oil, to be offered by fire to the LORD, a pleasing odor; and the drink offering with it shall be of wine, a fourth of a hin" as has already been said above. The Lawgiver (God) admonishes now, that from the crops of that year bread or corn may be eaten only after the sheaf has been brought on that very day, corresponding to His word:[37] "And you shall eat neither bread nor grain parched or fresh, until this same day, until you have brought the offering of your God: it is a statute forever throughout your generations in all your dwellings". His saying, "in all your dwellings" means that this command should be carried out in every land in which they are, and that it is not limited to the chosen place,[38] as the command relating to the passover offering, but God knows best. After that God said:[39] "And you shall count from the morrow after the Sabbath, from the day, that you brought the sheaf of the wave offering; seven full weeks shall they be"; so that the Sabbath which comes before the waving is not counted, instead the beginning of the counting shall be from the Sunday; this is the day on which the waving will be, so that there are seven full weeks in fulfilment of His saying at the end of His statement:[40] "counting fifty days to the morrow after the seventh sabbath;" and in fact, so that the seven weeks shall comprise, forty-nine days, the Sunday of the eighth week will be the end of the fifty days. It is a feast, the harvest feast, and the offerings of that day are prescribed and plainly expressed. The first of these offerings is contained in God's word:[41] "then you shall present cereal offering of new grain to the LORD. You shall bring from your dwellings two loaves of bread. His word here "a cereal offering of new grain" means, that the cereal offering, which they shall bring out of their dwellings, should be from the corn of that year. It is important to mention that, because they could have stored up still some of the corn of previous years in their dwellings. From it, i.e. the crop of this year, they must bring bread, and in this case two loaves, in weight two-tenth parts (of an ephaḥ) of the finest flour, which they should bake as leavened bread and name firstlings, i.e. in place of the first of their corn. This is contained in the divine Word:[42] "two loaves of bread, [cakes (so Sam.)] to be waved, made of two-tenths of an ephah; they shall be of fine flour, they shall be baked with leaven, as first fruits to the LORD". Then they should offer together with the bread, seven perfect one year old lambs, a young bullock, and two perfect rams. That they shall bring to God as a burnt offering, and the drink offering belonging to it as a fire offering, i.e. they should let the whole go up in smoke on the altar of burnt offering; and it will be a sweet savor which God will accept from them wellpleased. And the following is the word of God:[43] "And you shall present with the bread, seven lambs a year old without blemish, and one young bull, and two rams; they shall be a burnt offering to the LORD, with their cereal offering and their drink offerings, an offering by fire, a pleasing odor to the LORD". And they shall prepare a kid for the sin offering and two one year old lambs for a peace offering according to the word of God:[44] And you shall offer one male goat for a sin offering, and two male lambs a year old as a sacrifice of peace offering". The word of God at the end of that excerpt reads:[45] "And the priest shall wave them with the bread of the first fruits as a wave offering before the LORD with the two lambs; they shall be holy to the LORD for the priest". He says first: [46]"And you shall present with the bread seven lambs etc." And then: [47] "they shall be a burnt offering to the LORD with their cereal offering and their drink offerings, an offering by fire, a pleasing odor to the LORD". So he has combined the bread with the seven lambs for the burnt offering, and here He says:[48] "And the priest shall wave them with the bread of the first fruits". The result of this is that together with the seven lambs, the burnt offering, the two-tenth parts of the finest flour, together with the peace offering, the two cakes, the first fruits, are brought which He had mentioned above; whereas we stated above[49] that the two cakes, the first fruits, should be in weight two-tenth parts of finest meal, nevertheless God does not state[50] this plainly, that they should be two-tenth parts of finest flour, but the context of the passage seems to prove it. God said:[51] "two loaves of bread to be waved of two-tenth parts (of an ephah) of fine flour", i.e. that the two cakes should be in weight of two tenth parts of the finest flour. But God knows best.

Next the Lawgiver commanded a holy convocation, on that day, i.e. the invocation of God in praise and thanks for His constant benevolence; they shall greatly praise magnify, and hallow His most lofty Name, the great and lofty One, and they shall sanctify themselves and they shall purify themselves in clothes and in body. That corresponds to the word of God:[52] "And you shall make proclamation on the same day; you shall hold a holy convocation". And on that day shall be abstention from all other work apart from the worship of God, according to the word of God:[53] "You shall do no laborious work". That day shall be to you a religious duty prescribed continually for all time, in every year at that season after the ordinance of the seven weeks which He has mentioned above has been carried out and also the command to bring the sheaf has been fulfilled. And that day is a pilgrimage feast to God and it is named the feast of weeks, a harvest feast and feast of the first fruits, according to the word of God:[54] "it is a statute for ever in all your dwellings throughout all generations".

After this the Creator repeats here the command that one

must not harvest the corners of the field of crops, and that the scattered corn should not be gleaned. The explanation is that this should be left behind for the poor and strangers, who have no corn and no inheritance; and the weak of the people and the strangers are those who are to take both these things (gleaning and corners) as their protection. This corresponds to the word of God:[55] "And when you reap the harvest of your land, you shall not reap your field to its very border, nor shall you gather the gleanings after your harvest; you shall leave them for the poor and for the stranger: I am the LORD your God". It is a glory for us, that He, to whom praise and honour be, always at the end of a command finishes it with the word, I am the LORD your God.

For the next feast, time must elapse, you must wait until the beginning of the seventh month comes along, for He has said that on it the making of the Tabernacle was finished and was itself erected, as has already been mentioned in the place where it occurs.[56] Here He (merely)[57] repeats the command at the end of the enumeration of the yearly prescribed feasts. Having finished with all these matters which are mentioned above, He continues:[58] "And the LORD said to Moses, 'Say to the people of Israel, In the seventh month, on the first day of the month, you shall observe a day of solemn rest, a memorial ...'" He opened the discourse with His statement[59] "And the LORD said to Moses", with the command to the children of Israel, that they should refrain from all work on the first day of the seventh month of the year. Moreover on that day there should be the memorial of blowing of trumpets for holiness, according to the word of God:[60] "a memorial proclaimed with blast of trumpets, a holy convocation". That means on that day men should with loud voices proclaim laud and praise of God, Exalted is He. They should proclaim in such a way that all the people should know of that day, even in the remotest dwelling places, and that all of them should raise unto God praise and glory with sanctification and honor, with acknowledgment of His unity and confession of His majesty; and that they prove themselves to be worthy of the approaching day of fasting through repentance and prayer for pardon. They should on that day do no work according to His word:[61] "You shall do no laborious work". On it they shall bring offerings by fire, i.e. burnt offerings to God, and they shall put them upon the altar according to His word.[62] "You shall present an offering by fire to the LORD".

The kinds of offering He does not mention,[63] presumably they are the offerings which are prepared for any new moon. And God knows best thereon.

As to His word:[64] "On the tenth day of this seventh month is this fast day (the day of atonement); it shall be a holy convocation for you". Already that day, its prescriptions, its means of atonement and its offerings have been mentioned above, in fact with mention of the command as to bringing of the offerings and how the bringing shall be done, and of its special prescriptions; here He mentions every set time with its offering, and calls special attention to that day together with the rest of the set times, and feasts, and the relation of them to the times of the other feasts. We have already earlier in this book of ours[65] in its proper place, discussed the wise reason for this day. It is the day[66] on which the fasts of God's messenger (Moses) were at an end; three fasts which were for one hundred and twenty days. Each fast lasted forty days, as is explained in the book "*The right path*".[67] Their beginning was after the end of the second month, and they lasted four months, so that they all were at an end after the sixth month. The nine days are those which fell between the abovementioned fasts. This is all explained in its proper place. The name "fast day" signifies, a day of pardon and expiation for the whole year.

NOTES ON THE CHAPTER OF THE PRESCRIBED FEASTS

1. Lev. 23:2.

2. The Samaritan vocalisation *Mo'ud* instead of the M.T. *Mō'ēd*

3. Deut. 16:6.

4. Gen. 18:14.

5. *Mō'īd* Samaritan pronunciation of *Mō'ēd*, which in the M.T. Hebrew vocalisation means festive season, festival *or* appointed time, appointment.

6. The distinction between *Mō'ūd* the set time for something (other than a feast) to happen and *Mō'īd* the prescribed Feast is *not* made in the M.T. text. *Mō'ēd* covers both.

6a. The weekly Sabbath is a feast. No fasting is allowed thereon.

7. Lev. 23:3.

8. The Torah, but could refer also to Ibrahim's commentary on Genesis and Exodus.

9. Ibrahim here refers to a piece of Samaritan Midrash which he gave in his Commentary on Gen. 1:26-27.

10. Gen. 2:1.

11. Gen. 2:2.

12. Gen. 2:4.

13. Gen. 2:5.

14. Gen. 2:7.

15. However the Malef 4a states: "On the 6th day He created on it our Father Adam".

16. i.e. non-Samaritan. The connection between Sabbath and Saturn was widely held from ancient times in the Ancient Near East see Hanover's note, *ibid.* p.57 note 31.

17. Lev. 23:4.

18. One would have expected the fourteenth.

19. Only one of numerous chronological systems used by the Samaritans, but not commonly used. Dating is usually according to the Era of the Creation, or according to the date of the entry of Israel into Canaan with Joshua. The Samaritans used also dating according to the era of Jezdegird, or dating according to the Seleucid era, or the era of Diocletian or most often the Muslim dating A.H.

20. Lev. 23:15.

21. Deut.16:5. The Samaritans still keep this law. If they cannot (as was sometimes the case for Israeli Samaritans between 1949 and 1967) ascend Mt. Gerizim for the Passover sacrifice, they do *not* offer a sacrifice elsewhere; nor do they hold a Passover Seder at home. This was a problem which confronted Samaritans from Greek and Roman times, but they never went beyond Deuteronomy in this.

22. Deut.16:6.

23. Deut.16:12.

24. See Exod.12:1-11.

25. The Samaritans are always careful to stress that the feasts of Passover and Unleavened Bread are not one feast (as in Judaism) but two; the climax of the seven days of *Maṣṣoṯ* is the *Hag* or pilgrimage to the Mountain.

26. Exod.12:39.

27. Lev. 23:6.

28. Lev. 23:6.

29. Lev. 23:7.

30. Lev. 23:8.

31. Lev. 23:8.

32. Lev. 23:10. The cutting of the Omer and the waving of it took place among the Sadducees and Samaritans on the morrow of the actual Sabbath after Passover on the basis of Lev. 23:11 The Pharisees regarded the Feast of Passover as a Sabbath and

held that the Omer should be cut and waved on the day following the Passover. This is one of the wellknown differences between Sadducees and Pharisees, and affects their dating of *Hag Shabuot* which falls on the fiftieth day of the Omer. The Samaritan and Sadducean exegesis of Lev. 23:11, 15-16 was the same, and as a result the Samaritan and Sadducean Hag Shabuot always fell on a Sunday (see Meg. Ta'an i; T.B. Men. 65a). That is not to say that the Samaritan and the Sadducean *Hag Sahbuot* fell on the same Sunday as their Passovers may not have been held at the same time: one sect probably calculating that Nisan fell one month later than the other and vice versa. cf. the relation between Samaritan and Jewish calendars at present.

33. Lev. 23:10.

34. Lev. 23:11.

35. Lev. 23:12.

36. Lev. 23:13.

37. Lev. 23:14.

38. i.e. Mt. Gerizim. Ibrahim's interpretation of "in all your dwellings" as meaning that this waving of the sheaf could be carried out elsewhere than at Mt. Gerizim really narrows down the command in Ex. 23:17: "Three times in the year all your males appear before the LORD God. Actually there are three pilgrimages to Mt. Gerizim in the year, that of *Hag Maṣṣot*, that of *Hag Ḳaṣir* (i.e.*Shabuot*) and that of *Hag Asif* (i.e. *Sukkot*) as the Book of the Covenant *ibid.* prescribes. Presumably even in Ibrahim's day when there were still scattered Samaritan communities in Syria and in Egypt, the command to appear three times before God (i.e. at Mt. Gerizim) could not have been enforced. This would be all the more the case in earlier times when the Samaritans had farflung settlements e.g. in Babylon and Rome see Montgomery *ibid.* p.150, 152.

39. Lev. 23:15.

40. Lev. 23:16 see note 32.

41. Lev. 23:16.

42. Lev. 23:17. The Samaritan Pentateuch inserts *hallot* which is not in M.T. Ibrahim spells it *'allot* but this is merely the Samaritan confusion of the gutturals. The Samaritan Pentateuch tends to harmonise parallel statements within its confines; in Lev. 24:5 there is a reference to cakes made from

fine flour and since we have a reference to fine flour here, the word 'cakes' has been inserted to show the shape of the loaves. Further in Num. 15:20 there is reference to cakes (of coarse meal however) as a first fruits offering.

43. Lev. 23:18.

44. Lev. 23:19.

45. Lev. 23:20.

46. Lev. 23:18a.

47. Lev. 23:18b.

48. Lev. 23:20.

49. Lev. 23:17b.

50. Ibrahim had earlier taken Lev. 23:17b as referring only to the loaves of bread baked as first fruits; the two tenths of an ephah, their bulk: the finest flour was what they were made of. Here he interprets Lev. 23:17b differently, and finds it dealing with two offerings; (1) the two-tenth parts of the finest flour are part of the peace offering: (2) the two cakes of bread as the first fruits. Now he admits that what he said earlier as to the weight of loaves and their contents is not explicit in the text but is merely assumed. As Hanover *ibid.* p.65 note 116 points out, the Rabbis knew of only one offering and did not find two referred to in this verse.

51. Lev. 23:17b.

52. Lev. 23:21a.

53. Lev. 23:21b.

54. Lev. 23:21c.

55. Lev. 23:22.

56. Ibrahim says here that the Tabernacle was finished and erected on the 1st Tishri. However as Hanover *ibid.* p.67/8 note 130 points out, in Ibrahim's commentary on Exod. 24:8 he states that the building of the Tabernacle was begun after the feast of Tabernacles and that five months were spent on the work. The Tabernacle according to Ibrahim in that other comment (i.e. that on Exod. 24:8) was not finished till 1st Nisan. Ibrahim therefore contradicts himself. In Exod. 40:2 it is said that God

commanded Moses to erect the completed Tabernacle on the first day of the first month. Exod. 40:7 says that this was done. The question is what was to be understood as the first month. The Samaritans do not accept that 1st Tishri, the first of the seventh month is Rosh ha-Shanah; it is all the more surprising that Ibrahim should regard the Tabernacle as having been set up on the 1st Tishri.

57. True, the command to observe the first of the seventh month occurs elsewhere see Num. 29:1f.

58. Lev. 23:23, 24.

59. Lev. 23:23.

60. Lev. 23:24 end.

61. Lev. 23:25.

62. Lev. 23:25.

63. But the offerings are mentioned in Num. 29:2-5 in addition to those for the new moon. See Num. 29:6.

64. Lev. 23:26 for the Day of Atonement and its ritual see Lev. 16.

65. P.79a-87b of the Berlin MS. cf. Hanover *ibid.* p.69 note 137.

66. The first fast of Moses started when he went up Sinai to receive the Law. Exod. 24:18 see also Deut.9:11. The second fast of 40 days was when he went up the mountain again after breaking the tables of the Law see Exod.32:30. Exod. 32:31 does not tell how long Moses made intercession for Israel, but Deut. 9:18 states that it was forty days and forty nights. The third fast is while he is on the mountain the third time to receive the new tables of the Law. See Exod.34:28.

Ibrahim makes the last of Moses' three fasts of forty days end on the Day of Atonement. His calculation that their termination took place on the Day of Atonement, while making use of some details of Biblical information, is strictly traditional lore.

67. An unknown work.

ABU'L HASAN AL-SURI'S KITAB AL TABBAH

Abu'l Hasan is author of *Kitab al-Tabbaḥ* "The Book of Slaughtering" or "The Book of the Cook (or of Cookery)", and a few liturgical pieces. His date is still uncertain, but we would not be far wrong in assigning him to the eleventh century. One of his liturgical pieces (*Elah Rab* Cow. Vol. 1 p.70) in good Aramaic still occurs in the Eve of Sabbath Service. Abu'l Hasan may be the father of Ab-Gelugah (so the Chronicles) who built a synagogue and was standardiser of the liturgy in the 12th century. Abu'l Hasan may have been one of the first Samaritans to interest himself in working towards an Arabic Bible translation, afterwards to be done by Abu Sa'id. His chief claim to fame is his abovementioned "Book of Cookery"; the only connection it has with cookery is that it is a hotch-potch, but the *Kitab-al-Tabbaḥ* is important. It is the earliest Samaritan compilation that has come down to us dealing with Oral Law; among the halakot treated there is some space given to the laws of slaughtering which have some connection with the title. Clean and unclean animals are also dealt with as is the question of leprosy (see Weiss's art. in John Rylands Bulletin, Vol.33 p.131-137, 1950), and Gonorrhea. The Calendar is treated in some detail and that of the Jews and Karaites criticised. There is a lengthy section of the description of the service and the sacrifice of Passover. In addition to such matters we find at the end of the work some sections devoted to Bible commentary on the last chapters of Deuteronomy. Such are important as they are the earliest Samaritan Bible commentary that has dome down to us, if we exclude the Memar Marḳa. Very important is his section on the angels. The whole work is in Arabic. The chapters I have translated are of some general interest as giving some glimpse of Samaritan theology.

On Abu'l Hasan As-Suri see Cowley, *Samaritan Liturgy*, Vol. II, pp.23-24; J. W. Nutt, *Samaritan Targum*, London, 1874, pp.139-140; M. Gaster, *The Samaritans*, London, 1925, pp.151-152; J. A. Montgomery, *The Samaritans*, Philadelphia, 1907, pp.296, 298.

SECTION ON THE EXPLANATION OF THE SHEMA[1]

That things should come into existence after there had been nothing at all indicates that they come from one wise artificer who has no second. Besides the absence of similarity between them proves that there is none like Him, nor similar to Him. And although the mind points to the confirming of His unity (Exalted is He), and His necessary existence, yet that cannot be known except by speculation and inference by a method which is impossible for many people to arrive at; so the Law came from God (Exalted is He) through one, the truth of whom, and the rightness of whose prophecy were demonstrated by wonders to provide information about His being One, that those who cannot arrive at the way through inference, might get knowledge of it; and it is said also that its (i.e. the Law's) coming down by revelation can be added to what the mind infers so that it should be like making two proofs of the one thing. And He began this verse with a word which directs obedience and compliance according to His saying: (Exalted is He) "Hear O Israel".[2] Since God made His worship compulsory on all the Creation, He began with all the creation in general, and Israel in particular, according to His saying: "The LORD *our* God is one LORD".[3] He repeated the name (LORD) to connect it with the word which indicates unity (i.e. "one") as He (Exalted is He) is one by Himself, and so that none of the nations would imagine that Israel has a LORD other than the LORD of (other) nations. By this saying He pointed out that He is the LORD of Israel and their Creator and likewise Creator of the world. Further since amongst people, love for one another arises because it is advantageous, God made it known in this section that love of Him arises in three ways - in the heart, in the body, and in the effort to devote money according to His saying: "And you shall love the LORD your God with all your heart, and with all your soul, and with all you might".[4] Knowledge of Him and of His prophets and of His law is achieved by understanding, and its place is the heart. He referred to it in His saying: "With all your heart". Worship of Him and obedience to His command and adherence to His way and fulfilling of His ordinance, that is carried out by the body and it is that which is referred to in His saying: "With all your soul". Now the bringing of offerings and alms and tithes and such things as purity of intention and genuineness of purpose and sincerity, all this comes about through spending money and effort, as God said (Exalted is He); "And with all your might". God made the keeping of His Law obligatory by His saying (Exalted is He): "And these words which I command you this day shall be upon your hearts."[4a] And He made obligatory the teaching of it to children in His saying: "And you shall teach them diligently to your children".[4b] He ordered that the Law be read and not anything else in days of leisure according to His saying: "And you shall talk of them when you sit in your house".[4c] And in walking and in all occupations according to His saying (Exalted is He): "And when you walk by the way".[4d] And at times of worship, I mean by that the two chosen times of offering prayers, at the beginning of the night called 'Between the two evenings' which is referred to in His saying (Exalted is He): "And when you lie down",[4e] meaning before "you lie down", and at the beginning of the day called 'morning' indicated in His saying: "And when you rise".[4f] He meant by that after you awake from your sleep. Since the management of one's practical affairs is done by the two bodily members (i.e. hands) He made it (the Law) a restraint on them (the hands) that they should not do what is not permissible for them according to His saying: "And you shall bind them for a sign upon your hand".[4g] It is also said that this ordinance in which it is said: "And you shall bind", that He means by it the making of the 'fringes'. He made obligatory the teaching of the Hebrew writing in which its words (i.e. those of the command) were recorded according to His saying: "And they will be as frontlets between your eyes".[4h] And He (Exalted is He) made the dwellings of Israel to resemble holy places and altars suitable for the remembrance of God (Exalted is He), and it is that which is indicated by his saying (Exalted is He): "And you shall write them on the doorposts of your house and on your gates".[4i] It is said regarding the reference to the "door posts" that He meant by the writing on them (to remind the Israelites of) the death of the Egyptian firstborn and of what God did during that night (i.e. the first Passover) in making an example of the idols and saving Israel from bondage and of all that He did to the Egyptians (who were) their enslavers, in order that they should ponder on that in their going in and out to produce thereby favor and well-being.

SECTION
THE DISCOURSE ON: "AND HE WENT UP"[5]

When information came to the Apostle (Peace be on him) from Him[5a] (Exalted is He) that He would effect signs with him exclusively according to His saying: "With you I will do marvels, such as have not been wrought in all the earth, nor in any nation: and all the people among which you are shall see the work of the LORD, for it is a terrible thing that I do with you".[6] He (Exalted is He) indicated by that three things; (i) The first of them was his staying a period of 40 days during which he did not feed even three times, such as that no human being could do - and (ii) the acquiring of the light on his face, which is referred to by "with a ray of light" after his abstaining from food - and (iii) seeing the land of Canaan with its encompassing borders of which it is said: "From the river of Egypt to the great river, the river Euphrates and to the hinder sea".[7] And his seeing that land was after the blessing of the tribes. And on that day He did for him (Moses) five signs. The first of which was that He called on the spiritual world. I mean the troops of Angels to inhabit the earth; and He commanded them to hear His word according to his saying: "Give ear you heavens and I will speak".[8] The second (sign) was that God (Exalted is He) provided him with help until 600,000 (Angels) not counting their followers, heard his words and what he said in his address, according to His saying: "And let the earth hear the words of My mouth".[9] The third (sign) was that he wrote the whole Law in one day. He was pointing with his hand to the scroll and the writing thereby took form. The fourth (sign) was his being carried in the air until he was facing the earth, and the strength of his sight and the clearing away of the vapor rising from the earth which stands between the eye and the things seen - since he was ordered to ascend the mountain according to His saying: "And Moses went up from the plains of Moab to Mount Nebo, to the top of Pisgah, which is opposite Jericho. And the LORD showed him all the land etc." down to His saying "to the hinder sea".[10] Then God informed him: "This land which you saw with all its boundaries is that which I promised Abraham, Isaac and Jacob; 'to your progeny I will give (it)'". And in that, is an announcement to him of His giving it to his progeny that he might be comforted for what vexed him (Peace be on him), because he was prevented from entering it. Have you considered his saying to Israel: "I shall not go over the Jordan... but you shall go over".[11] Thus He (Exalted is He) made known his sorrow (Peace be on him), about such a thing. But He made Israel very happy in what they were coming to, and which he (Moses) perceived by sight, according to His saying: "I have caused you to see it with your eyes, but you shall not go over thither".[12]

THE DISCOURSE ON 'AND HE (MOSES) DIES'[13]

Since information has previously been given about the Apostle (Peace be upon him) of that which does not pertain to a human being, Wisdom decreed to give information about his death (upon him be peace) and his translation, lest it would be imagined that he was joining the spiritual beings owing to his associating with them in what was allowable for them.

The explanation of that is His saying (Exalted is He) "So Moses died there"[14] And the demonstrative in "There" refers to Mount Nebo from where he had seen the land of Canaan. And His saying "The servant of the LORD"[15] is to honor him (Moses): and God (Exalted is He) informed that were it not for the command of God (Exalted is He) which came to him to die, he would have remained until this day of ours; because nature would not make him aged and there certainly would not be much wearing out in him, but he would remain all his life in a state of equilibrium.

And when one's condition is such, had not the command been (given) for him to die, then it would have been necessary for him to go on living. And God has made that clear to the people, by His saying "According to the word of the LORD".[16] And God took charge of him, by His own will, because of his great position, and he was buried in Mount Nebo; and it (Mt. Nebo) has four sides, each region having a title applied to it. The first is Mt. Abarim, the second is Mt. Nebo, the third is Gai, the fourth is the Pisgah. And no mortal was present to witness the manner of his death according to His saying (perfect peace be upon Him) "But no man knows his sepulchre to this day".[17] Now the way by which knowledge of his death came to Israel was what they heard while they were around the mountain from the troops of Angels honoring him and showing regard and weeping, during the space of time which is mentioned. And in it Israel imitated the lamentations for him for the period about which it is said "And the children of Israel wept for Moses in the plains of Moab thirty days".[18] Further it is said that the Apostle had fixed the length of time for them, and ordered them to lament during it by command of God (Exalted is He), before his going up; and so they could not increase nor diminish (it), because had it not been for that, they would have wept for him more than this space of time; and in His saying: "then the days of weeping and mourning for Moses were ended"[19] is a proof regarding the complete duration of the time about which the command has previously been mentioned. It is said that Joshua (Peace be upon him) gave information of it after the death of the apostle. And the holder of this opinion adduces as argument His saying, "And Joshua the son of Nun was full of the spirit of Wisdom for Moses had laid his hands upon him; so the people of Israel obeyed him, and did as the LORD had commanded Moses".[20] Yet in the acceptance of his (precedence over them and (in) following his) command, and coming under his obedience, as God commanded Moses, (they adduce) his saying "And there has not arisen a prophet since in Israel like Moses".[21]

AND THERE HATH NOT ARISEN (A PROPHET SINCE IN ISRAEL LIKE MOSES)[22]

How could Joshua (peace be upon him) have been endowed with a species of prophecy, when the mention has already been made of their seventy-two prophets, who prophesied by the hand of Lord Apostle, and it has been said about them: "They prophesied but they did do no more".[23] That was followed by the mention of the prophecy of Moses at the conclusion of the Law and the denial of any similarity to him in the past and the future in the nation of Israel who are the favourites of God, and the chosen from all the nations and peoples; and the denial is more so amongst others. This can be concluded from His saying: "And there hath not arisen a prophet since in Israel like Moses".[24] It was also said that when it has been mentioned before the Law in a clear text which gives the full sense of similarity to him according to His saying "I will raise up for them a prophet like you from among their brethren, and I will put my words in his mouth"[25] the intention of His saying, 'like you' was to honour the Lord Apostle. God made that clear in what He expressed, along with the denial of any comparison and the denial of it in all Israel in the past and the future, to remove the obscurity and prevent such an interpretation. And His saying "whom the LORD knew face to face"[26] established for him qualities of being in a class by himself different from all the other prophets by conversing mouth to mouth. It was also said that the speech when it came to him in Egypt was shared between the Lord Aaron and between the Lord Moses; but God (Exalted is He) explained that the speech came to Him talking mouth to mouth in all which He did through him in the land of Egypt in order that people might not imagine that the speech delivered to him in Egypt was of the same sort as that delivered to Aaron. God made clear the special aspect of talking mouth to mouth to Moses and no one else in His saying: "for all the signs and the wonders, which the LORD sent him to do in the land of Egypt"[27] and in His saying "and for all the mighty power".[28]

He means the speech delivered in Pharaoh's council with the news of the killing of the Firstborn in Egypt in the sight of his (Pharaoh's) attendants and servants. And he is the one spoken about in it. "And the man Moses was very great in the land of Egypt in the eyes of Pharaoh and in the eyes of the people".[29] And in what he did of the miracles of the sea;

which is referred to in his saying: "And in all the great spectacle which Moses wrought in the sight of all Israel."[30]

FOOTNOTES

1. Cf. Abu'l Hasan al-Suri, Kitab al Tabbaḥ, (J.R.Sam.9 f.136a).

2. Deut. 6:4.

3. Deut. 6:4.

4. Deut. 6:5.

4a. Deut. 6:6.

4b. Deut. 6:7.

4c. Deut. 6:7.

4d. Deut. 6:7.

4e. Deut. 6:7.

4f. Deut. 6:8.

4gh. Deut. 6:8. Sam. reading 'hands' referring to the ten fingers at whose fingertips should be the Ten Commandments.

4i. Deut. 6:9. The Samaritans have not the Jewish Mezuzah on the doorpost, but sometimes the Ten Commandments on the lintel.

5. Abu'l Hasan al-Suri, Kitab al-Tabbaḥ (J.R.Sam.9 ff.213-14).

5a. Viz. God.

6. Cf. Exod. 34:10. Note difference in the Sam. text from the M.T. at beginning.

7. The first part of the quotation is derived from Gen. 15:18, the second part from Deut. 11:24. The phrase 'the river Euphrates' occurs in both and serves as a bridge between the two.

8. Cf. Deut. 32:1.

9. *Ibid.*

10. Cf. Deut. 34:1, 2.

11. Cf. Deut. 4:22.

12. *Ibid.* 34:4.

Abu'l-Hasan al-Suri, *Kitab al-Tabbaḥ*, (J.R.Sam.9 f.216a).

13. Cf. Deut. 34:5.

14. Deut. 34:5.

15. Deut. 34:5.

16. Cf. Deut. 34:5.

17. *Ibid.*, 34:6.

18. *Ibid.*, 34:8.

19. Cf. Deut. 34:8.

20. *Ibid.*, 34:9.

21. *Ibid.*, 34:10.

22. Cf. Deut. 34:10.

23. Cf. Num. 11:25.

24. Cf. Deut. 34:10.

25. Cf. Deut. 18:18.

26. Cf. Deut. 34:10.

27. *Ibid.*, 34:11.

28. *Ibid.*, 34:12.

29. *Ibid.*, 34:11.

30. *Ibid.*, 34:12.

CHAPTER 4

THE DISCOURSE CONCERNING THE ANGELS *

It has been established by the proof of what has been revealed that God has creatures other than mankind who are capable of worshipping Him, and who exist to act as emissaries to those who are[1] subject to command, for their well-being, and who are ready to glorify and honour all those who are blessed in heaven. They are formed out of fire and air according to what the noble Book indicated as He said: "Now the appearance of the glory of the LORD was like devouring fire on the top of the mountain in the sight of the people of Israel".[2] This is the fiery kind. As for the airy, knowledge of it is derived from His saying: "And they saw *Elohe Yisra'el...*"[3] etc. The difference in description points to the diversity of those described. It is not possible for them to be composed of the kind of things man is composed of, otherwise it would have been necessary (for them) to have the same needs and requirements of food; and it would have been impossible for them to continue existing, on account of the contradiction,[4] and it is not possible for any of them who are made of air, to be composed of dust or of water; otherwise the law of universals would apply to the particulars with regard to weight and density and they would have to be attached to an appropriate centre; because the rule is that when part of the elements is separated (from them) involuntarily it would necessarily return to them, and that is not allowable for angels,[5] because they are extremely fine. So many learned people hold that they are spirits without bodies. But as for us, we go back in describing them to what the noble Book has informed us about their corporeal description, regarding their standing up and their mobility, and ability to talk and the organs of speech and hearing and the organs of seeing and (having) two hands and two feet according to what He has said regarding the Angel who talked to Abraham, viz. His saying:

"And the LORD said; 'Because the outcry against Sodom and Gomorrah is great and because their sin is very grave";[6] etc... down to His saying: 'I will go down now and see (whether they have done altogether) according to the outcry, which has come to Me'".[7] So he established in this section five parts, (lit. Divisions) viz; mobility, articulation, the organs of speech, hearing and sight. In the Angel which appeared to oppose Balaam, He proved standing up, and (the having) two hands, according to His saying in the story concerning Balaam, "And he saw the Angel of the LORD standing in the way, with his drawn sword in his hand".[8] He proved their having two feet in the previous section in which it is said: "And they saw *Elohe Yisrael;* and there was under his feet etc..."[9] They are described as having wings according to His saying (Exalted is He), "And the Spirit of God was brooding[10] upon the face of the waters".[11] And this is the description of the kind that flies. Consider His saying (Exalted is He) in the Comprehensive Address, when He gave a description of the eagle according to His saying, "Like an eagle that stirs up her nest, that flutters over her young".[12] And this is all that the noble Book described. As for the abdomen and the internal organs like the heart which is the source of heat and the abode of the soul, and the lung by which air can be breathed, and the stomach and the liver, and the gallbag, and the bowels and the spleen and the kidneys and the pores, these are all the organs of digestion and the organs of the spirit. They can dispense with them, because they (the Angels) came into existence before the class of things which could be used as nourishment. They (the angels) are not of flesh or blood, and because life cannot exist without blood which is fundamental to life, God put life in them whilst they have no flesh or blood, in order that it may be known from that, that God is able to create all kinds of creatures. They have no lust nor hatred because of the lack of sensible souls. They are not described as possessing intelligence because intelligence is an acquisitive quality, but they are described as possessing knowledge which may be affected by times, and intelligence is below the grade of knowledge. They have no incentive to do evil because they know its evil and because they can do without it, because they are the most learned of creation because they are not composite being, and are separated from an earthly nature. In addition to that, they do not need to show a proof with regard to the message they carry. They live in the high heavens according to the saying of the Apostle "Look down from Thy holy habitation, from heaven".[13]

Al-Ma'on: in Hebrew that is the name for 'homeland'. A home is not a home except for him who lives in it; and there is no one in the higher world who dwells in it and is considered worthy of worshipping God other than them (the angels). As to their forms; they are said to be divided into two groups; one of them, it is said, is of an unique shape. There is nothing in existence similar to compare with them, and they are those who are called the "Cherubim" and no mortal has seen them except the Apostle according to His saying (Exalted is He), "And he beholds the form of the LORD".[14]

It is said that their shapes are like those of human beings; a statement which is unacceptable in two respects: one of them is that had it been like that, His saying: "And he beholds the form of the LORD",[15] would have no meaning or point but His (form), because everyone can see human forms. The other is the fact of created beings coming into existence from God in the beginning without a comparable form. So when Wisdom decreed to give them a dwelling in the noble tabernacle erected by the hand of the Apostle, God (Exalted is He) commanded him that he should show their likeness to the artificers so that they should know that there were two cherubim, and the Veil,[16] and that the likeness thereon be comparable to what was described to him, so that the Angels would yearn for their image because every kind likes most its own shape and form. And this is all that research and knowledge could attain in the knowledge of the form of the upper world.

NOTES TO ABU'L HASAN'S DISCOURSE CONCERNING THE ANGELS

*Abu'l Hasan al-Suri, *Kitab al-Tabbaḥ,* MS. pp.124-7.

1. The people charged with messages from God.

2. Cf. Exod. 24:17.

3. *Ibid.* 24:10.

4. Viz. humans being mortal.

5. Viz. The Angels.

6. Cf. Gen. 18:20.

7. *Ibid.* 21.

8. Cf. Num. 22:31.

9. Cf. Exod. 24:10.

10. Cf. R.V.Marg.

11. Cf. Gen. 1:2.

12. Cf. Deut. 32:11.

13. Cf. Deut. 26:15.

14. Num. 12:8. Here *T^e^munah YHWH* the form of the LORD is interpreted as Cherubim.

15. Num. 12:8.

16. See Exod.26:31 for Cherubim on the Veil.

THE MEMAR MARKAH from which the following short extract is taken deserves inclusion in a work dealing with documents relating to Samaritan history, religion and life. Marḳah himself played a significant part in the development of study of the

Torah and the development of liturgy in the time of Baba Raba. The Memar Markah like Marka's hymns are in Samaritan Aramaic, the language of the Samaritan Targum, which latter is itself cited in the Memar Markah. Though the Samaritan Targum long ago fell into disuse in the Sabbath services, the Memar Markah which presupposes knowledge of that Targum, has continued till this day to be an important source of doctrine; perhaps this is in part due to the fact that it is by Markah whose hymns are still used in Divine Worship on the Sabbath.

The Memar Markah is not meant to be a commentary on the whole Pentateuch. Indeed it is questionable whether it was intended primarily as a commentary at all. Forty-six verses are quoted from Genesis: one hundred and thirty-one are cited from Exodus: fourteen from Leviticus: seventeen from Numbers, and sixty-two from Deuteronomy. It is clear that Exodus is the most cited, and if one looks more closely at the verses from Exodus - and from Deuteronomy too, the reason becomes clear. The Memar Markah is primarily about Markah's namesake Moses, for Markah is the surrogate for Mošeh, used by Samaritans and Jews among the Romans. The Memar Markah is a haggadic midrash about Moses and the Exodus, his call by God, his commissioning to confront Pharaoh who after eleven plagues lets Israel go only to pursue them to the sea where by the help of God Moses and Israel pass through victoriously and Pharaoh's army is overwhelmed. After a midrashic discourse on the Song of Moses, at the sea Markah treats us to a discourse regarding God's holy mountain - not Sinai, but Gerizim for which he finds thirteen names in the Torah, seven of which he finds in citations from Genesis, two from Exodus and four from Deuteronomy. The second book of the Memar Markah ends with a eulogy of Moses. Books three and four are important as containing Markah's haggadic midrash on the teaching which Moses from God gave to the people of Israel. While there is some halakah here it is dealt with in homiletic fashion; when one remembers the amount of halakah in the Torah, it is all the more significant how much Markah does not deal with. Book four is basically a midrash on Deut. 32 which chapter is given such prominence in Samaritan religion containing as it does the great song of Moses, in which they find the teaching on the Day of Vengeance and Recompense. Book five of the Memar deals with the death of Moses and gives Markah further opportunity to eulogise Moses by gathering together citations and allusions throughout the Torah which to his mind establish the uniquè glory of Moses. As if this were not enough book six is an alphabetic midrash after the manner of the Jewish Midrash of R. Akiba, but devoted to the praise of Moses by every one of the twenty-two letters of the Hebrew Alphabet.

The short extract which follows is from Book four on The Day of Vengeance as this enshrines specifically Samaritan eschatology. While the Memar Markah was composed in Samaritan Aramaic in the fourth century A.D. and manuscripts of the Memar are still copied out in Aramaic which is a long dead language for Samaritans, it is perhaps not surprising that a Hebrew translation of the Memar Markah exists. It is to be found written alongside of the Aramaic text in the Moses Gaster MS. 825 in the John Rylands Library. While it would be rash to claim any antiquity for the Hebrew translation any more than for Hebrew translations of the Samaritan Joshua, yet it probably shows not only how a Samaritan priestly Scribe at the beginning of the twentieth century understood Markah to mean, but indeed how according to the Samaritan priestly tradition the Memar Markah was to be understood in Hebrew. In my opinion this is not unimportant and I have therefore used this bilingual manuscript for the translation here appended.

MARKAH ON THE DAY OF VENGEANCE

The Seventh Discourse is a discourse in which there is both comfort[1] and affliction;[2] it is on the phrase "and their doom comes swiftly".[3] He who had previously done evil deeds, shall be requited with penalties,[4] and he who previously had done good (will be rewarded) with the like, as He said:[5] but showing steadfast love to thousands of those who love Me and keep My commandments; visiting the inquity of their fathers upon the children to the third and fourth generation of those who hate Me". We ought to renew repentance so that we find rest, and be secure against punishment.

A day of vengeance[6] it is for all sinners: but a day of recompense for all the good: a day of standing up,[7] it is for all men:[8] a day of regret[9] it is for all evil men: a day of reckoning of all deeds: a day of giving of recompense for the righteous and the wicked: a day of questioning[10] about the bloodguilt[11] arising from the deeds of all creatures: a day of slipping for all feet:[12] a day of trembling for all limbs: a day of reckoning for all deeds: a day on which every one receives its reward: a day of judgment, a day of weeping, a day of deliverance, a day of gathering, a day of truth, a day of terror, a day of vengeance, a day of standing, a day of coming forth from under the earth; a day of grief for all wicked men, a day of joy for all the obedient, a day on which the Lord of the world reveals himself and declares: I, even I, am He, and there is no other beside Me.[13] He calls His creatures as He[14] wishes. The earth splits open in great dread, and all are spread forth as in the twinkling of an eye, and they arise at one time. When it is split open above the good, an odor of precious myrrh[15] arises: a pleasing odor[16] ascends to the lofty[17] dwelling.

But the evil,[18] a smell of dust arises as is said:[19] You return to the ground. He returns[20] and with him is sulphur and fire. And when these[21] are brought together, see the difference between the two of them.

The good - their odor is acceptable and their clothes are new as He said:[22] "Your clothes have not worn out upon you". And Adam and Noah and the meritorious[23] ones of the world are before them, and the angels of Divine Favor[24] are around them and the dews of mercy are distilled upon them and light[25] illumines them; and the great prophet Moses[26] glories in them; and Aaron the priest rejoices on their account, and his son Eleazar is glad for them and Phinehas sings their praises; and Joshua and Caleb and the seventy elders glorify them: and the Favor of the Lord rests on them and proclaims on their account.[27] "So Israel dwelt in safety alone". These are the things that befall the good, the possessors of merit because they kept the statutes which God decreed and forsook them not.

But the wicked are the opposite (of them), because an evil odor arises from the dust which returns, and pitch and fire are mixed with it, and it is not acceptable, and their clothes are tattered, and their faces troubled. It is said of them:[28] "Why are your faces downcast today?" And Cain[29] and Lamech and the men of the Flood, and the men of Sodom, and the men of Babel and the Egyptians, and the Amalekites, and Korah all his company smite them with their hands, (for) they are met together against them; the angels[30] of Wrath surround them, and dust and ashes fall upon them, and their eyes are dimmed. The great prophet Moses vindicates himself against them, and Aaron and his sons rage at them and the great fire destroys their corpses: and God has no pity on them. And they are weeping and the world is shut against them. And the Truth says[31] "I will make my arrows drunk with blood, and my sword shall devour flesh". These are the punishments of the guilty on the Day of the Great Judgement.

The good rejoice and none of their clothes have worn out

upon them, because they loved the stranger and gave him bread and clothing; and their faces shine because they did not turn their faces away from him who supplicated: their hands too are full of light, because they did not refuse him alms. Their hearts are full of light for they did not speak worthless things, and their souls are pure because they loved[32] their Lord with soul and heart and might, as He said: "And you shall love the LORD your God.[33] Their feet have not become swollen[34] for they went after the LORD as He said[35] "You shall walk after the LORD". All that shall be revealed on the Day of Recompense.

But the wicked are in great strife, and their clothes are torn because they seized in pledge the widow's rag;[36] their faces are blackened because they turned away from every poor and needy person: their hands are cut off, because they refused him alms; their hearts are mournful because they did not serve the LORD with joy and gladness and with goodness of heart. The sons of Belial[37] reigned over them and their souls are given in pledge, for they were not fully devoted to the LORD; and their understandings are troubled, for they went a-whoring after them. Their strength is feeble, because they did not cleave to the commandments, and he smote them from hand to foot, because they went about with slander, and were not afraid, because of doing this, of the Day of Vengeance, which is prepared for all such deeds. He who commits a transgression in the world, and does not turn back therefrom, there is there no deliverance for him. Woe to the transgressor for what he has done against himself. A devouring fire is prepared which will consume him. Happy are the meritorious ones in what they have acquired; and dew and blessing give rest to him: dew from the Garden, and blessing from heaven are his: these are refreshment for him. Oh a great portion is the portion of merit:[38] whoever is despised shall be in great glory in this world and the next. The great Apostle Moses is glorified because his LORD sanctified him and set him on a degree to which no man[39] of the seed of Adam had approached nor will ever after him approach.

The tenth discourse: When the great prophet Moses informed Israel of the Day of Vengeance, he gave them good news of their deliverance from it; but the good news and the deliverance were only for the sons of merit, and the doers of good deeds, and the keepers of the commandments who walk in the path of Truth. In peace the Taheb[40] comes who will rule in the place which God chose for those good ones. (When) the elder of his father's house was a boy, he increased in wisdom and his heart was full of knowledge of what he was taught and it was said of him:[41] "a perfect man, dwelling in tents": mighty was his knowledge (which he showed) in a meritorious reign. And Joseph came. Therefore he was rewarded with the[42] kingdom after his slavery; and those who oppressed him, they sought his glory: his brothers did not right in what they did, but he[43] did right in what he did. Where is there one like Joseph enlightened, wise in whom was the spirit of God.[44] He was king of the Place.[45] Therefore his bones were carried[46] by the prophet, the faithful[47] one of the house of the LORD. There is no king like Joseph and there is no prophet like Moses. Both of them ruled in two high degrees: Moses is king of prophecy and Joseph is king of the blessed mountain. Neither is greater than the other. Praise be to our God who eternally by Himself rules the worlds. And there is none with Him, other than He. Holy is the prophet who was hallowed by the hand of God, and by whose hand was revealed various very glorious things. And[48] there has not arisen a prophet like Moses nor will there ever arise, he who was lifted up above[49] all the camp of men and attained to being grouped[50] with the angels, as is said of him: I will gather[51] for you My angels. Where is there one like Moses who trod the fire? Where is one like Moses who rent the heavens? Where is one like Moses who approached the thick darkness? Where is one like Moses to whom God said:[52] "And do you stand here with Me". Where is there a prophet like Moses with whom God spoke[53] mouth to mouth? Where is there a prophet like Moses who fasted forty[54] days and forty nights; he neither ate nor drank. And he came down bearing two tables of stone[55] written with the finger of God. And besides he said other words, all of them good tidings to those who do good. May the Taheb come[56] in peace who rules the city of[57] the perfect and reveals the Truth.

NOTES TO MARKAH'S COMMENTARY ON DEUT. 32:35

1. M. Heidenheim Bib. Sam. iii, p.143,cf. also p.202 note 719 takes *Pugguhon* as if from *Pg'*. This is quite wrong. The Hebrew translation in MS. J.R.G. 825 (Hebrew column) translates as 'good tidings'. Cowley, *Ibid.* Vol. II p.xvi gives the meaning of *Pug(po)* as 'to relieve, comfort'.

2. *Maduhon.* MS. J.R.G. 825 (Heb.) *neamot*,cf. however Jastrow *ibid.* p.733-*Madwah* ('afflication'). We are to understand that Markah is saying that in the Biblical phrase which he is about to quote there is good news for good people about the Last Day, but grievous tidings of punishment for the wicked.

3. Deut. 32:35 Markah's method of commenting on a Biblical verse is not like that of Ibrahim ibn Ya'kub. Markah in true haggadic midrashic style uses a Biblical phrase as a peg on which to hang a lengthy discourse. Whereas we might compare the method of commenting used by Ibrahim ibn Ya'kub to that of Mekilta or Sifra, Markah's manner of comment is like that of Midrash Rabba. This portion of Deut. 32:35 is the word *'miltah'*. The expression *'miltah'* is also used of the discourse for which Deut. 32:35d forms the text. It is as if one word stood for both 'phrase' and 'discourse': cf. Memar Markah, which is the title of Markah's whole commentary, it literally means 'the word of Markah'.

4. MS. J.R.G. 825 (Heb.) 'shall be rewarded with punishment' which gives the sense. If *waw* has been interchanged in the original for *beth* (as frequently happens in Samaritan orthography) 'penalties' is the correct translation the root being *gbh*.

5. Cf.Exod.20:6. The Samaritan Targum as given by Markah literally says 'doing good' instead of 'showing steadfast love', and 'remembering' instead of 'visiting' the iniquity

of fathers.

6. The title of the Day of Vengeance derived from this Biblical verse Deut. 32:35 (Sam. reading i.e. Yom Naḳam instead of *li Naḳam*,i.e. 'for the Day of Vengeance' instead of 'Vengeance is mine'. This different Samaritan reading also affects the 'and recompense' (*ibid.*) which follows. The full name of the Day of Vengeance, is 'The Day of Vengeance and Recompense'. Undoubtedly, Samaritan Eschatology is founded on Deut. 32 and this verse in particular.

7. Cf. the Arabic *yaum al-Qiyamat* for the day of resurrection; one wonders if the Jewish expression *Yom ha-Ma'amad* applied to the day of the giving of the Law at Sinai to Israel, has influenced this Samaritan epithet of the Resurrection Day. All men, not Israel alone, stand to receive God's judgment. If so, it would not primarily be the arising from their graves that is referred to here.

8. *Bar Nashaya* i.e. human beings.

9. *Anhamuṯa* from the root *nhm* would seem to give the opposite meaning: comfort. On the other hand it is not impossible to obtain from it the meaning: regret. Heidenheim, *ibid.* p.202 note 723,would read Anḳamuṯa (vengeance) but there is no doubt as to the reading Anhamuṯa: further *heṯ* and *ḳof* do not interchange even in Samaritan orthography.

10. Heidenheim(*ibid.* p.144)inexplicably translates this as 'ein Auferstehungstag'.

11. Heidenheim(*ibid.* p.202 note 724)emends his text to give the sense of *Verschuldungen* reading *ma'a̅samaya*. The proper reading is *ma'adamaya* which I understand as 'bloodguilt'. J.R.G. 825 (Heb. col.) *metomim* would imply a translation: soundness, integrity of the deeds etc.

12. Cf. Deut. 32:35.

13. Cf. Deut. 32:39 'other' instead of the explicit mention of a god as in the Heb. Bible text.

14. i.e. the time and manner of the resurrection is entirely in God's contol.

15. One should compare the *Šira Yetima* stanza *Heṯ* for a description of the Resurrection as set out here. Although the *Šira Yetima* was written in the fourteenth century by Abisha ben Phinehas,i.e. one thousand years after Marḳah's Memar, the description of the events of the Resurrection Day are very

similar. For section *het* of *Šira Yetima*, cf. Cowley *ibid.* Vol. II, pp.515-516; for an English translation, cf. M. Gaster's: *Samaritan Oral Law and Ancient Traditions* Vol. 1, Eschatology pp.97-101 l.3 (the rest of p.101 is from stanza *Tet*). The *Šira Yetima* is still used in the modern Samaritan Day of Atonement Services.

16. The common phrase in the Pentateuch for the smell of an acceptable sacrifice, cf. Gen. 8:21 etc. There is a Medieval Jewish idea that a pleasant odor is emitted by the bones of the pious, cf. Heidenheim, *ibid.* p.202 note 724a.

17. The *Ma'on 'ala'ah* God's heavenly habitation.

18. Cf. *Šira Yetima* (Gaster *op.cit.* p.100). In the *Šira Yetima* it is quite clear that all non-Samaritans are the wicked. There is a hardening of attitude towards outsiders manifested in the fourteenth century account of the End. Perhaps it is understandable as the Samaritan community had suffered so much by then and was already dwindling.

19. Gen. 3:19 the original Aramaic is *haṣart* but *sameḥ* and *zayin* can interchange (cf. Cowley *ibid.* Vol. II p.xxxvi). If the verb is from the root *ḥazar* to return the reference is naturally to Gen. 3:19. One difficulty is that *ya'azor*, he returns, occurs in Marḳah's text in the same line: i.e. the same root is spelt with an initial *'ayin* and an initial *het* in close proximity. It may be that Marḳah when citing the Targum to Gen. 3:19 follows its orthography however, and reverts to his own way of writing the word 'to return' when the quotation is finished.

20. He (i.e. the wicked man) returns (at the resurrection). Heidenheim (*op. cit.* p.144) makes the earth return and quite misses the point.

21. The reference is to the evil smelling resurrected wicked, reeking of dust, sulphur and fire; when they meet the fragrant good people, the bad and the good are easily differentiated.

22. Deut. 8:4, 29:5.

23. The patriarchs. Frequent mention is made in the Samaritan Liturgy, of the merits of the patriarchs.

24. The angels of divine favor (*Raẓon*) must be the Angels of the Presence.

25. Perhaps a reference to the light of the first day of

creation cf. *Malef* beginning.

26. He had been their intercessor. Cf. *The Assumption of Moses* 12:6.

27. Deut. 33:28.

28. Gen. 40:7.

29. Cain (etc.), is listed as the extreme type of wickedness. The men of Babel must be those who built the tower of Babel. Cf. Gen. 11:1-9. For the Amalekites cf. especially Exod.17:16.

30. Angels who expressed the Divine Wrath by punishing sinners.

31. Deut. 32:42.

32. Cf. Deut. 6:5.

33. Deut. 6:5.

34. Deut. 8:4.

35. Deut. 13:4.

36. Deut. 24:17.

37. Cf. Deut. 13:13 for the expression, sons of Belial rendered in R.S.V. 'base fellows'. The expression can however have for the Samaritan a more definite connotation, cf. the use of the term 'Sons of Belial' in the Malef *passim*.

38. Markah clearly teaches that there is reward and punishment at the Day of Judgement for everything that has been done on earth. Just as almsgiving produces much merit, so the refusal to be generous to widows and the poor brought punishment on the Day of Judgement but there is more than this. Markah has tried to show that the kind of person one has been is clearly shown forth, e.g. the good with their shining faces and the wicked with theirs blackened. People in effect assess themselves; their deeds make them what they are. But Markah while teaching reward and punishment in the future does end by acknowledging here that virtue is its own reward here and now.

39. This is not quite what is taught by Markah in the section setting out the privileges etc., of the priesthood. There Aaron and Moses are on at least an equal level.

40. The Taheb or Samaritan Messiah is the prophet like Moses cf. Deut. 18:18. According to the *Šira Yetima* (cf. note 15) the Taheb comes earlier than the Day of Vengeance. But here 'those good ones' over whom he is the rule are obviously the resurrected pious. In other words the Taheb is clearly associated here with the final drama.

41. Gen. 25:27. The reference is to Jacob - R.S.V. "A quiet man dwelling in tents".

42. Cf. Gen. 42:6.

43. Cf. Gen. 42:7f Markah hints at the contrast of Joseph's treatment of his brothers with that of them to him. cf. Gen. 37:20-24.

44. Cf. Gen. 41:38.

45. Mount Gerizim.

46. Cf.Exod. 13:19. The tomb of Joseph is near Mount Gerizim.

47. i.e. Moses: the faithful one etc. It is a common designation of Moses in the Samaritan Liturgy.

48. Cf. Deut. 34:10.

49. This could be a reference to Moses' going up Mount Sinai to receive the Law. Certainly the Samaritans have elevated Moses above all the human race.

50. When Moses went up Sinai.

51. As if the angels were an army and were marshalled for Moses' benefit. In Gen. 32:1 Jacob says of the angels that met him on the way "This is God's army".

52. Cf.Exod.33:21.

53. Cf. Num. 12:8.

54. Cf.Exod.34:28.

55. Cf.Exod.31:18.

56. Mention of the Taheb coming after this recital of the praises of Moses must mean that the Taheb is closely associated with Moses, cf. Deut. 18:18, if not Moses redidivus.

57. 'The city of the perfect' must refer to the Samaritan equivalent of the heavenly Jerusalem. Cf. Rev. 21:2. There is no reason for regarding the Taheb as in any way associated with Joseph simply because reference is made by Markah above to Joseph as King of the Blessed Mountain. The Taheb's position vis-a-vis the city of the perfect is not unlike that of the Lamb in the New Jerusalem.

Be that as it may, Alpha and Omega's statement (Rev. 22:12) that he is coming soon 'bringing recompense, to repay every one for what he has done' is not absolutely unlike what Markah on the basis of Deut. 32:35 believes God is saying. Rev. 22:14 combines in the same way as Markah the idea of Paradise as being both garden with the Tree of Life and a City.

INTRODUCTION TO PHINEAS ON THE TAHEB.

The following extract is from the composition of Phinehas, Samaritan priest of the nineteenth century; the manuscript available was the John Rylands Manchester, Samaritan Gaster 876. The manuscript is on modern paper 6" x 4" and is written in black ink in a semi-cursive hand. The MS. has 18 folios. Only the first five folios however are devoted to Phinehas' composition; the rest is taken up with a liturgical composition by Jacob, another nineteenth century priest. Even of Phinehas' composition, short though it be, enough is as good as a feast; e.g. I do not propose to give any translation of the messianic calculations etc. of folios 4 and 5. The section which is given here in translation is an allegory about the Taheb. It may seem to us a very stilted allegory, but that may be because Westerners do not look at the Bible in quite the same way as Samaritans. Bunyan in his *Pilgrim's Progress* could make use of Biblical ideas, but freely adapt his material for the sake of giving a coherent and interesting story. The Samaritan allegorist is tied to the words of the Bible, and the Bible story which he is adapting is the story he tells practically word for word as in the Bible.

The allegory deals with the coming of the Taheb - the

Samaritan Messiah (cf. Deut. 18:18 'I will raise up for them a prophet like you (Moses) from among their brethren; and I will put My words in his mouth, and he shall speak to them all that I command him'). There are two derivations of the word Taheb. He is either the returning one in which case he would be Moses rededivus or the restorer. In either case he would be like Elijah who was to return (not as Messiah however, but as the forerunner of the Messiah) and who was to restore the scattered stock of Israel (cf. M. Eduyot 8:7). The Samaritans know nothing of Elijah however. The Taheb is the Samaritan Messiah, and, of course, has nothing to do with any Messiah of David's stock. David as the king who made Jerusalem his political and religious centre is beyond the Samaritan Pale. The Taheb is of the stock of Moses. When he comes he will restore Divine Favor, and end the current period of Divine Disfavor which has lasted since Eli's setting up a tabernacle at Shiloh, in opposition to the true tabernacle at Mount Gerizim. This schismatic act caused God's Favor, which had been shown to Israel from the Lawgiving at Sinai till Eli's time, to come to an end. When the Taheb comes he will find the Tabernacle vessels, Moses' staff and the pot of manna and the altar of incense, and the true Zadokite priesthood, which the Samaritans claim to have perpetuated, will make a valid atonement for Israel (i.e. the Samaritan Community). There is not much information given in Samaritan sources about the Taheb. The best statement is in Abisha b. Phinehas' hymn (Cowley, *Sam. Lit.* II, pp.511-519, especially p.515) used on the Day of Atonement, and which incorporates in my view two different traditions about the Taheb.[1] The composition of which I am giving an abstract is some five hundred years later than Abisha b. Phinehas' hymn about the Taheb. The picture of the Taheb drawn by Phinehas b. Isaac owes nothing to the teaching of the 14th century Abisha b. Phinehas. Since however there is so little information on the Taheb it is worthwhile including this relatively modern and highly artificial composition. It may be argued that the allegory of the Taheb is not actually modern, although at first sight the composition of a Samaritan of fairly recent times. The Samaritans are not given to original compositions, but re-state what has been handed down.

This allegory is based on the idea that what will mark the Taheb's coming and ministry will be repentance. The Biblical Hebrew word Šuḇ means to return or repent; likewise the Aramaic Taḇ has both meanings. The Taheb could be the penitent one, or the one who makes or calls to repentance. The idea that men could hasten the time of the coming of the Messiah by repentance was advocated by some Rabbis of early times (cf. M. Sotah 9:15).

Our writer has chosen the story of the Flood as the Biblical basis of his allegory.[2] The Ark saved Noah and his family from the Flood. The Hebrew word *Tebah* ark has the same consonants as Taheb. The Samaritan has a literal faith in the verbal inspiration of the Pentateuch. If one changes the order of the consonants in *tbh* (ark) to *thb* (Taheb) one is not interfering with the letters, but only with their order. To the Samaritan it would appear that there is a real indication of a Divine message to be conveyed to us by this accidental fact that the word for Ark in Hebrew and the word for the (Samaritan) Messiah in Aramaic (Taheb) have the same consonants though in different order. The fact too that Noah was commanded to cover the ark inside and out with pitch (the word 'cover' in the Hebrew here being '*kafar*' and pitch being *kofer*) seemed significant. The Taheb, it was known, when he came, would, with the priest, make atonement. The word 'make atonement' was the same word as that used with regard to Noah's covering the ark with pitch. It therefore seemed obvious to the Samaritan who was looking for teaching about the Taheb in the Pentateuch (which must contain in his eyes all instruction), that Noah was a type of the Taheb. He therefore retells the story of the Flood in the Biblical language and in the exact words of the Bible where he can, but reading Taheb for Noah, and Repentance for Ark. Repentance was to be the Ark which with the Taheb and his household of faith would deliver them from the Flood of Divine Disfavor, just as the Ark with Noah as captain had delivered the faithful few from the Flood of Waters caused by God's wrath. After all, what had been would be again, especially if it was in the Law. The interesting thing is that the Taheb is modelled here on Noah, not on Moses, though usually the Taheb is understood to be the one like Moses. God in the Bible(Gen. 9:15)covenanted with man not to destroy them all again by water. Our writer however dares to apply the metaphor of the Flood to Divine Disfavor, but even so is careful to say that not all flesh would be overwhelmed by the Flood of wickedness on earth, because of God's promise to Noah. This is an indication of how tightly he felt himself bound by Biblical details, and that such must be safeguarded even when used allegorically.

The following translation endeavours(where the allegory follows the Flood narrative)to keep to the Revised Standard Version's words where possible, and to note the slight changes which the allegorist has allowed himself.

Noah was interpreted allegorically by some of the early Church Fathers as a type of Christ, and the Ark as a type of the Church. This may point to the fact that the idea of Noah as the type of the Taheb, and the Ark as the type of repentance was not original to our author; not that he is likely to have consulted the works of Church Fathers, but rather to have perpetuated an old Samaritan tradition.

FOOTNOTES

1. *The Journal of Jewish Studies* Vol. VI, No.2 1955,

pp.63-72 *Early Samaritan Eschatology*, John Bowman.

2. On this compare also The Taheb (or Šaheb) *Samaritan Oral Law and Ancient Traditions*. M. Gaster Vol. 1 *Eschatology* The Search Publishing Company, 1932, ch. IX, pp.221-277.

PHINEAS ON THE TAHEB

Blessed is the LORD who spake and allowed mitigation[1] by means of repentance. And the Šaheb[2] is the Taheb. Then he will begin to proclaim in the name of the LORD: 'Israel[3] repentant return to the LORD'. This is he[4] who will console us for our work and the labor of our hands which the LORD increased because of the Divine Disfavor.[5] For now the LORD will comfort us and make us fruitful in another land, and there be Divine Favor and sowing[6] of desolate places, to answer for the testing, to do good to us at the Latter End.

May the LORD do good to us, and deliver us from Divine Disfavor soon. Amen, I am, that I am. Blessed is the LORD who created the heart[7] and sanctified it, and established it, and loved it. The Taheb, a man righteous[8] and perfect will he be in his generations. With God the Taheb will walk,[9] and at the command of the LORD he will establish the Holy Tabernacle,[10] as God said: "And you shall do all My commands"; and the LORD will establish His covenant[11] with Abraham, and with Isaac and with Jacob as the LORD commanded[12] Moses, the peace of the LORD be upon him. And the children of Israel will perform the festivals[13] of the LORD, and the offerings of the LORD, they will eat, and will do obeisance before the LORD. And the LORD will bless Israel, and they will encamp according to their standards,[14] with the messengers[15] between them according to their number:[16] and all[17] priests and the house of Joseph, and the children of Israel, shall see the Tabernacle[18] of the LORD and the pot of manna[19] and the staff of Moses:[20] and the LORD will bless him! Blessed is the LORD.

And God shall say to the Taheb: "Make for yourself a mighty repentance:[21] You shall make the Repentance, and you shall make atonement both[22] within and without. And this is that which you shall do:[23] The length of the year of Repentance is three hundred[24] ordinary days; its breadth[25] fifty Sabbath days, and seven festivals of the LORD, holy convocations, and the Day of Atonement. That is the (full) account of the year fully outspread. Its height[26] is the months. Righteousness you shall make for Repentance, and finish it to righteousness[27] above;[28] and set the door[29] of Repentance in its side; make it with righteousness, uprightness and goodness.[30] For behold, I will bring repentance[31] upon the earth that Israel may live and be gathered from under all the heavens, and that (God) may fulfil His covenant with Abraham and with Isaac and with Jacob; and you shall come into Repentance, you, and your household, and all the house of Israel with you. And you shall take (people) from every congregation and prayer[32] meeting and bring them out; and that which is pure, which you declare pure,[33] gather to you, and it shall[34] serve for Repentance for you and them. And the Taheb[35] shall do this; he shall do all that God commanded him.

The Ark delivered Noah from the Flood of Destruction, and repentance will deliver the Taheb and all the children of Israel from the Flood of Divine Disfavor. And God will say to the Taheb:[36] Go into the goodly land you and all your household, for I have seen that you are righteous before Me in this generation. Take[37] with you myriads of all clean animals, the male and his mate to keep their kind alive upon the face of the earth.

And it shall be in the six-thousandth[38] year, and the Flood of Divine Disfavor had been on the earth; then the Taheb[39] with his sons and the children of Israel will enter Repentance, to the goodly land away from the Flood of Divine Disfavor.

Myriads and[40] myriads will enter into Repentance the Šaheb and the good land just as the Lord commanded Moses. And it shall be for the repentance of Israel; and the waters[41] of repentance will have been upon the land in the six-thousandth[42] year from the creation of the world. By the life of Israel, in the first month in the first of the month, on that day all the fountains of the great deep will have burst forth, and the windows of Repentance have been opened. And there[43] will be Divine Favor upon the earth forty days, day by day for a year. On the very same[44] day the Taheb and his household, and the house of Israel with them will enter Repentance and the goodly land, they and all[45] the peoples will pass before them according to their families, likewise the sojourner according to his kind, and all the clean cattle and every clean bird for their offerings. And they will go into Repentance with the Šaheb[46] and with the priest two by two for a sin offering and a burnt offering as[47] the LORD commanded Moses. And the LORD will have shut up[48] Divine Disfavor.

And the Flood[49] of Divine Disfavor will continue two thousand and nine hundred and forty-four years; and the sinners[50] will increase and lift up their head, and rise high above the earth. And the sinners[51] will prevail and increase greatly upon the earth. And the[52] nations and the wicked will go and cover the sign on the face of all the earth. And the sinners[53] will prevail so mightily upon the earth, that all the good, the hills, the anointed ones, the truth, under the whole heaven were covered; for two[54] thousand nine hundred and forty-four years the sinners will have reigned and prevailed, and the wicked have covered (the earth). And[55] all flesh died from upon the earth; birds, cattle, beasts, and the fruit of the earth will be diminished. As to the Flood, all flesh expired thereby: but as to the Flood[56] of Divine Disfavor, all flesh will not expire thereby among the righteous; (that is) in remembrance of the covenant of the LORD with Abraham, and Isaac and Jacob, as the LORD said:[57] Yet for all that, when they are in the land of their enemies, I will not spurn them, neither will I abhor them so as to destroy them utterly and break My covenant with them; for I am the LORD their God; but I will for their sake remember the covenant with their forefathers, whom I brought forth out of the land of Egypt in the sight of the nations, that I might be their God: I am the LORD". And He will spare[58] the Šaheb and those who will be with him in repentance. And[59] the sinners will prevail upon the earth two thousand and forty nine years.

The God[60] will remember His covenant with Abraham, and with Isaac and with Jacob, and He will send the Taheb. And God will cause a spirit of zeal, to pass over the Taheb, and the waters of Divine Disfavor will subside; the fountains[61] of the dark deep will be closed; sin and violence will be restrained from the earth. But the righteous[62] shall dwell upon the earth. And in the first month on the first of the month, the She<u>k</u>inah[63] will come to rest upon the holy Mount Gerizim. And you shall see glorious sights.[64] On the tenth (of the month) the beginnings of Repentance shall be seen.

And such will be the Flood of Divine Disfavor. And the Taheb shall open[65] the window of repentance and he shall send forth the doves (and) the voices from it to see if sin had subsided from the face of the ground; but the voices[66] will find no place to set their feet, and the voices will come (back) to him. And he will wait[67] another seven days, and again he will send forth the voices; and the voices[68] shall come (back) to him in the evening of Divine Displeasure, and lo, the leaf of a good voice in their mouth. So the[69] Taheb knew that the sinners had subsided from the earth. And they[70] shall call Israel before the LORD God; and in the first month in the first of the month, the glory of the LORD shall fill the whole earth.

The raven[71] shall hover on the land of Canaan, two are righteous, and two are liars.

FOOTNOTES

1. Mitigation of the punishment due to men's sin.

2. Šaheb is a known form of the name Taheb. It (Šaheb) is an Aramaic pe'el participle form made from the Hebrew *Šub*; one finds more often the form Taheb derived from the cognate Aramaic *Tub*. Both Šaheb and Taheb mean either the Returning One or Penitent One.

3. Literally: Israel to repentance, to the LORD.

4. The Taheb: the very thought of his coming is a comfort to the Samaritans.

5. Divine Disfavor, i.e. *Panuta*, literally turning away. The Samaritan doctrine of Divine Disfavor is based on Deut. 32:20. 'I will hide My face from them'. We are still under *Panuta* and have been since Eli's time, say the Samaritans. The year of Grace and the consequent era of Grace has not yet come. Raẓon, Divine Favor, will come again with the Taheb.

6. The word rendered 'sowing' is *Zarutah*. But the interchange of ayin and waw is to be found in Samaritan MSS. so I take the word as from *Z R'*.

7. The heart, i.e. the heart of man.

8. Gen. 6:9 'a righteous and blameless man in his generation'. This is applied in the Bible to Noah, but here to the Taheb. With this verse begins the allegory of the Taheb based on Noah and the Flood story.

9. Cf. Gen. 6:9; Noah walked with God.

10. 'The Holy Tabernacle': according to the usual Taheb story based on Abisha b. Phinehas' hymn, the Taheb finds the Tabernacle vessels and the holy Tabernacle is set up again on Mt. Gerizim. In 2 Macc. 2:6, 7 there is a similar story of how when Jerusalem was taken, Jeremiah hid the ark, and the Tabernacle and the altar of incense so that they could be restored in the future when the LORD revealed them. In Josephus *Antiq.* XVIII IV 1 we hear how Pontius Pilate punished a Samaritan who led a crowd of people up Mt. Gerizim to find the Tabernacle

vessels; presumably this Samaritan claimed he was the Taheb. The interesting thing is that the Ark here is allegorically equated with the Holy Tabernacle, cf. the references in the early Church Fathers to the Ark as the type of the Church. Later in Phinehas' allegory the Ark and repentance are equated. This reference to the Taheb establishing the Holy Tabernacle at the command of God, in the setting of the Biblical Noah story, would be a general reference to Gen. 6:14-16. A more detailed reference follows in the allegory.

11. Covenant, cf. Gen. 6:18 where the covenant which God makes is with Noah and his family.

12. As the Lord commanded Moses. cf. Exod. 6:4.

13. The festivals enumerated in Lev. 23.

14. Standards, cf. Num. 10:18, 22, 25 for mention of some of the standards, e.g. Num. 10:18 'And the standard of the camp of Reuben set forward according to their armies' a reference to the arrangement of the tribes of the children of Israel in the Wilderness journeyings and encamping.

15. The messengers, i.e. the spies who went up to report on the land of Canaan, cf. Num. 13.

16. The number of the spies: twelve, cf. Num. 13:4-16.

17. Literally: 'the number of the priests' in the sense of the total number, the complete priestly body.

18. On the Taheb's coming the Samaritans believe the Tabernacle, which had been hidden on Mount Gerizim, would once more appear.

19. Cf. Exod. 16:33-34.

20. Moses' staff whereby he worked miracles was by the Samaritans believed to have been Adam's staff which he had brought from the Garden of Eden. Jewish tradition knew likewise of Moses' staff as the rod which Adam had taken out of the Garden of Eden (cf. Pirke de R. Eliezer, *ibid.* p.312). Jewish tradition went further and held that the rod was one of the things created in the twilight of the first Sabbath eve, cf. Pirke de R. Eliezer, *ibid.* Samaritan tradition knew of the preservation of the staff in the Tabernacle. When the Tabernacle was rediscovered the staff would be there with the other Tabernacle treasures.

21. This verse 'Make yourself mighty repentance' is simply Gen. 6:14 with 'a mighty repentance' instead of 'an ark of Gopher wood'.

22. 'You shall make atonement both inside and out' is instead of the Biblical 'and cover it inside and out with pitch'. As stated in our introduction to this extract, play is made of the fact that 'to make atonement' and 'to cover with pitch' come from the same Hebrew root *KPR*. Once the initial 'identification' of ark and repentance was made (since they have the same letters though in different order), it was an easy matter for the Samaritan theologian to make atonement serve the place of pitch in his good ship Repentance. In any case the Taheb with the true (i.e. Samaritan) priesthood was to make with them atonement for Israel at the rediscovered Tabernacle on what would be the greatest day of Atonement. 'Inside and out' could be taken by the allegorist as referring to what the High Priest does on the Day of Atonement both outside and within the Holy of Holies. Lev. 16:12, 15 tells of the atonement within the veil, i.e. inside the Holy of Holies made by the High Priest on the annual Day of Atonement. The High Priest also made atonement without the veil, i.e. at the altar; e.g. when he made atonement for it(Lev. 16:18-19). The High Priest also made atonement for himself and his household, cf. Lev. 16:6, 11. Is this personal atonement referred to in Phinehas' allegory when the Taheb is told to make repentance for himself(cf. note 21)?

23. Exact quotation of Gen. 6:15a.

24. The number 300 days is of course taken from the three hundred cubits. 'Three hundred ordinary days' are substituted for 'three hundred cubits'. Instead of 'the length of the ark' Phinehas writes in his allegory 'the length of the year of Repentance'. It would seem more than fortuitous that 300 cubits were mentioned as the length of the ark. It would seem near enough to the number of ordinary days in the year; therefore he would argue that that was the hidden meaning, which the Samaritan is convinced underlies every word of the Law. After all Akiba was able by his exegesis to find *asmaḵtoṯ*, Biblical support for many a mishnah that had lacked such before; but in the realm of Jewish haggadah the controlling influence of even *ribbui umiut* and the 13 *middoṯ* of Ishmael was not in evidence. The difference is that Samaritans made an orthodoxy out of haggaḏoṯ, Jews did not.

25. Its breadth, cf. Gen. 6:15 'its breadth of fifty cubits'. Fifty Sabbath days and seven festivals and the day of Atonement constitute the breadth of the good ship Repentance. Fifty Sabbaths would correspond with the fifty cubits of the

Ark's breadth, without seven festivals and the Day of Atonement.

26. The height of the ark was thirty cubits. Here the months make up the height of the good ship Repentance, on the basis of the number of days in a calendar month being thirty!

27. 'Do righteousness for Repentance', cf. Gen. 6:16. Righteousness stands for the roof of the Ark.

28. Gen. 6:16 'and finish it to a cubit above', becomes in the allegory 'and finish it to righteousness above'.

29. The Ark, cf. Gen. 6:16, had a door in its side. In the allegorical ark (Repentance) there is to be the door of Repentance.

30. The ark, cf. Gen. 6:16, was to have three decks. The allegorical ark 'Repentance' likewise has three decks: righteousness, uprightness and goodness.

31. This section down to 'And the Taheb shall do this; he shall do all that God commanded him' [cf. Gen. 6:22 (reading Taheb instead of Noah)], summarises briefly in allegorical form Gen. 6:17 - Gen. 6:22. Only in the last sentence is the relationship close, but there are points of contact throughout. Repentance stands here for Flood, and therefore the first sentence: "For behold, I will bring repentance upon the earth" is not unlike Gen. 6:17a. But there are some interesting alterations. Gen. 6:17b, to destroy all flesh in which is the breath of life from under heaven, becomes in the allegory: 'that Israel may live and be gathered from under all the heavens'. The last clause of Gen. 6:17 (everything that is in the earth shall die) is not represented in the allegory.

Gen. 6:18 is represented in the allegory, changed, of course, from 'But I will establish my covenant with you; and you shall come into the ark, you, your sons, your wife, and your sons' wives with you' to 'And that (God) may establish His covenant with Abraham and with Isaac and with Jacob; and you shall come into Repentance, you and your household, and all the house of Israel with you'. Naturally latter day saints would refer to the covenant with Abraham and with Isaac and with Jacob instead of the covenant with Noah, since the three holy ones were patriarchs of Israel, and the covenants with them were national. In the next sentence the differences are not great; here again the ark is allegorically termed Repentance; the national note is struck; all the house of Israel, not just the Taheb's kith and kin as in the case of Noah, are to be saved. One should note that Israel to the Samaritans means only the Samaritans who claim they are the true Israel. In Abisha b. Phinehas' hymn on the Taheb it is clear that Jews and Christians and others have no share in Paradise.

In Gen. 6:19, 20 Noah was commanded to bring two of all flesh (v.19) two of each kind of bird, of each kind of animal and of each kind of creeping thing; (v.20) to keep them alive. In our allegory the Taheb is commanded to take from every *Ma'amad*, station, or division. The word originally was used of the stopping-places in the wilderness march. In the Second Temple period, the Ma'amad was the division of representatives of the people who were in duty in the temple to read, e.g. the verses of Genesis 1 at the times of sacrifice, cf. M. Tamid 3:7. The word here must mean, however, congregation.

32. Literally Prayer, but prayer meeting is understood. Presumably in the case of Ma'amad and prayer meeting, it refers to such groups within Israel, the Samaritan Israel. The reference to the Ma'amad,in the Biblical sense of desert stopping-place, would fit in with the grouping of Israel according to standards. Cf. note 14 above. On the other hand we note that our writer is allegorizing verse by verse the second part of Gen. 6. Immediately before this he allegorized Gen. 6:18; it is therefore possible that this sentence about taking from every ma'amad and prayer meeting and bringing them with him (the Taheb) refers not to selections for all the house of Israel, but to "the lesser breeds without the Law". This is possible as this sentence would be an allegory of Gen. 6:19, 20 where pairs of animals, birds and creeping things are to be brought into the ark. There is therefore some hope for non-Samaritans.

33. 'the pure which you declare pure' would be the fit persons from every Ma'amad and prayer meeting either of Israel or from the outside world, depending on the terms of reference of Ma'amad and prayer meeting.

34. 'And it shall serve as Repentance for you and for them'. Our author tries to allegorize verse by verse the Biblical story; as a result the allegory is considerably hampered. This verse is the last part of Gen. 6:21 with one alteration 'repentance' instead of 'food'. Repentance in the allegory basically applies to the ark. In v.17 the word 'repentance' was substituted for 'flood', here for food. The writer by endeavouring to be faithful to the Biblical story and at the same time to keep a consistent allegory is on the horns of a dilemma. Here the matter is not serious. Later on in his allegory, it does lead to inconsistency.

35. Cf. Gen. 6:22 reading Taheb for Noah.

36. Cf. Gen. 7:1. The sentence in the allegory is a verbatim quotation of Gen. 7:1 reading however 'goodly land' for 'ark'. Here repentance is not the allegorical substitute for ark.

37. This sentence is virtually Gen. 7:2, 3 reading however myriads instead of the Biblical seven pairs (of clean animals) Gen. 7:26 which enjoins that a pair of each kind of unclean animals should be taken too is omitted in the allegory; likewise the first part of 7:3 is omitted, with its reference to seven pairs of birds of each kind to be taken into the Ark. The final part of Gen. 7:3 'to keep their kind alive upon the face of all the earth' follows immediately after Gen. 7:2a.

38. In the six thousandth year. The section which follows paraphrases allegorically Gen. 7:6-10. It commences with an adaptation of Gen. 7:6; instead of a statement as to the age of Noah, we are given the date of the Taheb's coming. The six-thousandth year is interesting as pointing to a seven day system of world ages, the seventh being the milleniary period of Tanna de Be Eliyahu etc. This system is found too in Samaritan Eschatology, cf. Bowman, *Journal of Jewish Studies* VI 2, 1955; Early Samaritan Eschatology p.63-72. The rest of the sentence is the same as Gen. 7:6 reading now, Flood of Divine Disfavor, instead of Flood of Waters. Note that earlier Gen. 6:17 Repentance stood for Flood of Waters.

39. This sentence corresponds to Gen. 7:7 Taheb being substituted for Noah; 'and the children of Israel' stands in place of 'and his wife and his sons' wives'. Repentance is here again the allegorical substitute for ark. In the allegory at the end of this sentence we find 'to the good land away from the Flood of Divine Disfavor' instead of 'to escape the waters of the Flood'.

40. This sentence is based on Gen. 7:8. The 'myriads and myriads' are presumably the allegorical equivalent of the clean animals. Above in the allegory based on Gen. 7:2 no allegorical equivalent to the unclean animals was mentioned. 'Went into Repentance with the Šaheb' represents in the allegory 'went into the Ark with Noah'. Reference in the allegory to the good land has no equivalent in the Biblical text of Gen. 7:9.

'As the LORD commanded Moses' agrees with the end of Gen. 7:9 except that Moses stands in place of Noah. Elsewhere in the allegory the Taheb stands in place of Noah, even earlier in this very verse Gen. 7:9. The existence of some sort of relationship of the Taheb to Moses is known; he is either the one like him, or Moses returning. The substitution of Moses for Taheb here in the allegory might point to identity.

41. This sentence is based on Gen. 7:10 with the substitution of 'for the repentance of Israel' for 'after seven days' Gen. 7:10; and the substitution of 'the Waters of Repentance' instead of 'the waters of the flood' Gen. 7:11. This latter alteration is to be noted. Here 'repentance' stands as the allegorical substitute for flood, and not for Ark; cf. the allegory's handling of Gen. 6:17. In this present case the substitution is not so felicitous, but rather confusing. In fact the writer is showing now that he has two interpretations of the Flood; (a) That of Divine Disfavor, (b) That of Repentance. Against the Flood of Divine Disfavor the Ark of Repentance is needed. In the second interpretation, the interpretation of the Ark is as Tabernacle(cf. note 43),though the allegorical interpretation of Ark as Repentance occurs. Actually apart from occasional lapses,as in the section immediately following this, the Flood is conceived of as the Flood of Divine Disfavor.

42. This sentence is a fairly close allegorization of Gen. 7:11 'In the six-thousandth year from the creation of the world in the life of Israel' stands instead of 'in the six hundredth year of Noah's life'. In the life of Israel it may mean that what is to follow will happen when is Israel is still alive as a nation.

Significant is the alteration in the first month, in the first of the month instead of the Biblical 'in the second month, in the second of the month'. The Taheb we learn from this is to come at Nisan. Cf. the Jerusalem Targum Exod. 12:42 on the four significant nights of Passover, on the first, the world was created, on the second was the covenant with Abraham, on the third was the Exodus, and on the fourth significant Passover Messiah will come. Cf. also Memar Markah who gives the same haggada of the four nights.

Another change in the verse is the reading 'windows of Repentance' for 'windows of heaven'.

43. This sentence corresponds to Gen. 7:12. Divine Favor being substituted for 'rain' of the Biblical text. Another alteration is the insertion of 'day by day for a year' instead of 'and forty nights'. The allegorist wishes to keep the Biblical text as much as possible, and yet harmonize it with his concept of a year of repentance.

44. This sentence in the allegory is based on Gen. 7:13.

Taheb is read instead of Noah; 'and his household and the house of Israel with them' stand in place of the Biblical 'and his sons, Shem and Ham and Japheth, and Noah's wife and the three wives of his sons with them'. 'Repentance' is here again the allegorical designation for the Biblical 'Ark', though a little earlier, the Flood is regarded as 'the waters of Repentance', cf. note 41. 'And the aforementioned good land' features again in this allegory, though not of course in the Biblical text, cf. note 39.

45. This sentence is a loose allegorical rendering of Gen. 7:14. It is clear from his sentence that there is hope for the sojourner or proselyte, cf. note 32. Note that there is no reference to 'the creeping things' of the Biblical text in our allegory; the cattle and the fowl are defined in the allegory as clean cattle and clean fowl, though the qualification is not mentioned in Gen. 7:14. The allegory states a reason why such were included, not mentioned in the Biblical text, i.e. 'for their offerings'.

46. This sentence is interesting as showing that even when the Flood itself is interpreted as Divine Favor(cf. note 41)the Ark can still be allegorized as repentance. This sentence is based on Gen. 7:15. Šaheb(i.e. Taheb)is written instead of Noah, Repentance instead of ark. Note the allegorist's insertion of 'and with the priest' not in the Biblical text. Note also the omission of 'of all flesh in which there was the breath of life' Gen. 7:15 and the insertion after 'two by two' of 'for a sin offering and a burnt offering'. Here the allegorization of the ark as Repentance has the Tabernacle in view. See above for the discovery of the Tabernacle and the reinstitution of sacrifices there by Taheb and priesthood. Cf. also Origen's interpretation of the ark as a figure of the Church, cf. Homilies on Genesis II, 4ff.

47. Cf. Gen. 7:16 the earlier part of which is omitted but the second half of that verse is quoted; but again Moses is identified with the Taheb.

48. 'Divine Disfavor' is the one insertion into the otherwise exactly cited Gen. 7:16a. As the verse stands in the Bible text the LORD shuts Noah into the ark away from the flood. In the allegory the LORD shuts up Divine Disfavor away from the Taheb and penitents in (a state of) Repentance.

49. This sentence in the allegory corresponds to Gen. 6:17. The Flood is now interpreted again not as Divine Favor but as Divine Disfavor. Instead of a duration of forty days its duration is two thousand and nine hundred and forty-four years. It

is to be distinguished in the allegory from the allegorization of the rain, Gen. 7:12,which fell for forty days and according to our allegorist lasted a year, the rain being a Flood of Divine Disfavor.

The two thousand and nine hundred and forty-four years of the Flood of Divine Disfavor would be considered by our author as the length of *Panuṯa*.

50. The verse which is the basis of the allegorist's statement is still Gen. 7:17; 'sinners' are read instead of 'waters', 'their head' instead of 'ark'. The end of the sentence is verbally the same as the Biblical text, but the words can bear the different meaning given them by the allegorist.

51. The Biblical text for this sentence is Gen. 7:18a. 'Sinners' again stand in place of 'waters'. Gen. 7:18b is not represented in the allegory.

52. This sentence is not represented in the Biblical text. The Nations and the Wicked of the allegory represent the waters of the Flood. What is the connotation of 'the sign' is not clear. One might think it referred to Mount Gerizim, the holiest place on earth for Samaritans. But Samaritans hold that Mount Gerizim was not covered by the waters of Noah's Flood, so it is not likely that the allegorist would venture to suggest that Mount Gerizim was covered in his allegorical Flood. 'Sign' might refer to sign of the truth and be interpreted as referring to the Samaritan witness and the truth thereof.

53. In the allegory 'sinners' is read for 'waters'. Also we find 'all the high mountains' of the Biblical text allegorized into 'all the good, the hills, the anointed ones, the truth'. The good would refer to the good people, presumably Israel; the truth would likewise refer to the Samaritan version of the religion of Israel. The anointed ones may refer to the Samaritan high priests.

54. In the Biblical text Gen. 7:20 we are told of the depth of the water of the Flood. Here in the allegory we are told of the length of the period that the Flood of Divine Disfavor will continue.

55. Gen. 7:21 quoted. The first part of the verse is cited practically verbatim. Note substitution in the allegory of 'the fruit of the earth' for the Biblical 'all swarming creatures that swarm upon the earth'. Further the fruit of the earth will merely be diminished not exterminated. The Biblical text Gen. 7:21 includes 'every man' in the general destruction,

not so the allegory.

56. Cf. Gen. 7:22 which says 'everything on the dry land in whose nostrils was the breath of life died'; not so the allegory. There it is stated 'the Flood of Divine Disfavor will reduce thereby all flesh'. The allegory in the next sentence specifically qualifies the scope of the destruction of the Flood of Divine Disfavor because of the covenants later than Noah's time. Cf. Lev. 26:42.

57. Lev. 26:44, 45. This seemed the most certain proof for the honoring by God of the terms of the Covenants, because these verses are found at the end of the warnings of the punishments of disobedience in Leviticus.

58. This sentence is very similar to the last part of Gen. 7:23. Following on the citation of Lev. 26:45 the writer probably deliberately drops the *'ak* which is found before Noah in the Biblical text. 'Repentance' is again substituted in the allegory for 'ark' (Gen. 7:23).

59. Cf. Gen. 7:24 'sinners' again being substituted in the allegory for 'waters'. Two thousand and forty-nine years here appears in the allegory as the period of the duration of the Flood waters upon the earth, as against the Biblical Flood's hundred and fifty days. We note that the duration of the Flood in the allegory itself is now five years longer than as stated, cf. note 54.

60. We now pass in the allegory to Gen. 8:1. In the allegory the reason for the abatement of this Flood is again the covenant with Abraham, Isaac and Jacob. Whereas in the Biblical Flood narrative the reason given is God's remembering 'Noah and all the beasts and all the cattle that were with him in the ark'. The allegorist does not say that God remembers the Taheb, but that He sends the Taheb. The allegorist is not quite consistent here. The picture of the Taheb in the Ark is tacitly dropped at least momentarily. Then in the next sentence whereas in the Bible Gen. 8:1 God made a wind to blow over the earth, that the waters may subside, in the allegory God causes a spirit of zeal to pass over the Taheb. The allegory alters the sense of the Biblical Hebrew text, with the minimum of verbal change, e.g. adding *kina'a* for zeal, and reading Taheb instead of 'earth'. The Taheb not the wind is the immediate cause of the sinking of the Flood waters. Wind and spirit are two meanings of the one Hebrew word. Therefore since the Taheb is the agent of God in coping with the Flood of Divine Disfavor, the allegorist felt justified in altering the text to make the Taheb the immediate cause of the Flood's abatement. The end of the sentence is the same as in the

Biblical account, except that 'of Divine Disfavor' is added to specify the flood waters.

61. This sentence is based on Gen. 8:1. The allegory qualifies the Deep as dark. Thereafter the beginning of the sentence was similar to Biblical text, the rest is very different, e.g. 'the fountains of the deep and the windows of heaven were closed, the rain from the heavens was restrained' becomes in the allegory 'sin and violence will be restrained from the earth'. The allegorization of 'rain' in Gen. 7:12 when the windows of heaven Gen. 7:11 were opened, was quite different. There the rain was Divine Favor, here Divine Disfavor. I point this out once again to underline the ambivalence in our author's mind regarding the Flood. Sometimes he can employ the metaphor in a favorable sense, cf. note 43, more often in an unfavorable.

62. 'and the righteous shall dwell upon the earth,' the allegorist's rendering of Gen. 8:3. Because the waters were abating, the righteous could live on the earth again, in fact were doing so, he tells us. This again points to confusion of metaphor in his allegory; the only folk, even righteous folk alive were in the Ark of Repentance with the Taheb; the good ship Repentance had not yet landed and disembarked her passengers. The allegorist is not consistent and has not made up his mind where the righteous are.

63. Cf. Gen. 8:4. A further example of inconsistency on the part of the allegorist. The Ark of the Biblical Flood story, allegorized elsewhere by our author as Repentance, now is metamorphosed into the Shekinah. This fits in with the comment in note 62 that the allegorist thought the righteous were already on the earth, not in the Ark Repentance. The Shekinah, God's abiding presence, was and is withdrawn in the period of Divine Disfavor; the Shekinah returns on the renewal of Divine Favor. In the Bible the glory of the LORD is used to express what later Judaism meant by the Shekinah. The 'glory of the Lord filled the Tabernacle', cf. Exod.40:34, and the glory of the Lord filled Solomon's Temple, cf. 1 Kings 8:11. For the withdrawal of God's presence from the Temple, cf. Ezek. 11:25; and for the return of His presence, cf. Ezek 43:2-5. On the first of the first month, i.e. at the termination of the year of Repentance, see above note 42. The allegorist alters the Biblical Flood dating understandably to conform with his allegory; but it is significant that he did so. There is in Judaism a certain doubt as to whether the Messianic redemption will be in Tishri (seventh month) or Nisan (the first month). Our author obviously believed it would be in Nisan.

Instead of Ararat the resting place of the Biblical Ark, the allegorist naturally substitutes Mount Gerizim here. The Shekinah was to return to Mount Gerizim when the Taheb came. It would almost appear as if the allegorist thought of Mount Gerizim itself as having been inundated in the Flood of Divine Disfavor, spared though it had been in Noah's Flood according to Samaritans.

64. This sentence is the allegory's rendering of Gen. 8:5. There is nothing in the Biblical text corresponding with seeing visions. Mount Gerizim (Bethel) has been associated in Samaritan thought with Jacob's vision at Bethel. Not only Jacob but the Samaritan High Priest Abisha (14th century) saw visions there, cf. Abisha's vision. Cowley, Samaritan Liturgy Vol. II, p.514f. Oxford, 1909.

The Biblical date of Gen. 8:5 is altered from the first day of the tenth month to the tenth (day of the first month); 'beginnings of repentance' cf. Gen. 8:5 'the tops of the mountains' *Rošē* heads can also mean beginnings.

Repentance is read in the allegory here for the mountains though Repentance in the allegory mainly stood in place of Ark.

65. This sentence in the allegory is based quite clearly on Gen. 8:6-8. Just as Noah opened the window of the ark, the Taheb in the allegory opens the window of Repentance. Noah sent forth a raven (v.7) and then a dove (v.8); the Taheb sends for 'doves and voices'. Noah's dove was sent forth 'to see if the waters had subsided from the face of the ground'; the Taheb's 'doves and voices' likewise are sent forth to see if the sinners had lessened. With slight verbal alterations despite the combining of Gen. 8:7 and 8 the allegorist keeps close to the Biblical text. 'At the end of forty days' Gen. 8:6 is omitted, as also is 'which he had made' at end of v.6. The main omission is the whole of v.7b. 'doves and voices' *ha-'Aṯūrim ha-Ḳoloṯ. ha-'Aṯurim* like Noah's raven v.7 are mentioned only once. The 'aleph in 'Aṯurim is the prosthetic *'aleph* which occurs in Samaritan pronunciation, and is not part of the root.

66. This sentence is based on Gen. 8:9, the voices being substituted in the allegory for the dove. (Gen. 8:9). The allegorist omits Gen. 8:9b, 9c, d with the exception of briefly noting the return of the voices to the Taheb. 'And the voices shall come to him' for the Biblical 'she (the dove) returned to him to the ark' etc.

67. This sentence in the allegory agrees with Gen. 8:10 so

far as it goes, but omits the final words 'out of the ark' which it does not attempt to allegorise. This may be significant as the same omission occurs in the previous sentence.

68. Cf. Gen. 8:11 to which this sentence is very similar. The differences are 'voices' instead of 'dove': the addition of 'of Divine Disfavor' to evening (Gen.8:11). The allegory substitutes 'a good voice' for 'a freshly plucked olive leaf' Gen. 8:11, but retains 'in her mouth' Gen. 8:11. The allegory is a bit strained here, voices go out and come back with 'a good voice in their mouth' (sic.).

69. This sentence is the same as Gen. 8:11b reading however Taheb for Noah, and sinners for waters.

70. Gen. 8:12 is omitted in the allegory. The sentence under our notice is remotely based on Gen. 8:13. The reference of 'they shall call' (in our allegory) is not clear; it probably refers to the voices. The date in our allegory is that of the Biblical text, so far as month and day are concerned. The allegory puts in place of the Biblical 'the waters were dried from off the earth' - the glory of the LORD shall fill the whole earth. i.e. The Flood of Divine Disfavor was past and God's Sheḵinah, His glorious abiding presence abode with men showing His Divine Favor. The allegorist may have based his idea of a year of repentance on the dates in Gen. 7:11 and Gen. 8:13. True in the Bible not a whole year intervenes, but it was all but a year.

71. Whereas one might compliment the allegorist on his worthy finish of the Flood with the glory of God filling the whole earth, cf. Num. 14:21, this last sentence is bathos, and the effect is spoiled. It is indefensible, unless the allegorist was a realist. The consonants of *'oreḇ* raven are also those of *'ereḇ* mixed multitude. Though the raven is mentioned in the Flood Story, there is a mixed multitude when he was writing; yes, and he felt even in the glorious future it could not help being the same.

In translating this allegory an attempt has been made to keep to the Revised Standard Translation where the text of allegorist and of the Bible agree. Tenses have had, however, to be changed. The Samaritan does not in the first place use the waw consecutive (b) the allegory is about something which will happen in the future. Perfects have therefore been regarded as prophetic perfects.

MOLAD MOSHEH

THE BIRTH OF MOSES:

SELECTIONS FROM THE BIRTH STORY

Such is the adoration accorded to Moses among the Samaritans that they celebrate his birth by the holding of special services. The John Rylands Library, Manchester, Gaster Samaritan MS. No. 865 gives the form of the service. The manuscript in question is on roughish paper, size per page approximately 8" x 6". The manuscript is not old. The scribe's name is not given, unless he, and the translator of the actual birth story from Arabic into Hebrew, be the one and the same. It appears, however, from a rubric on f.35b that the scribe was a son of Phinehas. Phinehas ben Isaac was the translator. The service begins with a hymn praising Moses. Then the congregation responds by repeating a scriptural verse. The reading of the ten verses of the Biblical birth story of Moses follows. Then the extra-Biblical account of the birth story is read to the congregation. This story begins with creation, for even before the heavens and earth were created the light of Moses had been called into existence. Moses also is the image or likeness of God. There is briefly recapitulated in the early pages of the birth story the way in which the light of Moses was conveyed from Adam to Amram(Moses' father)through the holy chain of patriarchal ancestors. Hereafter follows the birth story of Moses himself (folios 5b-8b) cf. the translation which is here given. From folio 9a-20a are the praises of the heavenly hosts lauding God and Moses. There is some similarity between this last section and the praises of Moses given by the elements and the letters of the alphabet in Book VI of the Memar Marḳaḥ; however such praises there take place at the end of Moses' life, here at the beginning. After the conclusion of the birth story and the praises of the heavenly hosts, there follow two separate sections dwelling on the excellencies of

Moses; the first from folio 20b-25a is constantly punctuated with the refrain 'Verily thus was Moses! And who is like Moses?' From folio 28b-29b we have a hymn of praise to God by Phinehas ben Isaac who made the Hebrew translation of the Samaritan Arabic version of the birth story. On folio 30 is a hymn to God by Amram the priest (d. 1291 A.H.).

From a rubric on f.33a it is stated that a final declaration of thanksgiving to God was read if there was a reading of the birth of Moses in the seven days of Tabernacles. This would seem to imply that the birth story with its accompanying hymns etc. was not reserved for use only on the actual birthday of Moses.

TRANSLATION OF THE BIRTH STORY OF MOSES FOLIOS 5B-8B

Now Amram[1] sprang from Levi's holy line[2] and became great in Egypt and exalted. He was one of the greatest[3] of the men who were with Pharaoh, high in his service. He was a doctor[4] for every disease in Egypt, and God aided him. Now the people of Israel at that time were in great distress because of the violence of the accursed wicked Pharaoh. For he increased their onerous servitude and afflicted them by the way in which he treated them. And the Egyptian the wicked people, evil entreated them, and sought to make the congregation of the people that were saved, despair.[5] Under tyranny and the lash they set them to build for Pharaoh, Nahshah,[6] store cities, Pithom[7] and Raamses, especially great cities, and made their life bitter with harsh slavery. Now there was with the wicked Pharaoh a sorcerer who had come in contact with knowledge of the Book of Signs;[8] and he knew the science of divination and omens. Now Amram had gone up with Pharaoh. A councillor (the Sandik)[9] saw this man and said: "Who is the lawyer[10] who has gone up to the house of Pharaoh?" He (the sorcerer) said to him: "This is one of the Hebrews who has come out." He said[11] "yea, this man is strong, and the light shines from his face, and a faithful upright apostle shall proceed from him and shine forth. Then there shall be release from oppression for the people of Israel, and the kingdom of the Egyptians shall be weakened[12] by his hand, and Pharaoh and all his host shall be of no worth. But to every stranger he gives light, for he is the righteous one with God, and the milk of Law[13] he shall suck". Now this diviner was called Pilti.[14] So this word was told to Pharaoh the accursed, and he sent and called the abovementioned Pilti; and they brought him in haste. (He said) "Indeed I have heard about you, and what you have proclaimed about him". Now Amram was dwelling with Pharaoh. Then Pharaoh asked after Pilti.

And he turned his face to Amram and began to say: "Respect belongs to this man for he will have much honour, because from him shall arise the light[15] from which the heavens and earth are illumined. For from his loins[16] shall come forth the chosen apostle;[17] and at his hand shall his people be relieved from all affliction. By his hand shall his kingdom be great for he distributes freely. Every lying word shall cease, and the powers of heaven[18] and earth shall serve him." When Pharaoh heard this word he arose in haste, and was afraid, and said to Pilti: "Well have you answered and well have you seen that I might know by your divination. So cause me to understand your reports. What you declare affrights me". Pilti pondered and said to Pharaoh: "Banish your fears. Hearken to the replies to your question. If what I say is right, the destruction of your kingdom is near, and you and your council shall perish. For I have seen the star of Israel[19] in the ascendant, and his kingdom growing strong. Nigh is the apostle that is sent to them and the way of his star is on high, and at his hand shall be redemption for them. And his enemy shall be in the lowest part of Sheol. Only I have seen something about the wondrous event of it; my knowledge is faint. For I have seen the Apostle[20] cast into the sea; and fire[21] and water are scattered by him, and in the midst of the sea his people stand. This is the vision which tells and shows that Israel shall be cast into the sea."[22] And violently he arose and was angry the whole of forty days. Now the child which was to be born did not (then) exist; and this is known from the reckoning, and sealed with sorcery. Pharaoh said to him: "What shall we do that the child be not born?" He ordered Pilti the enchanter: "Bring out from where you are, a speaker; let him say that the men of Israel are to be prevented from approaching a woman,[23] lest he be born. But let Amram remain with you till the end of forty days; and declare that any man that approaches his wife shall perish". Pharaoh did so, and set over Israel overseers[24] hard of heart and feelings. He commanded that if any man went in to his wife, he should be separated, and that Amram should never go out from the house of Pharaoh. By his excellence and his power, this is the thing which he did. He forbade the women to go into the men and he set all of them in one place and they suffered banishment. But against the will of God he could not stand. And by the hand of the Lord the Helper a man[25] went and joined together Amram and Jochebed; by this one a meeting was arranged between them, and Amran knew his wife and God aided him and the light of glory[26] passed from Amram. Now Jochebed[27] was advanced[28] in age. She was the daughter of Levi who was born to Jacob. But she became pregnant with Moses and was great with child, and the light[29] was present. And God enveloped her with the glory[30] ... Remember Jochebed for good, the grape from which came he who raised the sanctity of the Law. Let Him[31] be praised who completed all that He wished to do. And after 19 days, evidence was established that the child from his father had been begotten in the womb of his mother. A star[32] showed his glory in the heavens, and the Egyptians were astonished at this appearance, and all the wizards arose in haste;

Pilti came to Pharaoh in great alarm[33] and said to him, "The boy has been brought into contact with the womb of his mother. Vain was what you strove (to do) and your reckoning that you would watch him was wide of the mark". So after this Pharaoh convened an assembly and he called every wizard and sorcerer and magician and was violent concerning the reports of this affair. Now all of them stood by this decree: "If any child be born[34] to the Hebrew people let them cast him into the midst of the river". This order went forth from Pharaoh. Pharaoh also sent and called the midwives[35] of the people of Israel. The name of one was Shiphrah and the name of the other was Puah, just as God said in the Law. And the king of Egypt told the midwives of (the decree) which has been mentioned above. "Every son[36] that is born to the Hebrews you shall cast into the Nile, but you shall let every daughter live". So said the mighty tyrant. However the midwives who feared God, the righteous and upright God, did not do so as the wicked and overbearing Pharaoh commanded, but secretly let the male children live. And the midwives said[38] to Pharaoh with much talk, "because the (Hebrew women) are not like the Egyptian women, princess or slave: for they are vigorous and are delivered before the midwives come to them, indeed much earlier". This matter seemed to Pharaoh to be true (and) not a lie. So afterwards the people multiplied in number, and as for the midwives, God honored them, and their houses[39] He profited, and He kept a reward with Him for them. But Pharaoh did not know about them, and he was against the people of Israel who were growing powerful. So in everything he spread abroad evil for them, and they drank the waters of bitterness. The princess[40] of the Hebrew people was likewise in distress, for when she was pregnant and the time of her giving birth came, that she might bring forth the prince- lest it be spread abroad - they went apart into the wilderness.[41] If the woman in childbirth saw a daughter, she would return with the girl child. But if a son, he was left in the wilderness and God protected him, and He suckled him with honey out of the rock and oil out of the flinty rock. And when the boy was grown up, these[42] would pass with him to his father's house. So the people multiplied and they became very strong. All of them trusted in God that He would deliver them from their trouble. And they remembered how he should preserve (them) in bringing from their number a man, and (how) he would lead them to the Holy Land, and how there should be revealed at his hand every sign in abundance. All the people were gladdened by this that He remembers ~~the~~ covenant with the Meritorious[43] Ones. And on account of this, they silently hoped. And God remembered the covenant which He had made with the pious, and hastened to bring Moses from the hidden[44] world. And he was protected in the womb; and the holy firstborn[45] was kept seven months as our lord Markah[46] explained in his book. But his mother went her full term with him in the seventh month, and the great prophet Moses was born. Good is the mention of him. In the month of Nisan[47] in the fifth day thereof on the sabbath day that he should be protected by its holiness, she raised him up. Good is remembrance of her.

And God said to the Hosts of Heaven: He is born for whom[48] I created my world, and for whose sake (I created it) out of nothing. My good pleasure[50] is in him who surpasses (all), who is mightiest of every female[51] and male, and highest of all creatures (created) either hitherto[52] or to be created hereafter, revealed or concealed.

The Galaxies[53] were shown to be in exceeding great joy, and all of them did obeisance to him, for his light[54] was the origin of theirs. The house of Amram[55] were dwelling in light, and the fullness (of the light) was directed on him. Everyone was saying to his fellow: "The prophet of the Lord is born in whom is His Favor: The select[56] of all creation is born: the man[57] of God is born and he that is trusted[58] over all His house: the servant[59] of the Lord is born and His inheritance: the one chosen out of all His prophets[60] is born: the prophet of the world and of its End[61] is born, for the crown of the prophets is born. You shall desire his prophecy in detail. The master of signs[62] has come, the master of the covenants; the master of prayer[64] has come; the choicest of all creatures; He has come to reveal glories: he has come to receive the holiest[65] of all laws: he has come because our Lord has trusted him over all the world of hidden things: the prophet of all generations has come:[66] he has come to redeem the choicest of families:[67] he has come, he on account of whom and for whose sake He[68] remembered the covenants; he[69] has come, he for whose sake the oaths were established; he has come, he the most select[70] of all spirits: the portion of the God of all spirits has come; he who received the two tablets[71] of the testimony has come: he who reveals the treasures has come: he who tells of life and of different sorts of good things has come. The mother[72] of lights has come.

FOOTNOTES

1. Amram, Father of Moses, son of Kohath, and grandson of Levi. Exod. 6:18-20, Num. 3:19; 26:58, 59.

2. His holy line, i.e. Levi's stock through Kohath. His holy line, literally 'his holy genealogy' *Toledoto ha-Kᵉdošah.*

This concept of the holy stock is fundamental in Samaritan thought, e.g. cf. the careful genealogies of their priests from Adam to the present which the chronicle Tolidah claims to present. The reader should compare the Malef for the immediate interest of the author of the Birth story of Moses in showing that Moses' father was of the holy stock. The reason was that in Adam, even fallen Adam, was some of the light which had been created by the first word of God on the first Day. This light was the Holy Spirit, and was Moses. The true line passed on the light from Father to Son till it came to its fullness in Moses.

3. Jewish tradition knows of Amram as the head of the Jewish high-court, cf. J.E. Vol. I, art. Amram p.533.

4. Presumably as a Rabbi he would likewise be a doctor.

5. Literally: "be withered" or "dry in soul", i.e. "to despair".

6. Nahshah; as the name of the Pharaoh; this name is not given in Jewish tradition. There is a Jewish tradition that Pharaoh's name was Malol, cf. L.Ginzberg, The Legends of the Jews, Vol. II, p.248. (Philadelphia 1946).

7. Pithom and Raamses, cf. Exodus 1:11.

8. The Book of Signs: one of the books inscribed on the Rod which Adam took from Paradise, cf. Malef. According to Samaritan tradition Balaam and Jethro knew of this book. But cf. Pirke de R. Eliezer (*ibid.* p.313) Adam's rod came into the hands of Jethro. Because of his having this book Adam was able to do wonders (Asatir II 7, 12, 36).

9. Sandiḳ. It is not quite clear to whom Sandiḳ refers. The sentence is clumsy in construction in the Hebrew. Literally it is: 'He saw him this man the Sandiḳ'. The Sandiḳ cannot be either the magician or Amram as is clear from what follows. The magician tells him, some third party, presumably the Sandiḳ, who Amram is. The sentence must therefore be translated The Sandiḳ saw this man (meaning Amram). The *yateh* him after the verb merely anticipates the object 'this man' as in Mishnaic style. Sandiḳ cf. Gk. Sundikos an advocate, judge.

10. Nomik, i.e. Gk. Nomikos, lawyer.

11. The speaker is still the magician.

12. msḳ but cf. Arabic *mazzaḳa* to destroy.

13. The milk of the Law. Cf. the New Testament phrase 'the milk of the word'.

14. Pilti. Cf. the Asatir. Rabbinic tradition does not know Pilti as the name of the magician who foretold the birth of Moses. Instead we hear of two wizards. Jannes and Jambres, who foretold the birth of Moses "the destroyer of the land of Egypt" and thereby caused as did Pilti in our source, the cruel decree of Pharaoh against the Israelites; T.B. Soṭah 11a; Sanh, 106a. cf. also II Tim. iii:8 for the same two magicians' names. In Pirke de R. Eliezer (*ibid.* p.377) the magicians are reported as having told Pharaoh of the birth of the as yet unborn Moses.

The names of the magicians are not there given. For other references to the prophecy of the Egyptian priests as to the birth of Moses cf. Josephus *Antiq.* Bk.II.IX.2 - Bk. II.X.2. also Exod.R. i. Targ. Jer. to Exod.1:14. In some Jewish sources Miriam also foretells that a son would be born to her father who would liberate Israel; T.B. Soṭah 11b, 12a; Meg. 14a. Ex. R. i.24. cf. also Josephus Antiq.Bk. II·IX.3 where Amram is assured by God in a vision that he will be father of two famous sons.

15. The light cf. Gen. 1:3. To understand the connection of the light of the first day and Moses cf. Malef beginning. The light was the Holy Spirit and the pre-existent Moses. For the pre-existence of Moses cf. The Assumption of Moses i. 12-14 XI II, 17. Charles (*Apocrypha and Pseudepigrapha*) Vol. II, p.415, Oxford 1913.

16. i.e. Amram's loins.

17. The chosen apostle is Moses.

18. The powers of heaven shall serve him. This may be a reference (a) to the Angels hailing his birth (cf. the end of translated extract) and (b) to the homage he received even from the angels when he went up Sinai to receive the Law. To the latter's homage there is frequent reference in the Samaritan liturgy. Jewish tradition knows of how Moses refused to give the angel of death his soul, cf. T. B. Sotah 13b. Moses overcomes the angels at Sinai, cf. Pirke de R. Eliezer *ibid.* p.361 who thought the Law was given for them.

19. Star of Israel. Cf. Num. 24:17. A star out of Jacob.

20. Cast into the sea. A reference to Moses being put into the Nile. Exod. 2:3.

21. 'Fire and water' seem hardly a reference to any of the plagues. The fire may be a reference to the pillar of fire and the water to the cleaving of the sea to allow the Israelites to pass, cf.Exod.14:21-22. The word *tizdarmi* translated 'overcome' is uncertain, cf. Arabic *zrm* 'to stop', hence the word in our text may mean 'are stopped' or 'are overcome'.

22. The reference is to Israel's crossing of the Red Sea Exod.14:21-23. The irony of Pilti's vision was that in fact Egypt, and not Israel was cast into the sea Exod.14:28.

23. The Exodus narrative tells us nothing of this decree of Pharaoh separating the Israelite men from their wives, nor of Pharaoh's keeping Amram in his Palace away from Jochebed.

There is in Rabbinic literature (cf. J.E. Vol. I article Amram,' p.533) reference to Amram separating himself from his wife, when Pharaoh issued the decree (Exod.1:22) that every male child of the Hebrews sould be cast into the river. T. B. Soṭah 12a.

24. According to the Biblical account the overseers were not appointed for this purpose but to be taskmasters.

25. The man is unknown to the Biblical account and to Rabbinic tradition.

26. This light was the light of the first Day Gen. 1:3. It had been handed down from Adam through the holy patriarchs to Amram, and it was to shine in the face of Moses.

27. Jochebed, sister of Kohath, Amram's father. Amram married his aunt Jochebed, Exod. 6:20.

28. According to Rabbinic tradition cf. J.E. Vol. I art. Amram, p.538. Jochebed was 130 years old when Moses was conceived. Cf. also Pirke de R. Eliezer *ibid.* p.375 for Jochebed being 130 years old when she bare Moses.

29. The light was intensely bright. The rendering intensely bright for *zbd* is uncertain. But compare Ar. *zbd* the IVth form of which is to be intensely white. Rabbinic tradition cf. Pirḳe de R. Eliezer *ibid.* p.378 speaking presumably of the child when born, says that his parents saw the child in the form of an angel of God. There is the tradition too that a glorious light filled the whole house when he was born, showing that he was worthy of the gift of prophecy, T.B. Soṭah 12a.

30. In Soṭah 12a we hear of Amram when he decided to resume marital relations with his wife (despite Pharaoh's decree against male children) celebrating his wedding for a second time with his 130 years old wife, who under the marriage canopy becomes like a young maiden. The word *rebid* rendered 'enveloped' in our text is uncertain, but cf. *rbd* in Arabic to confine.

31. God who despite the plans of Pharaoh brought the redeemed Moses.

32. Cf. the star in Balaam's prophecy Num. 24:17; cf. the star of Bethlehem. Matt. 2:2.

33. *b^e rab dush.* The root *duš* is to trample, thresh in Hebrew. *Raušah* in Arabic means uproar. Perhaps the word can be translated 'alarm'. The Scribe may have written *daleth* for *resh.*

34. Cf. Exod.1:22. Pharaoh according to the Samaritan

account having failed in his earlier decree which was to prevent the union of Hebrew male and female, lest the liberator be born, now attempts to destroy any fruit of that union. In this respect Pharaoh according to the Samaritan story now acts in much the same way as Herod in slaughtering the innocents of Bethlehem. Matt. 2:16. There is a certain similarity between the two stories. In Pirḳe de R. Eliezer *ibid.* p.378 Pharaoh rescinds his order to cast male children into the river when he knows Moses is born. He only gave the command hoping Moses would be among the infants drowned. When Pharaoh knew that Moses had been safely born and not drowned at birth, he then apparently (according to Pirḳe de R. Eliezer) changed his policy and determined on embittering the lot of the Hebrews with hard labour.

35. The Hebrew midwives cf. Exod.1:15-21. The names of the midwives in the Samaritan birth story of Moses are as in the Bible Ex. 1:15.

36. M.T.Exod. 1:22 lacks 'to the Hebrews'. In the Bible, however, this is said by Pharaoh to all his people, not to the midwives. In Ex. 1:16 the midwives are to kill the male child when being born. The method of killing is not specified.

37. This is an exact quotation of Exod.1:17 with the addition of the epithets after God and Pharaoh respectively, and the further addition of 'secretly' as to how they managed to let the children live. The root *Amar* is used, however, instead of the root *Dabar* in reference to Pharaoh's command to them.

38. Pharaoh's query as to why the midwives were nevertheless letting the male children live cf. Exod. 1:18, is not quoted in our story. The text here assumes the question and proceeds to quote the midwives' excuse, cf. Exod. 1:19. This is also an exact quotation of the Biblical text apart from the addition of 'with much talk' after 'to Pharaoh' and 'prince and slave' after Egyptian women, and the closing 'indeed much earlier'. The Birth Story does not quote the verses 20, 21 of Exod.1, but merely paraphrases very loosely their substance.

39. The word *Battim* could be rendered 'families' as in the American Revised Standard Version. Exod. 1:21.

40. The word rendered here princess is literally prince so also 'princess and slave' above; but in neither case can the word mean anything but princess. In this case it very definitely refers to Jochebed.

41. Here follows a Samaritan haggadic interpretation of

Deut. 32:13 end, 'and he made him suck honey out of the rock, and oil out of the flinty rock'.

42. The rock and flinty rock.

43. The meritorious ones, i.e. Abraham, Isaac and Jacob. For God's covenants with them, cf. Gen. 15:18; 17:4 (with Abraham); with Isaac Gen. 26:3 with Jacob 35:9-12.

44. This is not a reference to his life in his mother's womb, but to Moses as already existing in the Unseen world as he had been from before the creation of the earth.

45. But Moses was not Jochebed's firstborn; her firstborn child was Miriam. The only way the use of the expression firstborn can be understood, is to understand it as meaning her first son.

46. Markah, the famous priest of the 4th century A.D. who in addition to composing liturgical hymns still used in the modern Samaritan Liturgy, wrote the famous Memar Markah. The Memar is now incomplete. This reference to the seven month gestation of Moses may come from a portion of the work now lost. There is no birth story of Moses in the extant Memar, though it is obvious that there must have been such at one time. The Memar Markah is not primarily a commentary on the Pentateuch, though there are pieces of Bible commented on *passim*. The Memar centers round Moses. Its interest in the events and personages before Moses are only in so far as they can be shown as leading up to Moses. Cf. the writer's paper given to the Dutch Old Testament Society's International Congress, Leiden, 1950. A comparison of Samaritan and Rabbinic Biblical Exegesis.

47. T. B. Meg. 13b., Mek. Beshallah Wayissa' (ed. Weiss p.60a) say that Moses died on Adar 7, the day on which he was born.

48. i.e. Moses. Heaven and earth were created for his sake. Lev. R. XXXVI.4 gives a Jewish parallel to the Samaritan belief. But one should note that in Judaism such a haggadic statement as cited above, has not, nor never had, any recognition accorded to it such as the statement in the Samaritan Birth Story of Moses has had among the Samaritans. The Samaritans did believe and were expected to believe such a statement; it was not an individual expression of opinion.

50. Cf. the Bath Qol or heavenly voice at the baptism of Jesus: 'This is my beloved Son, with whom I am well pleased'. Matt. 3:17.

51. i.e. mightier than all creation male and female.

52. This goes much further than Deut. 34:10 which applied only to prophets.

53. The word is *gltkim* which I understand as from Gk. *Galaksias* (galaxy), and in reference to the hosts of heaven the word would not be out of place.

54. The light of Moses being the light of the first day of creation. See above note 26.

55. Cf. Sefer Yashar p.112b and T. B. Soṭah 12a.

56. The select or elect of all creation is a common enough epithet of Moses as early as Marḳah.

57. "Moses the man of God" is a Biblical expression (Deut. 33:1).

58. The trusted one over all His house is a common enough expression in the Old Defter (Samaritan Liturgy), cf. Cowley *The Samaritan Liturgy*, Vol. II, p. L, Oxford, 1909).

59. Moses the servant of the Lord. Deut. 34:5.

60. Cf. Deut. 34:10; the reading in our text is literally, prophecy.

61. Of its End. Cf. Deut. 32:35 Sam. Version not 'vengeance' but day of Vengeance. The Samaritans base their eschatology on this verse in the Law of Moses.

62. A reference to the wonders worked by Moses at Pharaoh's court and in Egypt, at the crossing of the Sea and in the Desert.

63. The pillars of fire and cloud. Exod. 13:21, 22; Exod. 14:19, 24.

64. Cf. the Covenant at Sinai Exodus 24.

65. The master of prayer. Moses is called such because of the efficacy of his prayer in turning away the wrath of God when He wished to blot out Israel, cf. Exod. 32:30f. because of the sin of making the golden calf.

66. Cf. Deut. 34:10.

67. i.e. Israel.

68. God

69. Moses

70. Moses was the spirit of God according to Samaritan teaching of Malef, beginning.

71. i.e. the two tablets of the Ten Commandments, cf. Exod. 31:18 and Exod. 32:19.

72. i.e. Moses as the light of the First Day, Gen. 1:3.

CHAPTER 5

THE HILLUK

To the late Haham Gaster belongs the credit of having brought the attention of the learned world to the *Hilluk* or Code of Laws. In the Gaster Collection of manuscripts in the John Rylands Library, Manchester, there are three copies of this work; one is in Arabic and two are in Hebrew. The work is frankly fairly recent. Gaster (*'The Samaritans'* O.U.P. 1925, p. 153) admits 'a modern writer may claim to be the author'. Priest Amram b. Isaac when Secretary of the Samaritan Community told me that his father wrote it. While I cannot say with Gaster: "I am still inclined to believe that it dates from a much older time", I am convinced that the practices and doctrines set forth in the *Hilluk* are indeed old. The compilation itself may be recent, but the material included in it old. I am led to this conclusion by comparing matters treated in the *Hilluk* with the same subjects in the eleventh century *Kitab al-Tabbaḥ* of Abu'l Hasan al-Surī. Seven centuries and more separate these two works, but any individual topic which occurs in both is handled identically. The *Hilluk*, like the *Kitab al-Tabbaḥ*, is very careful to draw the distinction between the Samaritan and the Jewish way of doing things. In both works the element of polemic is prominent.

One manuscript J.R.G. 1811 (the *Sefer Hilluk*) describes itself as giving information about the worship of the Samaritans on Sabbaths and Festivals and about the statutes relating to circumcision. But that title is inadequate. The first section of the *Hilluk* states how and why Samaritans are a separate community from the Jews. This chapter contains interesting historical allusions to the fortunes of the Samaritan sect.

The second section states that "the Chosen Place" is

Mount Gerizim, and how the *Shekinah* was upon it in the days of Joshua the son of Nun; afterwards the Jews turned to another place - Shiloh.

The third section deals with the Sabbath and Sabbath Observance among the Samaritans. Differences between them and the Jews as to its observance are discussed. The fourth section is concerned with Circumcision as practised by the Samaritans. Again we have polemic against the Jews.

The fifth section discussed the Samaritan way of observing the Festivals and Passover in particular. Differences between Samaritans and Jews are underlined.

The sixth section details the laws relating to purity and impurity, male and female.

The seventh section sets out the laws relating to the slaughtering of animals and birds. It discusses in some detail what kinds are permissible and in what condition. Again we have anti-Jewish polemic.

The eighth section treats Samaritan marriage laws, and explains what unions are lawful and unlawful. In this section we have a description of the marriage ceremony. Divorce proceedings are dealt with next.

The ninth section is concerned with the permanence of the Torah and its legislation.

The tenth section commences by treating legislation relating to death and burial, and then passes on to give Samaritan teaching on Paradise and Hell and the question of the Resurrection and eternal punishment. The tenth section of the *Hilluk* has been translated by the late Ḥaḥam Gaster in *Samaritan Oral Law and Ancient Traditions* Vol. I, The Search Publishing Company, 1932, pp.129-187.

Here I give translations of pieces taken from the sections on marriage and circumcision. The texts available to me have been two manuscripts of the *Hilluk* in Hebrew. These Manuscripts are Gaster MSS. Nos. 1811, 1193 in the John Rylands Library Manchester. Unfortunately these MSS. have been damaged in part by water during the Second World War, and the ink has run; sometimes the readings are not clear. I have chosen selections from the sections dealing with marriage and circumcision as the state of the text of these sections was reasonably good, but not for this reason only. In these sections we have good examples of Samaritan Halakah. Both topics show how Biblical, nay Pentateuchal, the Samaritan usage still is; especially in this case with circumcision. One can see also how the Samaritan unimaginatively carries out the Torah's injunctions *au pied de lettre*. In the case of the laws relating to marriage, one finds that while Samaritan usage is primitive, it is not entirely based on the Bible text. Here we have some genuine Samaritan Halakah based on the communal usage, and not altogether drawn from the Pentateuch.

THE HILLUK ON MARRIAGE

To take a woman in marriage is one of the best of the Commandments that appears in the book of Genesis: "And said to them: Be fruitful and multiply".[1] And likewise there appears in this book: "It is not good that man should be alone.[2] I will make him a helper fit for him."

Even if the brideprice[3] of a virgin among the Community of the Samaritans is small - it is fifty shekels of silver[4] - yet the man also gives to her garments and ornaments as shall be determined by the father of the girl or her guardian. Now at the time when the man seeks to bind (in marriage) the girl to himself, he gathers to him as many men as he chooses and they go to the house[5] of the father of the girl. Before them is a man from the priest's house or many of the kind. The girl's father or her guardian sit on the left of the priest while his son-in-law (to be) who is seeking to marry the girl, sits before him, and begins by saying to the girl's father: "I ask you, Sir, or my friend So and So, to give your daughter, the young virgin, to me according to the ordinances of the LORD (blessed be He) and those of His servant our lord Moses, the peace of God be upon him, for the brideprice which he stipulated, four thousand and nine hundred *keritas*;[6] whereof is given first two thousand four hundred *keritas*, then later two thousand five hundred *keritas*; with over and above, the garments and ornaments which you settled for me (to provide) according to the usages of the daughter of the Ben Israel which they follow in this matter.[7] Will you give her to me and accept my request according to the ordinances[8] of the LORD, Blessed be He, and His servant Moses the son of Amram, upon him be peace?"

And the father of the girl takes the brideprice from his son-in-law (to be) and puts his hand in his hand; and afterwards the priest puts his hand on the hands of both of them and begins to speak in the hearing of all the men who are met together there saying: "The covenant of Abraham and Isaac and Jacob, Peace be upon them, bind them rightly and completely according to the holy Torah by the ordinances of the LORD, Blessed be He, and His servant Moses the son of Amram, upon him be peace. He is to be praised for he is the Righteous One, and He it is who consecrates everything that is consecrated. Afterwards[9] he reads the chapter[10] from the Book of the sacred Torah beginning: "For I will[11] proclaim in the name of the LORD and ascribe greatness to our God. The Rock His work is perfect, for all His ways are justice. A God of faithfulness without iniquity, just and right is He. Blessed is our God for ever and blessed is His name for ever. Then[12] the LORD said, "It is not good that man should be alone. I will make him a helper fit for him. So[13] the LORD God caused a deep sleep to fall upon the man and while he slept took one of his ribs and closed up its place with flesh. And[14] the rib which the LORD God had taken from the man he made into a woman, and brought her to the man. Then[15] the man said: "This at last is bone from my bone and flesh from my flesh. This shall be called Woman because she was taken out of Man." Therefore[16] a man leaves his father and his mother and cleaves to his wife, and there shall be from[17] the two of them one flesh. God is to be praised. There is no God but One.[18] Hear O Israel. The[19] LORD our God is One LORD. Blessed is His glorious Name for ever and ever.

And the LORD commanded us to do all these statutes, to fear the LORD our God, for our good always and that He might preserve us alive, as at this day. And[20] it will be righteousness for us, and if we are careful to do all this commandment before the LORD our God as He commanded us.

When[21] Moses commanded us a law as a possession of the assembly of Jacob. God is to be blessed; blessed is our God for ever and blessed is his name for ever.

The men that are met together answer saying with the joy known among the congregation of the Samaritans "We proclaim and say there is no God but One.
We proclaim and say there is no God but One.
We proclaim and say there is no God but One.
There is no God but One.
There is a God[22] merciful and gracious, slow to anger, and abounding in steadfast love and faithfulness:

The priest proclaims: Blessed art Thou, O LORD our God". And he blesses the bridegroom and his bride, and the men that are gathered together, the bridegroom and all his relatives. After this the bridegroom or his father bring the men that are gathered together, food or sweet drink, and tney praise the name of the Lord, blessed is He; and everybody comes to his house. And at the time[23] the bridegroom seeks to go to his bridal bed, he makes a big banquet according to his means, with great joy for seven days.[24] The priest writes for them a document of

Marriage,[25] in the holy language, Hebrew, the language known among them. This is the ordinance of marriage among the Samaritan community.

NOTES ON THE HILLUK
THE SECTION ON MARRIAGE

1. Gen. 1:28.

2. Gen. 2:18.

3. *Maher* so the Samaritans pronounce *Mohar*. The Mohar was the marriage present given for the bride to the prospective father-in-law cf. Gen. 34:12.

4. The minimum payable under ketubah was two hundred *zuzim* for virgins, and one hundred *zuzim* for women who were not virgins; the sum was mentioned in the Ketubah. Also mentioned was the amount of her dowry which she brought, and the addition thereto made by the husband-to-be. Here there is no mention of a dowry brought by the bride, but only the brideprice and the additional presents given by the bridegroom. It is doubtful whether the Samaritan community ever established as a regular feature the wise practice ordained by the Rabbis that a man give some of his property to his daughter on her marriage.

5. Cf. Gen. 24:32-52 for the way in which Eleazar Abraham's servant arranged for the marriage of Rebecca to Isaac.

6. Cf. the Mi<u>k</u>tab *Hadebikah* (Ketubah) of a virgin translated in the present book. *Kesitah*, cf. Gen. 33:19 translated in the Revised Standard Version as "piece of money".

7. While the Samaritans claim to follow the Torah and that alone as rule of faith and action, it is obvious that not all contingencies of life are covered therein. They have not developed an elaborate Oral Law, but they have indeed developed some extra-Biblical laws; such laws may not have the sanction of the Divine Law, but have at least the sanction of communal usage; such is the case with the ritual of arranging marriages.

8. A reference to Gen. 2:24 where the Samaritan Text reads "and they *both* shall become one flesh". Cf. Matt. 19:5, 6; Mark 10:7, 8, for the stress in Samaritan marriage is on this becoming one flesh. After fixing the dowry as Gaster says (*The Samaritans*,1925,p.72):"the contract is drawn up called the

Mikhtab Hadebikah,'the writing of joining', the word being taken from the text of the Bible in Gen. 2:24, where it says 'a man shall cleave'. The Karaites considered that husband and wife are legally one person. Cf. J. E. Art. Incest. Vol. VI, p.594.

9. i.e. the priest.

10. Here again we see how fundamental in Samaritan Liturgy is the reading of the Law. Cowley in his *The Samaritan Liturgy* (Oxford, 1909, Vol. II, pp.818-851) gives hymns for weddings and circumcisions. Actually it is quite impossible to form from these pages in Cowley any idea of the Samaritan wedding service; here we have the Samaritan wedding service proper at the Betrothal. The hymns in Cowley are for the seven days of the Bridal Feasts.

11. A favourite Biblical quotation in the Liturgy usually introducing Biblical readings. Deut. 32:3-4 (with Samaritan reading in v.3).

12. Gen. 2:18.

13. Gen. 2:21 (omitting "with flesh").

14. Gen. 2:22.

15. Gen. 2:23.

16. Gen. 2:24.

17. Note the different Samaritan reading instead of the Jewish Bible's "they shall become one flesh".

18. 'There is no God but One' reminds one of the Muslim credal statement. There is however no reason to see this as a borrowing from Islam. The phrase is constantly to be found at the end of hymns of Markah, the fourth century Samaritan writer, three centuries prior to the rise of Islam. Public confession of God being One, is as old as the Shema. The oldest element in the Samaritan Liturgy is the reading of passages from the Law. Between such passages and at the end of such reading it is customary for the Samaritans *inter alia* to proclaim the Oneness of God, which is the first article of their Creed. Not only is the phrase earlier than Islam, but earlier than the inclusion of Markah's hymns into the Liturgy for it is already found in connection with the earliest level of the Liturgy - the readings from the Law.

19. Deut. 6:24.

20. Deut. 6:25.

21. Deut. 33:4. This verse usually concludes readings from the Law in the Samaritan Liturgy, especially at the end of each of the Ḳetafim of the five books of the Law in the Sabbath morning service.

22. Cf. Exod. 34:6.

23. What has been described above was the betrothal, which however, as in Biblical practice, is an actual but incomplete marriage, cf. Deut. 22:23, 24 where a betrothed virgin is regarded as legally the wife of the man to whom she is betrothed, though not yet married to him. The Samaritan practice is that of the Pentateuch. While the Betrothed is legally the wife of the Bridegroom she may not become actually his Bride for a considerable period. It is this to which out author goes on to tell us. Judaism for long preserved the distinction between the *Erusin* and the *Nissu'in*. However now *Erusin* and *Nissu'in* (betrothal and home-taking) are syncopated into one marriage ceremony, instead of being two separate ceremonies. The becoming engaged, and the celebration of an engagement among modern Jews is not the same as the old *Erusin*, but resembles the old custom of *shiddukin*, cf. *J.E.* Vol. III, art. "Betrothal", pp.125-127.

24. But cf. Gen. 29:23, 27 where the feast may have been only on the first day, and "her week" v.27 have been the equivalent of a honeymoon.

25. This is the Mik̲tab Hadebikah, cf. Gaster *ibid.* p.72 who rightly states that this is drawn up at the Betrothal when the dowry is fixed. We cannot take this reference to the Document of Marriage here as implying that it only was when the Bridegroom took his bride to his house that he received this document; nor is the Document of Marriage anything other than the Mik̲tab Hadebikah.

THE HILLUK̲ ON CIRCUMCISION

The fourth section about Circumcision and the law thereon among the community of the children of Israel,[1] the Shomrim (i.e. "Observers of the Law") and mention of the points of difference which are between them and the Jewish community in regard to this commandment. From the earliest times the community of the Samaritans have been wont to observe the time of the birth of a boy child. If it were after the setting of the sun,[2] they would count for him seven days from the morrow (thereof). But if it were before the setting of the sun they would count from the very day of the birth, and on the eighth day they would circumcise him. Circumcision with them is always on the eighth day only. They, in the morning of this day, from the rising of the sun begin to circumcise the boy's foreskin. And he who is not circumcised[3] on the eighth day will be lost, and is not called by the name of Hebrew, nor is he clean.[4] So they do not delay circumcising a boy till another day, on account of persecution or sickness; nor (is it delayed) if his father is not to be found in the city of his birth, as do the community[5] of the Jews; nor if it fell on the Sabbath day, or on a feast day, nor on account of any matter. Only on the eighth day is he to be circumcised, and it is not to be postponed. But the Jewish community delay circumcision of a boy up to thirty days. But in the book of the Law which is in the hands of the community of the Samaritans (there is written) in the commandment which the Name commanded our father Abraham, upon him be peace: Gen. 17:14 "And the uncircumcised male child[6] whose flesh of his foreskin is not circumcised on the eighth day that soul shall be cut off from his people." They say that the reason for this is that he who is not circumcised on the eighth day is not an Israelite in the world to come. But in the book of the Law which is in the hands of the Jews it is thus: "and the uncircumcised male child, whose flesh of his foreskin is not circumcised that soul shall be cut off from his people". And they omit therefrom 'on the eighth day'. Therefore they can delay the circumcision.[7]

The community of the Samaritans on the seventh day purify the child with water. Then on the morning of the eighth day, the boy's father or his near relative sends to invite to him the priest and all his relatives and friends. Then the priest[8] who is to circumcise and all the men whom he has invited come to the boy's father's house.[9] The priest and all the men who are met together stand, and the priest begins a prayer which is called among them the prayer of circumcision.[10] And this prayer begins with the praises to the Name, Blessed is He. Afterwards there is mention of the creation of the world,[11] and passages[12] from the book of the Torah mentioning the first righteous ones,[13] (are read) and then passages mentioning the commandment of circumcision, and mention of the covenant,[14] and the blessings (involved). When they finish therewith, the circumciser arises, and circumcises the flesh of the boy's foreskin.[15] And afterwards they read a song in the language of the Targum[16] by the lord Markah[17] the priest who lived two thousand years[18] ago; he Markah was in those days high priest of the community of the Shomrim on the death of the priest 'Akbon.[19] Then when the circumcision of the boy is over, the priest says to the boy's father: what is the name of the boy?[20] He says to him: 'your servant So and So." Then the priest replies to the boy's father with: "Blessed be he".

The community of the Samaritans is accustomed to make a big feast on account of the keeping of this commandment. And if the eighth day were to fall on the Sabbath day, or on the Day of Atonement, or on a feast day, the boy is circumcised on it. They do not postpone the circumcision to the next day as does the Jewish[21] community. And the testimony to which they bear witness is that which comes in the book of Leviticus chapter 12 (v.3): "And in the eighth day the flesh of his foreskin shall be circumcised."

NOTES ON THE HILLUK

THE FOURTH SECTION: ABOUT CIRCUMCISION

1. i.e. The Samaritans.

2. The day begins with the evening, cf. Gen. 1:5

3. Cf. Gen. 17:12 'He that is eight days old among you shall be circumcised'. Cf. also Lev. 12:3: 'and on the eighth day the flesh of his foreskin shall be circumcised'. M. Shab. 19:1 shows that with the Jews too, circumcision overrode the Sabbath. Whereas the Jews did and do try to circumcise on the eighth day if at all possible, it could be postponed because of sickness or weakness of the child. But even were a Jew not to have been circumcised, he is a full Jew by birth (cf. T. B. Hull. 4b; T.B. Ab. Zar. 27a; Shulhan 'Arukh, Yoreh de'ah 264,1).

4. Cf. The Book of Jubilees 15:26-27 which says that the uncircumcised are 'sons of Belial' and 'children of doom and eternal perdition'.

5. Hardly fair to Judaism. For Judaism's noble record in circumcising even under severe persecution,cf. T. B. Shab. 130a, T.B.B.B. 60b, Mekilta Yitro, Ba-Ḥodesh, VI.

6. The M.T. Hebrew text has not 'on the eighth day'.

7. The allegation is that the Jewish scribes omitted the words so as to give Biblical sanction for delay in circumcision; this is not very feasible. What is much more likely is that the Samaritans inserted the words to emphasize the eight days mentioned in Gen. 17:12 and to bring it into line with Lev. 12:3.

8. Only the priest could circumcise a Samaritan baby. According to Rabbi Meir, if a Jewish Mohel were not available, a Jewish child could be circumcised by a non-Jewish physician; even women, slaves and children could officiate. Cf. T.B.Ab. Zar. 26b; T.B.Men. 42a.

9. Circumcision remained with the Samaritans a home ceremony.

10. Unidentifiable under this name but perhaps it is the prayer by Marḳah on p.846 in Cowley's *Samaritan Liturgy*, Oxford, 1909, Vol. II.

11. This refers to the Ḳiṣe ha-Beriah cf. above p. 3. Cf. also Cowley *ibid.* Vol. II, p.846,lines 7f. (Cowley only gives the beginning, and as usual with his edition, omits the portions read from the Law.)

12. It would appear that in the Circumcision Service whole Ḳaẓim are read from the Torah, and not a Ḳaṭaf of scriptural phrases. Cf. above p. 27. A similar sort of service is the preparatory service before the Eve of Sabbath service; it consists

of the *Ḳise ha-Beria* followed by whole *Ḳaṣim* or *paraṡiyyot* taken from throughout the Torah. (All of such *Ḳaṣim* in that service having some bearing on the Sabbath).

13. i.e. The Patriarchs.

14. With Abraham cf. Gen. 17.

15. There is no mention of the Sandek or godfather as holding the child as in the Jewish rite. There would be of course no Elijah's Chair beside the Sandek's chair. We do not hear of the *peri'ah* without which circumcision according to M. Shab 30:6 was of no value. Kaufmann Kohler, *J.E.*, Vol. IV, art. "Circumcision", p.93 suggests that the Rabbis after the war of Bar Kokbah instituted the *peri'ah*; but in view of the attempts of Hellenized Jews to conceal their circumcision in the gymnasium cf. 1 Macc. 1:15, this may be much earlier. We have no information that *meṣiṣah* ever was part of Samaritan circumcision, which seems to have consisted purely of *milah*.

16. i.e. Aramaic.

17. The hymn of Markah commemorates the goodness of Germon the Roman overseer or Bishop who allowed Aḳbon to circumcise his son with impunity, despite the strict Roman prohibition of the rite. For the story of Germon and Aḳbon see p.161 in the section of this book relating to Samaritan Chronicles: the story is told of Abu'l Fath. For the text of the hymn see A. E. Cowley, *ibid.*, Vol. II, p.846, esp. l.26.

18. The figure two thousand can only be taken as a round number. Everything points to Markah belonging to the fourth century A.D.

19. Markah was never High Priest. Aḳbon was succeeded by Nathanel cf. p. 139 in the translated extracts from Abu'l Fath.

20. Not only a Samaritan custom.

21. Nor necessarily would the Jew postpone the ceremony.

SAMARITAN KETUBOT MARRIAGE DOCUMENTS

Marriage documents are not of Biblical authority but they, on a priori grounds, would be of high antiquity, among both Samaritans and Jews. Dealing with origin of the Jewish Ketubah T.B. Ket. 10a and 82b tell us that "the wise men long before Simeon b. Shetaḥ instituted the ketubah for the daughters of

Israel". Nor need we stop with Maimonides (Yad. Ishut xvi) who believed that the ketubah was established by the Great Sanhedrin in order that a Jewish wife should not be lightly regarded in her husband's eyes. (J.E. Vol. VII art.Ketubah, p.474). As to when the Great Synagogue met we cannot be certain, but even if it were first convened in the days of Ezra, a form of Ketubah was already employed by the schismatic Jews of Elephantine (cf. *Aramaic Papyri of the Fifth Century B.C.*, A.E.Cowley, Oxford, 1923, pp.44-47) and it is not likely that they borrowed it from the post-exilic community in Jerusalem. The Samaritans, and those other schismatics whose schism was of more recent origin might well be expected to have been influenced in their drafting of their Ketubot by the example of Jewish prototypes. Unfortunately we have no prototypes from either party. We do know that Simeon ben Shetaḥ of the time of Alexander Jannaeus and Queen Alexandra (Salome) legislated in order to curtail freedom of hasty divorce, that the husband might use the sum mentioned in the Ketubah, but that his entire fortune should be held liable for it P.T. Ket. VIII 32c, and he must pay therefrom the equivalent amount in event of divorce. It is possible too from Mishnah Ketubot to form a fairly exact picture of the complete contents of the Jewish Ketubah in the first two centuries of this era. With the Samaritans it is another matter. Of the early form of the Samaritan Ketubah we have no information. I publish here two Samaritan Ketubot, one of the eighteenth century, the other of the nineteenth. The operative kernel, the actual marriage agreement, is the same in both even to the exact words used. One difference there is. The first Ketubah, the earlier, is that of a woman who had been married before, the other that of a virgin. Therefore the Brideprice of the first is half that of the second, as in Jewish usage, cf. M. Ket.1:2. In both however the bridegroom give 49% before he married her and 51% he retains. He is for this 51% left under obligation to his wife; and if she is divorced she may take it, as much thereof as she chooses. Presumably the Samaritan husband's property is under lien to this amount - 51% of the Brideprice. It would be foolhardy to see in this regulation any influence of Simeon b. Shetaḥ.

As in the Jewish Ketubot so in the Samaritan, now obsolete money-terms are used in the assessing of the dowry; this in itself is a testimony to the relative antiquity of both forms. The Samaritan Ketubah mentions two Biblical texts Ex. 21:10 and Gen. 2:24; the first to sum up the husband's duties to her, and the second to underline the Divine purpose of marriage. In Gen. 2:24 the Samaritan Pentateuch has a somewhat different reading from the Hebrew Massoretic, but the New Testament quotations of this verse seem to postulate a reading similar to the Samaritan.

Like the Jewish Ketubah, the Samaritan gives name, description and residence of the two parties to the marriage, and date thereof, and is careful to impress the binding nature of the document. What one does not find in a Jewish Ketubah, but in the Samaritan, is that the husband has power to annul his wife's vows, and she must owe him absolute obedience.

The preamble to the Samaritan Ketubot takes us back to the root of the matter, God, and the creation of the world and Adam and Eve, and leads up in deftly syncopated history to the happy couple.

The terms used to describe the happy man and his immediate forbears, and the blushing bride's male forbears are standard and in fact the vocabulary of this section and indeed of the historical preamble, were used in the 14th century in liturgical compositions of Abdallah b. Solomon; however these compositions are not to be regarded as the source of the phraseology, but they themselves would seem to reflect the language and phraseology of the Ketubah. We may infer that the Ketubot in the 14th century at least were the same as in the 18th century. There is a distinct possibility that the form of Ketubah like the institution itself is very much older and dates from at least the beginning of this era, when Greek was familiar to the Samaritans; witness the occurrence of two Greek terms in the Ketubah.

It remains to add that betrothal makes the bride-to-be the lawfully wedded wife of the husband.

SAMARITAN KETUBAH[1] (OF A WOMAN MARRIED FOR THE SECOND TIME)

In the name of the LORD God of Israel we begin and end. Blessed be the LORD our God, and the God of our Fathers the meritorious ones[2] our ancestors that possessed merit - the exalted King who makes night and day to alternate. Blessed be His name for ever on account of the renewal of the seasons.[3] He the Unique, who came first, and forever is exalted. Who teaches[4] every mouth, in proclamation of His praise, Who is separate in His Unity, Who is omnipotent in His Dominion, Who created His creation by the Ordinance of His Wisdom.[5] In the beginning, what did He create? He nipped[6] off the light from the darkness, and made a[7] separation between what is above and below the firmament, and what is around it. The waters[8] into one place He collected, and He revealed the dry land; and the earth brought forth grass,[9] herbs which bear seed, (and) trees. And He set in the heavens stars,[10] those which move, and those which are fixed, and two great[11] lights whose rule should be perpetual, and He created moving[12] creatures, and birds from the waters, and from the earth, living souls of three kinds, wild beasts, domestic animals and creeping things. And at the end of creation[13] He established man in His[14] likeness and made him rule by intelligence,[15] and He made Eden[16] his place of rest. And He said in the abundance of His goodness and mercy "It is not[17] good that the man should be alone. I will make him a helper fit for him". And He formed Eve from his rib(s).[18] And from him He raised up the meritorious and perfect ones, every meritorious one perfect in his generation, (until the time of) him[19] who was lord of the ages and the light of prophecy, the scribe of[20] life, the priest[21] of the angels, and who received the Tablets (of the Ten Commandments), and revealed the Faith, revealing the words of the Torah, and explained the ordinance of marriage,[22] and (that there would be) for Israel dominion at the Day of the End.[23]

Now therefore in the year 1157 of the dominion of the sons of Ishmael,[24] in the month of the first Jamad, occurred the betrothal[25] of a man, good, honorable, scholarly and devout, a master of[26] calculation and of writing, and illustrious and well-informed, and discriminating, practised in eloquence[27] and in (sacred) song, and in exegesis,[28] (or, and who is a shrewd judge of affairs) and one of the eyes of the community and one who directs[29] the reading of scripture and who calculates[30] the true calculation (of the calendar), a pillar of the congregation, an Archon[31] of the congregation and a doer of good, to wit - ISHMAEL the son of the elder, the good, the honorable, the scholarly, the devout, the one skilled in calculation and in writing, the illustrious, well-informed and discriminating, practised in eloquence and in (sacred) song, and who is one of the eyes of the community and one who directs the reading of scripture, and who calculates the true calculation (of the calendar) and is a father to the orphan and widow and a support of the congregation and an Archon thereof, and who does good - ISHMAEL of the sons of Denaftah[32] of the inhabitants of Shechem - to the virtuous woman MIRIAM the daughter of the elder, the good and honourable, scholarly and devout, a master of astronomical calculation and of writing, illustrious and discriminating, practised in eloquence and (sacred) song, and who is one of the eyes of the community and is a priest and minister of the GREAT[33] NAME and THE HOLY[34] SCRIPTURE and the HOLY[35] PROPHETS, and is greatest[36] among the priests the sons of Levi[37] at this time, and is a support of the congregation and an Archon thereof, and one who does good - the lofty priest the good JOSEPH the son of the elder, the good and honorable, scholarly and devout, master of calculation, and of writing, the illustrious well-informed and discriminating, practised in eloquence and in (sacred) song, and who is a priest and one of the eyes of the congregation, and a servant of THE GREAT NAME and the Holy Scripture and the Holy Prophets, and greatest of the priests the sons of Levi at this time, and a support of the congregation and an Archon thereof, and one who does good, the gracious and noble priest ABRAHAM of the sons of Levi, of the inhabitants of Shechem.

After the abovementioned man had sought[38] her from the abovementioned father of the woman, and he answered his request with full knowledge, whole-heartedly and willingly; she being at that time a virtuous[39] woman, who had reached puberty; he shall therefore do to her according to the law of wives according to the ordinance of the sturdy and honoured daughters of Israel, even as was Eve who was created from the rib of Adam for a helper fit for fruitfulness[40] and increase, - for a bride-price consisting of 2450 Egyptian Keritas. He gave to her before he took her 1200 Egyptian Keritas that he should marry her, and she should become his wife, excluded and withheld from every man apart from him. And he shall be her husband it being incumbent on him (that he should) do to her after the law of women, as the LORD said by His servant Moses:[41] "He shall not diminish her food, her clothing, or her marital rights". And he may confirm[42] her vows and her interdictions, or may invalidate them. And unto him she is bound by the bond of marital love; she shall listen[43] to his words and not go against what he says; and she shall be a helper fit for him.[44] And he has á residual obligation towards her of 1250[45] Egyptian Keritas because of their union. She may take them from him, when she is set free as much as she chooses. But he should cleave to her as the LORD said: "Therefore a man leaves his father and his mother,[47] and cleaves to his wife, and there shall become from the two of them , one flesh." And the writer of this document and the congregation of witnesses shall be against him so as to constitute perfectly incontrovertible evidence, and it is the LORD who grants prosperity to all who walk in His paths and who fulfil His ordinances: to Him be thanksgiving forever, from the beginning to the end; and blessed be our God forever, and blessed be His Name forever, and the peace of the LORD be upon the righteous, perfect, pure and faithful prophet Moses, the son of Amram, the Man of God.

I have written this document and I have testified to its content as the writer thereof. And I am the poor servant Solomon[48] the son of Jacob, the son of Ab Sakwah the sons of Denafṯah. May God forgive me the order of my sins. Amen.

Witnesses to what is set forth therein: the servant, Ebed Hanunah, Ebed Hafatah the children of Ishmael the son of Ebed Hanunah the Danfite. May the Lord forgive them Amen, and him who wrote this at their command. With regard to what is set forth therein, I acknowledge (it) I too, the wretched servant, whose sin is great, Abraham[49] the son of Jacob the Danfite. May God, my strength and my song, forgive me, Amen.

Witness to what is set forth, the servant Zedaḳah[50] the son of Ab Zehutah, who is of the sons of Habumtah. May the Lord forgive him, and him who wrote this at his dictation.

Witness to what is set forth in it and its writer (or its writing): the servant Šelah[51] the son of Isaac and Danfite. May the Lord forgive him, Amen.

Witness to what is set forth (and) its writer (or its writing) the servant Jacob[52] the son of the abovementioned

Isaac. May the Lord forgive him, Amen. Witness to what is set forth in it: the servant Šelah[53] the son of Abraham, the son of Zedakah the Danfite. May the Lord forgive him and him who wrote it at his dictation.

Witness to what is set forth in it: the servant Jacob[54] the son of the abovementioned Abraham. May the Everlasting God forgive him and him who wrote at his command.

NOTES ON THE FIRST KETUBAH

1. This Ketubah for a woman previously married and the accompanying one for a virgin are taken from J. Wilson's: *Land of the Bible*,1843. On p.688 *ibid.* Wilson gives a facsimile of this Ketubah; on p.689-691 he gives a transcription into Hebrew square character; on p.691-694 an English translation follows, faulty in not a few points. I have included my own translation of this Ketubah here, as it is the earliest Samaritan Ketubah which has come to my notice. It is dated 1157 A.H. = 1757 A.D. This Ketubah relates to a marriage of priestly families.

2. The meritorious ones are the Patriarchs Abraham, Isaac and Jacob. At every Sabbath morning service the Ḳataf of the Meritorious ones is said. The Samaritans believe strongly in the merit of the Fathers especially in the merit of the Patriarchs and of Joseph and Moses.

3. Wilson quite wrongly has 'on account of his boundless existence'. The word I have translated 'seasons' is literally 'times' but clearly the reference(following as it does the alternation of night and day) is to the revolution of the seasons.

4. Wilson's 'who gives wisdom to every mouth' does not give the proper sense; in any case the root *hakam* in Samaritan Hebrew is to know' in the first form, and means 'to teach' when it appears in the intensive as here. Other points of divergency between my translation and Wilson's are too numerous to list here.

5. Cf. Targ. Jer. Gen. 1:1 and Prov. 8:22-31.

6. This is the literal translation of Ḳaraṣ. To translate it by 'separated' would not be strong enough. Since we have here in the preamble to the Ketubah a statement of a Samaritan cosmogony, it is best not to blur their distinctive ideas merely

for the sake of easier English. It could perhaps be rendered "he portioned off the light from the darkness" cf. *Keres* division partition, Jastrow, *A Dictionary of the Targumim...*, p. 1425; but this rendering would imply a different origin for the light.

7. Cf. Gen. 1:6, 7 although here there is no mention of the waters as being separated by the firmament.

8. Cf. Gen. 1:9.

9. Cf. Gen. 1:11, 12.

10. Cf. Gen. 1:16 which however does not distinguish between stars and planets.

11. Cf. Gen. 1:14-18 which does not mention (though it may be inferred) that the rule of the two great lights was to be perpetual.

12. Cf. Gen. 1:20-25. This sentence briefly summarizes what was created on the fifth and sixth days of Creation up to and before the creation of Man.

13. Literally 'the creation'. The phrase could be translated perhaps as 'Last of created things'.

14. Cf. Gen. 1:26, 27.

15. Wilson *op. cit.* has quite missed the point when he translated this phrase as 'he made him like himself in understanding'. The reference is to Gen. 1:28 where man is given dominion over every living thing. The Ketubah adds a little midrashic note that man rules intelligence.

16. Gen. 2:8.

17. Gen. 2:18.

18. Cf. Gen. 2:21.

19. The Ketubah preamble teaches the usual Samaritan doctrine of the Holy Chain of pious and worthy ancestors stretching from Adam to Moses. Wilson *ibid.* p.692 has erred badly in not seeing that the expression "him who was lord of the ages etc." referred to Moses; instead he translated it "the mighty ones of the world". The Ketubah preamble's cosmogony though differing from that at the beginning of the Malef does imply that creation led up to Moses.

20. i.e. As writer of the Law.

21. The reference is to the Lawgiving at Sinai; according to Samaritan Midrash, when Moses went up the Mountain he was led past the angels to God's presence. In the Samaritan Liturgy there is often reference to this glorification of Moses by God and how even the angels had to do him obeisance. I know of no explicit reference to Moses elsewhere however in Samaritan sources as priest of the angels. Even in Marḳah Aaron the priest tends to be elevated qua priest above Moses.

22. Cf. Hilluḵ *op. cit.* and Gen. 2:18, 23, 24. Gen. 1:28.

23. Cf. Dt. 32:35. Samaritan reading: "To Me belongs the Day of Vengeance". In Gen. 1:28 all mankind are told to be fruitful and multiply and have dominion over every living thing. At the end dominion belongs to Israel alone, Israel signifying the Samaritan Community.

24. i.e. 1157 A.H. = 1757 A.D. A Jewish Ketubah does not have the lengthy preamble dealing with Creation and Lawgiving.

25. Note that the Ketubah deals with the betrothal which (cf. Hilluḵ on 'marriage' p.302 above) is the legal marriage ceremony with the Samaritans. The word for betrothal in our text is *ma'arisah*.

26. Calculation. Since the bridegroom was a priest he would be expected to know some mathematics as well as how to read and write the Samaritan languages, Hebrew, Aramaic and Arabic. The priests are the learned folk among the Samaritans. It may refer to astronomical calculation in connection with the calendar which the priests issued (and still issue) every six months. Wilson *op. cit.* is wrong in translating *Hašobah* as 'respected'. In any case the form is that of the Samaritan active participle.

27. Our text has *'Rhetor'*. The use of the Greek word probably denotes that the form of the Ketubah was drafted in a time when Greek was still known.

28. Paṯorah i.e. 'The one who interprets', is 'practised in interpretation'; since the reference is mainly to things religious I have translated as "(practised) in exegesis" i.e. interpretation of the Bible text. It could however be a reference to translation of the Hebrew Bible text in Aramaic for the Targum.

If however the reference to religious affairs is not

stressed one might translate as 'and is a shrewd judge of affairs'. This would link up with his being 'one' of the eyes of the community.

29. Reading *mtknh* not *mtgnt*. Wilson *op. cit.* is wrong in taking the phrase 'as skilled in learning' (so he renders *maḳarta*). Maḳarta is the one standard term for the reading of scripture.

30. Wilson *op. cit.* makes this: 'and a reckoner of the reckoning of the *Kasitah*'. Ḳoštah has nothing to do with *Kasitah*, but means true. Therefore I translate this as 'who calculates the true calculation' (of the calendar). On the 'true calculation' cf. the extract from the Tolidah p.39, cf. 41. The phrase 'true calculation' in Samaritan literature is always applied to the calendar; it was most important for the Samaritans to have priests who could calculate the calendar efficiently, as one of the strong props of Samaritan Dissent was that they kept their Festivals on the right days, while the Jews did not; therefore Jewish Festivals were condemned as worthless in Samaritan eyes.

31. It reminds one of the New Testament usage cf. Luke 8:41, 'a ruler of the synagogue'.

32. For a genealogy of the Danfi Family, cf. Cowley '*The Samaritan Liturgy*' Vol. II, p.XLVII. Ishmael the son of Abraham is there mentioned. The Danfi family was a great scribal family and many MSS written by members of that family are extant.

33. i.e. God. While it is true that the expression 'the Name' is used in Samaritan circles as in Jewish as a surrogate, nevertheless the Samaritans do know that the pronunciation of the divine name is *Yahwah* cf. e.g. Cowley *ibid.* Vol. II, p.830 line 1. The person described as minister of the Great Name is as will be shown below, of the High Priestly family. The reference to him as minister of the Great Name may refer to the High Priest's function in pronouncing the priestly blessing Num. 6:22-27. The priest puts God's name thereby on the people. Cf. v.27.

34. The Holy Scripture refers to the Abisha' Scroll in particular, guarded by the High Priest in his house at Shechem.

35. The Holy Prophets do not refer to those whom Jews and Christians call prophets, but to the seventy elders, who on receiving a portion of Moses' spirit prophesied, cf. Num. 11:24-25. Gaster, *The Samaritans* plate 13, reproduces the colophon of a Pentateuch MS. referring to the handing down of the Torah from

these seventy elders.

36. 'The greatest of the priests', means that Joseph was High Priest; but Joseph does not appear as the name of the High Priest at this time, cf. Cowley *ibid.* Vol. II, p.XLVI (the Levitical Family). Abraham is mentioned later in the Ketubah as the father of Joseph. Now Abraham was High Priest in the century to which the Ketubah belongs, but according to Cowley *ibid.* had died in 1145 A.H. Our Ketubah dates the betrothal in 1157. Abraham the bride's grandfather may have been dead at the time of her second marriage. We note that whereas the document says of Joseph that he was greatest of the priests 'at this time', it says of Abraham that he was greatest of the priests 'in his time'. There is no doubt that Abraham here described had been High Priest. The titles etc. which are applied to him are applied also to Joseph. It does appear that here we have a Ketubah of the marriage of the then reigning High Priest's daughter. It is not customary in Samaritan Ketubot to give a longer pedigree of either bride or bridegroom than mention (and eulogy) of the father and statement as to his clan. The priestly lists do not say that so-and-so was High Priest at such and such a time; they refer to him as priest. We note that the bridegroom's family were of priestly stock but no mention is specifically made as to the bridegroom being a priest; to have said so would have implied he was of the high priestly family. But Abraham the High Priest is called a priest, and so is his son Joseph the bride's father. There was a Joseph about this time who was nephew of Abraham. However Abraham had a son Levi who succeeded him as High Priest and died in 1165 A.H. (cf. Cowley *ibid.* p.XLVI). Levi, according to Chronicle Adler, (*R.E.J.*, 1903, 46-47, p.136) had no son. I am of the opinion that our Ketubah refers to the marriage of the then ruling high priest's daughter and that it shows who really succeeded the High Priest Abraham.

37. The last of the Samaritan Cohen family had died out in 1623-4 A.D., that is slightly more than a century and a quarter before this Ketubah was written. However the Levis stepped in to the breach. The transition was easy in that the Samaritans had always maintained that their priests were the priests the Levites (cf. Marḳah on the rights of the priesthood p.261 note 39 above).

38. Cf. the extract from the Hilluk on marriage p.300 which tells how the bridegroom-to-be approaches the bride's father who is accompanied by the priest, and makes this request.

39. It is not stated that she was virgin; this and the reduced brideprice show that she had been married before.

40. Cf. Gen. 1:28.

41. Ex. 21:10.

42. Nothing like this sentence appears in the Jewish Ketubah.

43. Nor is this stated in the Jewish Ketubah.

44. While this injunction is influenced by the Biblical language of Gen. 2:18, there is little doubt that this aspect is emphasized in the Samaritan Ketubah. True, reference is made earlier in the Samaritan Ketubah to the honored daughters of Israel (the Samaritan Community), but the husband-to-be does not promise explicitly in the Ketubah to honor his wife as does the husband in the Jewish Ketubah.

45. In all he gives her 2450 Keritas. Actually he gives her outright before taking her as wife 1200 Keritas. This takes the place of the 200 Zuzim mentioned in the Jewish Ketubah. However in the Jewish Ketubah the bride brings a dowry, and the bridegroom doubles it by giving a further like amount. The Jewish Ketubah makes it clear that the wife has a lien on her husband's property up to and including all the money mentioned in the Ketubah.

46. Wilson *ibid.* p.693 translates this as "at whatsoever time she may need them, as she chooses" implying that the wife could draw on the 1250 Keritas which remained, whenever she pleased. The sentiment may be laudible but the original does not warrant it. "When she is set free" means when she is divorced. Then she can claim the 1250 Keritas which remain. The Samaritan woman is not as well provided for under her Ketubah as the Jewish wife under hers. On the other hand the 1200 Keritas given to the High Priest's daughter before marriage are hers; her husband has only the use of half of the brideprice. That the residue of the brideprice can only become the woman's at divorce is clear from the statement in the Bill of Divorce which we include in this book, p.329.

47. Gen. 2:24. The Samaritan Ketubah,having dealt with the question of divorce, now hastens to reaffirm that marriage should be a permanent union.

48. Cf. Cowley *ibid.* Vol. II, p.XLVII. Solomon the son of Jacob the son of Murjan (= Ab Sakhwah) like his grandfather before him was a good scribe of liturgical manuscripts. Solomon was uncle of the bridegroom.

50. There was a Zedakah cf. Cowley *ibid.* who was brother to Abraham and Solomon, but this is hardly he, unless Ab Zehutah was Jacob's kunya.

51. Cf. Cowley *ibid.* Šelah son of Isaac was cousin of the witnesses Solomon and Abraham.

52. Cf. Cowley *ibid.* Jacob was Šelah's brother.

53. This name cannot be traced. One could assume he was a brother of the bridegroom; the only trouble is that his father's father was not Zedakah but Jacob. If this Šelah is Abraham's son, he is nephew to Zedakah.

54. Jacob, according to Cowley's list (*ibid.*) is the nephew of Abraham, and is Zedakah's son. Perhaps these last two notes show that Cowley's genealogical table of the Danfi Family needs correction. Contemporary marriage documents are more reliable than the Chronicles from which he mainly derived his information.

SAMARITAN KETUBAH[1] (OF A VIRGIN)

IN THE NAME OF THE LORD THE GOD OF ISRAEL, WE BEGIN AND WE END.

I begin with the name of the Lord who reigns[2] in the height and in the depth, the Mighty, the Eternal who in His Unity preceded (all things). Blessed be He and blessed be His name. How great and mighty are the multitudes of His creation which He ordained by His wisdom. The most merciful of the merciful, and the mightiest of the mighty, the God of the Earth and the Heavens, who revealed to us His commandments, the Mighty and the Great, who bears[3] the world. He has neither (time)[4] period nor (special) limit. Let us praise and exalt Him. He who rules in the height and in the depth, the Mighty and the Awesome. His laws let us keep, and let us thank Him for His goodness; the God who created (all) creation in six[5] days by the decree of the wisdom of the LORD, and the seventh day He sanctified. He made Adam by himself,[6] then He made a help[7] fit for him and married[8] them in Eden, and clothed[9] him with the Likeness and the Image (of God); until there arose[10] from them the meritorious ones, the chain[11] of the pure ones, the righteous, the faithful, and the possessors of merit. His mercies are on those in Machpelah,[12] with whom Thou has remembered the covenant of Circumcision;[13] their head is he who circumcised the first, Abraham whose merit is high; his LORD visited him and set him apart,[14] and above all creatures treasured him. And He sought from him Isaac[15] that he should offer him. And on the holiest of soil[16] his LORD gave to him[17] a crown of virtual martyrdom. And there arose from him Jacob Israel and he came to Bethel[18] and set up his pillar on his departure from Beer-Sheba, yea he erected the pillar. And there arose from him every good man and he who interpreted his dream, Joseph the righteous to whom the eleven bowed down;[19] from whom is the priestly[20] Levite whom the LORD treasured. And there arose from him[21] the Prophet Moses who delivered his people from the hand of the harsh Pharaoh, with signs and wonders. And He gave him the Law and the commandments, and many statutes, among them is the goodly statute of marriage, the first of His commandments.[22]

Now therefore in the year 1250[23] of the dominion of the sons of Ishmael in the month .... there was the betrothal of the bridegroom, the good,[24] honorable, scholarly, and devout, and master of calculation, all of whose acts are worthy; and he is the choicest[25] of the priests, andthe most handsome of bridegrooms, who does all good things .....X... the son of the elder the good, and honourable, and scholarly, the master of calculation and of writing and well informed and discriminating, and practiced in eloquence and in (sacred) song, and[26] an exponent of the teaching of the Elders of Prayer, and one who does good deeds ...Y... the son of an elder, honorable, scholarly, devout, master of calculation and of writing illustrious and skilled in (sacred) song and who is one of the eyes[27] of the community, and support of the congregation and an Archon thereof, and a doer of all good deeds ...Z... of the children sons of Denaftah[28] and all of them of the inhabitants of Shechem to the Bride ...A... the daughter of the elder, the good, honorable, scholarly and devout, master of calculation and writing, and who is one of the eyes of the community and one of the elders thereof, and one who is practised in eloquence and (sacred) song, and a great pillar (of the congregation) and Archon, and one who does what is good ...B... the son of the elder, the good and the honorable, the scholarly and devout who is a master of calculation and of writing and is an exponent of the teaching of the Elders of Prayer and who does all good deeds ...C... of the sons of Denaftah, and all of them are of the inhabitants of Shechem.

After that the abovementioned bridegroom[29] had sought her from the abovementioned father of the bride, and he had answered his request with full knowledge, wholeheartedly and willingly, she being at that time a young woman, a virgin who had reached puberty; he shall do to her according to the law of women according to the ordinance of the (sturdy and honoured) daughters of Israel even as was Eve who was created from the rib of Adam for a helper fit for fruitfulness and increase - for a brideprice consisting of 4900[30] Keritas. He gave to her before he took her 2400 Egyptian Keritas that he should marry her, and she should become his wife, excluded and withheld from every man apart from him. And he shall be her husband, it being incumbent on him (that he should) do to her after the law of wives as the LORD said by His servant Moses:[31] 'her food, her raiment, and her marital rights, shall he not diminish'. And he may confirm her vows and her interdictions or may invalidate them. And unto him she is bound by the bond of marital love, she shall listen to his words and not go against what he says: and she shall be a helpmeet for him. And he has a residual obligation towards her of 2500 Egyptian Keritas because of their union. She may take them from him when she is set free and as much as she chooses. But he should cleave to her as He said:[32] "A man leaves his father and his mother and cleaves to his wife: and there shall become from the two of them, one flesh".

And the writer[33] of this document and the congregation of witnesses shall be against him so as to furnish rightly constituted and perfectly uncontrovertible evidence, and it is the LORD who grants prosperity to all who walk in His paths and who fulfil His ordinances from the beginning even unto the end; and blessed be our God for ever, and blessed be His Name for ever. And the peace of the LORD be upon the righteous, perfect, pure and faithful prophet Moses the son of Amram, the man of God.

NOTES ON THE SECOND KETUBAH

1. The preamble to this Ketubah is different from the other, but like it starts off with creation and ends with Moses. More attention is given to Adam and Eve, and less to the acts of creation which preceded that of him. Further more attention is given to the Patriarchs as links in the Holy Chain between Adam and Moses. The text (in transcription) of this Ketubah is to be found in Wilson *ibid.* p.694-695. Wilson's translation thereof is given p.696-697. Space does not allow for reference to all Wilson's mistranslations. It is a pity that Wilson did not give in the text of his transcriptions of this Ketubah the names of the contracting parties and the names of the witnesses. However the Ketubah is of interest because of the midrashic preamble.

2. Wilson *ibid.* p.695 contrives quite wrongly to make this read 'the king of the lowly and the exalted'.

3. i.e. sustains (cf. Cowley *ibid.* Vol. I, p.17, line 2 in the first Markah hymn).

4. Literally 'he had neither end nor limit'. But Ḳeṣ, the word translated 'end', can have the sense of 'designated time', (cf. Jastrow *ibid.* p.1403) whereas *Gebul* the word translated 'limit' has more of a spatial significance. What the Ketubah is trying to make clear is that God is not restricted by time or space.

5. In this Ketubah the total number of the days of

Creation are mentioned, but the acts of creations are not listed. In the previous Ketubah the latter are mentioned, but there is no reference to the time taken to complete Creation, nor is there any mention of the Sabbath. Wisdom as in the other Ketubah is God's instrument in creation.

6. *Sa'ar* - *yasar* cf. Cowley *ibid.* Vol. II, p.lxviii, lit. he formed; *Baddo* = *le baddo* alone, by himself. Note that in the other Ketubah while there is reference regarding Adam and Eve to Gen. chapter 2, the story of creation is basically that of Gen. chapter 1 where all creation is listed and man comes as the end of creation. Here in this Ketubah there is mention of creation in six days, and of the Divine Sabbath of the seventh day. Only thereafter we hear of the creation of Adam. The time sequence should not be pressed, but it is as if here the creation of Adam is deliberately distinguished from that of the rest of creation.

7. Gen. 2:18.

8. Cf. Pirke de Rabbi Eliezer. G. Friedlander, London, 1916. pp.89-90, cf. also Gen. Rab. xviii 2. But cf. the Malef on Creation of Man and his Fall. According to this section of the Malef, Adam could not have consummated marriage in Eden.

9. Lit. the Likeness and the Image (of God) was his (Adam's) clothing. The word translated his clothing is *Al(e)busuto*. The 'a' is not usually written but is inserted in speech at the beginning of words especially when two consonants come together. This statement that Adam was clothed in the Likeness and Image of God ought to be compared with the statement in the Malef regarding pre-fallen man.

10. We have no mention of the Fall of Man, and the expulsion from Eden. Cf. however the Malef *op. cit.*

11. This refers to the Holy Chain of those descended from Adam and Eve and which reached to Moses.

12. Where Abraham, Sarah, Isaac, Rebeccah, Jacob and Leah were buried.

13. Wilson *ibid.* p.696 "Salt", must have misread *milah* for *melah*. Cf. Gen. 17:9-14 for the Covenant of Circumcision.

14. Cf. Gen. 12:1-3.

15. Cf. Gen. 22:1, 2.

16. The Samaritans believe that the Aḳedah was on Mount Gerizim not Mount Moriah.

17. i.e. Isaac.

18. With the Samaritans this means Mount Gerizim which they usually call Mount Gerizim Bethel. For Jacob's dream cf. Gen. 28:10-22.

19. Cf. Gen. 37:7.

20. i.e. Aaron.

21. This must refer back to Abraham, or at least Jacob.

22. Cf. Gen. 1:28, Gen. 2:18, Gen. 2:24.

23. 1250 A.H. = 1834 A.D.

24. The epithets applied to this bridegroom are the same - so far as they go - as those applied to the bridegroom of the first Ketubah. The omissions are significant however. Wilson maintained *ibid.* p.694 that this was a non-priestly wedding. In this he was mistaken; it is a non-high priestly wedding, but a marriage of a young priest nevertheless. We note that the bridegroom is 'master of calculation' but we are not told that he was one "who calculates the true calculation" (of the calendar); but this latter was a high-priestly concern.

25. Wilson(*ibid.*, p.696) renders this: "an eminent youth". In his transcription of the phrase *Bahur ha-Karnaim*, he seems to have understood the K as equivalent to Ḳ and then read Ḳarnaim. It would be better to emend Wilsons's text and read Bahur ha Kohanim, reading h for r. It is more likely that the bridegroom is referred to here as one of the priestly class than that the unusual phrase *Bahur ha-Karnaim* be applied to him.

26. There is a longer description of the bridegroom's father's qualities than of his sons's. *So far as they go* the epithets used agree with those of the other Ketubah; here however is one which does not occur there. Wilson *ibid.* 696 freely translates it "skilled in learning among the elders of the Church". It is literally: "one who expounds the study of the elders of prayer". This I understand means that the bridegroom's father, who was of the Danfi family, was like many of that family a good liturgiologist. 'The elders of prayer' could be a reference to the great liturgical writers Markah and Amram Darah, whose compositions being in Aramaic cannot be understood by the ordinary Samaritan. Their hymns and prayers are still

used in the Samaritan synagogue however with accompanying Arabic (or as in Israel Hebrew) translation. Note that nothing is said of the bridegroom's father regarding direction of reading of the scripture or exegesis thereof, as is said of the members of the high priestly family.

27. This and the following epithets descriptive of the bridegroom's grandfather are employed in describing members of the priestly and high priestly families mentioned in the first Ketubah (cf. p.313f).

28. I have kept the form of the name as it appears in the Ketubah. Both the contracting parties in this Ketubah were of the Danfi family.

29. For notes on this the main section of the Ketubah see notes to the first Ketubah. There are only two differences (a) she was a virgin and (b) the amount of the brideprice because she was a virgin.

30. The brideprice of the high priest's daughter was exactly half of this as she had been married before. The sum is divided in much the same proportions in both cases. The high priest's daughter received 1200 of her 2450 Keritas, whereas the virgin daughter mentioned in this Ketubah receives 2400 of her 4900 Keritas, i.e. half of the brideprice plus 50 Keritas remains in the case of the previously married woman in her husband's hands only to be claimed by her on being divorced; whereas half of the brideprice plus 100 Keritas remains in the case of the woman who marries for the first time. According to the Hilluk on marriage (cf. p.300 above) the minimum brideprice for a virgin was 50 shekels of silver.

31. Ex. 21:10.

32. Gen. 2:24 Samaritan reading.

33. This ending is similar in both Ketubot, though not word for word identical.

THIS IS THE BILL OF DIVORCE[1]

We begin in the name of the Lord the Righteous: the King, the Upright God. O God, the God of the Spirits of all the Flesh,[2] His great Name is to be hallowed[3] every evening and morning. Israel[4] He chose as His servants from (among) all the peoples, generation after generation. He sent to them Moses the Prophet, the son of Amram the choicest of all Flesh.[5] through him the perfect Law was established for the righteous people. He explained in it commandments and judgments and statutes and laws. Among them is the statute of[6] joining together in marriage (lit. cleaving together) and divorce (lit. dismissal).[7] (It, the Law is) a crown for Israel which is found in every place. It is thus as follows:

Because of this in such and such a year, in such and such a month was the judgment of divorce of N the son of M of the sons of O of the inhabitants of Shechem (given)[8] to his wife P the daughter of Q, as a result of great quarrels between them, and there had come between them abominable and evil things and likewise occasions of immorality[9] are found. And the two of them by mutual consent separated and the above-mentioned woman acquired what was hers of what was reserved for her, by the Marriage Document.[10] 2500 Egyptian Keritas which he gave her prior to her dismissal; and he gave to her all which was hers of garments and furniture, and nothing of hers was left with him either great or small as testified by the witnesses. And her document which is the Bill of Divorce he put in her hand as the Lord said by the hand of His servant Moses:[11] When a man takes a wife and marries her, if then she find no favor in his eyes, because he has found some indecency in her, he writes her a bill of divorce and puts it in her hand and sends her out of his house, and she departs out of his house.[12] And neither of them shall have any matrimonial relations with the other, for the abovementioned woman he sent away; she is withheld from him. And as for the document[13] - this is the document, and the testimony of the witnesses is in it to furnish rightly constituted and perfectly incontrovertible evidence. The Name of the LORD be blessed from everlasting to everlasting. And blessed is our God forever and blessed is His Name forever.

NOTES ON THE BILL OF DIVORCE

1. The Samaritans do not call the Bill of Divorce the *Get*, but retain the Biblical name Sefer Keritut. cf. Deut. 24:1, 3.

2. Cf. Num. 16:22.

3. The Samaritan daily prayer is evening and morning.

4. According to the Samaritans, Israel is represented by themselves.

5. The choicest of all flesh, a common description of Moses throughout the Samaritan Liturgy.

6. Cf. Biblical references in connection with preceding Ketubot.

7. Cf. note 1.

8. Only the Priest could give the Samaritan husband power to divorce his wife.

9. The Samaritans like Beth Shammai (M. Git. 9:10) interpreted Deut. 24:1 very strictly.

10. Cf. the second Ketubah included in this book p.322-325. The residual sum of 2,500 Keritas shows that the total brideprice must have been 4,900 Keritas. This we know from the second Ketubah was the brideprice of a virgin. 2,400 Keritas were given before marriage and 2,500 kept by the husband to give the wife on her being divorced.

11. Here follows a quotation of Deut. 24:1-2a. Verse 2b and the whole of v.3 dealing with subsequent marriage to a third party and death of second husband are omitted.

12. This sentence is a paraphrase of Deut. 24:4.

13. i.e. The bill of divorce mentioned in Deut. 24:1.

14. Cf. the ending of the Marriage Documents; the language is exactly that of the second Ketubah. There is of course no reference however to God granting prosperity to all who walk in His paths and who fulfil His ordinances.

EPILOGUE

FOUR PRAYERS FROM THE SAMARITAN LITURGY

The following four pieces are from the Defter, the old Samaritan liturgy which was the sole liturgical collection of the Samaritans until the development of the large festival liturgies in the fourteenth century and later. However even with the later special festival liturgies, the core of the liturgy is still the old Defter.

The first piece[1] given here is said silently at the beginning of all Samaritan public prayer on Sabbath and on Festivals. The second piece[2] is actually from morning prayer on a week day. It is number seven in the important early collection of prayers in the Defter called the Durran; traditionally the Durran was composed by Amram Darah the father of Markah. The Durran pieces are in the same Samaritan Aramaic as Markah's.

The third piece is the second[3] of Markah's twelve hymns all of which are used regularly in Samaritan public worship. It should be noted that the Samaritans call the pieces by Amram Darah and Markah "Prayers". This second prayer by Markah is at present used in the morning service of the first Sabbath in the month.

The fourth piece the Kadišah[4] has two different forms according to the Sabbath in the month. The form given below is said on the second and fourth Sabbaths. The Kadišah is also used in the Festival Liturgy.

All four of these ancient Samaritan prayers are still used today.

FOOTNOTES

1. See A. E. Cowley: *The Samaritan Liturgy*, Clarendon Press, Oxford 1909 Vol. 1, p.3.

2. Cf. *ibid.* p.41.

3. Cf. *ibid.* p.17-18.

4. Cf. *ibid.* p.11.

1. In the Name of Yahweh the Great we begin and we end. Before Thee I stand at the gate of Thy mercies, Yahweh my God and God of my fathers to speak Thy praise and Thy glory according to my poor strength and my weakness. I know today and I have placed (it) at my heart that Thou Yahweh art the God in the heavens above, and on the earth beneath there is no other. Here before Thee I stand and I face the chosen place Mount Gerizim, Bethel-Luzah, the mountain of the inheritance and place which Thou hast made for Thee to dwell, O Yahweh, the sanctuary of Yahweh which Thine hands have established.

Yahweh shall reign for ever and ever, for Yahweh is greater than all the gods. Righteous and upright is He.

May this prayer ascend to the place of Life in the unseen world before the Knower of hidden things. Where is there a god who helps his worshippers but Thou? Blessed is the Name of Thy Holiness for ever. There is no god but One.

2. When you rise up in the morning and see the (sun)-light has come up and is illuminating all the world, cry out all of you and say: Praised be (God) the Light who for the world kindled a lamp which never grows dim; it passes through the firmament and lightens all the world, at the order of the Lord of all. He kindled for the world a lamp which never grows dim. In the beginning a storehouse was made for the lights, heaven and earth the structure of which not being (as) the sons of the great light is like the foundation. Light early every morning speaks plainly to the world. Light proclaims to the children of men: Rise from your sleep, see the light and praise its Maker. Let God be praised. There is no God but One.

3. Thou art our God. and the God of our fathers:
the God of Abraham. and Isaac and Jacob:
In the height and in the depth. Thy power is great and dominant:
in the unseen world and the seen. Thou art a merciful God.
Thy great might. who can espy it or know it:
mighty and awesome One to all the generations of the world.
Thou who wert before the world was. didst set it up in majesty
and Thou didst make it a witness to Thy greatness. that Thou art God eternally.
Where is there a trusty person, good. or near like Thee:
or where are belongings. except what Thou ownest-
And Thou in Thy greatness. art a God who changest not:
and he who seeks apart from Thee. searches and finds not.
Righteousness is Thine. the righteous are those who love Thee:
no time and no season. are we silent concerning Thy goodness.
Heaven Thou hast spread out. the world Thou hast established:
dreams Thou hast sent. to comfort those who love Thee.
Blessed is the world. for Thou art the Lord and director:
blessed are Thy commands. blessed they who keep them.
Unique One who wert first. to eternity Thou remainest:
Thou who givest gifts. to Thee be thanks for Thy greatness
All Thou seest. but nothing can see Thee:
all Thy works are good. our Lord, but Thou art better than they.

Ever Thou art merciful. ever Thou art compassionate.
Thy majesty we adore. Thou who exaltest those who adore Thee
Believers are we. that Thou art our God, and happy are we:
From us to Thee are praises. from Thee to us is the gift.
Guide of the world. after Thee we walk;
Guardian of the living. in Thy goodness Thou comest near.
Much is Thy goodness. many are those who love Thee:
many are they. thy wonders for which Thou art to be praised.
Thy great works. submit themselves to Thee:
Thy servants rule. in Thy service is all glory.
Thou hast opened Thy treasury. the world was set free:
mouths praise Thee. without end
We need Thee. living and dead:
Prayers in truth. to Thy Name are to be said.
Before Thy holiness. we cry out. O El Elyon!
Thou art near to those who worship Thee. without showing Thyself to them.
Beginning without end. are the ascriptions of praise to Thee:
Love of all. Thy loving kindness if life.
Thy Name is awesome. for Thou art glorious and terrible:
Powerful are Thy messengers. and in their hands is a command from Thee.
Thou shalt be praised to eternity. for all which is Thine praises Thee
Thou shalt be blessed to eternity. for Thou blessest the World.

There is no God but One.

4. O Thou Holy Glorious One who separated us Thy holy ones and revealed to us Thy chosen ones and hast given to us, (the) Holy Sabbath for rest, the Book of Life with wisdom and glory and majesty. Thou hast raised up for us an altar for worship of Thy Name in order that we should know that Thou art our Creator and our God and our Lord. O our Lord in Thy mercy help us. O Merciful, send down Thy blessing on our houses and on all our hands are put to. O Merciful, withhold every affliction and all anger and all plague from us. O Merciful, make Thyself master over him who has the mastery over us: strengthen us against fear O Merciful, heal our wounds. O Merciful, make our children grow. O Merciful, restore our sanctuary. O Merciful, have mercy on our dead. O Merciful, make blessed this Sabbath day and every Sabbath day which is coming, and bless us with righteousness, and forgive us and our fathers in Thy abundant loving kindness; for the sake of Moses Thy Prophet turn Thy face from hot anger according as Thou are wont. Ever pity (us) and do good to us and free (us), O Our God the Merciful and Compassionate.

INDEX

Beer-Sheba: p.32.
Beisan: p.143, 169.
Benjamin: p.58, 83, 90, 93, 100.
Belial: p.256, 261.
Ben-Zebi 1., former President of Israel: p.14.
Berechiah: p.92, 107.
Beth Dagan: p.198.
Bethel: p.32, 34, 36, 106, 282, 332.
Bethlehem: p.82, 284.
Beth Namara: p.198.
Beth Peor: p.91.
Beth-Porek: p.94.
Beth Shammai: p.330.
Betrothal: : p.304, 305, 312, 313.
Bezaleel: p.48, 86.
Bible: p.238.
Birtah: p.94.
Bir Ya'ḳub: p.9, 11, 12, 14.
Blau, O: p.10.
Book of the Covenant: p.221, 235.
Book of the Signs: p.285.
Bridegroom: p.302, 305, 324, 327.
Brideprice: p.300, 301, 310, 321, 328.
British Museum: p.253.
Buḥḳi: p.48, 59, 86, 90, 91.
Bunyan, John: p.263.
Burnt offering: p.229, 230, 278.
Bustunus: p.183, 213.
Caesarea: p.160.
Cain: p.255, 261.
Caleb: p.73, 79, 82, 255.
Calendar: p.238, 313, 318, 319, 327.
Canaan: p.17, 35, 40, 41, 42, 43, 75, 86, 87, 92, 97, 99, 103, 105, 242, 243, 271, 272.
Canaanites: p.24, 25.
Caracalla: p.193.
Castro, P.: p.58.
Chaldeans: p.98, 99.
Charles, R.H.: p.50, 54.
Cherubim: p.250, 251.
Christ: p.266.
Cohens: p.195.
Chronological systems: p.234.
Church: p.266, 272.
Circumcision: p.299, 305, 306, 307, 308, 309, 323.
Commodus: p.136, 139, 192, 193.
Commentary: p.252.
Constantinople: p.68, 151, 156-158, 201, 202, 205.

173, 176, 180, 185, 186, 187, 189, 205, 209, 211, 212, 223, 231, 237, 242, 243, 244, 245, 252, 255, 256, 257, 258, 261, 262, 264, 267, 269, 272, 276, 277, 284, 287, 289, 292, 295, 296, 297, 301, 302, 314, 315, 318, 324, 325, 329, 335.
Mosul: p.148.
Mt. Abarim: p.43.
Mount Gerizim: (see also Gerizim): p.262, 264, 271, 279, 282.
Mount Nebo: p.242, 243.
M.T. p.246.
Na'aneh: p.91, 94.
Nabiḥ (Nobah): p.64.
Nablus: p.1, 37, 38, 52, 58, 67, 79, 81, 87, 118, 122, 123, 124, 135, 136, 137, 140, 148, 149, 152, 155, 162, 166, 171, 174, 177, 179, 191, 195, 200, 204, 210, 214.
Nablus Decalogue Inscription: p.11, 12, 13, 14.
Nahshah: p.285, 291.
Nebuzaradan: p.98.
Nadab: p.81, 93.
Nahor: p.46, 56.
Nahum: p.99.
Namara: p.137, 146, 149, 158, 159, 200.
Naphtali: p.82, 83, 96.
Nasi' Ha-'ob: p.207.
Nathanael, Nathanel: p.44, 67, 79, 80, 82, 83, 91, 98, 137, 138, 139, 158, 167, 193, 194, 202, 206.
Nazareth: p.207.
Neapolis: p.174, 193, 203.
Nebat: p.93.
Nebuchadnezzar: p.65, 98, 99, 110, 111, 112.
Nehemiah: p.17, 101, 102.
Neo-Caesarea: p.203.
Neubauer : p.38, 58, 120, 194.
Nicea: p.203.
Niger Pescennius: p.193.
Nimshi: p.95.
Nin: p.171, 179, 209, 210.
Nisan: p.39, 40, 43, 49, 236, 277, 281.
Noah: p.31, 38, 39, 46, 49, 55, 56, 255, 265, 266, 271, 272, 274, 275, 277, 278, 280, 282, 283.
Nobah: p.91, 94.
Northern Kingdom: p.17.
Notarikon: p.2, 28.
Numa: p.97, 111.
Numbers (Biblical Book): p.252.
Nun: p.62, 72, 73, 91.
Nutt, J.W.: p.69, 239.
Og: p.18.

Sadducees: p.234, 235.
Ṣadoḳ: p.172, 180, 212.
Ṣadūkaī: p.170, 209.
Ṡaftanah: p.169.
Šaheb: p.267, 268, 270, 271, 276, 278.
Sailun: p.83.
Sȧkta b. Tabrin b. Nin: p.180.
Saktu: p.209, 210.
Salem: p.146, 198.
Salem The Great: p.90.
Šallum: p.91, 95, 97.
Salus: p.97.
Šalyah: p.171, 172, 179-181, 209-213.
Samaria: p.63, 91, 93, 110, 179.
Samaritanism: p.220.
Samaritan Joshua: p.253.
Samaritan Pentateuch: p.235, 311.
Samaritan vocalisation: p.233.
Samaritan Woman: p.21.
Samson: p.64, 73, 75, 80, 84, 89, 104.
Samuel: p.64, 0, 105.
Sanballat: p.17, 65, 107, 113, 177, 183.
Sandek: p.309.
Sar: p.97.
Sarafin: p.144.
Sarbah: p.97.
Šarsar: p.100.
Sasan: p.136.
Sa'ud: p.91.
Saul: p.77, 90, 91, 146.
Scaliger: p.61.
Sebaste: p.135, 191.

Segi'an: p.91, 94.
Segiel: p.94.
Seleucid: p.234.
Seligsohn: p.87-89.
Semekh: p.91.
Seraiah: p.98, 111, 113.
Seror: p.90.
Serpius Tullius for Servius Tullus: p.98, 112.
Serug: p.46, 56.
Seth: p.31, 38, 45, 54.
Sethur: p.90.
Seṯumoṯ: p.3, 4.
Severus: p.137, 193, 199, 202.
Shalmaneser: p.96.
Shamagar: p.81, 82.
Shaubak: p.64.

INDEX OF
BIBLICAL AND POST-BIBLICAL
REFERENCES

GENESIS

GENESIS (cont.)

6:8 p.31.
6:9 p.31, 271.
6:14 p.272, 273.
6:15 p.272, 273.
6:16 p.272, 274.
6:17 p.274, 276, 277.
6:18 p.272, 274.
6:19 p.274, 275.
6:20 p.274, 275.
6:21 p.274, 275.
6:22 p.31, 274, 275.
7:1 p.276.
7:2 p.276.
7:3 p.276.
7:5 p.31.
7:6 p.55, 276.
7:7 p.276.
7:8 p.276.
7:9 p.276.
7:10 p.276, 277.
7:11 p.49, 277, 281.
7:12 p.277, 279, 281.
7:13 p.277.
7:14 p.278.
7:15 p.278.
7:16 p.278.
7:17 p.279.
7:18 p.279.
7:20 p.279.
7:21 p.279.
7:22 p.280.
7:23 p.31, 280.
7:24 p.49, 280.
8:1 p.31, 280, 281.
8:3 p.281.
8:4 p.49, 281.
8:5 p.49, 282.
8:6 p.282.
8:7 p.282.
8:8 p.282.
8:9 p.282.
8:10 p.282.
8:11 p.283.
8:12 p.283.
8:13 p.283.
8:18 p.31.
8:19 p.31.
8:20 p.32.
8:21 p.32, 39, 49, 260.
8:22 p.32.
9:1 p.32.
9:15 p.266.
10:10-15 p.55.
11:1-9 p.260.
11:16-26 p.56.
11:32 p.56.
12:1 p.326.
12:2 p.32, 326.
12:3 p.32, 326.
12:6 p.32, 58.
12:7 p.32.
12:8 p.32.
13:1 p.32.
13:17 p.32.
14:5 p.220
14:18 p.106.
14:19 p.32.
14:22 p.32.
15:1 p.32.
15:5 p.32.
15:6 p.32.
15:18 p.295.
17:4 p.295.
17:9 p.326.
17:10 p.326.
17:11 p.326.
17:12 p.308, 326.
17:13 p.326.
17:14 p.326.
17:21 p.32.
18:14 p.233.
18:19 p.32.
18:20 p.251.
18:21 p.251.
19:19 p.32.
20:7 p.32.
20:17 p.32.
21:5 p.56.
21:22 p.32.
21:25 p.220
21:33 p.32.
22:1 p.32, 326.
22:2 p.186.
22:4 p.32, 326.

GENESIS (cont.)

22:5 p.33.
22:9 p.33.
22:14 p.33.
22:17 p.33.
22:18 p.33.
24:2 p.220.
24:5 p.220.
24:7 p.33.
24:9 p.220.
24:12 p.33.
24:32-52 p.303.
24:40 p.33, 303.
24:48 p.33, 303.
24:52 p.220, 303.
24:53 p.220.
24:63 p.33.
25:4 p.56.
25:11 p.33.
25:21 p.33.
25:26 p.56.
25:27 p.262.
26:3 p.33, 295.
26:4 p.33.
26:5 p.33.
26:12 p.33.
26:22 p.33.
26:24 p.33.
26:29 p.33.
27:28 p.34.
27:29 p.34.
28:3 p.34.
28:4 p.34.
28:10-22 p.327.
28:17 p.34.
28:19 p.106.
28:20 p.34.
28:22 p.34.
29:23 p.305.
29:27 p.305.
29:30 p.49.
30:35 p.17.
31:11 p.17.
31:12 p.17.
31:13 p.17, 34.
32:1 p.262.
32:8 p.34.
32:10 p.34.
32:11 p.34.
32:13 p.34.
33:18 p.34.
33:19 p.34.
33:20 p.34.
34:12 p.303.
34:25 p.194.
34:26 p.194.
35:2 p.34.
35:3 p.34.
35:7 p.34.
35:9 p.295.
35:10 p.295.
35:11 p.34, 295.
35:12 p.295.
35:13 p.34.
35:14 p.34.
35:28 p.56.
37:2 p.34.
37:3 p.34.
37:5 p.34.
37:7 p.327.
37:2o-24 p.262.
37:34-35 p.187.
37:36 p.34.
39:1 p.35.
39:2 p.35.
40:7 p.260, 262.
40:30 p.202.
41:38 p.262.
42:6 p.262.
43:14 p.35.
47:28 p.57.
48:3 p.35.
48:15 p.35.
48:16 p.35.
49:18 p.35.
49:25 p.35.
49:26 p.35.
50:24 p.35.
50:25 p.35.
50:26 p.35.

EXODUS

LEVITICUS (cont.)

25:29 p.222.
25:39 p.76, 220, 222.
25:40 p.220, 221.
25:41 p.221.
25:42 p.221.
25:50-52 p.76.
25:55 p.221.
26:1 p.212.
26:42 p.280.
26:44 p.280.
26:45 p.280.

NUMBERS

1:50 p.77.
1:51 p.77.
2:1 p.78.
2:2 p.78.
2:14 p.78.
2:16 p.78.
3:4 p.81.
3:19 p.290.
5:16 p.77.
5:17 p.77.
5:18 p.77.
5:19 p.77.
5:20 p.77.
5:21 p.77.
5:22 p.77.
6:14 p.78.
6:15 p.78.
10:10 p.19.
10:18 p.272.
10:22 p.272.
10:25 p.272.
10:35 p.3, 12, 14.
10:36 p.12, 14.
11:16 p.188.
11:24 p.188, 319.
11:25 p.188, 247, 319.
12:8 p.251.
12:16 p.19.
13:4-16 p.272.
13:33 p.19.
14:21 p.283.
14:40 p.19.

NUMBERS (cont.)

15:20 p.236.
16:1ff. p.105.
16:22 p.330.
18:10 p.207.
18:17 p.204.
18:21ff. p.76.
18:24 p.75.
18:26-28 p.76.
19:16 p.187.
19:19 p.187.
20:13 p.19.
21:11 p.19.
21:12 p.19.
21:20 p.19.
21:22 p.19.
21:23 p.19.
21:33f. p.18, 22.
21:35 p.18.
22:31 p.251.
24:17 p.292, 293.
25:7-12 p.194.
25:10-13 p.48.
26:58 p.290.
26:59 p.290.
27:18 p.19.
27:21 p.50.
28:4 p.79.
28:6 p.78.
28:10 p.78.
28:15 p.78.
29:1f. p.237.
29:2-5 p.237.
29:6 p.237.
33:39 p.57.
34:16 p.81.
35:2 p.47, 58.
35:13 p.77.
35:24-25 p.77.

DEUTERONOMY

1:6 p.19.
1:7 p.19.
1:8 p.19.
1:13 p.76.
1:14 p.76.
1:15 p.76.
1:16 p.76.
1:17 p.76.
1:20 p.19.
1:21 p.19.
1:22 p.19.
1:23 p.19.
1:27 p.19.
1:28 p.19.
1:29 p.19.
1:30 p.19.
1:31 p.19.
1:32 p.19.
1:33 p.19.
1:42 p.19.
2:2 p.19.
2:3 p.19.
2:4 p.19.
2:5 p.19.
2:6 p.19.
2:9 p.19.
2:17 p.19.
2:18 p.19.
2:19 p.19.
2:21 p.19.
2:24 p.19.
2:25 p.19.
2:28 p.19.
2:29 p.19.
2:31 p.19.
3:1f. p.18, 22.
3:3 p.18.
3:20 p.222.
3:24 p.19.
3:25 p.19.
3:26 p.19.
3:27 p.19.
3:28 p.19.
4:2 p.16.
4:22 p.247.
5:4 p.26.
5:5 p.26.

DEUTERONOMY (cont.)

5:6 p.26.
5:7 p.26.
5:8 p.26.
5:9 p.26.
5:10 p.26.
5:11 p.26.
5:12 p.19, 26.
5:13 p.26.
5:14 p.19, 26.
5:15 p.19, 26, 220.
5:16 p.26.
5:17 p.26.
5:18 p.26.
5:19 p.26.
5:20 p.26.
5:21 p.19, 26.
5:24 p.20, 24, 185.
5:25 p.20, 24, 185.
5:26 p.20, 24, 185.
5:27 p.20, 24, 185.
5:28 p.20, 21, 25, 185.
5:29 p.20, 21, 25, 185.
5:30 p.21, 25, 185.
5:31 p.21, 25, 185.
6:4 p.47, 246.
6:5 p.49, 246, 261.
6:6 p.47, 246.
6:7 p.47, 246.
6:8 p.47, 246.
6:9 p.47, 246.
6:10 p.47.
6:11 p.237.
6:24 p.304.
6:25 p.305.
8:4 p.260
10:5 p.52.
10:6 p.81.
11:24 p.246.
11:29 p.20, 23, 25.
11:30 p.20, 24, 26, 58.
12:1 p.114.
12:5 p.186.
12:6 p.186.
12:7 p.186.
12:11 p.185.
12:14 p.185.
12:18 p.185.

DEUTERONOMY (cont.)

12:21 p.185.
12:26 p.185.
12:32 p.188.
13:1 p.114.
13:4 p.261.
13:13 p.261.
14:5 p.76.
14:22 p.76, 186.
14:23 p.76, 185.
14:24 p.76, 185.
14:25 p.76, 185.
14:26 p.76.
14:27 p.76.
14:28 p.76.
14:29 p.76.
15:1 p.51.
15:12 p.76, 221, 222.
15:20 p.185.
16:1 p.49.
16:2 p.185.
16:3 p.77.
16:4 p.77.
16:5 p.234.
16:6 p.185, 233, 234.
16:7 p.185.
16:11 p.185.
16:12 p.234.
16:15 p.185.
16:16 p.185.
17:8 p.185.
17:10 p.185.
18:1 p.76.
18:4 p.76.
18:6 p.185.
18:10 p.76.
18:11 p.76.
18:12 p.76.
18:18 p.21, 25, 185, 247, 264.
18:19 p.25, 185.
18:20 p.25, 185.
18:21 p.25, 185.
18:22 p.25, 185.
19:10 p.205.
19:19 p.191, 203.
21:5 p.77.
22:23 p.305.
22:24 p.305.

DEUTERONOMY (cont.)

23:16 p.185.
24:1 p.330.
24:2 p.330.
24:3 p.330.
24:4 p.330.
24:17 p.261.
25:1 p.191.
25:3 p.191.
26:15 p.251.
27:2 p.19, 20, 24.
27:3 p.14, 19, 20, 24, 26, 28.
27:4 p.12, 14, 16, 19, 20, 24, 26, 28, 186.
27:5 p.12, 14, 19, 20, 24, 26.
27:6 p.19, 20, 24, 26.
27:7 p.19, 20, 24, 26.
27:8 p.12, 14.
27:13 p.200.
28:66 p.194.
28:67 p.194.
29:5 p.260.
31:11 p.185, 186.
31:14 p.186.
32:1 p.246.
32:3 p.304.
32:4 p.304.
32:11 p.251.
32:13 p.296.
32:15 p.86.
32:16 p.86.
32:17 p.86.
32:18 p.86.
32:20 p.104, 271.
32:32 p.187.
32:33 p.187.
32:34 p.187.
32:35 p.187, 259 (Sam. reading) p.296, 318.
32:39 p.187, 259.
32:42 p.261.
32:43 p.187.
33:1 p.296.
33:4 p.13, 14, 212, 305.
33:8 p.77.
33:15 p.187.

DEUTERONOMY (cont.)

33:28 p.261.
33:29 p.200.
34:1 p.216, 247.
34:2 p.247.
34:4 p.247.
34:5 p.186, 247, 296.
34:6 p.247.
34:8 p.247.
34:9 p.247.
34:10 p.47, 58, 188, 247, 296.
34:11 p.247.
34:12 p.247.

JOSHUA

7:14 p.77.
8:32 p.28.
14:1 p.79, 81.
14:2 p.79.
19:51 p.79.
24:1 p.79.
24:25 p.48, 79.
24:26 p.48, 79.
24:29 p.81.

JUDGES

11:26 p.81.

RUTH

4:19 p.81.
4:20 p.81.

I SAMUEL

1:1 p.105.
4:15 p.103.
7:1 p.105.
7:2 p.105.
9:1 p.105.

2 SAMUEL

6:2 p.105.
24:24 p.107, 113.
24:25 p.107, 113.

1 KINGS

8:11 p.281.
11:1-3 p.107.
11:42 p.107.
12:1 p.107.
12:17 p.107.
12:20 p.107.
12:25 p.108.
12:28 p.108, 204.
14:20 p.107.
15:1 p.107, 108.
15:8-10 p.108.
15:27-28 p.108.
16:6, 8 p.108.
16:9-15 p.108.
16:24 p.108.
16:28 p.109.
16:31 p.109.
22:40 p.109.
22:41-42 p.109.
22:50 p.109.
22:51 p.109.

2 KINGS

2:1 p.56, 109.
4:38 p.56.
8:25-26 p.109.
9:24 p.109.
10:36 p.109.
10:35 p.109.
11:2 p.109.
12:1 p.109.
13:1 p.109.
14:2 p.109.
14:16 p.109.
14:17 p.109.
14:21 p.109.
14:22 p.109.
14:23 p.109.

2 KINGS (cont.)

14:29 p.109.
15:8 p.109.
15:10 p.109.
15:13 p.109.
15:14 p.110.
15:17 p.110.
15:19-20 p.110.
15:22-23 p.110.
15:25 p.110.
15:27 p.110.
15:29 p.110.
15:32-33 p.110.
16:1-2 p.110.
17:1 p.110.
17:3-4 p.110.
17:5 p.110.
17:6 p.110.
17:24 p.112.
18:1-2 p.111.
21:1 p.111.
23:30 p.111.
23:31 p.111.
23:34 p.111.
23:36 p.111.
24:6 p.111.
24:8 p.111.
24:12 p.111.
24:17-18 p.111.
25:1 p.112.
25:5-7 p.112.
25:8 p.112.
25:9-11 p.112.
25:18 p.111.

1 CHRONICLES

5:30 (RSV6:4) p.48.
5:31 (RSV6:5) p.59.
5:32 (RSV6:6) p.59.
6:1-14 p.175.
6:3 (RSV6:51) p.59.
6:5 p.59, 103.
6:15 p.114.
6:35 (RSV6:50) p.59.
6:36 (RSV6:51) p.59.
6:51 p.103.

EZRA

4:1-3 p.175.
5:16 p.175.
7:4 p.59.
7:5 p.59.
9-10 p.175.

NEHEMIAH

8:6 p.176.
8:7 p.176.
8:8 p.36, 176.
11:11 p.111.
12:10 p.114.
13:28 p.177, 183.
13:29 p.177.

ESTHER

9:2 p.114.

EZEKIEL

11:25 p.281.
26:7 p.112.
43:2-5 p.281.

MARK

8:29 p.207.

LUKE

10:1 p.207

JOHN

3:34 p.212.
7:39 p.212.
19:51 p.48.

ACTS

5:39 p.207.
6:2 p.207.

EPHESIANS

6:12 p.209.

REVELATIONS

21:2 p.262.
22:12 p.262.
22:14 p.262.

JOSEPHUS. War of the Jews.

Josephus, War I. II. 6 p.191.
II. VII. 2 p.189.
II. VIII.4 p.189.
II. VIII.9 p.189.

JOSEPHUS, Antiquities of the Jews.

Josephus Antiq. II. IX. 2 - X.2 p.292.
II. IX. 3 p.292.
IX. XIV. 3 p.175.
XI. III.8 p.118.
XI. IV. 1-9 p.118.
XI. IV. 3-4 p.118.
XI. IV. 9 p.175.
XI. III-IV.1-9 p.174.
XI. VII. 2 p.177.
XI. VIII. 8 p.66.
XII. II. 1,4,11,14 p.184.
XII. II. 13 p.187.
XII. IV. 1 p.177.
XIII. III. 4 p.185, 210.
XIII. V. 9 p.188.
XIII. VI. 4, 7 p.174.
XIII. IX. 1 p.191.
XIII. X. 2 p.191.

JOSEPHUS, Antiquities of the Jews (cont.)

Josephus Antiq.	XIII. X. 5	p.189, 190.
	XIII. X. 6	p.176.
	XVIII. IV. 1	p.208, 271.

Pirke de R. Eliezer. ed. & trans. G. Friedlander, London 1916.

Pirke de R. Eliezer,	p.34.	p.299.
	p.89-90.	p.326.
	p.299 (ch.xxxviii)	p.28, 179, 204.
	p.312.	p.272.
	p.361.	p.292.
	p.377.	p.291.
	p.378.	p.293, 294.
	p.375.	p.293.

APOCRYPHA AND PSEUDEPIGRAPHA

MACCABEES

1 Macc. 1:15 p.309.
2 Macc. 2:5 p.105.
2 Macc. 2:6 p.105, 271.
2 Macc. 2:17 p.105, 271.

JUBILEES

Jubilees 15:26-27 p.308.

ASSUMPTION OF MOSES

Assumption of Moses 1:12-14 p.292.
12:6 p.261.

RABBINIC

MISHNAH

M. Ber. 3:4 p.207.
M. Ber. 9:5 p.12.
M. Shek. 5:2 p.78.
M. Shab. 30:6 p.309.

MISHNAH (cont.)

M. Ta'an. 4:3 p.35.
M. Meg. 3:6 p.35.
M. RH 1:1 p.51.
M. RH 4:8 p.51.
M. Sheb. 10:3 p.188.
M. Git. 9:10 p.330.
M. Sot. 7:8 p.28.
M. Sot. 9.10 p.188.
M. Sot. 9.15 p.265.
M. Abot 1:1 p.188.
M. Abot 5:1 p.1.
M. Eduyot 8:7 p.264.
M. Nid. 1:1-3 p.179.
M. Nid. 4:1 p.211.

Megillat Ta'anit i p.235.

Babylonian Talmud.

T. B. Shab. 130a p.308.
T. B. Meg. 3a p.184.
T. B. Meg. 13b p.295.
T. B. Meg. 14a p.292.
T. B. Ket. 10a p.309.
T. B. Ket. 82b p.39.
T. B. Sot. 11b p.292.
T. B. Sot. 12a p.292, 293.
T. B. Sot. 13b p.292.
T. B. Sot. 35b p.36.
T. B. Sot. 48a p.188.
T. B. B. Ḳ. 92b p.182.
T. B. B. Ḃ. 145b p.204.
T. B. Ab.Zar.27a p.308.
T. B. Makk. 2b p.191.
T. B. Hor. 13b p.196.
T. B. Hul. 46 p.308.
T. B. Tam. 32a p.66.
T. B. 'Ar. 32b p.52.
T. B. Men. 65a p.235.
T. B. Sof. 1:18

Palestinian Talmud.

P. T. AZ 3:1 p.66.
P. T. Ket. VIII 32c p.310.

MAIMONIDES Yad Hazakah Ishut XVI p.310.

Shulhan 'Arukh Yoreh de'ah 264, 1 p.308.

Targ. Jer. to Exod. 1:14 p.292.
Ex. R. i 24 p.292.
Lev. R. XXVI 4 p.295.
Mekilta Beshallah Wayissa' 60a p.295.
Mekilta Yitro, Ba-Hodesh 130a p.308.
Sefer Yashar p.112b, p.295.

SHORT BIBLIOGRAPHY

Adler, E. N. & Séligsohn, M. "Une Nouvelle Chronique Samaritaine", *Revue des Etudes Juires*, 44-46 (1902-3).

Ben-Zebi, Y. "Eben mĕzuzah šomronit̲ mi-kĕfar, Bīlō", *Yedi'ot ha-Heb̲rah le-Hakirat̲ Ereṣ Yisrā'el we'atiḳot̲eha,* xviii, p.223-229, 1954.

Blau, O. "Der Dekalog in einer samaritanischen Inschrift aus dem Tempel des Garizim", *Zeitschrift der Deutschen Morgenlandischen Gesellschaft*, (1859), 275-281.

Bowman, J. "The Exegesis of the Pentateuch among the Samaritans and among the Rabbis", *Oudtestamentische Studiën* 8, Leiden, 1950.

---------. *Transcript of the Original Text of the Samaritan Chronicle Tolidah (with a critical introduction)*, University of Leeds, Department of Semitic Languages, 1954.

---------. *The Hebrew Text of a Samaritan Allegory by Phinehas on the Taheb.* University of Leeds, Department of Semitic Languages, 1955.

---------. "Early Samaritan Eschatology", *The Journal of Jewish Studies,* VI, (1955), 63-72.

---------. *The Samaritan Problem: Studies in the Relationships of Samaritanism, Judaism, and Early Christianity.* Franz Delitzsch Lectures 1959. Translated by Alfred M. Johnson, Jr. Pittsburgh Theological Monograph Series. Pittsburgh, Pennsylvania, The Pickwick Press, 1975.

Buchanan, Gray G. *Numbers* (International Critical Commentary). Edinburgh, T. & T. Clark, 1912.

Charles, R. H. *Apocrypha and Pseudepigrapha of the Old Testament.* 2 vols. Oxford, Clarendon Press, 1913.

——————. *The Book of Jubilees.* London, A. C. Black, 1902.

Cowley, A. E. *The Samaritan Liturgy.* 2 vols. Oxford, Clarendon Press, 1909.

——————. *Aramaic Papyri of the Fifth Century B.C.* Oxford, Clarendon Press, 1923.

——————. "The Samaritan Doctrine of the Messiah", *Expositor*, 5th series, I, (1895), 161 - 174.

——————. "The Samaritan Liturgy and the Reading of the Law, *Jewish Quarterly Review*, 7 (1894), 121-140.

De Sacy, S. *Chrestomathie arabe.* Paris, Imprimerie Royale, 1826-1827.

Eusebius. *Praeparatio Evangelica.* J. Sirineli, La préparation évangelique par Eusèbe de Césarée, v. 1-7 (Sources Chrétiennes, 206). Paris, Editions du Cerf, 1974.

Friedlander, G. *Pirke de R. Eliezer.* London, R. Kegan Paul, 1916.

Von Gall, A. F. *Der Hebraische Pentateuch der Samaritaner.* Giessen, A. Töpelmann, 1918 [1966].

Gaster, M. *The Samaritans.* Oxford, Oxford University Press, 1925.

——————. *Samaritan Oral Law and Ancient Traditions.* Vol. I, Eschatology. New York, The Search Publishing House, 1932.

——————. *Asātīr, The Samaritan Book of the "Secrets of Moses".* London, Royal Asiatic Society, 1927.

Ginzberg, L. *The Legends of the Jews.* 7 vols. Philadelphia, Jewish Publication Society, 1946.

Hanover, S. *Das Festgesetz der Samaritaner nach Ibrahim ibn Jakub.* Edition und Ubersetzung seines Kommentars zu Lev. 23. Berlin, 1904.

Field, F. *Origenis Hexaplorum.* 2 vols. Oxford, Clarendon Press, 1875.

Heidenheim, M. "Der Traum des Priesters Abischa", *D.V.J.*, ii, 81. "Der Dekalog in der samaritanischen Liturgie", *D.V.J.*, iii, 486.

------------. *Bibliotheca Samaritana: iii Der Commentar Merqah's des Samaritaners.* Weimar, 1896.

Jastrow, M. *A Dictionary of the Targumim, the Talmud Babli and Yerushalmi and the Midrashic Literature.* New York, Pardes, 1950.

Juynboll, T. G. J. *Chronicon Samaritanum, arabice conscriptum, cui titulus est liber Josuae.* Leyden, 1848.

Kahle, P. *The Cairo Geniza.* Oxford, University Press, 1947.

--------. "The Abisha Scroll of the Samaritans", *Studia Orientalia Goanni Pederson dicata.* Copenhagen, 1953.

Kippenberg, H. G. *Garizim und Synagoge.* Berlin, de Gruyter, 1971.

Klumel, M. *Mischpatim. Ein samaritanisch-arabischer Commentar zu Ex 21-22, 15 von Ibrahim ibn Jakub.* Berlin, 1902.

Macdonald, J. *Theology of the Samaritans.* London, S.C.M. Press, 1964.

------------, ed. & tr. *Memar Marqah.* 2 vols. Berlin, Verlag Alfred Topelmann, 1963.

Montgomery, J. A. *The Samaritans. The Earliest Jewish Sect. Their History, Theology and Literature.* New York, Ktav, 1907 [1968].

Petermann, J. H. *Reisen im Orient*, Vol. I. Leipzig, 1860.

Pfeiffer, R. H. *Introduction to the Old Testament.* London, A. C. Black, 1952.

Rosen, G. "Ueber samaritanische Inscriften", *Zeitschrift der Deutschen Morgenlandischen Gesellschaft* 14 (1860), 622-631.

Vilmar, E. *Abulfathi Annales Samaritani.* Gotha, 1865.

Weiss, P. R. "Abū'l Hasan al-Sūrī: Discourse on the Rules of Leprosy in Kitab al-Tabbah. Rylands Samaritan Codex IX", *Bulletin of the John Rylands Library*, 33, (1950-51), 131-137.

Wilson, J. *Lands of the Bible*. Edinburgh, 1843.

Zacuto, Abraham ben Samuel. *Yuhasin ha-shalom*. Filipowski's edition, Freimann, Alfred (ed.). Frankfurt am Main, 1924.

CPSIA information can be obtained
at www.ICGtesting.com
Printed in the USA
LVHW080959020820
662182LV00014B/804

9 780915 138272